The British Navy

Nelson receiving the swords of the Spanish officers on board the "San Joseph."

The British Navy
Accounts of Naval Warfare from
Damme 1213 to Trafalgar 1805

Alfred H. Miles

The British Navy
Accounts of Naval Warfare from Damme 1213 to Trafalgar 1805
by Alfred H. Miles.

First published under the title
Fifty-Two Stories of the British Navy, from Damme to Trafalgar

Leonaur is an imprint of Oakpast Ltd

Copyright in this form © 2012 Oakpast Ltd

ISBN: 978-1-78282-036-9 (hardcover)
ISBN: 978-1-78282-037-6 (softcover)

http://www.leonaur.com

Publisher's Notes

The views expressed in this book are not necessarily those of the publisher.

Contents

Prefatory	7
The Beginnings of the British Navy	9
The Story of the Cinque Ports	16
The Story of Sir Edward Howard	28
The Story of Sir Thomas Howard and Sir Andrew Barton	33
The Story of Sir John Hawkins	37
The Worthy Enterprise of John Fox	48
The Story of Sir Francis Drake	59
The Voyage Made to Tripolis in Barbary	67
A True Report of a Worthy Fight	77
The Story of the Spanish Armada	86
The Story of the "Revenge"	99
The Story of Admiral Blake	108
The Story of the First Dutch War	119
Stories of the Second Dutch War	130
The Destruction of the Algerine Navy	143
The Story of Sir John Berry	147
The Story of the Third Dutch War	152
The Battle of Beachy Head	165
The Victory of La Hogue	170
The Story of Sir George Rooke	175

Off Gibraltar	186
The Story of Admiral Benbow	189
Defeat of the Spanish Fleet in the Faro off Messina	198
The Story of Captain Hornby and the French Privateer	203
Off Cape Finisterre	207
The Loss of H.M.S. "Namur"	210
The Loss of H.M.S. "Pembroke"	213
The Story of Admiral the Honourable John Byng	220
In Indian Seas	232
The Story of the "Glorious Fifty-Nine" and the Battle of Quiberon Bay	237
The Story of Lord Rodney	242
The Loss of the "Ramilies"	250
The Loss of H.M.S. "Centaur"	258
The Loss of the "Royal George"	271
The Mutiny of the "Bounty"	275
The Story of Lord Exmouth	286
The Glorious First of June	291
Triumph in Retreat	298
The Mutiny of 1797	302
The Battle of Camperdown	309
The Loss of H.M.S. "Repulse"	314
The Story of Nelson's Boyhood	321
First Steps Up the Ladder	328
On Board the "Agamemnon"	333
The Evacuation of Corsica and the Battle of Cape St. Vincent	338
The Story of Santa Cruz	347
The Story of the Battle of the Nile	351
The Bombardment of Copenhagen	363
The Story of the Battle of Trafalgar	376

Prefatory

This volume contains fifty-two stories of the British navy from Damme to Trafalgar. These stories are arranged chronologically, and, without pretending to be a complete history of the British Navy, provide fifty-two consecutive links of the chain which for a thousand years has bound the sovereignty of the seas to the British throne.

In preparing this series many historical and biographical works have been laid under contribution. Of these Dr. Campbell's *Lives of the British Admirals and Naval History*, Southey's *Life of Nelson*, Giffard's *Deeds of Naval Daring*, Creasy's *Fifteen Decisive Battles of the World*, Green's *History of the English People*, Hakluyt's *Voyages*, and Sir Walter Raleigh's prose epic *The Truth of the Fight about the Isles of Azores* are the most important.

When a story has been adequately told once there is little to be gained by retelling it in other words; hence the "Story of the *Revenge*" is given from Sir Walter Raleigh's account with but slight abbreviation, and the "Story of the Spanish Armada" from Sir Edward Creasy's book with but similar abridgment. Many of the stories taken from Dr. Campbell's work and that of Robert Southey have been subject to the same treatment, and the editor believes they have, for present purposes, gained by condensation.

The editor desires to acknowledge his indebtedness to his friend, Mr. A. J. Pattle, who collaborated with him in the editorship of his *Fifty-two Stories of the Indian Mutiny*, published in 1895 with so much success, and who has rendered valuable service in the production of this work.

He also desires to acknowledge the courtesy of Messrs. Cassell and Co., whereby he is enabled to use the engraving which forms the frontispiece of this volume, from *The Story of the Sea* published by them.

Stories of the sea are always welcome to British boys and girls, and the editor has no fear for the reception of this collection.

A. H. M.

September 1st, 1896.

The Beginnings of the British Navy
A Saxon Chronicle

The founders of the English nation were a maritime people. Before they settled in the British Isles they had to dare the dangers of the deep, and though for nearly four hundred years after their first arrival they were too much occupied with internal strife to think of external enterprise, no sooner had they apparently completed the subjugation of the Britons and effected a settlement of their own differences by uniting the country under one crown, than they were called upon to give vigorous attention to maritime affairs.

Egbert, king of the West Saxons, who, by the conquest of Mercia and Northumbria, became the first overlord of all England, *A.D.* 828, was soon compelled to deal seriously with the Danes. According to old chroniclers, threatened with invasion in the south, he engaged these formidable foes at Charmouth in Dorsetshire, but sustained defeat. Two years later, however, when they returned and landed on the coast of Wales, uniting with the disaffected Britons in a powerful armament, Egbert proved equal to the occasion, met them in a general engagement at the Battle of Hengestesdun, routed their entire forces, and compelled the Britons to seek safety in their mountains and the Danes to return to their ships.

Desultory warfare supervened for some time with ever-varying success until, according to the Saxon Chronicle, the Danes were defeated off Sandwich in a desperate battle in which nine of their ships were taken by the English, and the rest compelled to seek safety in flight. After this they again returned, this time with a fleet of three hundred and fifty sail, devastated the south country and took Canterbury and London by storm.

Hitherto the English had made the fatal mistake of allowing their enemies to land before attempting to grapple with them, and even the disasters which followed naturally upon such a policy did not arouse them to a sense of the necessity of maintaining an efficient fleet. On the contrary, dispirited by their failures, the English seem to have abandoned all thoughts of naval armament, and to have contented themselves with fortifying their cities and defending them against enemies whom they passively allowed to land. This unhappy condition of things continued through the reigns of Ethelbald, Ethelbert and Ethelred; during which time the Danes conquered Northumbria and East Anglia, and invaded Wessex. In *A.D.* 867 they took York, and in the following year Nottingham. In 870 they defeated and put to death Edmund, king of East Anglia, whose burial-place was named St. Edmundsbury—Bury St. Edmunds—and during the same year fought no less than nine battles in Wessex. Abbeys, churches and monasteries were burnt, and the whole country was given up to fire and the sword.

In the year 871 Alfred came to the throne and found himself a monarch without a people, a king without a country. The long-continued struggle with the Danes, who, like locusts, *"came without number and devoured the fruits of the land,"* had reduced the people to a state of despairing servitude. The wealth, strength, and spirits of the English, who had sometimes been compelled to fight as many as ten or twelve battles in the course of a year, had become exhausted, and instead of attempting to defend themselves further, they began everywhere to submit to the Danes; preferring a settled slavery to a precarious freedom. Although the country had been brought to this low condition, the young king did not despair of its restoration, but with equal vigour and prudence applied himself to the prosecution of the war and the conduct of public affairs.

Encouraged by his example and inspired by his spirit, the English at length took heart again, and ultimately—led by his skill and wisdom—defeated the Danes at Exeter in 877, and at Edington in the following year, securing the peace of Wedmore, which, while it gave them little more than the kingdom of Wessex as a possession, ensured them what they needed much more than land, a period of rest and repose, which, but for one short interval, lasted for fifteen years. This period Alfred employed in pursuing the arts of peace and preparing himself for the eventualities of war. In the year *A.D. 883* he sent envoys to Rome and India; and in 886 he took and refortified the city of London. From 893 to 897 he was once more engaged with his old enemies the Danes. This protracted campaign was by no means a light undertaking.

Hasting, the Danish leader, pitched his camp on the hills gently sloping above Benfleet, in Essex, and sent two hundred and fifty Danish ships cruising along the south-west coast of Kent; while he proceeded himself with eighty ships along the Thames estuary. Having formed a camp at Milton, near Sittingbourne, he ventured up the River Lea where he found himself unexpectedly entrapped; for Alfred hit upon the expedient of draining the river, and by this means left the Danish ships high and dry. Retreating to Benfleet, Hasting discovered that in his absence his camp had been attacked and captured by one of Alfred's aldermen. Alfred drove Hasting out of Wessex in 894, and out of Essex in 896, after which the Danish leader appears to have had enough of English hospitality; for he returned to Denmark in the following year.

From 897 to the end of his reign, Alfred devoted much time to the construction of ships and the equipment of a fleet; a purpose which he effected with so much success that he earned for himself the title of "The Father of the British Navy." Alfred seems to have been the first of the English kings to realise that the true principle of insular defence is to meet one's enemies upon the sea, and destroy them before they have time to effect a landing. Once realised, however, he made every effort to carry out this sagacious and far-sighted policy, a policy in which, for a thousand years, he has been followed by the wisest and best of his successors. To do this, the creation and maintenance of a national fleet became an imperative necessity.

According to Dr. Campbell, Alfred reflected that, as the fleets of his enemies were frequently built in a hurry, hastily drawn together, meanly provided with victuals and rigging and overcrowded with men, a few ships of a larger size, built in a new manner of well-seasoned materials, thoroughly supplied with food and arms, and manned by expert seamen must, at first sight, surprise, and, in the course of an engagement destroy many with but little danger to themselves; and with this view he constructed a number of ships in most points twice the size of the largest ships then in use, and furnished with accommodation for double the number of rowers. These vessels were longer, higher, and yet swifter than the vessels in common use among the Danes; so that Alfred was able always to engage his enemies at advantage, and, when necessary, to escape them by flight. As, moreover, these vessels were built upon a new model, they were wholly strange to the enemy, who were a long time learning the way to board them; hence their courage and seamanship did not avail them much.

Alfred was not long in finding employment for his infant navy. Soon after the earlier of these ships were built, six large pirate ships of unusual size appeared off the Isle of Wight and the coast of Devonshire. The king immediately despatched nine of his new vessels in quest of them, with orders to get, if possible, between them and the shore, and to give and take no quarter. On sighting the king's ships three of the pirates ran aground, while the others stood out to sea and boldly offered battle. Of these, two were taken and the whole of their crews destroyed, while the third escaped with five men only. Turning their attention to the ships that had grounded, the king's men destroyed the greater part of their crews, and when the tide floated them, brought the ships to the coast of the South Saxons, where the remainder of their crews endeavoured to escape. They were, however, captured and carried to Winchester, where they were hanged by order of the king. This may be regarded as one of the first engagements of the British navy—that is, of ships built on purpose for defensive warfare; though of course there were many famous sea fights of earlier dates. Dr. Campbell says:

> If it should be asked how this superiority at sea was lost, we must observe that it was very late in the king's life before his experience furnished him with light sufficient for this noble design, which very probably his successors wanted skill to prosecute; though, as history shows, they were moved by his example to make great efforts for preserving their territories on shore by maintaining the sovereignty of the sea.

Alfred the Great died in the year 901, and was succeeded by Edward the Elder. Opposed by his cousin Ethelwald, who laid claim to the crown and who invited the Danes over to help him in securing it, Edward was unable to prevent the Northmen from landing; but marching into Kent he engaged the united forces of his enemies in a desperate battle in which his cousin Ethelwald and Eric, the King of the Danes, were slain. Still troubled by successive hordes of Northmen, who—like the heads of the fabled giants—seemed to multiply as they were destroyed, Edward had recourse to his fleet, and gathering a hundred ships upon the coast of Kent, totally defeated the invaders; forcing most of their ships upon the shore, and destroying their commanders on the spot. Athelstan, who succeeded his brother in 925, was also a wise and powerful ruler.

Called upon to defend himself against a confederacy which included Constantine, King of the Scots, Anlaff, a Danish prince, settled in Ireland, and a host of disaffected Britons, he attacked them both by sea and land at the same time with equal valour and success. In this battle, fought in 938, there fell five kings and seven Danish chiefs. It is said to have been the bloodiest engagement which up to that time had ever taken place in England; and, as a result, Athelstan became the most absolute monarch that had ever reigned in Britain. Edmund, Edred, and Edwy followed in lineal succession, but without adding anything of importance to our naval annals.

In Edgar, who came to the throne in 958, Alfred had a successor who proved himself worthy of carrying on his great traditions. He thoroughly understood and successfully pursued the maxims of his great ancestor, and applied himself from the beginning of his reign to the raising of an efficient maritime force. It is said that his fleet was far superior to those of any of his predecessors, as well as much more powerful than those of all the other European princes put together. This navy—variously estimated by the monkish chroniclers to number from three thousand to four thousand ships—he is said to have divided into three fleets each of twelve hundred sail, which he stationed respectively on the north, the east, and the west coasts of England. Not content with making these provisions, it is said that:

> Every year after Easter, he went on board the fleet stationed on the eastern coast, and, sailing west, scoured all the channels, looked into every creek and bay, from the Thames mouth to Land's End in Cornwall; there, quitting these ships, he went on board the western fleet, with which, steering his course northward, he did the like not only on the English and Scotch coasts, but also on those of Ireland and the Hebrides—which lie between them and Britain; then meeting the northern fleet, he sailed in it to the mouth of the Thames. Thus surrounding the island every summer, he rendered invasion impracticable, kept his sailors in continual exercise, and effectually asserted his sovereignty over the sea.

In the winter, Edgar is said to have travelled by land through all parts of his dominion to see that justice was duly administered, to prevent his nobles from becoming oppressors, and to protect the meanest people from suffering wrong. By these arts he secured tranquillity at home while he engendered respect abroad. By being always ready for war he avoided it, so that in his whole reign there happened but one disturbance, and that through the Britons, who, while he was in the north, committed disorder in the west. It is further said of this prince that "he reigned sixteen years without a thief being found in his dominions on land, or a pirate being heard of at sea."

Edgar died in 975, and was succeeded by Edward the Martyr, who reigned three years, and then gave place to Ethelred the Unready. Then followed the period of decadence which prepared the way for Danish supremacy. Ethelred adopted the fatal plan of buying off his invaders, the effect of which policy was to increase the numbers and the demands of his enemies. Accordingly, in 994, Sweyn, son of the King of Denmark, and Olaf, King of Norway, made a descent upon London and devastated Kent, Sussex, and Hampshire. Olaf was bought off with a payment of £16,000, but the Danes were insatiable. A truce, purchased by Ethelred in 1002, was brought to an abrupt conclusion by his own weakness and cruelty; for in that year he planned and effected the massacre of all the Danes in his dominions, on St. Brice's day. Among the victims was a sister of Sweyn of Denmark, and Sweyn's revenge was sharp and swift. In 1003 he laid Exeter waste, and in 1004 destroyed Norwich; and when two years later the "great fleet" of the Danes arrived off Sandwich, Ethelred was obliged to purchase peace with a supply of provisions and a sum of thirty thousand pounds.

Great efforts were made during this truce to reconstruct the navy. The king commanded ships to be built throughout the country and levied taxes to pay for them. Within a year it is said that eight hundred ships, equipped with thirty thousand men, were ready for the national defence. But no armament can be strong that is directed by weak hands, and the want of a wise and vigorous leader led to internal quarrels, which effectually destroyed Ethelred's chances of successfully resisting the Danes.

In 1013 Sweyn was practically king of England, and Ethelred fled to Normandy. In 1016 the death of Ethelred left Edmund Ironside his son, and Canute, the son of Sweyn of Denmark, rival candidates for the throne. After fighting two battles, they agreed to divide the kingdom between them; but the death of Edmund the same year left Canute the master of the whole. Under Canute, peace prevailed and commerce began to thrive.

> Men from the Rhineland and from Normandy moored their vessels along the Thames, on whose rude wharves were piled

a strange medley of goods: pepper and spices from the far East, crates of gloves and gay cloths, it may be from the Lombard looms, sacks of wool; ironwork, from Liège, butts of French wine and vinegar, and with them the rural products of the country itself—cheese, butter, lard and eggs, with live swine and fowls.

Such was Canute's influence that it became unnecessary to maintain more than forty ships for the protection of the coast, and this number was afterwards reduced to sixteen. With the death of Canute the Danish rule began to collapse, and with the accession of Edward the Confessor the Danes resumed their aggressive expeditions, though with but little success. William of Normandy found England without a fleet, for Harold had been compelled to disband the navy from want of supplies; and, as he destroyed his own ships after he had effected a landing, he began his reign without means of maritime defence.

The Story of the Cinque Ports

The history of the English navy from the Conquest to the fifteenth century is, in effect, the history of the great and powerful corporation known as "The five Cinque Ports and two Ancient Towns"—Hastings, Sandwich, Dover, Romney, Hythe, Winchelsea, and Rye. In the Domesday Book only three such ports are mentioned—Sandwich, Dover, and Romney—but in the charters and royal writs mention is always made of, and precedence assigned to, Hastings. Winchelsea and Rye were added to the first five soon after the Conquest, but the title of "Cinque" Ports was retained. In addition to the seven head ports there were eight "corporate members"—Deal, Faversham, Folkestone, Fordwich, Lydd, Pevensey, Seaford, and Tenterden—and twenty-four non-corporate members, which included Birchington, Brightlingsea, Bulverhithe, Grange, Kingsdown, Margate, Ramsgate, Reculver, Sarre, and Walmer, all of which were called Cinque Ports.

Some writers have endeavoured to connect the Cinque Ports with the five Roman fortresses which guarded the south-eastern shores of Britain, and the Lord Warden of the Cinque Ports with the *Comes Littoris Saxonici*—the count of the Saxon Shore, but it seems sufficiently clear that the confederation of the ports was of Teutonic origin. Originally, trading communities banded together to protect and control the herring-fishery, the principal industry and food-supply of the people; the regular descents of the Danes supplied the motive for the military character the union afterwards assumed.

The Danish invasion, which ended in Canute's supremacy, raged most fiercely round Sandwich, which was the head-quarters of the Danish fleet, and acquired the title of "the most famous of all the English ports."

As far back as the year 460, Hengist the Saxon conferred the office of Warden of the Cinque Ports upon his brother Horsa, and since the time of Godwin, Earl of Kent, who died in the year 1053, nearly one hundred and fifty persons have held that distinguished office. These include many whose names are illustrious in English history, amongst them being Odo, Bishop of Bayeux, Eustace, Earl of Boulogne, William Longchamps, Hubert de Burgh, Sir Stephen de Pencester, Edmund Plantagenet, King Henry V., Simon de Montfort, Richard III., Prince Henry, afterwards Henry VIII., James II., and Prince George of Denmark. William Pitt was Lord Warden in 1792, and from that date until the year 1896 the holders of the office have been the Earl of Liverpool, the Duke of Wellington, the Marquis of Dalhousie, Lord Palmerston, Earl Granville, Mr. W. H. Smith, the Marquis of Dufferin and the Marquis of Salisbury.

The privileges and distinctions of the inhabitants of the ports in those days were of a very substantial character. Amongst other things "pains and penalties" were imposed on anyone entering or quitting the kingdom from or for the Continent except by way of Dover. The Grand Court of Shepway, at which the Lord Warden takes the oath of office, in the presence of the "barons," was formerly held in the open air at Lympne, a Roman port, the remains of which are now several miles inland, in the neighbourhood of Hythe, but the site of the court was removed to Dover as a more convenient place in 1693.

To Edward the Confessor may be attributed the incorporation of the Cinque Ports in the form of a Royal Navy bound to stated service. To attach them to the throne he granted them lands and franchises, in return for which they undertook, on a stated notice, to provide ships for fighting purposes for a specified time. The Domesday Book, for instance, records that:

> Dover, in the time of King Edward, rendered eighteen pounds, of which moneys King Edward had two parts, and Earl Godwin the third. The burgesses gave the king twenty ships once a year for fifteen days, and in each ship were twenty men. This they did in return for his having endowed them with sac and soc—(the right of independent jurisdiction and free courts).

Soon after the Norman conquest, the Danes once more threatened invasion with a powerful fleet, and Dover, Sandwich, and Romney were called upon to provide, at their own expense, twenty vessels equipped for sea, each with a crew of twenty-one men and provisions for fifteen days. Rye and Winchelsea rendered similar assistance, and in return received privileges similar to those enjoyed by the older ports.

The fleet thus provided was so fully maintained by William Rufus that England's maritime supremacy may be dated from that early period. But, for more than a century after the Conquest, English ships seldom ventured beyond the Bay of Biscay or the entrance to the Baltic.

The reign of Henry I. was marked by the tragic death of Prince William in the year 1120 while crossing from Normandy to England in *The White Ship*. The rowers, hilarious with wine, ran *The White Ship*—probably an undecked or only partially decked vessel, of not more than fifty tons burden steered by two paddles over the quarter—violently on to a ledge of rocks, now called Ras de Catteville. The sea rushed in, and all on board, except two men, were lost. As soon as his ship struck, the prince and a few others got into a small boat and pushed off, but, returning to the aid of his sister, many persons jumped in the boat and all were drowned. The prince's body was carried away by the current and never recovered.

Fitzstephen, the captain, whose father had carried William the Conqueror to England, and who held his office by virtue of providing a passage for his sovereign, rose once to the surface and asked, "What has become of the king's son?" Being answered, "We have not seen him, nor his brother, nor his sister, nor any of their companions," he exclaimed, "Woe is me!" and sank back into the sea. For three days no one ventured to break the news to Henry who, the old chroniclers say, was so stricken with the tidings that he fainted away and was never seen to smile again.

Not until the time of the Crusades, however, did maritime commerce undergo any marked development, and England take her place among sea-faring peoples. Whatever the Crusades may have done for the Cross, they gave the first impetus to English maritime enterprise, and European industry progressed with the conquests of the Crusaders. On ascending the throne Richard Cœur de Lion made vast levies to equip an expedition to the Holy Land. The fleet numbered one hundred vessels, the most of which had been collected from the south and west of England, and from the continental ports of the House of Anjou, Richard's own ship being named *Trenche-le mer*, presumably because it was a swift sailer. It was from Messina, on March 27th, 1190, that Richard dated his charter to the Cinque Ports.

The reign of Richard marked another epoch in the naval history of Britain, for he issued the first articles for the government of an English fleet. If any man slew another on board a ship, he was to be fastened to the dead body and thrown with it into the sea; if the murder was committed on shore, he was to be bound to the corpse, and buried with it. If anyone was convicted by legal testimony of drawing his knife upon another, or of drawing blood in any manner, he was to lose his hand. For giving a blow with the hand without producing blood, the offender was to be plunged three times into the sea. If anyone reviled or insulted another, he was on every occasion to pay to the offended party an ounce of silver. A thief was to have his head shaven, boiling pitch poured upon it, and feathers shaken over him, as a mark by which he might be known; and he was to be put ashore at the first land at which the ship might touch.

In the reign of John a close approach was made to a regular naval establishment, and a kind of dockyard appears to have existed at Portsmouth, for the Sheriff of Southampton was commanded to cause the docks at Portsmouth to be enclosed with a strong wall to preserve the king's ships and galleys, and to cause pent-houses to be erected for their stores and tackle. The king had galleys, long ships, and great ships; all allusions to which, however, make it clear that the largest vessels had only one mast and sail. But no admiral or commander of the fleets appears to have been created, and the chief management of the navy was for many years entrusted to William de Wrotham, Archdeacon of Taunton, who was designated "Keeper of the King's Ships," and also "Keeper of the Seaports."

The expulsion of John from his dominions in Normandy in 1203 opened a new chapter in English history and brought the Cinque Ports prominently into notice, as frequently repeated orders were issued to the barons of the ports to "guard the seas." By their vigilant guard, it is alleged, the excommunication which followed the Pope's Interdict in 1208 was so long prevented from making its way across the Channel, and they were certainly the moving spirits in the great maritime exploit which help to redeem the gloom of John's reign.

Philip of France, obeying the exhortation of the Pope to assist in dethroning John, had made extensive preparations for the invasion of England, and when in 1213 John became the Pope's vassal Philip did not like the idea of giving up the project. John, therefore, found it necessary to adopt retaliatory measures. All men capable of bearing arms were ordered to assemble at Dover "for the defence of the king's and their own heads, and the land of England," and the bailiffs of all the ports were forbidden to suffer any ship to sail without the king's express authority.

The French king entered Flanders to punish the count, who had refused to join the expedition against John, and despatched all the ships which he had collected to the port of Damme, the harbour of which, though of "wonderful size," could not contain all the French ships, which are said to have numbered one thousand seven hundred sail. Thither the English fleet, of five hundred sail the greater portion consisting of ships from the Cinque Ports, under William Longsword, proceeded at the urgent summons of the count.

On the arrival of the English they found that the French had landed and were ravaging the surrounding country, whereupon they attacked the fleet in the harbour, and three hundred vessels laden with corn, wine, and arms, fell into English hands. The cables of the captured vessels were cut, and the wind being off the land, they were soon on the passage to England. About a hundred others were burnt, and the first great naval victory recorded in English annals was complete.

The attitude of the Cinque Ports during the period immediately preceding the granting of the Great Charter of English Liberties is obscure. They are mentioned as guaranteed in their franchises when the Charter took its final shape under Henry III., and it is clear that, when the baronage invited Louis of France to depose the faithless King of England, the ports resolved to stand by the House of Plantagenet. John's unexpected death in 1216, at a time when London and a great part of Kent were in the power of Louis, found the Cinque Ports—though Sandwich had been burnt by the French—staunch to the loyal Earl of Pembroke—marshal of the kingdom, and supporters of the boy-king, Henry III.

The following year, however, was destined to become memorable in the history of naval warfare, for in August, 1217, the French fleet of one hundred vessels put to sea with a view to a descent upon the Thames. Hubert de Burgh, with the seamen of the Cinque Port ships, assembled in Dover Harbour, and as the hostile fleet was descried from Dover Cliffs, on the 24th forty ships dashed out of the harbour to challenge French supremacy in England by engaging in the first regular sea-fight of modern history. Sir W. H. Nicholas says:

> It appears that the wind was southerly, blowing fresh; and the French were going large steering round the North Foreland, little expecting any opposition. The English squadron, instead of directly approaching the enemy, kept their wind as if going to Calais, which made Eustace, the French commander, exclaim, 'I know that those wretches think to invade Calais like thieves;

but that is useless, for it is well defended!' As soon as the English had gained the wind of the French fleet, they bore down in the most gallant manner upon the enemy's rear; and the moment they came close to the sterns of the French ships they threw grapnels into them, and, thus fastening the vessels together, prevented the enemy from escaping—an early instance of that love of close fighting for which English sailors have ever since been distinguished.

The action commenced by the English cross-bowmen and archers pouring volleys of arrows into the enemy's ships with deadly effect; and to increase their dismay, the English threw unslaked lime, reduced to a powder, on board their opponents, which being blown by the wind into their eyes, completely blinded them. The English then rushed on board; and cutting away the rigging and halyards with axes, the sails fell over the French 'like a net over ensnared small birds.' . . . Thus hampered, the enemy could make but a feeble resistance; and after an immense slaughter were completely defeated. Though the French fought with great bravery, very few among them were accustomed to naval tactics; and they fell rapidly under the lances, axes, and swords of their assailants. In the meantime, many of their vessels had been sunk by the galleys, which, running their own prows into them, stove their sides.

Of the whole French fleet, fifteen vessels only escaped; and as soon as the principal persons had been secured, the English taking the captured ships in tow, proceeded in triumph to Dover, 'victoriously ploughing the waves,' and returning thanks to God for their success. . . . The battle was seen with exultation by the garrison of Dover Castle, and the conquerors were received by the bishops and clergy in full sacerdotal habits, bearing crosses and banners in procession.

Though the ships, compared with those of the present age were small, yet the mode of attack, the bravery displayed, and the great superiority of the enemy render the event worthy of an honourable place in the list of our naval victories. It was actually a hand-to-hand fight against double the number of ships, and probably four times the number of men. The political effect of the battle was that Louis relinquished all hopes of the English crown. England was saved. "The courage of the sailors who manned the rude boats of the Cinque Ports first made the flag of England terrible on the seas." For this celebrated action, which saved England from the domination of France, the Cinque Ports obtained further privileges, amongst which was liberty to "annoy the subjects of France"—in other words, to plunder as they pleased the merchant vessels of that country.

Few naval events of any importance occurred for many years after the signal victory off Dover. The Cinque Ports were at their highest tide of prosperity during the reign of Edward I., who, in 1300, took thirty of their ships with him in his expedition against Scotland. During the reign of Edward II. the ports did not lack employment on the king's service, though they acted merely as coast-guards. The sovereignty of the Channel was gradually challenged in this reign by the French, who were encouraged by the revolutions and disorders of the time, and Edward III. had not been many years on the throne before it became evident that the nation must bestir itself in view of the increasing power of the French fleet.

A formal proclamation declaring England's sovereignty of the seas was issued. A new spirit at once declared itself, but not a moment before it was necessary; for in 1339 the French fleet burnt Portsmouth, inflicted severe disaster upon Southampton, threatened Sandwich, and, diverging to Rye, landed and ravaged the immediate neighbourhood. On the approach of the English fleet the French took to flight and were chased into Boulogne. The English gallantly entered the harbour, captured several French vessels, hanged twelve of their captains, burnt part of the town, and returned with their prizes to England.

Towards the end of 1339 a new invasion was planned. The French ships and galleys assembled off the town of Sluys, in Flanders, and their crews solemnly vowed not to return to their own ports till they had taken one hundred English ships and five hundred English towns. In view of this invasion parliament was summoned in January 1340 "to adopt various measures relating to the navy." The sailors of the Cinque Ports undertook to have their ships ready, and in due course a fleet of two hundred vessels was formed, and more soldiers and archers assembled than could be employed.

On his arrival on the coast of Flanders, Edward found that the various sections of his fleet had met, and discovered the French fleet of one hundred and ninety ships, manned by thirty-five thousand Normans and Genoese, lying at anchor off Sluys. The French fleet was in four divisions, their ships being fastened to each other by iron chains and cables. To the masts a small boat was suspended, filled with stones, which were to be hurled by the soldiers stationed on the tops. Trumpets and other martial instruments resounded from the French ships. The fight was long and fierce, for "the enemy defended themselves all that day and the night after." In one French ship alone four hundred dead bodies were found, the survivors leaping headlong into the sea.

Only twenty-four of the French ships escaped, and no less than twenty-five thousand French and Genoese perished. The English loss was, perhaps, four thousand men, and all writers agree that it was one of the most sanguinary and desperate sea-fights recorded in the pages of history. Edward's modest letter regarding this victory is the earliest naval despatch in existence. Though the annihilation of the French fleet at Sluys did not surpass in importance the victory off Dover in the preceding century, it established the maritime supremacy of England.

To supply a covering force for the army which was besieging Calais in 1347 and to guard the Channel, England made a general demand for ships and seamen. The total number of ships mustered was seven hundred and ten; these were equipped with a full complement of fighting men. The "five Cinque Ports and two Ancient Towns," together with Seaford, Faversham, and Margate, contributed one hundred and five ships; London sent twenty-five ships, Fowey forty-seven, and Dunwich six. Three years later on August 29th, 1350, the battle known as *"Lespagnols-sur-mer"* was fought off Winchelsea, when Edward defeated a Spanish squadron of forty sail which had plundered several English ships, capturing twenty-six large vessels, the crews of which were put to death. This action firmly established the reputation of Edward III. as the King of England, whose name is more identified with the naval glory of England than that of any other sovereign up to the sixteenth century.

But reverses of fortune clouded the end of what had promised to be a glorious reign. In 1371 an engagement with the Flemings resulted in the capture of twenty-five ships by the English, but in June, 1372, the Spaniards completely defeated the English fleet of forty sail under the Earl of Pembroke off La Rochelle; the Spaniards not only having the advantage of size and numbers in their ships, but also in being provided with cannon, said to have been first used at sea in this battle. Immediately upon Edward's death an overwhelming fleet of French and Spanish ships swept the Channel, and Winchelsea, Rye, Hastings, Plymouth, Portsmouth and other ports suffered from the fury of the invaders.

The reign of Richard II. was redeemed from absolute barrenness in naval affairs by the victory of the Earl of Arundel in 1387. Taking advantage of the absence from England of John of Gaunt, Duke of Lancaster, who had sailed the year before to enforce his claim upon the crown of Spain, the French raised a powerful armament with a view to invading the British Isles. These preparations were made upon a most extensive scale, and were said to have included an army of a hundred thousand men and a fleet of ships which, if laid side by side, would have reached from Calais to Dover. The news of this terrible armament caused great excitement in England, and various preparations were made to receive it.

The Earl of Arundel was made high admiral and was dispatched to sea with instructions to destroy the ships of the enemy as they disembarked; while the people on shore laid waste the country, and dealt with them as opportunity served. The winds and the waves, however, fought on England's side, and under stress of weather the army was disbanded and the enterprise abandoned. The Earl of Arundel, taking advantage of the situation, attacked the French fleet with great vigour, captured a hundred and sixty vessels, and proceeding to the Port of Sluys, destroyed the ships that had taken refuge there, and laid waste the country for ten leagues round.

The reign of Henry IV. was likewise characterised by abortive invasions on the part of the French. In 1403-4, La Marche, a young French prince, made a descent upon Falmouth with a view to helping Owen Glendower, the leader of the Welsh rebellion; but the attempt was an entire failure. In the spring of 1405, however, a second French fleet, consisting of a hundred and twenty sail and carrying large numbers of cavalry, bore down upon our southern coast. Once more our old allies, the winds and the waves, did us good service; for most of the horses fell victims to the rigours of the journey, and no sooner were the ships moored off Milford Haven than they were attacked by the squadron of the Cinque Ports, which burnt fifteen ships, captured six transports laden with food and ammunition, and cut off all supplies at sea. The French were rather more successful on land, but before the end of the year they were glad of an excuse for sailing back to France.

But the corporation of the Cinque Ports had practically fulfilled its purpose, and was now to give way to other organisations better adapted to the requirements of the times. Even at this early date some of the ports had begun to suffer from "the sea change," which eventually caused the majority of them to be deserted by the routes of commerce; and Henry V., finding that their harbours were no longer capable of building or sheltering the large ships which were required in his time, determined to establish a King's Royal Navy. So successful was he, that in his fleet which invaded France in 1415, and which consisted of one thousand four hundred vessels, carrying about six thousand men-at-arms and twenty-four thousand archers, were twenty-seven royal ships, some perhaps of the size of five hundred tons.

After the return of Henry V. from the Battle of Agincourt, and during the negotiations which were to settle the relationships of England and France for the future, the Count of Armagnac, who had succeeded D'Albret, slain at Agincourt, as Constable of France, determined to attempt the recapture of Harfleur, held for the king by the Earl of Dorset, and with this view laid siege to the town by land, and sent the French fleet with a number of Genoese *caracks* and Spanish ships hired for the occasion to blockade the port from the sea. Henry V. in a great rage dispatched his brother, the Duke of Bedford, to deal with this formidable armament. The duke assembled his ships at Rye in August 1416, and on the 14th of the same month reached the mouth of the Seine, at the head of a fleet said to number four hundred sail and to carry twenty thousand men. He found the Genoese galleys so tall that the largest of his ships could not reach to their upper decks by a spar's length, while the Spanish ships far out-matched his own for size and for the number of their crews.

Notwithstanding the disparity of the forces the duke determined to attack the enemy on the following day; and on the morning of August 15th, 1416, taking advantage of the wind, he engaged the combined fleets with such vigour that he succeeded in capturing or destroying nearly five hundred ships, his men clambering up the Genoese galleys like so many squirrels and boarding them in gallant style. Having destroyed the fleet, the duke joined his forces with those of the garrison in repelling the attacks on land and sea, and compelled the Count of Armagnac to raise the siege and retire. The duke remained long enough to see the town placed in a state of defence and then returned to England.

In 1417 the Earl of Huntingdon being sent to sea with a strong squadron, met with the united fleets of France and Genoa, which he fought and defeated, though they were much superior to his—not only in number, but in the strength and size of their ships—taking the French admiral prisoner, and capturing four large Genoese ships, containing a quarter's pay for the whole navy.

The reign of Henry VI. added but little to the naval glory of England. In August 1457 a fleet fitted out in Normandy made a descent upon the coast of Kent and landed nearly two thousand men about two leagues from Sandwich, with instructions to attack the port by land while the fleet engaged it from the sea. In this case the English were taken by surprise, and the town pillaged and burnt, with great loss on both sides. Other attempts of the kind were also made at other parts of the coast. In the following year, Warwick, the King Maker, having been made admiral, caused several squadrons to be put to sea, to the officers of which he gave such instructions as he thought proper.

On Trinity Sunday, 1458, one of these squadrons fell in with the Spanish fleet and quickly came to hostilities; with the result that the English captured six ships laden with iron and other merchandise and destroyed twenty-six others. A year later Warwick himself put to sea from Calais with fourteen sail, when he encountered five large ships in the English Channel, three of which were Genoese and two Spanish, all of them being richly laden with merchandise. After an engagement which lasted two days he succeeded in capturing three of these, which were hauled into Calais, where their cargoes realised £10,000. It is said that in this engagement Warwick lost fifty men and the enemy nearly a thousand.

Jealous of the successes of Warwick, the French queen of Henry VI. sent Lord Rivers down to Sandwich to seek the assistance of the Cinque Ports in depriving the earl of the government of Calais; but when the ships were almost ready, Warwick sent a squadron under Sir John Dineham, which captured the whole fleet, carrying away Lord Rivers and Anthony Woodville, his son, who long remained prisoners in Calais. After this, one Sir Baldwin Talford undertook to burn the earl's fleet in the haven of Calais; this, however, proved but a vain vaunt.

At last the Duke of Exeter, who had been made admiral, received information that the Earl of Warwick had set sail for Ireland, and stood out to sea to intercept him; the sailors in the king's ships, however, showed so much coldness in the cause, that it was not judged safe to risk an engagement, and Warwick, not wishing to destroy the king's fleet, passed by without molesting it. Later, Warwick, on an invitation from Kent, made a descent upon the country and encountered Sir Simon de Montfort, then warden of the Cinque Ports, with his squadron off Sandwich, which he attacked, defeated and destroyed, Sir

Simon being killed in the engagement.

Thenceforward the decline of the Cinque Ports fleet as a fighting force was sure. It was called out occasionally for the transport of royal personages and was employed by Henry VII. and Henry VIII. to transport troops to France; it furnished some of the ships which harassed the Armada in its passage up the Channel; but that was its final effort. The King's Navy with difficulty survived the chaos of the reign of Henry VI., but it never wholly disappeared. The revival of commerce in the reigns of Edward IV. and Henry VII., both of whom were engaged largely in mercantile speculations, created additional interest in maritime affairs; but it was left to Henry VIII. to make the vital change which firmly established the Royal Navy as an organisation independent of the merchant service.

The Story of Sir Edward Howard
By John Campbell

Sir Edward Howard was the second son of Thomas, Earl of Surrey, afterwards Duke of Norfolk, and treasurer to Henry VIII. He seems to have begun early in life to testify his inclination for the sea service, and we find him employed in the Flanders expedition in 1492, when King Henry VII. thought fit to assist the Duke of Burgundy against his rebellious subjects.

The Flemings, naturally a brave people and fond of freedom, grew uneasy under the yoke of the House of Austria, and under the command of the Baron de Ravenstein began to throw off allegiance. In doing this, they seized the town and harbour of Sluys, whence they fitted out a number of vessels of considerable force; and, under colour of pursuing their enemies, took and plundered vessels of all nations without distinction. As the English trade with Flanders was then very extensive, English ships suffered at least as much as any others; and this was the reason why King Henry, upon the first application of the Duke of Burgundy, sent a squadron of twelve sail to his assistance under the command of Sir Edward Poynings, with whom went out Sir Edward Howard, then a very young man, to learn the art of war. The Duke of Saxony, in consequence of his alliance with the Duke of Burgundy, marched with an army into Flanders, and besieged Sluys by land; and Sir Edward Poynings thereupon blockaded it by sea.

The port was defended by two strong castles, which the Flemings, who had nothing to trust to but force, defended with unparalleled obstinacy; insomuch, that though Poynings attacked them constantly every day for twenty days successively, yet he made no great impression, till at last, through accident, the bridge of boats, by which the communication between the castles was preserved, took fire; whereupon the besieged were glad to surrender their city to the Duke of

Saxony, and their port and castles to the English. After this expedition Sir Edward was made a knight for extraordinary bravery, of which quality he gave many proofs during the reign of Henry VII., so thoroughly establishing his reputation that Henry VIII., on his accession, made choice of him for his standard-bearer, which in those days was considered not only as a mark of particular favour, but as a testimony also of the highest confidence and esteem.

In the fourth year of the same reign he was created lord high-Admiral of England, and in that station convoyed the Marquis of Dorset into Spain. The admiral, after the landing of the forces, put to sea again; and, arriving on the coasts of Brittany, landed some of his men about Conquet and Brest, who ravaged the country and burnt several of the small towns. This roused the French, who began immediately to fit out a great fleet, in order, if possible, to drive the English from their coasts; and, as this armament was very extraordinary, King Henry sent a squadron of five-and-twenty tall ships, which he caused to be fitted out under his own eye at Portsmouth, to the assistance of the admiral.

Among these were two capital ships; one called the *Regent*, commanded by Sir Thomas Knevet, master of the horse to the king; and the other, which was the *Sovereign*, by Sir Charles Brandon, afterwards Duke of Suffolk. When these vessels had joined the admiral, his fleet consisted of no less than forty-five sail, with which he immediately resolved to attack the enemy, who were by this time ready to come out of the harbour of Brest. Authors differ much as to their number, though they agree pretty well as to the name of the admiral, whom they call Primauget; yet it seems they agree in a mistake, for the historians of Brittany assure us they have no such name in that province, and that undoubtedly it ought to be Porsmoguer.

Whatever his name was, or whatever the force of his fleet might have been (our writers say it consisted of thirty-nine, and the French only of twenty, sail), he was certainly a very brave man. The ship he commanded was called the *Cordelier*, and was so large as to be able to carry twelve hundred fighting men, exclusive of mariners. At this time there were nine hundred on board; and, encouraged by their gallant officer, they did their duty bravely. Sir Thomas Knevet, in the *Regent*, which was a much smaller ship, attacked and boarded the *Cordelier*, and the action lasted for some time with equal vigour on both sides. At last, both flag ships took fire and burnt together, wherein the two commanders and upwards of sixteen hundred valiant men were lost.

It seems this accident struck both fleets with amazement; so that they separated without fighting, each claiming the victory, to which probably neither had a very good title.

In the beginning of the next April the admiral put to sea again with a fleet of forty-two men-of-war, besides small vessels, and forced the French into the harbour of Brest, where they fortified themselves, in order to wait the arrival of a squadron of six galleys from the Mediterranean. Sir Edward Howard, having considered their position, resolved, since it was impossible to attack them, to burn the country round about; which he accordingly did, in spite of all the care they could take to prevent it; and yet the French lay still under the cover of their fortifications and of a line of twenty-four large hulks lashed together, which they proposed to have set on fire in case the English attempted to force them to a battle.

While the admiral was thus employed, he had intelligence that M. Pregent, with the six galleys from the Mediterranean, had arrived on the coast, and had taken shelter in the Bay of Conquet. This circumstance induced him to change his plans; and he now resolved first to destroy the galleys, if possible, and then to return to the fleet. Upon his advancing to reconnoitre Pregent's squadron, he found them at anchor between two rocks, on each of which stood a strong fort; and, what was likely to give him still more trouble, they lay so far up in the bay that he could bring none of his ships of force to engage them. The only way open to him now was to put the bravest of his sailors on board two galleys which were in his fleet, and with these to venture in and try what might be done against the six.

This being resolved on, he went himself, attended by Sir Thomas Cheyne and Sir John Wallop, on board one of the galleys, and sent Lord Ferrers, Sir Henry Sherburn, and Sir William Sidney on board the other; and, having a brisk gale of wind, sailed directly into the bay, where, with his own galley, he attacked the French admiral. As soon as they were grappled, Sir Edward Howard, followed by seventeen of the bravest of his sailors, boarded the enemy, and were very gallantly received; but it so happened that, in the midst of the engagement, the galleys sheered asunder, and the French, taking advantage of this circumstance, forced the English overboard, except one seaman, from whom they quickly learned that the English admiral was among the slain.

Lord Ferrers, in the other galley, did all that was possible for a very brave man to do; but, having spent all his shot, and perceiving, as he thought, the admiral retire, he likewise made the best of his way out of the harbour.

In Lord Herbert's *Life and Reign of Henry VIII., 1513*, there are some very singular circumstances given relating to this unlucky adventure. He says that Sir Edward Howard having considered the position of the French fleet in the haven of Brest, and the consequences which would attend either defeating or burning it, gave notice thereof to the king, inviting him to be present at so glorious an action; desiring rather that the king should have the honour of destroying the French naval force than himself; a loyal, generous proposition—supposing the honour, not the danger, too great for a subject, and measuring (no doubt very justly) his master's courage by his own; the only standard men of his rank and temper of mind ever use.

But, his letter being laid before the council, they were altogether of another opinion; conceiving it was much too great a hazard for His Majesty to expose his person in such an enterprise; and therefore they wrote sharply to the admiral, commanding him not to send excuses, but to do his duty. This, as it well might, piqued him to the utmost; and as it was his avowed maxim that a seaman never did good who was not resolute to a degree of madness, he took a sudden resolution of acting in the manner he did. When he found his galley slide away and saw the danger to which he was exposed, he took his chain of gold nobles which hung about his neck, and his great gold whistle, the ensign of his office, and threw them into the sea, to prevent the enemy from possessing the spoils of an English admiral. Thus fell the great Sir Edward Howard, on April 25th, 1513, a sacrifice to his too quick sense of honour in the service, and yet to the manifest and acknowledged detriment of his country; for his death so dejected the spirits of his sailors that the fleet was obliged to return home.

Sir Edward Howard, we are assured, was very far from being either a mere soldier or a mere seaman, though so eminent in both characters; but he was what it became an English gentleman of so high a quality to be—an able statesman, a faithful counsellor, and a free speaker. He was ready at all times to hazard his life and fortune in his country's quarrels; and yet he was against her quarrelling on insufficient occasion or against her interests. He particularly dissuaded a breach with the Flemings, for the wise and strong reasons that such a war was prejudicial to commerce abroad; that it diminished the customs, while it increased the public expenses; that it served the French, by constraining the inhabitants of Flanders to deal with them against their will; and that it tended to the prejudice of our manufactures, by interrupting our intercourse with those by whom they were principally improved.

Thus qualified, we need not wonder he attained such high honours, though he died in the flower of his age. Henry conferred upon him many titles and other rewards, making him Admiral of England, Wales, Ireland, Normandy, Gascony, and Aquitaine, for life, and causing him to be chosen Knight of the Garter; believing that he should thereby command, as indeed he did, not only the utmost service of Sir Edward, but also all the force and interest of his potent family; an interest in later years which he but ill requited. As soon as the news of his unfortunate death reached the ears of his royal master he was succeeded in his high office by Sir Thomas Howard, his elder brother.

The Story of Sir Thomas Howard and Sir Andrew Barton
By John Campbell

In the third year of the reign of Henry VIII., Sir Andrew Barton, a Scots seaman, with two stout vessels—the *Lion* and the *Jenny Perwin*—ranged the coasts of England and interrupted all trade and navigation; his authority being letters of reprisals against the Portuguese, granted him by James III., late King of Scotland, under which he did not hesitate to attack and appropriate ships of all nations, alleging that they had Portuguese goods on board. On complaint of these grievances being made to the Privy Council of England, the Earl of Surrey, afterwards Duke of Norfolk, treasurer to Henry VIII. and father of Sir Edward Howard referred to in the previous story, and of Sir Thomas Howard, who forms the subject of this sketch, said the narrow seas should not be so infested while he had estate enough to furnish a ship and a son capable of commanding it.

Upon this, two ships were immediately fitted out by the brothers, probably at their own, or at their father's cost; for if they had gone with the king's commission they would most likely have sailed at the head of a squadron. Upon an expedition of this kind, however, they needed no commission, for pirates being *hostes humani generis*, enemies to mankind in general, every man was at liberty to act against them.

The brothers having been some days at sea, were separated by a storm, which gave Sir Thomas Howard an opportunity of coming up with Sir Andrew Barton in the *Lion*, whom he immediately engaged. The fight was long and doubtful; for Barton, who was an experienced seaman, and who had under him a determined crew, made a most desperate defence; cheering his men with a boatswain's whistle to his last breath. On the loss of their captain, however, they were induced to submit, and were received to quarter and fair usage. In the meantime, Sir Edward fought and took the consort of the *Lion*, which was likewise a strong vessel, and exceedingly well-manned. Both these ships, with as many men as were left alive, being in number one hundred and fifty, they brought on August 2nd, 1511, into the River Thames, as trophies of their victory.

King James IV., who then governed the Scots, exceedingly resented this action, and instantly sent ambassadors to Henry to demand satisfaction; on which the king gave the memorable answer: "That punishing pirates was never held a breach of peace among princes." King James, however, remained still dissatisfied; and, from that time to his death was never thoroughly reconciled to the king or English nation.

Sir Thomas Howard accompanied the Marquis of Dorset in his expedition against Guienne; which ended in King Ferdinand's conquering Navarre; and the commander-in-chief falling sick, Sir Thomas succeeded him, and brought home the remains of the English army. He had scarcely returned, however, before the news arrived of the death of his brother, Sir Edward the lord-Admiral; whereupon the king instantly appointed him his successor. The French ships were at that time hovering about the English coasts; but Sir Thomas quickly scoured the seas, so that not a barque of that nation durst appear; and, on July 1st, 1513, landing in Whitsand Bay, he pillaged the country adjacent and burnt a considerable town. Henry VIII. was at this time engaged in Picardy, and in the absence of the king and his admiral, James IV. seized the opportunity to invade England with a mighty army, supposing he should find it without defence.

Thomas, Earl of Surrey, father of the admiral, however, quickly convinced him of his mistake, marching towards Scotland with a powerful army, which strengthened as it moved; while Sir Thomas Howard, returning, on the news of the invasion, landed five thousand veterans, and made haste to join his father. The Earl of Surrey despatching a herald to bid the Scots king battle, the lord-Admiral sent him word, at the same time, that he was come in person to answer for the death of Sir Andrew Barton. This defiance produced the famous Battle of Flodden Field,[1] which was fought on September the 8th, 1513, when Sir Thomas Howard commanded the van-guard, and, by his courage and conduct, contributed not a little to the glorious victory in which James IV. of Scotland fell, with the flower of his army.

---

1. *The Battle of Flodden Field* by Robert Jones, also published by Leonaur.

King Henry, for this and other services, restored Thomas, Earl of Surrey, to the title of Norfolk, and created the lord-Admiral Earl of Surrey.

The war being ended with France, the admiral's martial talent lay some time unemployed; but certain disturbances in Ireland calling for redress, the active Earl of Surrey was sent thither, with a commission as lord-deputy, where he suppressed Desmond's rebellion, humbled the O'Neals and O'Carrols, and, without affecting severity or popularity, brought all things into good order, leaving, when he quitted the island, peace and a parliament behind him, and carrying with him the affections of the people.

The pretence for recalling him was the breaking out again of a French war. Before it was declared, the French ships of war interrupted (according to custom) the English trade, so that we suffered as their enemies, while their ambassadors were treated as our friends. The lord-Admiral, on his arrival, immediately fitted out a small squadron of clean ships, under a vigilant commander, who soon drove the French privateers from the sea. In the spring, Sir William Fitz-William, as vice-Admiral, put to sea, with a fleet of twenty-eight men-of-war, to guard the narrow seas; and it being apprehended that the Scots might add to the number of the king's enemies by sea as well as by land, a small squadron of seven frigates sailed up the Firth of Forth, and burned all such vessels as lay there and were in a condition of going to sea.

In the meantime, the admiral prepared a Royal Navy, with which that of the Emperor Charles V. (of Spain) was to join; and as it was evident that many inconveniences might arise from the fleets having several commanders-in-chief, the Earl of Surrey, by special commission from Henry VIII., received the emperor's commission to be admiral also of the united navy, which consisted of one hundred and eighty tall ships.

With the united fleets, the admiral sailed over to the coast of Normandy, and landed some forces near Cherbourg, wasted and destroyed the country; after which they returned. This seems to have been a feint; for, in a few days, the admiral landed again on the coast of Bretagne a very large body of troops, with which he took and plundered the town of Morlaix; and having gained an immense booty, and opened a passage for the English forces into Champagne and Picardy, he first detached Sir William Fitz-William with a strong squadron to scour the seas and to protect the merchants, and then returned to Southampton, where the emperor, Charles V., who had visited England to confer with Henry VIII. and Cardinal Wolsey, embarked on board his ship, and was safely convoyed to the port of St. Andero, in Biscay.

The Earl of Surrey succeeded to the office of Lord Treasurer on the retirement of his father, and on the duke's death was appointed to command an army against the Scots and employed on various other commissions of importance.

Towards the close of his reign the king was led to believe that he (now Duke of Norfolk) and his son, Henry, Earl of Surrey, the most distinguished poet of his time, were in a plot to seize upon his person, and to engross the government into their own hands. For these supposed crimes, he and his son were imprisoned and attainted almost on suspicion. Henry, Earl of Surrey, lost his head in his father's presence; nor would the duke have survived him long, if the king had not died at that critical juncture and thereby opened a door of hope and liberty. After all these sufferings, he survived King Edward VI. and died in the first year of Queen Mary, at the age of sixty-six, when his attainder was repealed, and the act thereof taken from amongst the records.

The Story of Sir John Hawkins

And the troublesome voyage made with the *Jesus* of Lubeck, the *Minion*, and four other ships to the parts of Guinea and the West Indies, in the years 1567 and 1568 by Master John Hawkins.

Sir John Hawkins was born at Plymouth about the year 1520. He was from his youth devoted to the study of navigation, and began very early to carry his knowledge into practice by making voyages to Spain, Portugal and the Canaries, voyages which were in those days great undertakings. In 1562 he made his first voyage to Guinea for slaves, and then to Hispaniola, St. John de Porto Rico, and other Spanish islands, for sugars, hides, silver, etc. His venture proving financially successful he made another voyage in 1564 with a like purpose, with the same success, arriving on his return at Padstow in Cornwall, on September 20th, 1565.

Towards the end of the year 1567, he started on the unfortunate voyage made with the *Jesus*, the *Minion* and four other ships to the ports of Guinea and the West Indies, his own personal account of which is thus recorded in Hakluyt's *Voyages*.

> The ships departed from Plymouth October 2nd, 1567, and had reasonable weather until the seventh day, at which time, forty leagues north from Cape Finisterre, there arose an extreme storm which continued four days, in such sort that the fleet was dispersed and all our great boats lost, and the *Jesus*, our chief ship, in such case as not thought able to serve the voyage. Whereupon in the same storm we set our course homeward, determining to give over the voyage; but the eleventh day of the same month the wind changed, with fair weather, whereby we were animated to follow our enterprise, and so did, directing our course to the islands of Grand Canaries, where, according to an order before prescribed, all our ships, before dispersed,

met in one of those islands, called Gomera, where we took water, and departed from thence on November 4th towards the coast of Guinea, and arrived at Cape Verde, November 18th, where we landed one hundred and fifty men, hoping to obtain some negroes; where we got but few, and those with great hurt and damage to our men, which chiefly proceeded from their envenomed arrows; although in the beginning they seemed to be but small hurts, yet there hardly escaped any that had blood drawn of them but died in strange sort, with their mouths shut, some ten days before they died, and after their wounds were whole; where I myself had one of the greatest wounds, yet, thanks be to God, escaped.

From thence we passed the time upon the coast of Guinea, searching with all diligence the rivers from Rio Grande unto Sierra Leone till January 12th, in which time we had not gotten together a hundred and fifty negroes: yet, notwithstanding, the sickness of our men and the late time of the year commanded us away: and thus having nothing wherewith to seek the coast of the West Indies, I was with the rest of our company in consultation to go to the coast of the Myne, hoping there to have obtained some gold for our wares, and thereby to have defrayed our charge. But even in that present instant there came to us a negro sent from a king oppressed by other kings, his neighbours, desiring our aid, with promise that as many negroes as by these wars might be obtained, as well of his part as of ours, should be at our pleasure.

Whereupon we concluded to give aid, and sent one hundred and twenty of our men, which January 15th assaulted a town of the negroes of our allies' adversaries which had in it eight thousand inhabitants, and very strongly impaled and fenced after their manner; but it was so well defended that our men prevailed not, but lost six men, and forty hurt, so that our men sent forthwith to me for more help; whereupon, considering that the good success of this enterprise might highly further the commodity of our voyage, I went myself, and with the help of the king of our side assaulted the town, both by land and sea, and very hardly with fire (their houses being covered with dry palm leaves) obtained the town, and put the inhabitants to flight, where we took two hundred and fifty persons, men, women, and children, and by our friend the king of our side there were taken six hundred prisoners, whereof we hoped to have our choice, but the negro (in which nation is seldom or never found truth) meant nothing less; for that night he removed his camp and prisoners, so that we were fain to content us with those few which we had gotten ourselves.

Now had we obtained between four and five hundred negroes, wherewith we thought it somewhat reasonable to seek the coast of the West Indies, and there, for our negroes, and our other merchandise, we hoped to obtain whereof to countervail our charges with some gains, whereunto we proceeded with all diligence, finished our watering, took fuel, and departed the coast of Guinea, on February 3rd, continuing at the sea with a passage more hard than before hath been accustomed till March 27th, which day we had sight of an island called Dominique, upon the coast of the West Indies, in fourteen degrees; from thence we coasted from place to place, making our traffic with the Spaniards as we might, somewhat hardy, because the king had straightly commanded all his governors in those parts by no means to suffer any trade to be made with us; notwithstanding we had reasonable trade, and courteous entertainment from the Isle of Marguerite and Cartagena, without anything greatly worth the noting, saving at Capo de la Vela, in a town called Rio de la Hacha, from whence come all the pearls.

The treasurer who had the charge there would by no means agree to any trade, or suffer us to take water. He had fortified his town with divers bulwarks in all places where it might be entered, and furnished himself with a hundred harquebusiers, so that he thought by famine to have enforced us to have put on land our negroes, of which purpose he had not greatly failed unless we had by force entered the town; which (after we could by no means obtain his favour) we were enforced to do, and so with two hundred men brake in upon their bulwarks, and entered the town with the loss only of eleven men of our parts, and no hurt done to the Spaniards, because after their volley of shot discharged, they all fled.

Thus having the town, with some circumstance, as partly by the Spaniards' desire of negroes, and partly by friendship of the treasurer, we obtained a secret trade; whereupon the Spaniards resorted to us by night, and bought of us to the number of two hundred negroes; in all other places where we traded the Spaniard inhabitants were glad of us, and traded willingly.

At Cartagena, the last town we thought to have seen on the coast, we could by no means obtain to deal with any Spaniard, the governor was so straight, and because our trade was so near finished, we thought not good either to adventure any landing or to detract further time, but in peace departed from thence on July 24th, hoping to have escaped the time of their storms, which then soon after began to reign, the which they call *Furicanos*; but passing by the west end of Cuba, towards the coast of Florida, there happened to us, on August 12th, an extreme storm, which continued by the space of four days, which so beat the *Jesus*, that we cut down all her higher buildings; her rudder also was sore shaken, and, withal, was in so extreme a leak, that we were rather upon the point to leave her than to keep her any longer; yet, hoping to bring all to good pass, sought the coast of Florida, where we found no place nor haven for our ships because of the shallowness of the coast.

Thus, being in greater despair, and taken with a new storm, which continued other three days, we were enforced to take for our succour the port which serveth the city of Mexico, called St. John de Ullua, which standeth in nineteen degrees, in seeking of which port we took in our way three ships, which carried passengers to the number of one hundred, which passengers we hoped should be a means to us the better to obtain victuals for our money and a quiet place for the repairing of our fleet. Shortly after this, on September 16th, we entered the port of St. John de Ullua, and on our entry, the Spaniards thinking us to be the fleet of Spain, the chief officers of the country came aboard us, which, being deceived of their expectation, were greatly dismayed, but immediately, when they saw our demand was nothing but victuals, were recomforted.

I found also in the same port, twelve ships, which had in them, by the report, 200,000 *livres* in gold and silver, all which (being in my possession with the King's Island, as also the passengers before in my way thitherward stayed) I set at liberty, without the taking from them the weight of a groat; only, because I would not be delayed of my despatch, I stayed two men of estimation, and sent post immediately to Mexico, which was two hundred miles from us, to the presidents and council there, showing them of our arrival there by the force of weather, and the necessity of the repair of our ships and victuals, which wants we required, as friends to King Philip, to be furnished of for our money, and that the presidents in council there should, with all convenient speed, take order that at the arrival of the Spanish fleet, which was daily looked for, there might no cause of quarrel rise between us and them, but, for the better maintenance of amity, their commandment might be had in that behalf.

This message being sent away on September 16th, at night, being the very day of our arrival, in the next morning, which was the sixteenth day of the same month, we saw open of the haven thirteen great ships, and understanding them to be the fleet of Spain, I sent immediately to advertise the general of the fleet of my being there, giving him to understand that, before I would suffer them to enter the port, there should be some order of conditions pass between us for our safe being there and maintenance of peace. Now, it is to be understood that this port is a little island of stones, not three feet above the water in the highest place, and but a bow-shot of length any way. This island standeth from the mainland two bow-shots or more.

Also it is to be understood that there is not in all this coast any other place for ships to arrive in safety, because the north wind hath there such violence, that, unless the ships be very safely moored, with their anchors fastened upon this island, there is no remedy for these north winds but death; also, the place of the haven was so little, that of necessity the ships must ride one aboard the other, so that we could not give place to them nor they to us; and here I began to bewail the which after followed: 'For now,' said I, 'I am in two dangers, and forced to receive the one of them.' That was, either I must have kept out the fleet from entering the port (the which, with God's help, I was very well able to do), or else suffer them to enter in with their accustomed treason, which they never fail to execute where they may have opportunity, or circumvent it by any means.

If I had kept them out, then had there been present shipwreck of all the fleet, which, amounted in value to six millions, which was in value of our money 1,800,000 *livres*, which I considered I was not able to answer, fearing the Queen's Majesty's indignation in so weighty a matter. Thus with myself revolving the doubts, I thought rather better to abide the jutt of the uncertainty than the certainty. The uncertain doubt was their treason, which by good policy I hoped might be prevented; and therefore, as choosing the least mischief, I proceeded to conditions.

Now was our first messenger come and returned from the fleet with report of the arrival of a viceroy, so that he had authority, both in all this province of Mexico (otherwise called Nova Hispania) and in the sea, who sent us word that we should send our conditions, which of his part should (for the better maintenance of amity between the princes) be both favourably granted and faithfully performed, with many fair words how, passing the coast of the Indies, he had understood of our honest behaviour towards the inhabitants, where we had to do as well elsewhere as in the same port; the which I let pass, thus following our demand. We required victual for our money, and license to sell as much ware as might furnish our wants, and that there might be of either part twelve gentlemen as hostage for the maintenance of peace, and that the island, for our better safety, might be in our own possession during our abode there, and such ordnance as was planted in the same island, which was eleven pieces of brass, and that no Spaniard might land in the island with any kind of weapon.

These conditions at the first he somewhat misliked—chiefly the guard of the island to be in our own keeping, which, if they had had, we had soon known our fate; for with the first north wind they had cut our cables, and our ships had gone ashore; but in the end he concluded to our request, bringing the twelve hostages to ten, which with all speed on either part were received, with a writing from the viceroy, signed with his hand and sealed with his seal, of all the conditions concluded, and forthwith a trumpet blown, with commandment that none of either part should inviolate the peace upon pain of death; and, further, it was concluded that the two generals of the fleet should meet, and give faith each to other for the performance of the promises, which was so done.

Thus, at the end of three days, all was concluded, and the fleet entered the port, saluting one another as the manner of the sea doth require. Thus, as I said before, Thursday we entered the port, Friday we saw the fleet, and on Monday, at night, they entered the port; then we laboured two days, placing the English ships by themselves and the Spanish ships by themselves, the captains of each part, and inferior men of their parts, promising great amity of all sides; which, even as with all fidelity was meant of our part, though the Spanish meant nothing less of their parts, but from the mainland had furnished themselves with a supply of men to the number of one thousand, and meant the next Thursday, being September 23rd, at dinner-time, to set upon us of all sides.

The same Thursday, the treason being at hand, some appearance showed, as shifting of weapons from ship to ship, planting and bending of ordnance from the ship to the island where our men were, passing to and fro of companies of men more than required for their necessary business, and many other ill likelihoods, which caused us to have a vehement suspicion and therewithal sent to the viceroy to inquire what was meant by it, which sent immediately straight commandment to unplant all things suspicious, and also sent word that he, in the faith of a viceroy, would be our defence from all villainies. Yet we, not being satisfied with this answer, because we suspected a great number of men to be hid in a great ship of nine hundred tons, which was moored next unto the *Minion*, sent again unto the viceroy the master of the *Jesus*, which had the Spanish tongue, and required to be satisfied if any such thing were or not; on which the viceroy, seeing that the treason must be discovered, forthwith stayed our master, blew the trumpet, and of all sides set upon us.

Our men which were on guard ashore, being stricken with sudden fear, gave place, fled, and sought to recover succour of the ships; the Spaniards, being before provided for the purpose, landed in all places in multitudes from their ships, which they could easily do without boats, and slew all our men ashore without mercy, a few of them escaping aboard the *Jesus*. The great ship which had, by the estimation, three hundred men placed in her secretly, immediately fell aboard the *Minion*, which, by God's appointment, in the time of the suspicion we had, which was only one half-hour, the *Minion* was made ready to avoid, and so, loosing her headfasts, and hailing away by the sternfasts, she was gotten out; thus, with God's help, she defended the violence of the first brunt of these three hundred men. The *Minion* being passed out, they came aboard the *Jesus*, which also, with very much ado and the loss of many of our men, were defended and kept out.

Then were there also two other ships that assaulted the *Jesus* at the same instant, so that she had hard work getting loose; but yet, with some time, we had cut our headfasts, and gotten out by the sternfasts. Now, when the *Jesus* and the *Minion* were gotten two ship-lengths from the Spanish fleet, the fight began hot on all sides, so that within one hour the admiral of the Spaniards was supposed to be sunk, their vice-Admiral burned, and one other of their principal ships supposed to be sunk, so that the ships were little to annoy us.

Then is it to be understood that all the ordnance upon the island was in the Spaniards' hands, which did us so great annoyance that it cut all the masts and yards of the *Jesus* in such sort, that there was no hope to carry her away; also it sank our small ships, whereupon we determined to place the *Jesus* on that side of the *Minion*, that she might abide all the battery from the land, and so be a defence for the *Minion* till night, and then to take such relief of victual and other necessaries from the *Jesus* as the time would suffer us, and to leave her.

As we were thus determining, and had placed the *Minion* from the shot of the land, suddenly the Spaniards had fired two great ships which were coming directly to us, and having no means to avoid the fire, it bred among our men a marvellous fear, so that some said, 'Let us depart with the *Minion*;' others said, 'Let us see whether the wind will carry the fire from us.' But to be short, the *Minion's* men, which had always their sails in readiness, thought to make sure work, and so without either consent of the captain or master, cut their sail, so that very hardly I was received into the *Minion*.

The most part of the men that were left alive in the *Jesus* made shift and followed the *Minion* in a small boat, the rest, which the little boat was not able to receive, were enforced to abide the mercy of the Spaniards (which I doubt was very little); so with the *Minion* only, and the *Judith* (a small barque of fifty tons) we escaped, which barque the same night forsook us in our great misery. We were now removed with the *Minion* from the Spanish ships two bow-shots, and there rode all that night. The next morning we recovered an island a mile from the Spaniards, where there took us a north wind, and being left only with two anchors and two cables (for in this conflict we lost three cables and two anchors), we thought always upon death, which ever was present; but God preserved us to a longer time.

The weather waxed reasonable, and the Saturday we set sail, and having a great number of men and little victual, our hope of life waxed less and less. Some desired to yield to the Spaniards, some rather desired to obtain a place where they might give themselves to the infidels; and some had rather abide, with a little pittance, the mercy of God at sea. So thus, with many sorrowful hearts, we wandered in an unknown sea by the space of fourteen days, till hunger enforced us to seek the land; for hides were thought very good meat; rats, cats, mice, and dogs, none escaped that might be gotten; parrots and monkeys that were had in great prize, were thought there very profitable if they served the turn of one dinner.

Thus in the end, on October 8th, we came to the land in the bottom of the same bay of Mexico, in twenty-three degrees and a half, where we hoped to have found habitations of the Spaniards, relief of victuals, and place for the repair of our ship, which was so sore beaten with shot from our enemies, and bruised with shooting of our own ordnance, that our weary and weak arms were scarce able to defend and keep out the water. But all things happened to the contrary, for we found neither people, victual, nor haven of relief, but a place where, having fair weather, with some peril we might land a boat. Our people, being forced with hunger, desired to be set aland, whereunto I concluded.

And such as were willing to land I put apart, and such as were desirous to go homewards I put apart, so that they were indifferently parted, a hundred of one side and a hundred of the other side. These hundred men were set on land with all diligence, in this little place aforesaid, which being landed, we determined there to refresh our water, and so with our little remain of victuals to take the sea.

The next day, having on land with me fifty of our hundred men that remained, for the speedier preparing of our water aboard, there arose an extreme storm, so that in three days we could by no means repair our ships. The ship also was in such peril that every hour we looked for shipwreck.

But yet God again had mercy on us, and sent fair weather. We got aboard our water, and departed October 16th, after which day we had fair and prosperous weather till November 16th, which day, God be praised, we were clear from the coast of the Indians and out of the channel and gulf of Bahama, which is between the Cape of Florida and the Islands of Cuba. After this, growing near to the cold country, our men, being oppressed with famine, died continually, and they that were left grew into such weakness that we were scarcely able to manoeuvre our ship; and the wind being always ill for us to recover England, determined to go to Galicia, in Spain, with intent there to relieve our company and other extreme wants.

And being arrived the last day of December, in a place near unto Vigo, called Pontevedra, our men, with excess of fresh meat, grew into miserable diseases, and died a great part of them. This matter was borne out as long as it might be, but in the end, although there was none of our men suffered to go on land, yet by access of the Spaniards our feebleness was known to them. Whereupon they ceased not to seek by all means to betray us; but with all speed possible we departed to Vigo, where we had some help of certain English ships, and twelve fresh men, wherewith we repaired our wants as we might, and departing January 20th, 1568, arrived in Mounts Bay in Cornwall the 25th of the same month, praised be God therefore.

If all the misery and troublesome affairs of this sorrowful voyage should be perfectly and thoroughly written, there should need a painful man with his pen, and as great time as he had that wrote the *Lives and Deaths of the Martyrs*.

Sir John Hawkins rendered great service under Lord Howard in 1588, against the Spanish Armada, acting as rear admiral on board H.M.S. *Victory*, where we are told he had as large a share of the danger and honour of the day as any man in the fleet; for which he deservedly received the honour of knighthood, and was particularly commended by Queen Elizabeth. In 1590 he was sent, in conjunction with Sir Martin Frobisher—each having a squadron of men-of-war—to infest the coast of Spain, where they met with many adventures but not much success. Later, a proposition was made to the queen by Sir John Hawkins and Sir Francis Drake, to fit out an expedition for the West Indies to harry the Spaniards, a proposition which they backed with an offer to bear the greater part of the expense themselves. The queen favoured the design, and the two ablest seamen of the time sailed from Plymouth on August 28th, 1595, with a squadron of twenty-seven ships and barques, and a force of two thousand five hundred men. Divided counsels seem to have interfered with the success of this expedition, Sir John and Sir Francis not agreeing as to the course to be pursued.

A few days before their departure they received notice from the queen that the Plate fleet had safely arrived in Spain, with the exception of a single galleon, which, having lost a mast, had been obliged to return to Porto Rico; the capture of which she recommended to them as practical without interfering with the general design of the expedition. Sir John was for immediately executing the queen's commands, but Sir Francis inclined first to go to the Canaries, in which he prevailed over his friend and colleague, but not over his enemies. In the meantime the Spaniards had sent five stout frigates to bring away the damaged galleon from Porto Rico, which convoy, falling in with the *Francis*, the sternmost of Sir John's ships, captured her before she could receive assistance from the admiral. This is said to have so affected the veteran Sir John, that he died on November 21st, 1595, soon after his vessel had sighted the island of Porto Rico.

Dr. Campbel says:

> Sir John Hawkins was the author of more useful inventions, and introduced into the navy better regulations than any officer who had borne command therein before his time. One instance of this was the institution of that noble fund the *Chest of Chatham*, which was the humane and wise contrivance of this gentleman and Sir Francis Drake, and their scheme that seamen, safe and successful, should, by a voluntary deduction from their pay, give relief to the wants, and reward to those who are maimed in the service of their country, was approved by the queen, and has been adopted by posterity.

The Worthy Enterprise of John Fox

An Englishman, in delivering two hundred and sixty-six Christians out of the captivity of the Turks at Alexandria, the 3rd of January, 1577 written by by Richard Hakluyt.

Richard Hakluyt was born at Eyton in Herefordshire in 1553, and was educated at Westminster School and Christ Church, Oxford, where he graduated B.A. in 1574, and M.A. in 1577, and lectured publicly upon geography, showing "both the old imperfectly composed, and the new lately reformed maps, globes, spheres, and other instruments of this art."

In 1582 Hakluyt published his *Divers Voyages touching the Discovery of America and the Lands adjacent unto the same, made first of all by our Englishmen, and afterwards by the Frenchmen and Bretons; and certain Notes of Advertisements for Observations, necessary for such as shall hereafter make the like attempt.* In 1583, having taken orders, he went to Paris as chaplain to the English ambassador, Sir Edward Stafford, returning to England for a short time in 1584, when he laid before the queen a paper entitled "A particular Discourse concerning Western Discoveries, written in the year 1584 by Richard Hakluyt, of Oxford, at the request and direction of the right worshipful Mr. Walter Raleigh, before the coming home of his two barks."

In 1587 he translated and published in London *A Notable History containing Four Voyages made by certain French Captains into Florida.* In 1589 he published *The Principal Navigations, Voyages and Discoveries of the English Nation*—a work developed into three volumes folio, published in the years 1598, 1599, and 1600 as *The Principal Navigations, Voyages, Traffics, and Discoveries of the English Nation.* Hakluyt became Archdeacon of Westminster in 1603, and died in 1616. He was buried in Westminster Abbey.

Four stories from Hakluyt's voyages appear in this book. *The Troublesome Voyage of the Jesus*, which is included with *The Story of Sir John*

Hawkins, *The Voyage made to Tripolis in Barbary*, *A True Report of a Worthy Fight*, and *The Worthy Enterprise of John Fox* which here follows.

Among our merchants here in England, it is a common voyage to traffic to Spain; whereunto a ship called the *Three Half Moons*, manned with eight and thirty men, well fenced with munitions, the better to encounter their enemies withal, and having wind and tide, set from Portsmouth 1563, and bended her journey towards Seville, a city in Spain, intending there to traffic with them. And falling near the Straits, they perceived themselves to be beset round about with eight galleys of the Turks, in such wise that there was no way for them to fly or escape away, but that either they must yield or else be sunk, which the owner perceiving, manfully encouraged his company, exhorting them valiantly to show their manhood, showing them that God was their God, and not their enemies', requesting them also not to faint in seeing such a heap of their enemies ready to devour them; putting them in mind also, that if it were God's pleasure to give them into their enemies' hands, it was not they that ought to show one displeasant look or countenance there against; but to take it patiently, and not to prescribe a day and time for their deliverance, as the citizens of Bethulia did, but to put themselves under His mercy.

And again, if it were His mind and good will to show His mighty power by them, if their enemies were ten times so many, they were not able to stand in their hands; putting them, likewise, in mind of the old and ancient worthiness of their countrymen, who in the hardest extremities have always most prevailed, and gone away conquerors; yea, and where it hath been almost impossible. 'Such,' quoth he, 'hath been the valiantness of our countrymen, and such hath been the mighty power of our God.'

With such other like encouragements, exhorting them to behave themselves manfully, they fell all on their knees, making their prayers briefly unto God; who, being all risen up again, perceived their enemies, by their signs and defiances, bent to the spoil, whose mercy was nothing else but cruelty; whereupon every man took him to his weapon.

Then stood up one Grove, the master, being a comely man, with his sword and target, holding them up in defiance against his enemies. So likewise stood up the owner, the master's mate, boatswain, purser, and every man well appointed. Now likewise sounded up the drums, trumpets and flutes, which would have encouraged any man, had he never so little heart or courage in him.

Then taketh him to his charge John Fox, the gunner, in the disposing of his pieces, in order to the best effect, and, sending his bullets towards the Turks, who likewise bestowed their pieces thrice as fast towards the Christians. But shortly they drew near, so that the bowman fell to their charge in sending forth their arrows so thick amongst the galleys, and also in doubling their shot so sore upon the galleys, that there were twice as many of the Turks slain as the number of the Christians were in all. But the Turks discharged twice as fast against the Christians, and so long, that the ship was very sore stricken and bruised under water; which the Turks, perceiving, made the more haste to come aboard the ship: which, ere they could do, many a Turk bought it dearly with the loss of their lives. Yet was all in vain, boarded they were, where they found so hot a skirmish, that it had been better they had not meddled with the feast; for the Englishmen showed themselves men indeed in working manfully with their brown bills and halberds, where the owner, master, boatswain and their company stood to it so lustily, that the Turks were half dismayed.

But chiefly the boatswain showed himself valiant above the rest, for he fared amongst the Turks like a wood lion; for there was none of them that either could or durst stand in his face, till at last there came a shot from the Turks which brake his whistle asunder, and smote him on the breast, so that he fell down, bidding them farewell, and to be of good comfort, encouraging them, likewise, to win praise by death, rather than to live captives in misery and shame, which they, hearing, indeed, intended to have done, as it appeared by their skirmish; but the press and store of the Turks were so great, that they were not long able to endure, but were so overpressed that they could not wield their weapons, by reason whereof they must needs be taken, which none of them intended to have been, but rather to have died, except only the master's mate, who shrunk from the skirmish, like a notable coward, esteeming neither the value of his name, nor accounting of the present example of his fellows, nor having respect to the miseries whereunto he should be put. But in fine, so it was, that the Turks were victors, whereof they had no great cause to rejoice or triumph.

Then would it have grieved any hard heart to see these *infidels* so violently entreating the Christians, not having any respect of their manhood, which they had tasted of, nor yet respecting their own state, how they might have met with such a booty as might have given them the overthrow; but no remorse hereof, or anything else doth bridle their fierce and tyrannous dealing, but the Christians must needs to the galleys, to serve in new officer; and they were no sooner in them, but their garments were pulled over their ears and torn from their backs, and they set to the oars.

I will make no mention of their miseries, being now under their enemies' raging stripes. I think there is no man will judge their fare good, or their bodies unloaden of stripes, and not pestered with too much heat, and also with too much cold; but I will go to my purpose, which is to show the end of those being in mere misery, which continually do call on God with a steadfast hope that He will deliver them, and with a sure faith that He can do it.

Nigh to the city of Alexandria, being a haven town, and under the dominion of the Turks, there is a road, being made very fencible with strong walls, whereinto the Turks do customably bring their galleys on shore every year, in the winter season, and there do trim them, and lay them up against the spring-time; in which road there is a prison, wherein the captives and such prisoners as serve in the galleys are put for all that time, until the seas be calm and passable for the galleys; every prisoner being most grievously laden with irons on their legs, to their great pain and sore disabling of them to any labour; into which prison were these Christians put and fast warded all the winter season. But ere it was long, the master and the owner, by means of friends, were redeemed, the rest abiding still in the misery, while that they were all, through reason of their ill-usage and worse fare, miserably starved, saving one John Fox, who (as some men can abide harder and more misery than other some can, so can some likewise make more shift, and work more duties to help their state and living, than other some can do) being somewhat skilful in the craft of a barber, by reason thereof made great shift in helping his fare now and then with a good meal.

Insomuch, till at the last God sent him favour in the sight of the keeper of the prison, so that he had leave to go in and out to the road at his pleasure, paying a certain stipend unto the keeper, and wearing a lock about his leg, which liberty likewise five more had upon like sufferance, who, by reason of their long imprisonment, not being feared or suspected to start aside, or that they would work the Turks any mischief, had liberty to go in and out at the said road, in such manner as this John Fox did, with irons on their legs, and to return again at night.

In the year of our Lord 1577, in the winter season, the galleys happily coming to their accustomed harbourage, and being discharged of all their masts, sails, and other such furnitures as unto galleys do appertain, and all the masters and mariners of them being then nested in their own homes, there remained in the prison of the said road two hundred three score and eight Christian prisoners who had been taken by the Turks' force, and were of fifteen sundry nations. Among which there were three Englishmen, whereof one was named John Fox, of Woodbridge, in Suffolk, the other William Wickney, of Portsmouth, in the county of Southampton, and the third Robert Moore, of Harwich, in the county of Essex; which John Fox, having been thirteen or fourteen years under their gentle entreatance, and being too weary thereof, minding his escape, weighed with himself by what means it might be brought to pass, and continually pondering with himself thereof, took a good heart unto him, in the hope that God would not be always scourging His children, and never ceasing to pray Him to further His intended enterprise, if that it should redound to His glory.

Not far from the road, and somewhat from thence, at one side of the city, there was a certain victualling house, which one Peter Vuticaro had hired, paying also a certain fee unto the keeper of the road. This Peter Vuticaro was a Spaniard born, and a Christian, and had been prisoner above thirty years, and never practised any means to escape, but kept himself quiet without touch or suspect of any conspiracy, until that now this John Fox using much thither, they brake one to another their minds, concerning the restraint of their liberty and imprisonment. So that this John Fox, at length opening unto this Vuticaro the device which he would fain put in practice, made privy one more to this their intent; which three debated of this matter at such times as they could compass to meet together; insomuch that, at seven weeks' end they had sufficiently concluded how the matter should be, if it pleased God to further them thereto; who, making five more privy to this their device, whom they thought that they might safely trust, determined in three nights after to accomplish their deliberate purpose.

Whereupon the same John Fox and Peter Vuticaro, and the other five appointed to meet all together in the prison the next day, being the last day of December, where this John Fox certified the rest of the prisoners what their intent and device was, and how and when they minded to bring that purpose to pass, who thereunto persuaded them without much ado to further their device; which, the same John Fox seeing, delivered unto them a sort of files, which he had gathered together for this purpose by the means of Peter Vuticaro, charging them that every man should be ready, discharged of his irons, by eight of the clock on the next day at night.

On the next day at night, the said John Fox, and his five other companions, being all come to the house of Peter Vuticaro, passing the time away in mirth for fear of suspect till the night came on, so that it was time for them to put in practice their device, sent Peter Vuticaro to the master of the road, in the name of one of the masters of the city, with whom this keeper was acquainted, and at whose request he also would come at the first; who desired him to take the pains to meet him there, promising him that he would bring him back again. The keeper agreed to go with him, asking the warders not to bar the gate, saying that he would not stay long, but would come again with all speed.

In the mean-season, the other seven had provided them of such weapons as they could get in that house, and John Fox took him to an old rusty sword-blade without either hilt or pommel, which he made to serve his turn in bending the hand end of the sword instead of a pommel; and the other had got such spits and glaves as they found in the house.

The keeper being now come unto the house, and perceiving no light nor hearing any noise, straightway suspected the matter; and returning backward, John Fox, standing behind the corner of the house, stepped forth unto him; who, perceiving it to be John Fox, said, 'O Fox, what have I deserved of thee that thou shouldest seek my death?' 'Thou, villain,' quoth Fox, 'hast been a bloodsucker of many a Christian's blood, and now thou shalt know what thou hast deserved at my hands,' wherewith he lift up his bright shining sword of ten years' rust, and stroke him so main a blow, as therewithal his head clave asunder so that he fell stark dead to the ground. Whereupon Peter Vuticaro went in and certified the rest how the case stood with the keeper, and they came presently forth, and some with their spits ran him through, and the other with their glaves hewed him in sunder, cut off his head, and mangled him so that no man should discern what he was.

Then marched they toward the road, whereinto they entered softly, where were five warders, whom one of them asked, saying, who was there? Quoth Fox and his company, 'All friends.' Which when they were all within proved contrary; for, quoth Fox, 'My masters, here is not to every man a man, wherefore look you, play your parts.' Who so behaved themselves indeed, that they had despatched these five quickly. Then John Fox, intending not to be barren of his enterprise, and minding to work surely in that which he went about, barred the gate surely, and planted a cannon against it.

Then entered they into the gaoler's lodge, where they found the keys of the fortress and prison by his bedside, and there got they all better weapons. In this chamber was a chest wherein was a rich treasure, and all in *ducats*, which this Peter Vuticaro and two more opening, stuffed themselves so full as they could between their shirts and their skin; which John Fox would not once touch, and said, 'that it was his and their liberty which he fought for, to the honour of his God, and not to make a mart of the wicked treasure of the *infidels*.' Yet did these words sink nothing unto their stomachs; they did it for a good intent. So did Saul save the fattest oxen to offer unto the Lord, and they to serve their own turn. But neither did Saul escape the wrath of God therefore, neither had these that thing which they desired so, and did thirst after. Such is God's justice. He that they put their trust in to deliver them from the tyrannous hands of their enemies, he, I say, could supply their want of necessaries.

Now these eight, being armed with such weapons as they thought well of, thinking themselves sufficient champions to encounter a stronger enemy, and coming unto the prison, Fox opened the gates and doors thereof, and called forth all the prisoners, whom he set, some to ramming up the gate, some to the dressing up of a certain galley which was the best in all the road, and was called *The Captain of Alexandria*, whereinto some carried masts, sails, oars, and other such furniture as doth belong unto a galley.

At the prison were certain warders whom John Fox and his company slew, in the killing of whom there were eight more of the Turks which perceived them, and got them to the top of the prison, unto whom John Fox and his company were fain to come by ladders, where they found a hot skirmish, for some of them were there slain, some wounded, and some but scarred and not hurt. As John Fox was thrice shot through his apparel, and not hurt, Peter Vuticaro and the other two, that had armed them with the *ducats*, were slain, as not able to wield themselves, being so pestered with the weight and uneasy carrying of the wicked and profane treasure; and also divers Christians were as well hurt about that skirmish as Turks slain.

Amongst the Turks was one thrust through, who (let us not say that it was ill-fortune) fell off from the top of the prison wall, and made such a groaning that the inhabitants thereabout (as here and there stood a house or two) came and questioned him, so that they understood the case, how that the prisoners were paying their ransoms; wherewith they raised both Alexandria, which lay on the west side of the road, and a castle which was at the city's end next to the road, and also another fortress which lay on the north side of the road, so that now they had no way to escape but one, which by man's reason (the two holds lying so upon the mouth of the road) might seem impossible to be a way for them.

So was the Red Sea impossible for the Israelites to pass through, the hills and rocks lay so on the one side, and their enemies compassed them on the other. So was it impossible that the walls of Jericho should fall down, being neither undermined nor yet rammed at with engines, nor yet any man's wisdom, policy, or help, set or put thereunto. Such impossibilities can our God make possible. He that held the lion's jaws from rending Daniel asunder, yea, or yet from once touching him to his hurt, cannot He hold the roaring cannons of this hellish force? He that kept the fire's rage in the hot burning oven from the three children that praised His name, cannot He keep the fire's flaming blasts from among His elect?

Now is the road fraught with lusty soldiers, labourers, and mariners, who are fain to stand to their tackling, in setting to every man his hand, some to the carrying in of victuals, some munitions, some oars, and some one thing some another, but most are keeping their enemy from the wall of the road. But to be short, there was no time misspent, no man idle, nor any man's labour ill-bestowed or in vain. So that in short time this galley was ready trimmed up. Whereinto every man leaped in all haste, hoisting up the sails lustily, yielding themselves to His mercy and grace, in Whose hands is both wind and weather.

Now is this galley afloat, and out of the shelter of the road; now have the two castles full power upon the galley; now is there no remedy but to sink. How can it be avoided? The cannons let fly from both sides, and the galley is even in the middest and between them both. What man can devise to save it? There is no man but would think it must needs be sunk.

There was not one of them that feared the shot which went thundering round about their ears, nor yet were once scarred or touched with five and forty shot which came from the castles. Here did God hold forth His buckler, He shieldeth now this galley, and hath tried their faith to the uttermost. Now cometh His special help; yea, even when man thinks them past all help, then cometh He Himself down from Heaven with His mighty power, then is His present remedy most ready. For they sail away, being not once touched by the glance of a shot, and are quickly out of the Turkish cannons' reach. Then might they see them coming down by heaps to the water's side, in companies like unto swarms of bees, making show to come after them with galleys, bustling themselves to dress up the galleys, which would be a swift piece of work for them to do, for that they had neither oars, masts, sails, nor anything else ready in any galley.

But yet they are carrying into them, some into one galley, and some into another, so that, being such a confusion amongst them, without any certain guide, it were a thing impossible to overtake the Christians; beside that, there was no man that would take charge of a galley, the weather was so rough, and there was such an amazedness amongst them. And verily, I think their god was amazed thereat; it could not be but that he must blush for shame, he can speak never a word for dullness, much less can he help them in such an extremity. Well, howsoever it is, he is very much to blame to suffer them to receive such a gibe. But howsoever their god behaved himself, our God showed Himself a God indeed, and that He was the only living God; for the seas were swift under His faithful, which made the enemies aghast to behold them; a skilfuller pilot leads them, and their mariners bestir them lustily; but the Turks had neither mariners, pilot, nor any skilful master, that was in readiness at this pinch.

When the Christians were safe out of the enemy's coast, John Fox called to them all, telling them to be thankful unto Almighty God for their delivery, and most humbly to fall down upon their knees, beseeching Him to aid them to their friends' land, and not to bring them into another danger, since He had most mightily delivered them from so great a thraldom and bondage.

Thus when every man had made his petition, they fell straightway to their labour with the oars, in helping one another when they were wearied, and with great labour striving to come to some Christian land, as near as they could guess by the stars. But the winds were so contrary, one while driving them this way, another while that way, so that they were now in a new maze, thinking that God had forsaken them and left them to a greater danger. And forasmuch as there were no victuals now left in the galley, it might have been a cause to them (if they had been the Israelites) to have murmured against their God; but they knew how that their God, who had delivered Egypt, was such a loving and merciful God, as that He would not suffer them to be confounded in whom He had wrought so great a wonder, but what calamity soever they sustained, they knew it was but for their further trial, and also (in putting them in mind of their further misery) to cause them not to triumph and glory in themselves therefor. Having, I say, no victuals in the galley, it might seem one misery continually to fall upon another's neck; but to be brief the famine grew to be so great that in twenty-eight days, wherein they were on the sea, there died eight persons, to the astonishment of all the rest.

So it fell out that upon the twenty-ninth day after they set from Alexandria, they fell on the Isle of Candia, and landed at Gallipoli, where they were made much of by the abbot and monks there, who caused them to stay there while they were well refreshed and eased. They kept there the sword wherewith John Fox had killed the keeper, esteeming it as a most precious relic, and hung it up for a monument.

When they thought good, having leave to depart from thence, they sailed along the coast till they arrived at Tarento, where they sold their galley, and divided it, every man having a part thereof. And then they came afoot to Naples, where they departed asunder, every man taking him to his next way home. From whence John Fox took his journey unto Rome, where he was well entertained by an Englishman who presented his worthy deed unto the pope, who rewarded him liberally, and gave him letters unto the King of Spain, where he was very well entertained of him there, who for this his most worthy enterprise gave him in fee twenty pence a day.

From whence, being desirous to come into his own country, he came thither at such time as he conveniently could, which was in the year of our Lord God 1579; who being come into England went unto the court, and showed all his travel unto the council, who considering of the state of this man, in that he had spent and lost a great part of his youth in thraldom and bondage, extended to him their liberality to help to maintain him now in age, to their right honour and to the encouragement of all true-hearted Christians.

The Battle Off Dover.

The Story of Sir Francis Drake
By John Campbell

Francis Drake is said to have been born at Crowndale, near Tavistock, about the year 1540. Both his birth and his parentage are involved in obscurity; but it is probable that he was born of good family in reduced circumstances, for he was declared by the King of Arms in 1551 to have the right "by just descent and progeniture of birth" to bear the arms of the Drakes of Ash; while it is clear that he began life in a humble capacity. According to Camden, he was apprenticed at an early age to the master of a small coasting vessel, who, dying without issue, left the barque to him. We find also that at the age of eighteen he was purser on board a ship trading to Biscay, and at twenty he made a voyage to Guinea. At twenty-two he had the honour to be appointed captain of the *Judith*, in the harbour of St. John de Ullua, in the Gulf of Mexico, where he behaved most gallantly in the glorious action, fought there under his kinsman, Sir John Hawkins, described in the story of Sir John Hawkins, and afterwards returned with him into England with a great reputation, but not worth a single groat.

Upon this he conceived a design of making reprisals on the King of Spain, which, some say, was put into his head by the minister of his ship; and, to be sure, in sea-divinity, the case was clear; the King of Spain's subjects had undone Mr. Drake, and therefore Mr. Drake was at liberty to take the best satisfaction he could on the subjects of the King of Spain. This doctrine, how rudely soever preached, was very taking in England; and therefore he no sooner published his design than he had numbers of volunteers ready to accompany him, though they had no such pretence even as he had to colour their proceedings. In 1570 he made his first expedition with two ships, the *Dragon* and the *Swan*, and the next year in the *Swan* alone, wherein he returned safe, with competent advantages, if not rich; and, having now means sufficient to perform greater matters, as well as skill to conduct them, he laid the plan of a more important design with respect to himself and to his enemies.

This he put in execution on May 24th, 1572, on which day he sailed from Plymouth, himself in a ship called the *Pascha*, of the burden of seventy tons, and his brother, John Drake, in the *Swan*, of twenty-five tons burden, their whole strength consisting of no more than twenty-three men and boys; and, with this inconsiderable force, on July 22nd he attacked the town of Nombre de Dios, which he took in a few hours by storm, notwithstanding a dangerous wound he received early in the action; yet upon the whole he was no great gainer, for after a very brisk action he was obliged to betake himself to his ships with very little booty. His next attempt was to plunder the mules laden with silver which passed from Vera Cruz to Nombre de Dios; but in this scheme too he was disappointed. However, he attacked the town of Vera Cruz, carried it, and got some little booty. In returning, he met unexpectedly with a string of fifty mules laden with plate, of which he carried off as much as he could, and buried the rest.

In these expeditions he was greatly assisted by the Simerons, a nation of Indians who were engaged in a perpetual war with the Spaniards. The prince, or captain of these people, whose name was Pedro, was presented by Captain Drake with a fine cutlass, which he at that time wore, and to which he saw the Indian had a mind. Pedro, in return, gave him four large wedges of gold, which Drake threw into the common stock, saying, that "he thought it but just that such as bore the charge of so uncertain a voyage on his credit should share the utmost advantages that voyage produced." Then embarking his men with all the wealth he had obtained, which was very considerable, he bore away for England, and was so fortunate as to sail in twenty-three days from Cape Florida to the isles of Scilly, and thence without any accident to Plymouth, where he arrived August 9th, 1573.

His success in this expedition, joined to his honourable behaviour towards his owners, gained him a high reputation, and the use he made of his riches still a greater; for, fitting out three stout frigates at his own expense, he sailed with them to Ireland, where, under Walter, Earl of Essex (the father of the unfortunate earl who was beheaded), he served as a volunteer, and did many glorious actions. After the death of his noble patron he returned to England, where Sir Christopher Hatton, who was then vice-chamberlain to Queen Elizabeth, and a great favourite, took him under his protection, introduced him to Her Majesty, and procured him her countenance. By this means he acquired facilities for undertaking that glorious expedition which will render his name immortal. His first proposal was to voyage into the South Seas through the Straits of Magellan, an enterprise which hitherto no Englishman had ever attempted. This project was well received at court, and in a short time Captain Drake saw himself at the height of his wishes; for in his former voyage, having had a distant prospect of the South Seas from the top of a tree which he ascended for the purpose, he framed an ardent prayer to God that he might sail an English ship in them, which he found now an opportunity of attempting; the queen's permission furnishing him with the means, and his own fame quickly drawing to him a force sufficient.

The squadron with which he sailed on this extraordinary undertaking consisted of the following ships: the *Pelican*, commanded by himself, of the burden of one hundred tons; the *Elizabeth*, vice-Admiral, eighty tons, under Captain John Winter; the *Marygold*, a *barque* of thirty tons, commanded by Captain John Thomas; the *Swan*, a fly-boat of fifty tons, under Captain John Chester; and the *Christopher*, a pinnace of fifteen tons, under Captain Thomas Moon. In this fleet were embarked no more than one hundred and sixty-four able men, and all the necessary provisions for so long and dangerous a voyage; the intent of which, however, was not openly declared.

Thus equipped, on November 15th, 1577, about three in the afternoon, he sailed from Plymouth; but a heavy storm taking him as soon as he was out of port, forced him, in a very bad condition, into Falmouth, to refit; which, being expeditiously performed, he again put to sea on the 13th of December following. On the 25th of the same month he fell in with the coast of Barbary; and on the 29th with Cape Verd; the 13th of March he passed the equinoctial; the 5th of April he made the coast of Brazil in 30° N. Lat. and entered the river De la Plata, where he lost the company of two of his ships; but meeting them again, and having taken out of them all the provisions they had on board, he turned them adrift.

On August 20th, with his squadron reduced to three ships, he entered the Straits of Magellan; on September 25th he passed them; having then only his own ship, which, in the South Seas, he renamed the *Golden Hind*. It may not be amiss to take notice here of a fact very little known, as appearing in no relation of this famous voyage. Sir Francis Drake himself reported to Sir Richard, son to Sir John Hawkins, that meeting with a violent tempest, in which his ship could bear no sail, he found, when the storm sank, he was driven through or round the Straits into the latitude of fifty degrees. Here, lying close under an island, he went on shore, and, leaning his body over a promontory as far as he could safely, told his people, when he came on board, he had been farther south than any man living. This we find confirmed by one of our old chronicle writers, who farther informs us that he bestowed on this island the name of Elizabetha, in honour of his royal mistress.

On November 25th he came to Machao, in the latitude of thirty degrees, where he had appointed a rendezvous in case his ships separated; but the *Marygold* had gone down with all hands, and Captain Winter, having repassed the Straits, had returned to England. Thence he continued his voyage along the coasts of Chili and Peru, taking all opportunities of seizing Spanish ships, or of landing and attacking them on shore, till his crew were sated with plunder. While off the island of Mocha Drake landed with some of his men to seek water; but the inhabitants, mistaking them for Spaniards, attacked them, killed two of their number and wounded several others, including Drake himself, who was shot in the face with an arrow.

As the surgeon of the *Golden Hind* was dead, Drake had to be his own doctor as well as surgeon to his crew. Realising that the attack had been made in mistake, and not wishing to risk more casualties, Drake did not attempt to punish the natives, but put to sea and made his way to Valparaiso, where he made free with the stores and valuables he found, and then proceeded further in search of his missing vessels, and finding others which added to his booty; from one of which he took a number of charts of seas then utterly unknown to the English mariners. While pursuing this course he gained intelligence of a rich ship laden with gold and silver for Panama, which he fell in with off Cape Francisco on March 1st, 1579, and captured.

The booty in this case amounted to twenty-six tons of silver, eighty pounds of gold, thirteen chests of money and a quantity of jewels and precious stones; valued in all at nearly £200,000. Coasting North America to the height of forty-eight degrees, he endeavoured to find a passage back into our seas on that side, but being disappointed of what he sought, he landed, and called the country New Albion, taking possession of it in the name, and for the use of Queen Elizabeth; and, having trimmed his ship, set sail thence, on September 29th, 1579, for the Moluccas; choosing this passage round, rather than returning by the Straits of Magellan, owing to the danger of being attacked at a great disadvantage by the Spaniards, and the lateness of the season, whence dangerous storms and hurricanes were to be apprehended. On November 4th he sighted the Moluccas, and on December 10th made Celebes, where his ship unfortunately ran on a rock on the 9th of January; whence, beyond all expectation, and in a manner miraculously, they got off, and continued their course. On March 16th he arrived at Java, where he determined on returning directly home. On March 25th, 1580, he put this design in execution, and on June 15th doubled the Cape of Good Hope, having then on board his ship fifty-seven men and but three casks of water. On July 12th he passed the line, reached the coast of Guinea on the 16th, and there watered. On September 11th he made the island of Terceira, and on the 26th of the same month entered the harbour of Plymouth.

In this voyage he completely circumnavigated the globe, which no commander-in-chief had ever done before. His success in this enterprise, and the immense mass of wealth he brought home, naturally raised much comment throughout the kingdom; some highly commending, and some as loudly decrying him. The former alleged that his exploit was not only honourable to himself, but to his country; that it would establish our reputation for maritime skill amongst foreign nations, and raise a useful spirit of emulation at home; and that as to the money, our merchants having suffered deeply from the faithless practices of the Spaniards, there was nothing more just than that the nation should receive the benefit of Drake's reprisals.

The other party alleged that, in fact, he was no better than a pirate; that, of all others, it least became a trading nation to encourage such practices; that it was not only a direct breach of all our late treaties with Spain, but likewise of our old leagues with the house of Burgundy; and that the consequences of owning his proceeding would be much more fatal than the benefits reaped from it could be advantageous. Things continued in this uncertainty during the remainder of that, and the spring of the succeeding year.

At length they took a better turn; for on April 4th, 1581, Her Majesty, dining at Deptford in Kent, went on board Captain Drake's ship, where she conferred on him the honour of knighthood, and declared her absolute approbation of all that he had done, to the confusion of his enemies and to the great joy of his friends. She likewise gave directions for the preservation of his ship, that it might remain a monument of his own and his country's glory. In process of time, the vessel decaying, it was broken up; but a chair made of the planks was presented to the University of Oxford, and is still preserved.

In the year 1582 he was Mayor of Plymouth, and in 1584-5 a member of the House of Commons.

In 1585 he concerted a scheme of a West-Indian expedition with the celebrated Sir Philip Sidney. It was to be partly maritime and partly an invasion. The sea force was to be commanded absolutely by Sir Francis, the land troops by Sir Philip Sidney. The queen having required Sir Philip to desist from his scheme, Drake sailed, notwithstanding, to the West Indies, having under his command Captain Christopher Carlisle, Captain Martin Frobisher, Captain Francis Knollys, and many other officers of great reputation. In this expedition he took the cities of St. Iago, St. Domingo, Carthagena, and St. Augustine, exceeding even the expectation of his friends and the hopes of the common people, though both were sanguine to the last degree. Yet the profits of this expedition were but moderate; the design of Sir Francis being rather to weaken the enemy than to enrich himself. It was, to do him justice, a maxim from which he never varied, to regard the service of his country first, next the profit of his proprietors, and last, his own interest. Hence, though rich in wealth, he was richer still in reputation.

In 1587 he proceeded to Lisbon with a fleet of thirty sail, and having intelligence of a numerous fleet assembled in the Bay of Cadiz, which was to have made part of the Armada, he, with great courage, entered the port, and burnt upwards of ten thousand tons of shipping. Drake's policy was to attack the enemy in his own harbours and so prevent the possibility of his invading our coasts; and this policy he was continually pressing upon the home government, but without success. There can be little doubt that if he had been allowed to follow up his success in the Bay of Cadiz by carrying out this policy the Spanish Armada might have never set sail.

Not obtaining the support and authority he wanted, he now resolved to do his utmost to content the merchants of London, who had contributed, by a voluntary subscription, to the fitting out of his fleet. With this view, having intelligence of a large *carack* expected at Terceira from the East Indies, thither he sailed; and though his men were severely pinched through want of victuals, yet by fair words and large promises he prevailed upon them to endure these hardships for a few days. Within this time the East India ship arrived, and was found to contain wealth to the value of £100,000, which he took and carried home in triumph.

It was in consequence of the journals, charts, and papers, taken on board his East India prize, that it was judged practicable for us to enter into the Indian trade: for promoting which, the queen, by letters patent, in the forty-third year of her reign, founded our first India company. To this, we may also add that it was Drake who first brought in tobacco, the use of which was much promoted by the practice of Sir Walter Raleigh. How much this nation has gained by these branches of commerce, of which he was properly the author, I leave to the intelligent reader's consideration.

In 1588 Sir Francis Drake was appointed vice-Admiral, under Charles Lord Howard of Effingham, High-Admiral of England; here his fortune favoured him as remarkably as ever, for he made prize of a large galleon, commanded by Don Pedro de Valdez, who yielded on the bare mention of his name. In this vessel fifty thousand *ducats* were distributed among the seamen and soldiers. It must not, however, be dissembled that, through an oversight of his, the admiral ran the utmost hazard of being taken by the enemy; for Drake being appointed, the first night of the engagement, to carry lights for the direction of the English fleet, he being in full pursuit of some hulks belonging to the Hanse Towns, neglected it; which occasioned the admiral's following the Spanish lights, and remaining almost in the centre of their fleet till morning. However, his succeeding services sufficiently effaced the memory of this mistake; the greatest execution done on the flying Spaniards being performed by the squadron under his command.

The next year he was employed as admiral at sea over the fleet sent to restore Don Antonio, King of Portugal; the command of the land forces being given to Sir John Norris. They were hardly at sea, however, before these commanders differed; though it is on all hands agreed that there never was an admiral better disposed, with respect to soldiers, than Sir Francis Drake. The ground of their difference was this: the general was bent on landing at the Groyne, whereas Sir Francis and the sea-officers were for sailing to Lisbon directly; in which, if their advice had been taken, without question their enterprise would have succeeded, and Don Antonio would have been restored. For it appeared, on their invading Portugal, that the enemy had made use of the time they gave them to such good purpose that it was not possible to make any impression.

Sir John Norris, indeed, marched by land to Lisbon, and Sir Francis Drake, very imprudently, promised to sail up the river with his whole fleet; but when he saw the consequences which would have attended the keeping of his word, he chose rather to break his promise than to hazard the queen's navy; for which he was grievously reproached by

Norris, and the miscarriage of the whole affair was imputed to his failure in performing what he had undertaken. Yet Sir Francis fully justified himself on his return; for he made it manifest to the queen and council that all the service that was done was performed by him, and that his sailing up the river of Lisbon would have signified nothing to the taking the castle, which was two miles off; and without reducing that there was no taking the town.

In 1590 he seems to have devoted himself to civil engineering, for we find him contracting with the town of Plymouth to effect a water supply from the River Meavy, which he did by conducting a stream a distance of nearly twenty-five miles; after which he erected six mills for grinding corn in 1591. In 1593 he represented Plymouth in parliament.

His next service was the fatal undertaking in conjunction with Sir John Hawkins, in 1594, for the destroying of Nombre de Dios, referred to in the story of Sir John Hawkins, who died the day before Sir Francis made his desperate attack on the shipping in the harbour of Porto Rico. This was performed, with all the courage imaginable, on November 13th, 1595, and attended with great loss to the Spaniards, yet with very little advantage to the English, who, meeting with a more resolute resistance and much better fortifications than they expected, were obliged to sheer off. The admiral then steered for the main, where he took the town of Rio de la Hacha, which he burnt to the ground; a church and a single house belonging to a lady only excepted.

After this, he destroyed some other villages, and then proceeded to Santa Marta, which he likewise burnt. The like fate had the famous town of Nombre de Dios, the Spaniards refusing to ransom any of these places, and the booty taken in them being very inconsiderable. On December 29th Sir Thomas Baskerville marched with seven hundred and fifty men towards Panama, but returned on January 2nd, finding the design of reducing that place to be wholly impracticable. This disappointment made such an impression on the admiral's mind that it threw him into a lingering fever, of which he died on the 28th of January, 1596, just two months after his distinguished kinsman, Sir John Hawkins, with whom he had been so often associated, and with so much glory.

The Voyage Made to Tripolis in Barbary

In the year 1583, with a ship called the *Jesus*, wherein the adventures and distresses of some Englishmen are truly reported, and other necessary circumstances observed, written by Thomas Sanders.

This voyage was set forth by the Right Worshipful Sir Edward Osborne Knight, chief merchant of all the Turkish Company, and one Master Richard Stapers, the ship being of the burden of one hundred tons, called the *Jesus*; she was built at Farmne, a river by Portsmouth. About November 29th, 1584, she made sail from Portsmouth, and December 1st, by means of a contrary wind, we were driven to Plymouth. The 18th day then next following we made forthward again, and by force of weather we were driven to Falmouth, where we remained until January 1st, at which time the wind coming fair we departed thence, and about the 20th day of the said month we arrived safely at St. Lucas. And about March 9th next following we made sail from thence, and about the 18th day of the same month we came to Tripolis in Barbary, where we were very well entertained by the king of that country and also of the commons.

The commodities of that place are sweet oils; the king there is a merchant, and the rather (willing to prefer himself before his commons) requested our said factors to traffic with him, and promised them that if they would take his oils at his own price they should pay no manner of custom; and they took of him certain tons of oil; and afterward perceiving that they might have far better cheap, notwithstanding the custom free, they desired the king to license them to take the oils at the pleasure of his commons, for that his price did exceed theirs; whereunto the king would not agree, but was rather contented to abate his price, insomuch that the factors bought all their oils of the king's custom free, and so laded the same aboard.

In the meantime there came to that place one Miles Dickinson, in a ship of Bristol, who together with our said factors took a house to themselves there. Our French factor, Romaine Sonnings, desired to buy a commodity in the market, and, wanting money, desired the said Miles Dickinson to lend him a hundred *chikinoes* until he came to his lodging, which he did; and afterwards the same Sonnings met with Miles Dickinson in the street, and delivered him money bound up in a napkin, saying, "Master Dickinson, there is the money that I borrowed of you," and so thanked him for the same.

The said Dickinson did not tell the money presently, until he came to his lodging, and then, finding nine *chikinoes* lacking of his hundred (which was about three pounds, for that every *chikinoe* is worth seven shillings of English money), he came to the said Romaine Sonnings and delivered him his handkerchief, and asked him how many *chikinoes* he had delivered him. Sonnings answered, "A hundred"; Dickinson said "No"; and so they protested and swore on both parts. But in the end the said Romaine Sonnings did swear deeply with detestable oaths and curses, and prayed God that He might show His works on him, that other might take ensample thereby, and that he might be hanged liked a dog, and never come into England again, if he did not deliver unto the said Dickinson a hundred *chikinoes*.

There was a man in the said town a pledge, whose name was Patrone Norado, who the year before had done this Sonnings some pleasure there. The foresaid Patrone Norado was indebted unto a Turk of that town in the sum of four hundred and fifty crowns, for certain goods sent by him into Christendom in a ship of his own, and by his own brother, and himself remained in Tripolis as pledge until his said brother's return; and, as the report went there, he came among lewd company, and lost his brother's said ship and goods at dice, and never returned unto him again.

The said Patrone Norado, being void of all hope and finding now opportunity, consulted with the said Sonnings for to swim a-seaboard the islands, and the ship, being then out of danger, should take him in (as was afterwards confessed), and so go to Tallowne, in the province of Marseilles, with this Patrone Norado, and there to take in the rest of his lading.

The ship being ready May 1st, and having her sails all abroad, our said factors did take their leave of the king, who very courteously bid them farewell, and when they came aboard they commanded the master and the company hastily to get out the ship. The master answered that it was impossible, for that the wind was contrary and overblowed. And he required us, upon forfeiture of our bands, that we should do our endeavour to get her forth.

Then went we to warp out the ship, and presently the king sent a boat aboard of us, with three men in her, commanding the said Sonnings to come ashore, at whose coming the king demanded of him custom for the oils. Sonnings answered him that his highness had promised to deliver them customs free. But, notwithstanding, the king weighed not his said promise, and as an *infidel* that hath not the fear of God before his eyes, nor regard of his word, albeit he was a king, he caused the said Sonnings to pay the custom to the uttermost penny, and afterwards ordered him to make haste away, saying that the *janisaries* would have the oil ashore again.

These *janisaries* are soldiers there under the Great Turk, and their power is above the king's. And so the said factor departed from the king, and came to the waterside, and called for a boat to come aboard, and he brought with him the aforesaid Patrone Norado. The company, inquisitive to know what man that was, Sonnings answered that he was his countryman, a passenger. "I pray God," said the company, "that we come not into trouble by this man."

Then said Sonnings angrily, "What have you to do with any matters of mine? If anything chance otherwise than well, I must answer for all."

Now the Turk unto whom this Patrone Norado was indebted, missing him, supposed him to be aboard of our ship, presently went unto the king and told him that he thought that his pledge, Patrone Norado, was aboard on the English ship. Whereupon the king presently sent a boat aboard of us, with three men in her, commanding the said Sonnings to come ashore; and, not speaking anything as touching the man, he said that he would come presently in his own boat; but as soon as they were gone he willed us to warp forth the ship, and said that he would see the knaves hanged before he would go ashore.

And when the king saw that he came not ashore, but still continued warping away the ship, he straight commanded the gunner of the bulwark next unto us to shoot three shots without ball. Then we came all to the said Sonnings, and asked him what the matter was that we were shot at; he said that it was the *janisaries* who would have the oil ashore again, and willed us to make haste away. And after that he had discharged three shots without ball he commanded all the gunners in the town to do their endeavour to sink us; but the Turkish gunners could not once strike us, wherefore the king sent presently to the *banio* (this *banio* is the prison where all the captives lay at night), and promised that if there were any that could either sink us or else cause us to come in again, he should have a hundred crowns and his liberty.

With that came forth a Spaniard called Sebastian, which had been an old servitor in Flanders, and he said that, upon the performance of that promise, he would undertake either to sink us or to cause us to come in again, and thereto he would gage his life; and at the first shot he split our rudder's head in pieces, and the second shot he struck us under water, and the third shot he shot us through our fore-mast with a culverin shot, and thus, he having rent both our rudder and mast and shot us under water, we were enforced to go in again.

This Sebastian for all his diligence herein had neither his liberty nor a hundred crowns, so promised by the said king; but, after his service done, was committed again to prison, whereby may appear the regard that a Turk or *infidel* hath of his work, although he be able to perform it—yea, more, though he be a king.

Then our merchants, seeing no remedy, they, together with five of our company, went ashore; and they then ceased shooting. They shot unto us in the whole nine-and-thirty shots without the hurt of any man.

And when our merchants came ashore the king commanded presently that they, with the rest of our company that were with them, should be chained four and four to a hundred-weight of iron, and when we came in with the ship there came presently above a hundred Turks aboard of us, and they searched us and stripped our very clothes from our backs, and broke open our chests, and made a spoil of all that we had; and the Christian caitiffs likewise that came aboard of us made spoil of our goods, and used us as ill as the Turks did.

Then came the guardian *basha*, who is the keeper of the king's captives, to fetch us all ashore; and then I, remembering the miserable estate of poor distressed captives in the time of their bondage to those *infidels*, went to mine own chest, and took out thereof a jar of oil, and filled a basket full of white ruske, to carry ashore with me. But before I came to the *banio* the Turkish boys had taken away almost all my bread, and the keeper said, "Deliver me the jar of oil, and when thou comest to the *banio* thou shalt have it again;" but I never had it of him anymore.

But when I came to the *banio* and saw our merchants and all the rest of our company in chains, and we all ready to receive the same reward, what heart is there so hard but would have pitied our cause, hearing or seeing the lamentable greeting there was betwixt us? All this happened May 1st, 1584.

And the second day of the same month the king with all his council sat in judgment upon us. The first that were had forth to be arraigned were the factors and the masters, and the king asked them wherefore they came not ashore when he sent for them. And Romaine Sonnings answered that, though he were a king on shore, and might command there, so was he as touching those that were under him; and therefore said, if any offence be, the fault is wholly in myself and in no other. Then forthwith the king gave judgment that the said Romaine Sonnings should be hanged over the north-east bulwark, from whence he conveyed the forenamed Patrone Norado. And then he called for our master, Andrew Dier, and used few words to him, and so condemned him to be hanged over the walls of the westernmost bulwarks.

Then fell our other factor, named Richard Skegs, upon his knees before the king, and said, "I beseech your highness either to pardon our master or else suffer me to die for him, for he is ignorant of this cause." And then the people of that country, favouring the said Rickard Skegs, besought the king to pardon them both. So then the king spake these words: "Behold, for thy sake I pardon the master." Then presently the Turks shouted and cried, saying, "Away with the master from the presence of the king." And then he came into the *banio* where we were, and told us what had happened, and we all rejoiced at the good hap of Master Skegs, that he was saved, and our master for his sake.

But afterwards our joy was turned to double sorrow, for in the meantime the king's mind was altered: for that one of his council had advised him that, unless the master died also, by the law they could not confiscate the ship nor goods, neither make captive any of the men. Whereupon the king sent for our master again, and gave him another judgment after his pardon for one cause, which was that he should be hanged.

And when that Romaine Sonnings saw no remedy but that he should die, he protested to turn Turk, hoping thereby to have saved his life. Then said the Turk, "If thou wilt turn Turk, speak the words that thereunto belong;" and he did so. Then said they unto him, "Now thou shalt die in the faith of a Turk;" and so he did, as the Turks reported that were at his execution; and the forenamed Patrone Norado, whereas before he had liberty and did nothing, he then was condemned slave perpetual, except there were payment made of the foresaid sum of money.

Then the king condemned all of us, who were in number five-and-twenty, of which two were hanged (as you have heard) and one died the first day we came on shore by the visitation of Almighty God, and the other three-and-twenty he condemned slaves perpetually unto the Great Turk, and the ship and goods were confiscated to the use of the Great Turk; then we all fell down upon our knees, giving God thanks for this sorrowful visitation and giving ourselves wholly to the almighty power of God, unto whom all secrets are known, that He of His goodness would vouchsafe to look upon us.

Every five men had allowance but five *aspers* of bread in a day, which is but two pence English, and our lodging was to lie on the bare boards, with a very simple cape to cover us. We were also forcibly and most violently shaven, head and beard, and within three days after, I and five more of my fellows, together with fourscore Italians and Spaniards, were sent forth in a *galiot* to take a Greek *carmosel*, which came into Arabia to steal negroes, and went out of Tripolis unto that place which was two hundred and forty leagues thence; but we were chained three and three to an oar, and we rowed naked above the girdle, and the boatswain of the galley walked abaft the mast, and his mate afore the mast, and each of them a whip in their hands, and when their devilish choler rose they would strike the Christians for no cause: and they allowed us but half a pound of bread a man in a day, without any other kind of sustenance, water excepted.

And when we came to the place where we saw the *carmosel*, we were not suffered to have neither needle, bodkin, knife, or any other instrument about us, nor at any other time in the night, upon pain of one hundred *bastinadoes*: we were then also cruelly manacled, in such sort that we could not put our hands the length of one foot asunder the one from the other, and every night they searched our chains three times, to see if they were fast riveted. We continued the fight therehours, and then we took it, and lost but two of our men in that fight; but there were slain of the Greeks five, and fourteen were cruelly hurt; and they that were found were presently made slaves and chained to the oars, and within fifteen days after we returned again into Tripolis, and then we were put to all manner of slavery. I was put to hew stones, and others to carry stones, and some to draw the cart with earth, and some to make mortar, and some to draw stones (for at that time the Turks builded a church); and thus we were put to all kinds of slavery that was to be done.

Now, the king had eighteen captives, which three times a week went to fetch wood thirty miles from the town, and on a time he appointed me for one of the eighteen, and we departed at eight of the clock in the night; and upon the way, at midnight, or thereabouts, as I was riding upon my camel, I fell asleep, and the guide and all the rest rode away from me, not thinking but I had been among them. When I awoke, and finding myself alone, I durst not call nor holloa, for fear lest the wild Moors should hear me—because they hold this opinion, that in killing a Christian they do God good service—and musing with myself what were best for me to do: if I should return back to Tripolis without any wood or company I should be most miserably used; therefore, of the two evils, rather I had to go forth to the losing of my life than to turn back and trust to their mercy, fearing to be used as before I had seen others.

For, understanding by some of my company before how Tripolis and the said wood did lie one off another, by the North Star I went forth at adventure, and, as God would have it, I came right to the place where they were, even about an hour before day. There altogether we rested, and gave our camels provender, and as soon as the day appeared we rode all into the wood; and I, seeing no wood there but a stick here and a stick there, about the bigness of a man's arm, growing in the sand, it caused me to marvel how so many camels should be loaded in that place. The wood was juniper; we needed no axe nor edged tool to cut it, but plucked it up by strength of hands, roots and all, which a man might easily do, and so gathered together a little at one place, and so at another, and laded our camels, and came home about seven of the clock that night following; because I fell lame and my camel was tired, I left my wood in the way.

This king had a son which was a ruler in an island called Gerbi, whereunto arrived an English ship called the *Green Dragon*, of the which was master one M. Blonket, who, having a very unhappy boy on that ship, and understanding that whosoever would turn Turk should be well entertained of the king's son, this boy did run ashore and voluntarily turned Turk. Shortly after the king's son came to Tripolis to visit his father, and seeing our company, he greatly fancied Richard Burges, our purser, and James Smith. They were both young men, therefore he was very desirous to have them to turn Turks; but they would not yield to his desire, saying, "We are your father's slaves and as slaves we will serve him."

Then his father the king sent for them, and asked them if they would turn Turks; and they said: "If it please your Highness, Christians we were born and so we will remain, and beseech the king that they might not be enforced thereunto."

The king had there before in his house a son of a yeoman of our queen's guard, whom the king's son had enforced to turn Turk; his name was John Nelson. Him the king caused to be brought to these young men, and then said unto them, "Will you not bear this, your countryman, company, and be Turk as he is?" and they said that they would not yield thereunto during life. But it fell out that, within a month after, the king's son went home to Gerbi again, being five score miles from Tripolis, and carried our two foresaid young men with him, which were Richard Burges and James Smith.

And after their departure from us they sent us a letter, signifying that there was no violence showed unto them as yet; yet within three days after they were violently used, for that the king's son demanded of them again if that they would turn Turk. Then answered Richard Burges: "A Christian I am, and so I will remain." Then the king's son very angrily said unto him, "By Mahomet thou shalt presently be made Turk!" Then called he for his men and commanded them to make him Turk; and they did so, and circumcised him, and would have had him speak the words that thereunto belonged; but he answered them stoutly that he would not, and although they had put on him the habit of a Turk, yet said he, "A Christian I was born, and so I will remain, though you force me to do otherwise."

And then he called for the other, and commanded him to be made Turk perforce also; but he was very strong, for it was so much as eight of the king's son's men could do to hold him. So in the end they circumcised him and made him Turk. Now, to pass over a little, and so to show the manner of our deliverance out of that miserable captivity.

In May aforesaid, shortly after our apprehension, I wrote a letter into England unto my father, dwelling in Evistoke in Devonshire, signifying unto him the whole estate of our calamities, and I wrote also to Constantinople to the English ambassador, both which letters were faithfully delivered. But when my father had received my letter, and understood the truth of our mishap, and the occasion thereof, and what had happened to the offenders, he certified the Right Honourable the Earl of Bedford thereof, who in short space acquainted Her Highness with the whole cause thereof; and Her Majesty, like a most merciful princess tendering her subjects, presently took order for our deliverance. Whereupon the Right Worshipful Sir Edward Osborne, knight, directed his letters with all speed to the English ambassador in Constantinople to procure our delivery, and he obtained the Great Turk's commission, and sent it forthwith to Tripolis by one Master Edward Barton, together with a justice of the Great Turk's and one soldier, and another Turk and a Greek, which was his interpreter, which could speak beside Greek, Turkish, Italian, Spanish and English.

And when they came to Tripolis they were well entertained, and the first night they did lie in a captain's house in the town. All our company that were in Tripolis came that night for joy to Master Barton and the other commissioners to see them. Then Master Barton said unto us, "Welcome, my good countrymen," and lovingly entertained us: and at our departure from him he gave us two shillings, and said, "Serve God, for tomorrow I hope you shall be as free as ever you were." We all gave him thanks and so departed.

The next day, in the morning very early, the king having intelligence of their coming, sent word to the keeper that none of the Englishmen (meaning our company) should go to work. Then he sent for Master Barton and the other commissioners, and demanded of the said Master Barton his message. The justice answered that the Great Turk, his sovereign, had sent them unto him, signifying that he was informed that a certain English ship, called the *Jesus*, was by him the said king confiscated about twelve months since, and now my said sovereign hath here sent his especial commission by us unto you for the deliverance of the said ship and goods, and also the free liberty and deliverance of the Englishmen of the said ship whom you have taken and kept in captivity.

And further, the same justice said, I am authorised by my said sovereign the Great Turk to see it done; and therefore I command you, by the virtue of this commission, presently to make restitution of the premises or the value thereof. And so did the justice deliver unto the king the Great Turk's commission to the effect aforesaid, which commission the king with all obedience received; and after the perusing of the same, he forthwith commanded all the English captives to be brought before him, and then willed the keeper to strike off all our irons.

Which done, the king said, "You Englishmen, for that you did offend the laws of this place, by the same laws therefore some of your company were condemned to die, as you know, and you to be perpetual captives during your lives; notwithstanding, seeing it hath pleased my sovereign lord the Great Turk to pardon your said offences, and to give you your freedom and liberty, behold, here I make delivery of you unto this English gentleman."

So he delivered us all that were there, being thirteen in number, to Master Barton, who required also those two young men which the king's son had taken with him. Then the king answered that it was against their law to deliver them, for that they were turned Turks; and, touching the ship and goods, the king said that he had sold her, but would make restitution of the value, and as much of the goods as came unto his hands. And so the king arose and went to dinner, and commanded a Jew to go with Master Barton and the other commissioners to show them their lodgings, which was a house provided and appointed them by the said king. And because I had the Italian and Spanish tongues, by which there most traffic in that country is, Master Barton made me his caterer, to buy his victuals for him and his company, and he delivered me money needful for the same. Thus were we set at liberty April 28th, 1585.

A True Report of a Worthy Fight

Performed in the voyage from Turkey by five ships of London, against eleven galleys and two frigates of the King of Spain's, at Pantalarea, within the Straits, *anno* 1586, written by Philip Jones.

The merchants of London, being of the incorporation for the Turkey trade, having received intelligences and advertisements from time to time that the King of Spain, grudging at the prosperity of this kingdom, had not only of late arrested all English ships, bodies, and goods in Spain, but also, maligning the quiet traffic which they used, to and in the dominions and provinces under the obedience of the Great Turk, had given orders to the captains of his galleys in the Levant to hinder the passage of all English ships, and to endeavour by their best means to intercept, take, and spoil them, their persons and goods; they hereupon thought it their best course to set out their fleet for Turkey in such strength and ability for their defence that the purpose of their Spanish enemy might the better be prevented, and the voyage accomplished with greater security to the men and ships. For which cause, five tall and stout ships appertaining to London, and intending only a merchant's voyage, were provided and furnished with all things belonging to the seas, the names whereof were these:—

1. The *Royal Merchant*, a very brave and good ship, and of great report.
2. The *Toby*.
3. The *Edward Bonaventure*.
4. The *William and John*.
5. The *Susan*.

These five departing from the coast of England in the month of

November, 1585, kept together as one fleet till they came as high as the Isle of Sicily, within the Levant. And there, according to the order and direction of the voyage, each ship began to take leave of the rest, and to separate himself, setting his course for the particular port whereunto he was bound—one for Tripolis in Syria, another for Constantinople, the chief city of the Turk's empire, situated upon the coast of Roumelia called of old Thracia, and the rest to those places whereunto they were privately appointed.

But before they divided themselves, they altogether consulted of and about a certain and special place for their meeting again after the landing of their goods at their several ports. And in conclusion, the general agreement was to meet at Zante, an island near to the main continent of the west part of Morea, well known to all the pilots, and thought to be the fittest place for their rendezvous; concerning which meeting it was also covenanted on each side and promised that whatsoever ship of these five should first arrive at Zante, should there stay and expect the coming of the rest of the fleet for the space of twenty days. This being done, each man made his best haste, according as wind and weather would serve him, to fulfil his course and to despatch his business; and no need was there to admonish or encourage any man, seeing no time was ill-spent nor opportunity omitted on any side in the performance of each man's duty, according to his place.

It fell out that the *Toby*, which was bound for Constantinople, had made such good speed, and gotten such good weather, that she first of all the rest came back to the appointed place of Zante, and not forgetting the former conclusion, did there cast anchor, attending the arrival of the rest of the fleet, which accordingly (their business first performed) failed not to keep promise. The first next after the *Toby* was the *Royal Merchant*, which, together with the *William and John*, came from Tripolis in Syria, and arrived in Zante within the compass of the aforesaid time limited.

These ships, in token of the joy on all parts conceived for their happy meeting, spared not the discharging of their ordnance, the sounding of drums and trumpets, the spreading of ensigns, with other warlike and joyful behaviours, expressing by these outward signs the inward gladness of their minds, being all as ready to join together in mutual consent to resist the cruel enemy, as now in sporting manner they made mirth and pastime among themselves. These three had not been long in the haven but the *Edward Bonaventure*, together with the *Susan* her consort, were come from Venice with their lading, the sight of whom increased the joy of the rest, and they, no less glad of the presence of the others, saluted them in most friendly and kind sort, according to the manner of the seas.

In this port of Zante the news was fresh and current of two several armies and fleets, provided by the King of Spain, and lying in wait to intercept them: the one consisting of thirty strong galleys, so well appointed in all respects for the war that no necessary thing wanted; and this fleet hovered about the Straits of Gibraltar. The other army had in it twenty galleys, whereof some were of Sicily and some of the Island of Malta, under the charge and government of John Andreas Dorea, a captain of name serving the King of Spain. These two divers and strong fleets waited and attended in the seas for none but the English ships, and no doubt made their account and sure reckoning that not a ship should escape their fury. And the opinion also of the inhabitants of the Isle of Zante was, that in respect of the number of galleys in both these armies having received such straight commandment from the king, our ships and men being but few and little in comparison of them, it was a thing in human reason impossible that we should pass either without spoiling, if we resisted, or without composition at the least, and acknowledgment of duty to the Spanish king.

But it was neither the report of the attendance of these armies, nor the opinions of the people, nor anything else, that could daunt or dismay the courage of our men, who, grounding themselves upon the goodness of their cause, and the promise of God to be delivered from such as without reason sought their destruction, carried resolute minds notwithstanding all impediments to adventure through the seas, and to finish their navigation maugre the beards of the Spanish soldiers. But lest they should seem too careless and too secure of their estate, and by laying the whole and entire, burden of their safety upon God's Providence, should foolishly presume altogether of His help, and neglect the means which was put into their hands, they failed not to enter into counsel among themselves, and to deliberate advisedly for their best defence.

And in the end, with general consent, the *Royal Merchant* was appointed admiral of the fleet, and the *Toby* vice-Admiral, by whose orders the rest promised to be directed; and each ship vowed not to break from another whatsoever extremity should fall out, but to stand to it to the death, for the honour of their country and the frustrating of the hope of the ambitious and proud enemy.

Thus in good order they left Zante and the Castle of Grecia, and committed themselves again to the seas, and proceeded in their course and voyage in quietness, without sight of any enemy till they came near to Pantalarea, an island so called betwixt Sicily and the coast of Africa; into sight whereof they came on July 13th, 1586. And the same day, in the morning about seven o'clock, they descried thirteen sails in number, which were of the galleys lying in wait of purpose for them in and about that place.

As soon as the English ships had spied them, they by-and-by, according to a common order, made themselves ready for a fight, laid out their ordnance, scoured, charged, and primed them, displayed their ensigns, and left nothing undone to arm themselves thoroughly. In the meantime, the galleys more and more approached the ships, and in their banners there appeared the arms of the Isles of Sicily and Malta, being all as then in the service and pay of the Spaniard. Immediately both the admirals of the galleys sent from each of them a frigate to the admiral of our English ships, which being come near them, the Sicilian frigate first hailed them, and demanded of them whence they were; they answered that they were of England, the arms whereof appeared in their colours.

Whereupon the said frigate expostulated with them, and asked why they delayed to send or come with their captains and pursers to Don Pedro de Leiva, their general, to acknowledge their duty and obedience to him, in the name of the Spanish king, lord of those seas. Our men replied and said that they owed no such duty nor obedience to him, and therefore would acknowledge none; but commanded the frigate to depart with that answer, and not to stay longer upon her peril. With that away she went, and up came towards them the other frigate of Malta; and she in like sort hailed the admiral, and would needs know whence they were and where they had been. Our Englishmen in the admiral, not disdaining an answer, told them that they were of England, merchants of London, had been in Turkey, and were now returning home; and to be requited in this case, they also demanded of the frigate whence she and the rest of the galleys were. The messenger answered:

> We are of Malta, and for mine own part, my name is Cavalero. These galleys are in service and pay to the King of Spain, under the conduct of Don Pedro de Leiva, a nobleman of Spain, who hath been commanded hither by the king with this present force and army of purpose to intercept you. You shall therefore

do well to repair to him to know his pleasure; he is a nobleman of good behaviour and courtesy, and means you no ill.

The captain of the English admiral, whose name was Master Edward Wilkinson, now one of the six masters of Her Majesty's Royal Navy, replied and said, "We purpose not at this time to make trial of Don Pedro his courtesy, whereof we are suspicious and doubtful, and not without good cause;" using withal good words to the messenger, and willing him to come aboard him, promising security and good usage, that thereby he might the better know the Spaniard's mind. Whereupon he indeed left his frigate and came aboard him, whom he entertained in friendly sort, and caused a cup of wine to be drawn for him, which he took, and began, with his cap in his hand and with reverent terms, to drink to the health of the Queen of England, speaking very honourably of her majesty, and giving good speeches of the courteous usage and entertainment that he himself had received in London at the time that the Duke of Alençon, brother to the late French king, was last in England.

And after he had well drunk, he took his leave, speaking well of the sufficiency and goodness of our ships, and especially of the *Royal Merchant* which he confessed to have seen before riding in the Thames near London. He was no sooner come to Don Pedro de Leiva, the Spanish general, but he was sent off again, and returned to the English admiral, saying that the pleasure of the general was this, that either their captains, masters, and pursers should come to him with speed, or else he would set upon them, and either take them or sink them. The reply was made by Master Wilkinson aforesaid, that not a man should come to him; and for the brag and threat of Don Pedro, it was not that Spanish bravado that should make them yield a jot to their hindrance, but they were as ready to make resistance as he to offer an injury. Whereupon Cavalero, the messenger, left bragging, and began to persuade them in quiet sort and with many words; but all his labour was to no purpose, and as his threat did nothing terrify them, so his persuasion did nothing move them to do that which he required.

At the last he entreated to have the merchant of the admiral carried by him as a messenger to the general, that so he might be satisfied and assured of their minds by one of their own company. But Master Wilkinson would agree to no such thing; although Richard Rowit, the merchant himself, seemed willing to be employed in that message, and laboured by reasonable persuasions to induce Master Wilkinson to grant it—as hoping to be an occasion by his presence and discreet answers to satisfy the general, and thereby to save the effusion of Christian blood, if it should grow to a battle. And he seemed so much the more willing to be sent, by how much deeper the oaths and protestations of this Cavalero were, that he would (as he was a true knight and a soldier) deliver him back again in safety to his company. Albeit, Master Wilkinson who, by his long experience, had received sufficient trial of Spanish inconstancy and perjury, wished him in no case to put his life and liberty in hazard upon a Spaniard's oath; but at last, upon much entreaty, he yielded to let him go to the general, thinking indeed that good speeches and answers of reason would have contented him, whereas, otherwise, refusal to do so might peradventure have provoked the more discontentment.

Master Rowit, therefore, passing to the Spanish general, the rest of the galleys having espied him, thought, indeed, that the English were rather determined to yield than to fight, and therefore came flocking about the frigate, every man crying out, "*Que nuevas? que nuevas?* Have these Englishmen yielded?"

The frigate answered, "Not so; they neither have nor purpose to yield. Only they have sent a man of their company to speak with our general."

And being come to the galley wherein he was, he showed himself to Master Rowit in his armour, his guard of soldiers attending upon him, in armour also, and began to speak very proudly in this sort:

Thou Englishman, from whence is your fleet? Why stand ye aloof off? know ye not your duty to the Catholic king, whose person I here represent? Where are your bills of lading, your letters, passports, and the chief of your men? Think ye my attendance in these seas to be in vain, or my person to no purpose? Let all these things be done out of hand, as I command, upon pain of my further displeasure, and the spoil of you all.

These words of the Spanish general were not so outrageously pronounced as they were mildly answered by Master Rowit, who told him that they were all merchantmen, using traffic in honest sort, and seeking to pass quietly, if they were not urged further than reason. As for the King of Spain, he thought (for his part) that there was amity betwixt him and his Sovereign, the Queen of England, so that neither he nor his officers should go about to offer any such injury to English merchants, who, as they were far from giving offence to any man, so they would be loath to take an abuse at the hands of any, or sit down to their loss, where their ability was able to make defence. And as touching his commandment aforesaid for the acknowledging of duty in such particular sort, he told him that where there was no duty owing there none should be performed, assuring him that their whole company and ships in general stood resolutely upon the negative, and would not yield to any such unreasonable demand, joined with such imperious and absolute manner of commanding.

"Why, then," said he, "if they will neither come to yield, nor show obedience to me in the name of my king, I will either sink them or bring them to harbour; and so tell them from me."

With that the frigate came away with Master Rowit, and brought him aboard to the English admiral again, according to promise, who was no sooner entered in but by-and-by defiance was sounded on both sides. The Spaniards hewed off the noses of the galleys, that nothing might hinder the level of the shot; and the English, on the other side, courageously prepared themselves to the combat, every man, according to his room, bent to perform his office with alacrity and diligence. In the meantime a cannon was discharged from out the admiral of the galleys, which, being the onset of the fight, was presently answered by the English admiral with a culverin; so the skirmish began, and grew hot and terrible. There was no powder nor shot spared, each English ship matched itself in good order against two Spanish galleys, besides the inequality of the frigates on the Spanish side.

And although our men performed their parts with singular valour, according to their strength, insomuch that the enemy, as amazed therewith, would oftentimes pause and stay, and consult what was best to be done, yet they ceased not in the midst of their business to make prayer to Almighty God, the revenger of all evils and the giver of victories, that it would please Him to assist them in this good quarrel of theirs, in defending themselves against so proud a tyrant, to teach their hands to war and their fingers to fight, that the glory of the victory might redound to His name, and to the honour of true religion, which the insolent enemy sought so much to overthrow.

Contrarily, the foolish Spaniards, they cried out, according to their manner, not to God, but to our Lady (as they term the Virgin Mary), saying, "Oh, Lady, help! Oh, blessed Lady, give us the victory, and the honour thereof shall be thine." Thus with blows and prayers on both sides, the fight continued furious and sharp, and doubtful a long time to which part the victory would incline, till at last the admiral of the galleys of Sicily began to warp from the fight, and to hold up her side for fear of sinking; and after her went also two others in like case, whom all the sort of them enclosed, labouring by all their means to keep them above water, being ready by the force of English shot which they had received to perish in the seas. And what slaughter was done among the Spaniards the English were uncertain, but by a probable conjecture apparent afar off they supposed their loss was so great that they wanted men to continue the charging of their pieces; whereupon with shame and dishonour, after five hours spent in the battle, they withdrew themselves.

And the English, contented in respect of their deep lading rather to continue their voyage than to follow in the chase, ceased from further blows, with the loss of only two men slain amongst them all, and another hurt in his arm, whom Master Wilkinson, with his good words and friendly promises, did so comfort that he nothing esteemed the smart of his wound, in respect of the honour of the victory and the shameful repulse of the enemy.

Thus, with dutiful thanks to the mercy of God for His gracious assistance in that danger, the English ships proceeded in their navigation. And coming as high as Algiers, a port town upon the coast of Barbary, they made for it, of purpose to refresh themselves after their weariness, and to take in such supply of fresh water and victuals as they needed. They were no sooner entered into the port but immediately the king thereof sent a messenger to the ships to know what they were. With which messenger the chief master of every ship repaired to the king, and acquainted him not only with the state of their ships in respect of merchandise, but with the late fight which they had passed with the Spanish galleys, reporting every particular circumstance in word as it fell out in action; whereof the said king showed himself marvellous glad, entertaining them in the best sort, and promising abundant relief of all their wants; making general proclamation in the city, upon pain of death, that no man, of what degree or state soever he were, should presume either to hinder them in their affairs or to offer them any manner of injury in body or goods; by virtue whereof they despatched all things in excellent good sort with all favour and peaceableness.

The English, having received this good justice at the king's hands, and all other things that they wanted or could crave for the furnishing of their ships, took their leave of him and of the rest of their friends that were resident in Algiers, and put out to sea, looking to meet with the second army of the Spanish king, which waited for them about the mouth of the Strait of Gibraltar, which they were of necessity to pass. But coming near to the said strait, it pleased God to raise, at that instant, a very dark and misty fog, so that one ship could not discern another if it were forty paces off, by means whereof, together with the notable fair eastern winds that then blew most fit for their course, they passed with great speed through the strait, and might have passed, with that good gale, had there been five hundred galleys to withstand them and the air never so clear for every ship to be seen.

But yet the Spanish galleys had a sight of them when they were come within three English miles of the town, and made after them with all possible haste; and although they saw that they were far out of their reach, yet in a vain fury and foolish pride they shot off their ordnance and made a stir in the sea as if they had been in the midst of them, which vanity of theirs ministered to our men notable matter of pleasure and mirth, seeing men to fight with shadows and to take so great pains to so small purpose.

But thus it pleased God to deride and delude all the forces of that proud Spanish king, which he had provided of purpose to distress the English; who, notwithstanding, passed through both his armies—in the one, little hurt, and in the other, nothing touched, to the glory of His immortal name, the honour of our prince and country, and the just commendation of each man's service performed in that voyage.

The Story of the Spanish Armada
By Sir Edward Creasy

On the afternoon of July 19th, *A.D.* 1588, a group of English captains was collected at the bowling green on the Hoe at Plymouth, whose equals have never before or since been brought together, even at that favourite mustering-place of the heroes of the British navy. There was Sir Francis Drake, the first English circumnavigator of the globe, the terror of every Spanish coast in the Old World and the New; there was Sir John Hawkins, the rough veteran of many a daring voyage on the African and American seas, and of many a desperate battle; there was Sir Martin Frobisher, one of the earliest explorers of the Arctic seas in search of that North-West Passage which is still the darling object of England's boldest mariners; there was the High-Admiral of England, Lord Howard of Effingham, prodigal of all things in his country's cause, and who had recently had the noble daring to refuse to dismantle part of the fleet, though the queen had sent him orders to do so; resolved to risk his sovereign's anger, and to keep the ships afloat at his own charge, rather than that England should run the peril of losing their protection.

A match at bowls was being played, in which Drake and other high officers of the fleet were engaged, when a small armed vessel was seen running before the wind into Plymouth Harbour, with all sails set. Her commander landed in haste, and eagerly sought the place where the English lord-Admiral and his captains were standing. His name was Fleming; he was the master of a Scotch privateer; and he told the English officers that he had that morning seen the Spanish Armada off the Cornish coast. At this exciting information the captains began to hurry down to the water, and there was a shouting for the ship's boats: but Drake coolly checked his comrades, and insisted that the match should be played out. He said that there was plenty of time both to win the game and beat the Spaniards. The best and bravest match that ever was scored was resumed accordingly. Drake and his friends aimed their last bowls with the same steady calculating coolness with which they were about to point their guns. The winning cast was made; and then they went on board and prepared for action, with their hearts as light and their nerves as firm as they had been on the Hoe bowling green.

Meanwhile, the messengers and signals had been despatched fast and far through England, to warn each town and village that the enemy had come at last. In every seaport there was instant making ready by land and by sea; in every shire and every city there was instant mustering of horse and man. But England's best defence then, as ever, was her fleet; and after warping laboriously out of Plymouth Harbour against the wind, the lord-Admiral stood westward under easy sail, keeping an anxious lookout for the Armada, the approach of which was soon announced by Cornish fishing-boats, and signals from the Cornish cliffs.

The England of our own days is so strong, and the Spain of our own days is so feeble, that it is not possible, without some reflection and care, to comprehend the full extent of the peril which England then ran from the power and the ambition of Spain, or to appreciate the importance of that crisis in the history of the world. We had then no Indian or Colonial Empire save the feeble germs of our North American settlements, which Raleigh and Gilbert had recently planted. Scotland was a separate kingdom; and Ireland was then even a greater source of weakness, and a worse nest of rebellion than she has been in after times. Queen Elizabeth had found at her accession an encumbered revenue, a divided people, and an unsuccessful foreign war, in which the last remnant of our possessions in France had been lost; she had also a formidable pretender to her crown, whose interests were favoured by all the Roman Catholic powers; and even some of her subjects were warped by religious bigotry to deny her title, and to look on her as an heretical usurper.

On the other hand, Philip II. was absolute master of an empire so superior to the other states of the world in extent, in resources, and especially in military and naval forces, as to make the project of enlarging that empire into a universal monarchy seem a perfectly feasible scheme; and Philip had both the ambition to form that project and the resolution to devote all his energies, and all his means, to its realisation. Since the downfall of the Roman empire no such preponderating power had existed in the world.

Philip had also the advantage of finding himself at the head of a large standing army in a perfect state of discipline and equipment, in an age when, except some few insignificant corps, standing armies were unknown in Christendom. The renown of the Spanish troops was justly high, and the infantry in particular was considered the best in the world. His fleet, also, was far more numerous, and better appointed, than that of any other European power; and both his soldiers and his sailors had the confidence in themselves and their commanders which a long career of successful warfare alone can create.

One nation only had been his active, his persevering, and his successful foe. England had encouraged his revolted subjects in Flanders against him, and given them the aid in men and money without which they must soon have been humbled in the dust. English ships had plundered his colonies; had defied his supremacy in the New World as well as the Old; they had inflicted ignominious defeats on his squadrons; they had captured his cities, and burned his arsenals on the very coasts of Spain. The English had made Philip himself the object of personal insult. He was held up to ridicule in their stage-plays and masks, and these scoffs at the man had (as is not unusual in such cases) excited the anger of the absolute king even more vehemently than the injuries inflicted on his power. Personal as well as political revenge urged him to attack England. Were she once subdued, the Dutch must submit; France could not cope with him, the empire would not oppose him; and universal dominion seemed sure to be the result of the conquest of that malignant island.

There was yet another and a stronger feeling which armed King Philip against England. He was one of the sincerest and sternest bigots of his age. He looked on himself, and was looked on by others, as the appointed champion to extirpate heresy and re-establish the Papal power throughout Europe. A powerful reaction against Protestantism had taken place since the commencement of the second half of the sixteenth century, and Philip believed that he was destined to complete it. The Reform doctrines had been thoroughly rooted out from Italy and Spain. Belgium, which had previously been half Protestant, had been reconquered both in allegiance and creed by Philip, and had become one of the most Catholic countries in the world. Half Germany had been won back to the old faith. In Savoy, in Switzerland, and many other countries, the progress of the counter-Reformation had been rapid and decisive. The Catholic league seemed victorious in

France. The Papal court itself had shaken off the supineness of recent centuries; and, at the head of the Jesuits and the other new ecclesiastical orders, was displaying a vigour and a boldness worthy of the days of Hildebrand or Innocent III.

Throughout continental Europe, the Protestants, discomfited and dismayed, looked to England as their protector and refuge. England was the acknowledged central point of Protestant power and policy; and to conquer England was to stab Protestantism to the very heart. Sixtus V., the then reigning pope, earnestly exhorted Philip to this enterprise. And when the tidings reached Italy and Spain that the Protestant Queen of England had put to death her Catholic prisoner, Mary, Queen of Scots, the fury of the Vatican and Escurial knew no bounds.

The Prince of Parma, who was appointed military chief of the expedition, collected on the coast of Flanders a veteran force that was to play a principal part in the conquest of England. Besides the troops who were in his garrisons, or under his colours, five thousand infantry were sent to him from northern and central Italy, four thousand from the kingdom of Naples, six thousand from Castile, three thousand from Arragon, three thousand from Austria and Germany, together with four squadrons of heavy-armed horse; besides which he received forces from the Franche-Comté and the Walloon country. By his command, the forest of Waes was felled for the purpose of building flat-bottomed boats, which, floating down the rivers and canals to Meinport and Dunkerque, were to carry this large army of chosen troops to the mouth of the Thames, under the escort of the great Spanish fleet.

Gun-carriages, fascines, machines used in sieges, together with every material requisite for building bridges, forming camps, and raising fortresses, were to be placed on board the flotillas of the Prince of Parma, who followed up the conquest of the Netherlands whilst he was making preparations for the invasion of this island. His intention was to leave to the Count de Mansfeldt sufficient forces to follow up the war with the Dutch, which had now become a secondary object, whilst he himself went at the head of fifty thousand men of the Armada and the flotilla, to accomplish the principal enterprise—that enterprise, which, in the highest degree, affected the interests of the pontifical authority. In a bull, intended to be kept secret until the day of landing, Sixtus V., renewing the anathema fulminated against Elizabeth by Pius V. and Gregory XIII., affected to depose her from our throne.

Elizabeth was denounced as a murderous heretic whose destruction was an instant duty. A formal treaty was concluded (in June, 1587), by which the pope bound himself to contribute a million of *scudi* to the expenses of the war; the money to be paid as soon as the king had actual possession of an English port. Philip, on his part, strained the resources of his vast empire to the utmost. The French Catholic chiefs eagerly co-operated with him. In the sea-ports of the Mediterranean, and along almost the whole coast from Gibraltar to Jutland, the preparations for the great armament were urged forward with all the earnestness of religious zeal, as well as of angry ambition.

For some time the destination of the enormous armament of Philip was not publicly announced. Only Philip himself, the Pope Sixtus, the Duke of Guise, and Philip's favourite minister, Mendoza, at first knew its real object. Rumours were sedulously spread that it was designed to proceed to the Indies to realise vast projects of distant conquest. Sometimes hints were dropped by Philip's ambassadors in foreign courts that his master had resolved on a decisive effort to crush his rebels in the Low Countries.

But Elizabeth and her statesmen could not view the gathering of such a storm without feeling the probability of its bursting on their own shores. As early as the spring of 1587 Elizabeth sent Sir Francis Drake to cruise off the Tagus. Drake sailed into the Bay of Cadiz and the Lisbon roads, and burnt much shipping and military stores, causing thereby an important delay in the progress of the Spanish preparations. Drake called this "Singeing the King of Spain's beard." Elizabeth also increased her succours of troops to the Netherlanders, to prevent the Prince of Parma from overwhelming them, and from thence being at full leisure to employ his army against her dominions.

Meanwhile in England, from the sovereign on the throne to the peasant in the cottage, all hearts and hands made ready to meet the imminent deadly peril. Circular letters from the queen were sent round to the lord-lieutenants of the several counties requiring them "to call together the best sort of gentlemen under their lieutenancy, and to declare unto them these great preparations and arrogant threatenings, now burst forth in action upon the seas, wherein every man's particular state, in the highest degree, could be touched in respect of country, liberty, wives, children, lands, lives, and (which was specially to be regarded) the profession of the true and sincere religion of Christ; and to lay before them the infinite and unspeakable miseries that would fall out upon any such change, which miseries were evidently seen by the fruits of that hard and cruel government holden in countries not far distant."

The ships of the Royal Navy at this time amounted to no more than thirty-six; but the most serviceable merchant vessels were collected from all the ports of the country; and the citizens of London, Bristol, and the other great seats of commerce, showed as liberal a zeal in equipping and manning vessels as the nobility and gentry displayed in mustering forces by land. The seafaring population of the coast, of every rank and station, was animated by the same ready spirit; and the whole number of seamen who came forward to man the English fleet was 17,472. The number of the ships that were collected was a hundred and ninety-one; and the total amount of their tonnage 31,985.

There was one ship in the fleet (the *Triumph*) of eleven hundred tons, one of ten hundred, one of nine hundred, two of eight hundred each, three of six hundred, five of five hundred, five of four hundred, six of three hundred, six of two hundred and fifty, twenty of two hundred, and the residue of inferior burden. Application was made to the Dutch for assistance; and, as Stowe expresses it, "The Hollanders came roundly in, with threescore sail, brave ships of war, fierce and full of spleen, not so much for England's aid, as in just occasion for their own defence; these men foreseeing the greatness of the danger that might ensue, if the Spaniards should chance to win the day and get the mastery over them; in due regard whereof their manly courage was inferior to none."

We have more minute information of the numbers and equipment of the hostile forces than we have of our own. In the first volume of Hakluyt's *Voyages*, dedicated to Lord Effingham, who commanded against the Armada, there is given (from the contemporary foreign writer, Meteran) a more complete and detailed catalogue than has perhaps ever appeared of a similar armament.

> The number of mariners in the saide fleete were above eight thousand, of slaves two thousand and eighty-eight, of soldiers twenty thousand (besides noblemen and gentlemen voluntaries), of great cast pieces two thousand six hundred. The aforesaide ships were of an huge and incredible capacitie and receipt: for the whole fleete was large enough to containe the burthen of sixty thousand tunnes.
>
> The galeons were sixty-four in number, being of an huge big-

nesse, and very flately built, being of marveilous force also, and so high, that they resembled great castles, most fit to defend themselves and to withstand any assault; but in giving any other ships the encounter farr inferiour unto the English and Dutch ships, which can with great dexteritie weild and turne themselves at all assayes.

The upperworke of the said galeons was of thicknesse and strength sufficient to bear off musket-shot. The lower worke and the timbers thereof were out of measure strong, being framed of plankes and ribs foure or five foote in thicknesse, insomuch that no bullets could pierce them, but such as were discharged hard at hand; which afterward prooved true, for a great number of bullets were found to sticke fast within the massie substance of those thicke plankes. Great and well-pitched cables were twined about the masts of their shippes, to strengthen them against the battery of shot.

The *galliasses* were of such bignesse, that they contained within them chambers, chapels, turrets, pulpits, and other commodities of great houses. The galliasses were rowed with great oares, there being in eche one of them three hundred slaves for the same purpose, and were able to do great service with the force of their ordinance. All these, together with the residue aforenamed, were furnished and beautified with trumpets, streamers, banners, warlike ensignes, and other such like ornaments.

Their pieces of brazen ordinance were sixteen hundred, and of yron ten hundred.

The bullets thereto belonging were a hundred and twenty thousand.

Item of gun-poulder, five thousand six hundred quintals. Of matche, twelve hundred quintals. Of muskets and kalcivers seven thousand. Of haleberts and partisans, ten thousand.

Moreover they had great store of canons, double-canons, culverings and field-pieces for land services.

This navie (as Diego Pimentelli afterward confessed) was esteemed by the king himselfe to containe thirty-two thousand persons, and to cost him every day thirty thousand *ducates*.

While this huge Armada was making ready in the southern ports of the Spanish dominions, the Prince of Parma, with almost incredible toil and skill, collected a squadron of war-ships at Dunkirk, and his flotilla of other ships and of flat-bottomed boats for the transport to England of the picked troops, which were designed to be the main instruments in subduing England. Thousands of workmen were employed, night and day, in the construction of these vessels, in the ports of Flanders and Brabant. The army which these vessels were designed to convey to England amounted to thirty thousand strong, besides a body of four thousand cavalry, stationed at Courtrai, composed chiefly of the ablest veterans of Europe; invigorated by rest, and excited by the hopes of plunder and the expectation of certain conquest.

Philip had been advised, in the first instance, to effect a landing and secure a strong position in Ireland; his admiral, Santa Cruz, had recommended him to make sure, in the first instance, of some large harbour on the coast of Holland or Zealand, where the Armada, having entered the Channel, might find shelter in case of storm, and whence it could sail without difficulty for England; but Philip rejected both these counsels, and directed that England itself should be made the immediate object of attack; and on May 20th the Armada left the Tagus, in the pomp and pride of supposed invincibility, and amidst the shouts of thousands, who believed that England was already conquered. But steering to the northward, and before it was clear of the coast of Spain, the Armada was assailed by a violent storm, and driven back with considerable damage to the ports of Biscay and Galicia. It had, however, sustained its heaviest loss before it left the Tagus, in the death of the veteran admiral Santa Cruz, who had been destined to guide it against England.

Philip II. had replaced him by Alonzo Perez de Gusman, Duke of Medina Sidonia, one of the most powerful of the Spanish *grandees*, but wholly unqualified to command such an expedition. He had, however, as his lieutenants, two seamen of proved skill and bravery, Juan de Martinez Recalde of Biscay, and Miguel Orquendo of Guipuzcoa.

On July 12th, the Armada having completely refitted, sailed again for the Channel, and reached it without obstruction or observation by the English.

The orders of King Philip to the Duke de Medina Sidonia were, that he should, on entering the Channel, keep near the French coast, and, if attacked by the English ships, avoid an action, and steer on to Calais roads, where the Prince of Parma's squadron was to join him. The hope of surprising and destroying the English fleet in Plymouth led the Spanish admiral to deviate from these orders, and to stand across to the English shore; but, on finding that Lord Howard was coming out to meet him, he resumed the original plan, and determined to bend his way steadily towards Calais and Dunkirk, and to keep merely on the defensive against such squadrons of the English as might come up with him.

It was on Saturday, July 20th, that Lord Effingham came in sight of his formidable adversaries. The Armada was drawn up in form of a crescent, which from horn to horn measured some seven miles. There was a south-west wind; and before it the vast vessels sailed slowly on. The English let them pass by; and then, following in the rear, commenced an attack on them. A running fight now took place, in which some of the best ships of the Spaniards were captured; many more received heavy damage; while the English vessels, which took care not to close with their huge antagonists, but availed themselves of their superior celerity in tacking and manoeuvring, suffered little comparative loss. Each day added not only to the spirit, but to the number of Effingham's force. Raleigh, Oxford, Cumberland, and Sheffield joined him; and "the gentlemen of England hired ships from all parts at their own charge, and with one accord came flocking thither as to a set field, where glory was to be attained, and faithful service performed unto their prince and their country."

The Spanish admiral also showed great judgment and firmness in following the line of conduct that had been traced out for him; and on July 27th he brought his fleet unbroken, though sorely distressed, to anchor in Calais roads. But the King of Spain had calculated ill the number and activity of the English and Dutch fleets; as the old historian expresses it, "It seemeth that the Duke of Parma and the Spaniards grounded upon a vain and presumptuous expectation, that all the ships of England and of the Low Countreys would at the first sight of the Spanish and Dunkerk Navie have betaken themselves to flight, yeelding them sea-room, and endeavouring only to defend themselves, their havens, and sea coasts from invasion.

Wherefore their intent and purpose was, that the Duke of Parma, in his small and flat-bottomed ships should, as it were, under the shadow and wings of the Spanish fleet, convey over all his troupes, armour, and warlike provisions, and with their forces so united should invade England; or, while the English fleet were busied in fight against the Spanish, should enter upon any part of the coast which he thought to be most convenient. Which invasion (as the captives afterwards confessed) the Duke of Parma thought first to have attempted by the river of Thames; upon the banks whereof, having at the first arrivall landed twenty or thirty thousand of his principall souldiers, he supposed that he might easily have wonne the citie of London; both because his small shippes should have followed and assisted his land forces, and also for that the citie itselfe was but meanely fortified and easie to ouercome, by reason of the citizens' delicacie and discontinuance from the warres, who, with continuall and constant labour, might be vanquished, if they yielded not at the first assault."

But the English and Dutch found ships and mariners enough to keep the Armada itself in check, and at the same time to block up Parma's flotilla. The greater part of Seymour's squadron left its cruising ground off Dunkirk to join the English admiral off Calais; but the Dutch manned about five-and-thirty sail of good ships, with a strong force of soldiers on board, all well seasoned to the sea-service; and with these they blockaded the Flemish ports that were in Parma's power. Still it was resolved by the Spanish admiral and the prince to endeavour to effect a junction, which the English seamen were equally resolute to prevent: and bolder measures on our side now became necessary.

The Armada lay off Calais, with its largest ships ranged outside, "like strong castles fearing no assault; the lesser placed in the middle ward." The English admiral could not attack them in their position without great disadvantage, but on the night of the 29th he sent eight fire-ships among them, with almost equal effect to that of the fire-ships which the Greeks so often employed against the Turkish fleets in their late war of independence. The Spaniards cut their cables and put to sea in confusion. One of the largest *galeasses* ran foul of another vessel and was stranded. The rest of the fleet was scattered about on the Flemish coast, and when the morning broke, it was with difficulty and delay that they obeyed their admiral's signal to range themselves round him near Gravelines.

Now was the golden opportunity for the English to assail them, and prevent them from ever letting loose Parma's flotilla against England; and nobly was that opportunity used. Drake and Fenner were the first English captains who attacked the unwieldy leviathans: then came Fenton, Southwell, Burton, Cross, Raynor, and then the lord-Admiral, with Lord Thomas Howard and Lord Sheffield. The Spaniards only thought of forming and keeping close together, and were driven by the English past Dunkirk, and far away from the Prince of Parma, who in watching their defeat from the coast, must, as Drake expressed it, have chafed like a bear robbed of her whelps. This was indeed the last and the decisive battle between the two fleets. It is, perhaps, best described in the very words of the contemporary writer as we may read them in Hakluyt.

> Upon July 29th, in the morning, the Spanish fleet after the forsayd tumult, having arranged themselves againe into order, were, within sight of Greveling, most bravely and furiously encountered by the English; where they once again got the wind of the Spaniards; who suffered themselves to be deprived of the commodity of the place in Caleis road, and of the advantage of the wind neer unto Dunkerk, rather than they would change their array or separate their forces now conjoyned and united together, standing only upon their defence.
>
> And howbeit there were many excellent and warlike ships in the English fleet, yet scarce were there twenty-two or twenty-three among them all, which matched ninety of the Spanish ships in the bigness, or could conveniently assault them. Wherefore the English ships using their prerogative of nimble steerage, whereby they could turn and wield themselves with wind which way they listed, came often times very near upon the Spaniards, and charged them so sore, that now and then they were but a pike's length asunder: and so continually giving them one broadside after another, they discharged all their shot both great and small upon them, spending one whole day from morning till night in that violent kind of conflict, untill such time as powder and bullets failed them.
>
> In regard of which want they thought it convenient not to pursue the Spaniards any longer, because they had many great vantages of the English, namely, for the extraordinary bigness of their ships, and also for that they were so neerley conjoyned, and kept together in so good array, that they could by no meanes be fought withall one to one. The English thought, therefore, that they had right well acquitted themselves, in chasing the Spaniards first from Caleis, and then from Dunkerk, and by that meanes to have hindered them from joyning with the Duke of Parma his forces, and getting the wind of them, to have driven them from their own coasts.
>
> The Spaniards that day sustained great loss and damage, having many of their shippes shot thorow and thorow, and they discharged likewise great store of ordinance against the English;

who, indeed, sustained some hindrance, but not comparable to the Spaniard's loss: for they lost not any one ship or person of account, for very diligent inquisition being made, the English men all that time wherein the Spanish navy sayled upon their seas, are not found to have wanted above one hundred of their people: albeit Sir Francis Drake's ship was pierced with shot above forty times, and his very cabben was twice shot thorow, and about the conclusion of the fight, the bed of a certain gentleman lying weary thereupon, was taken quite from under him with the force of a bullet. Likewise, as the Earle of Northumberland and Sir Charles Blunt were at dinner upon a time, the bullet of a demy-culverin brake thorow the middest of their cabben, touched their feet, and strooke downe two of the standers by, with many such accidents befalling the English shippes, which it were tedious to rehearse.

It reflects little credit on the English Government that the English fleet was so deficiently supplied with ammunition, as to be unable to complete the destruction of the invaders. But enough was done to ensure it. Many of the largest Spanish ships were sunk or captured in the action of this day. And at length the Spanish admiral, despairing of success, fled northward with a southerly wind, in the hope of rounding Scotland, and so returning to Spain without a farther encounter with the English fleet. Lord Effingham left a squadron to continue the blockade of the Prince of Parma's armament; but that wise general soon withdrew his troops to more promising fields of action. Meanwhile the lord-Admiral himself, and Drake chased the vincible Armada, as it was now termed, for some distance northward; and then, when it seemed to bend away from the Scotch coast towards Norway, it was thought best, in the words of Drake, "to leave them to those boisterous and uncouth northern seas."

The sufferings and losses which the unhappy Spaniards sustained in their flight round Scotland and Ireland are well known. Of their whole Armada only fifty-three shattered vessels brought back their beaten and wasted crews to the Spanish coast, which they had quitted in such pageantry and pride. Some passages from the writings of those who took part in the struggle have been already quoted, to which may be added the following description of the defeat of the Armada, written in answer to some mendacious stories by which the Spaniards strove to hide their shame.

They were not ashamed to publish, in sundry languages in print, great victories in words, which they pretended to have obtained against this realm, and spread the same in a most false sort over all parts of France, Italy, and elsewhere; when, shortly afterwards, it was happily manifested in very deed to all nations, how their navy, which they termed invincible, consisting of one hundred and forty sail of ships, not only of their own kingdom, but strengthened with the greatest *argosies*, Portugal *caracks*, Florentines, and large hulks of other countries, were by thirty of Her Majesty's own ships of war, and a few of our own merchants, by the wise, valiant, and advantageous conduct of the Lord Charles Howard, High-Admiral of England, beaten and shuffled together even from the Lizard in Cornwall, first to Portland, when they shamefully left Don Pedro de Valdez with his mighty ship; from Portland to Calais, where they lost Hugh de Monçado, with the galleys of which he was captain; and from Calais driven with squibs from their anchors, were chased out of the sight of England, round about Scotland and Ireland. Where, for the sympathy of their religion, hoping to find succour and assistance, a great part of them were crushed against the rocks, and those others that landed, being very many in number, were, notwithstanding, broken, slain, and taken; and so sent from village to village, coupled in halters, to be shipped into England, where Her Majesty, of her princely and invincible disposition, disdaining to put them to death, and scorning either to retain or to entertain them, they were all sent back again to their countries, to witness and recount the worthy achievement of their invincible and dreadful navy.

Of which the number of soldiers, the fearful burthen of their ships, the commanders' names of every squadron, with all others, their magazines of provisions were put in print, as an army and navy irresistible and disdaining prevention: with all which their great and terrible ostentation, they did not in all their sailing round about England so much as sink or take one ship, bark, pinnace, or cockboat of ours, or even burn so much as one sheep-cote on this land.

The Story of the "Revenge"

A report of the truth of the fight about the Isles of Azores, this last summer, betwixt the *Revenge*, one of Her Majesties' ships, and an Armada of the King of Spain (London 1591), by Sir Walter Raleigh.

Because the rumours are diversely spread, as well in England as in the Low Countries and elsewhere, of this late encounter between Her Majesties' ships and the Armada of Spain; and that the Spaniards, according to their usual manner, fill the world with their vain-glorious vaunts, making great appearance of victories—when, on the contrary, themselves are most commonly and shamefully beaten and dishonoured—thereby hoping to possess the ignorant multitude by anticipating and forerunning false reports, it is agreeable with all good reason for manifestation of the truth to overcome falsehood and untruth, that the beginning, continuance and success of this late honourable encounter of Sir Richard Grenville, and other Her Majesties' captains with the Armada of Spain, should be truly set down and published without partiality or false imagination.

The Lord Thomas Howard, with six of Her Majesties' ships, six victualers of London, the bark *Ralegh*, and two or three pinnaces riding at anchor near unto Flores, one of the westerly islands of the Azores, the last of August in the afternoon, had intelligence by one Captain Middleton of the approach of the Spanish Armada, which Middleton, being in a very good sailer, had kept them company three days before, of good purpose both to discover their forces the more as also to give advice to my Lord Thomas of their approach. He had no sooner delivered the news but the fleet was in sight: many of our ships' companies were on shore in the island; some providing ballast for their ships, others filling of water and refreshing themselves from the land with such things as they could either for money or by force recover.

By reason whereof our ships being all pestered and romaging, everything out of order, very light for want of ballast, and that which was most to our disadvantage, the one half part of the men of every ship sick and utterly unserviceable. For in the *Revenge* there were ninety diseased: in the *Bonaventure*, not so many in health as could handle her mainsail. For had not twenty men been taken out of a bark of Sir George Caryes, his being commanded to be sunk and those appointed to her, she had hardly ever recovered England. The rest for the most part were in little better state.

The names of Her Majesties' ships were these as followeth: the *Defiance*, which was admiral; the *Revenge*, vice-Admiral; the *Bonaventure*, commanded by Captain Crosse; the *Lion*, by George Fenner; the *Foresight*, by M. Thomas Vavisour, and the *Crane*, by Duffeild. The *Foresight* and the *Crane* being but small ships; only the others were of the middle size; the rest, besides the bark *Ralegh*, commanded by Captain Thin, were victualers and of small force or none. The Spanish fleet, having shrouded their approach by reason of the island, were now so soon at hand, as our ships had scarce time to way their anchors, but some of them were driven to let slip their cables and set sail. Sir Richard Grenville was the last weighed, to recover the men that were upon the island, which otherwise had been lost.

The Lord Thomas with the rest very hardly recovered the wind, which Sir Richard Grenville not being able to do was persuaded by the master and others to cut his main sail and cast about, and to trust to the sailing of the ship: for the squadron of Sivill were on his weather bow. But Sir Richard utterly refused to turn from the enemy, alleging that he would rather choose to die than to dishonour himself, his country, and Her Majesties' ships, persuading his company that he would pass through the two squadrons in despite of them, and enforce those of Sivill to give him way. Which he performed upon divers of the foremost, who, as the mariners term it, sprang their luffe and fell under the lee of the *Revenge*. But the other course had been the better, and might right well have been answered in so great an impossibility of prevailing.

Notwithstanding, out of the greatness of his mind he could not be persuaded. In the meanwhile, as he attended those which were nearest him, the great *San Philip* being in the wind of him, and, coming towards him, becalmed his sails in such sort as the ship could neither make way nor feel the helm: so huge and high carged was the Spanish ship, being of a thousand and five hundred tons; who after laid the *Revenge* aboard. When he was thus bereft of his sails, the ships that were under his lee luffing up, also laid him aboard: of which the next was the admiral of the *Biscaines*, a very mighty and *puisant* ship commanded by Brittan Dona. The said *Philip* carried three tire of ordinance on a side and eleven pieces in every tire. She shot eight forth right out of her chase, besides those of her stern ports.

After the *Revenge* was entangled with this *Philip*, four other boarded her; two on her larboard and two on her starboard. The fight thus beginning at three of the clock in the afternoon continued very terrible all that evening. But the great *San Philip* having received the lower tire of the *Revenge* discharged with crossbar shot, shifted herself with all diligence from her sides, utterly misliking her first entertainment. Some say that the ship foundered, but we cannot report it for truth unless we were assured. The Spanish ships were filled with companies of soldiers, in some two hundred besides the mariners; in some five, in others eight hundred. In ours there were none at all beside the mariners, but the servants of the commanders and some few voluntary gentlemen only.

After many interchanged volleys of great ordinance and small shot, the Spaniards deliberated to enter the *Revenge*, and made divers attempts, hoping to force her by the multitudes of their armed soldiers and musketeers, but were still repulsed again and again, and at all times beaten back into their own ships or into the seas. In the beginning of the fight the *George Noble* of London, having received some shot through her by the Armados, fell under the lee of the *Revenge*, and asked Sir Richard what he would command him, being but one of the victualers and of small force: Sir Richard bid him save himself and leave him to his fortune. After the fight had thus without intermission continued while the day lasted and some hours of the night, many of our men were slain and hurt, and one of the great galleons of the Armada and the admiral of the hulks both sunk, and in many other of the Spanish ships great slaughter was made.

Some write that Sir Richard was very dangerously hurt almost in the beginning of the fight, and lay speechless for a time ere he recovered. But two of the *Revenge's* own company, brought home in a ship of lime from the islands, examined by some of the lords and others, affirmed that he was never so wounded as that he forsook the upper deck till an hour before midnight; and then being shot into the body with a musket as he was a-dressing, was again shot into the head, and withal his Chirurgion wounded to death. This agreeth also with an examination taken by Sir Frances Godolphin, of four other mariners of the same ship being returned, which examination, the said Sir Frances sent unto Master William Killigrue, of Her Majesties' privy chamber.

But to return to the fight; the Spanish ships which attempted to board the *Revenge*, as they were wounded and beaten off so always others came in their places, she having never less than two mighty galleons by her sides and aboard her. So that ere the morning, from three of the clock the day before, there had fifteen several Armados assailed her; and all so ill approved their entertainment, as they were by the break of day far more willing to hearken to a composition, than hastily to make any more assaults or entries. But as the day encreased so our men decreased, and as the light grew more and more by so much more grew our discomforts. For none appeared in sight but enemies, saving one small ship called the *Pilgrim*, commanded by Jacob Whiddon, who hovered all night to see the success; but in the morning, bearing with the *Revenge*, was hunted like a hare amongst many ravenous hounds, but escaped.

All the powder of the *Revenge* to the last barrel was now spent, all her pikes broken, forty of her best men slain and the most part of the rest hurt. In the beginning of the fight she had but one hundred free from sickness, and four score and ten sick, laid in hold upon the ballast. A small troop to man such a ship, and a weak garrison to resist so mighty an army. By those hundred all was sustained, the volleys, boardings and enterings of fifteen ships of war, besides those which beat her at large. On the contrary, the Spanish were always supplied with soldiers brought from every squadron: all manner of arms and powder at will. Unto ours there remained no comfort at all, no hope, no supply either of ships, men, or weapons; the masts all beaten overboard, all her tackle cut asunder, her upper work altogether rased, and in effect evened she was with the water, but the very foundation or bottom of a ship, nothing being left overhead either for flight or defence.

Sir Richard finding himself in this distress, and unable any longer to make resistance, having endured in this fifteen hours' fight the assault of fifteen several Armadoes, all by turns aboard him, and by estimation eight hundred shot of great artillery, besides many assaults and entries, and that himself and the ship must needs be possessed by the enemy, who were now all cast in a ring round about him, the *Revenge* not able to move one way or other but as she was moved with the waves and billows of the sea, commanded the master-gunner, whom he knew to be a most resolute man, to split and sink the ship, that thereby nothing might remain of glory or victory to the Spaniards, seeing in so many hours' fight and with so great a navy they were not able to take her having had fifteen hours' time, fifteen thousand men, and fifty and three sail of men-of-war to perform it withal, and persuaded the company, or as many as he could induce, to yield themselves unto God, and to the mercy of none else but as they had, like valiant, resolute men, repulsed so many enemies, they should not now shorten the honour of their nation by prolonging their own lives for a few hours or a few days.

The master-gunner readily condescended and divers others, but the captain and the master were of another opinion, and besought Sir Richard to have care of them, alleging that the Spaniards would be as ready to entertain a composition as they were willing to offer the same; and that there being divers sufficient and valiant men yet living and whose wounds were not mortal, they might do their country and prince acceptable service hereafter. And (that where Sir Richard had alleged that the Spaniards should never glory to have taken one ship of Her Majesties', seeing they had so long and so notably defended themselves) they answered that the ship had six foot water in hold, three shot under water which were so weakly stopped, as with the first working of the sea she must needs sink, and was besides so crushed and bruised as she could never be removed out of the place.

And as the matter was thus in dispute and Sir Richard refusing to hearken to any of those reasons, the master of the *Revenge* (while the captain wan unto him all the greater party) was conveyed aboard the general *Don Alfonso Bassan*, who, finding none over-hastie to enter the *Revenge* again, doubting least Sir Richard would have blown them up and himself, and perceiving by the report of the master of the *Revenge* his dangerous disposition, yielded that all their lives should be saved, the company sent for England, and the better sort to pay such reasonable ransom as their estate would bear, and in the mean season to be free from gally and imprisonment. To this he so much the rather condescended as well as I have said, for fear of further loss and mischief to themselves, as also for the desire he had to recover Sir Richard Grenville, whom for his notable valour he seemed greatly to honour and admire.

When this answer was returned and that safety of life was promised, the common sort being now at the end of their peril, the most drew back from Sir Richard and the master-gunner being no hard matter to dissuade men from death to life. The master-gunner, finding himself and Sir Richard thus prevented and mastered by the greater number, would have slain himself with a sword had he not been by force withheld and locked in his cabin. Then the general sent many boats aboard the *Revenge*, and divers of our men, fearing Sir Richard's disposition, stole away aboard the general and other ships. Sir Richard thus overmatched, was sent unto by Alfonso Bassan to remove out of the *Revenge*, the ship being marvellous unsavoury, filled with blood and bodies of dead and wounded men like a slaughter house. Sir Richard answered that he might do with his body what he list, for he esteemed it not, and as he was carried out of the ship he swooned, and reviving again, desired the company to pray for him.

The general used Sir Richard with all humanity, and left nothing unattempted that tended to his recovery, highly commending his valour and worthiness, and greatly bewailed the danger wherein he was, being unto them a rare spectacle, and a resolution seldom approved. To see one ship turn toward so many enemies, to endure the charge and boarding of so many huge Armados, and to resist and repel the assaults and entries of so many soldiers, all which and more is confirmed by a Spanish captain of the same Armada, and a present actor in the fight, who being severed from the rest in a storm, was by the *Lyon* of London, a small ship, taken, and is now prisoner in London.

The general commander of the Armada was Don Alphonso Bassan, brother to the Marquesse of Santa Cruce. The admiral of the Biscaine squadron was Britan Dona; of the squadron of Sivill, Marques of Arumburch. The hulks and fly-boats were commanded by Luis Cutino. There were slain and drowned in this fight well near two thousand of the enemies and two especial commanders, Don Luis de sant John and Don George de Prunaria de Mallaga, as the Spanish captain confesseth, besides divers others of special account, whereof as yet report is not made.

The admiral of the hulks and the ascention of Sivill were sunk by the side of the *Revenge*; one other recovered the road of Saint Nichels and sunk also there; a fourth ran herself with the shore to save her men. Sir Richard died, as it is said, the second or third day aboard the general, and was by them greatly bewailed. What became of his body, whether it was buried in the sea or on the land, we know not: the comfort that remaineth to his friends is that he hath ended his life honourably in respect of the reputation won to his nation and country, and of the same to his posterity, and that being dead he hath not outlived his own honour.

For the rest of Her Majesties' ships that entered not so far into the fight as the *Revenge*, the reasons and causes were these. There were of them but six in all, whereof two but small ships; the *Revenge* engaged past recovery; the Island of Flores was on the one side, fifty-three sail of the Spanish divided into squadrons, on the other, all as full filled with soldiers as they could contain. Almost the one half of our men sick and not able to serve; the ships grown foul, unroomaged, and scarcely able to bear any sail for want of ballast, having been six months at the sea before. If all the rest had entered all had been lost. For the very hugeness of the Spanish fleet, if no other violence had been offered, would have crushed them between them into shivers. Of which the dishonour and loss to the queen had been far greater than the spoil or harm that the enemy could any way have received.

Notwithstanding, it is very true that the Lord Thomas would have entered between the squadrons, but the rest would not condescend; and the master of his own ship offered to leap into the sea rather than to conduct that Her Majesties' ship and the rest to be a prey to the enemy where there was no hope nor possibility either of defence or victory. Which also in my opinion had ill-sorted or answered the discretion and trust of a general to commit himself and his charge to an assured destruction without any hope or any likelihood of prevailing, thereby to diminish the strength of Her Majesties' navy and to enrich the pride and glory of the enemy.

> The story of Sir Richard Grenville's last fight has been told many times in prose and verse. Sir Walter Raleigh tells it in the prose epic from which the foregoing is taken; Froude made it the subject of one of his essays, Gerald Massey and Lord Tennyson have both exploited it in ballads of power and beauty. These ballads are too long for quotation here, but there are some *stanzas* in Gerald Massey's poem which may be given.
>
> *Signalled the English admiral,*
> *'Weigh or cut anchors.' For*
> *A Spanish fleet bore down in all*
> *The majesty for war,*
> *Athwart our tack for many a mile,*
> *As there we lay off Florez Isle,*
> *With crews half sick; all tired of toil.*
> *Eleven of our twelve ships escaped;*

Sir Richard stood alone!
Though they were three and fifty sail—
A hundred men to one—
The old Sea Rover would not run,
So long as he had man or gun;
But—he could die when all was done.

Ship after ship like broken waves
That wash up on a rock,
Those mighty galleons fall back foiled
And shattered from the shock.
With fire she answers all their blows;
Again, again in pieces strows
The girdle round her as they close.

Through all that night the great white storm
Of worlds in silence rolled;
Sirius with green-azure sparkle,
Mars in ruddy gold.
Heaven looked with stillness terrible
Down on a fight most fierce and fell—
A sea transfigured into hell.

Some know not they are wounded till
'Tis slippery where they stand;
Then each one tighter grips his steel
As 'twere salvation's hand.
Grim faces glow through lurid night
With sweat of spirit shining bright:
Only the dead on deck turn white.

At daybreak the flame-picture fades
In blackness and in blood;
There, after fifteen hours' fight,
The unconquered sea-king stood,
Defying all the powers of Spain:
Fifteen armadas hurled in vain,
And fifteen hundred foemen slain.

About that little bark Revenge
The baffled Spaniards ride
At distance. Two of their good ships
Were sunken at her side;
The rest lie round her in a ring

As round the dying lion-king
The dogs afraid of his death-spring.

Old heroes who could gladly do,
As they could greatly dare;
A vesture very glorious
Their shining spirits wear,
Of noble deeds! God give us grace,
That we may see such face to face,
In our great day that comes apace.

We will only add here that the *Revenge* foundered a few days after the fight with two hundred Spaniards on board her, and conclude with Sir Richard Grenville's last words, "Here die I, Richard Grenville, with a joyful and quiet mind, for that I have ended my life as a true soldier ought to do, fighting for his queen, religion, and honour; my soul willingly departing from this body, leaving behind the lasting fame of having behaved as any valiant soldier is in his duty bound to do."—Original Ed.

The Story of Admiral Blake
By John Campbell

Robert Blake, who became the Admiral of the Commonwealth, was the eldest son of Mr. Humphrey Blake, a Spanish merchant who, having acquired a considerable fortune for the times in which he lived, purchased a small estate near Bridgewater, in which neighbourhood his family had been long settled.

Robert was born in the month of August, 1598, and was educated at a free school in Bridgewater. He afterwards removed to Oxford, where he was first a member of St. Alban's Hall and next of Wadham College. Having taken a degree and met with more than one disappointment in his endeavours to obtain academical preferment, he left the university after a stay of seven years.

During his residence in Oxford he displayed a temper usually grave, and in appearance morose, but inclined at times and with particular friends to be very cheerful, though still with a tincture of severity that disposed him to bear hard upon the pride of courtiers and the powers of churchmen; which rendered him very agreeable company to the good fellows of those days. This is certain, that his reputation for probity and his known aversion to persecution caused the Puritans to promote his election as a burgess for Bridgewater in the parliament which sat in April 1640.

This assembly was dissolved too early for Blake to make any discovery therein of his talents as a senator; and in the long parliament, which sat soon after, he lost his election. When the war broke out between the king and the parliament he declared for the latter, and took arms very early in their service; but where, and in what capacity, is not very clear. However, he was very soon made a captain of dragoons, in which position he showed himself as able and active an officer as any in the service; and as such was constantly employed upon occasions when boldness or dexterity were requisite.

In 1643 he was at Bristol, under the command of Colonel Fiennes, who entrusted him with a little fort on the line, in which he first gave the world a proof of his military prowess; for, on July 26th, when Prince Rupert attacked that important place, and the governor had agreed to surrender it upon articles, Blake still held out his fort and killed several of the king's forces. This exasperated Prince Rupert to such a degree that he talked of hanging him, and would probably have carried out his threat had not some friends interposed and excused the young officer on account of his want of experience in war, and then prevailed upon him to give up the fort.

After this Blake served in Somersetshire under the command of Popham, who was governor of Lyme, to whose regiment he was lieutenant-colonel. While here, in conjunction with Sir Robert Pye, he surprised Taunton for the parliament, capturing ten pieces of cannon and a great deal of ammunition. In 1664 he was made governor of the town, an important appointment, as Taunton contained the only garrison the parliament had in the west. The works about it, however, were far from being strong, and the garrison was by no means numerous; yet by keeping a strict discipline, and treating the townsmen well, he made shift to keep it, though no great care was taken to furnish him with supplies, and he was often besieged and blocked up by the king's forces.

At length General Goring attacked Taunton with nearly ten thousand men, carried all the outworks, and actually took a part of the town. Blake, however, held the rest of it and the castle with wonderful obstinacy till relief came; for which extraordinary service the parliament gave the garrison a bounty of two thousand pounds, and honoured Colonel Blake with a present of five hundred pounds. All who have preserved the memory of the signal events in this unhappy war allow this to have been a singularly gallant and soldier-like action.

In April, 1646, Colonel Blake marched with a detachment from his garrison, and reduced Dunster Castle, a seat belonging to the ancient family of Lutterel, the troops posted therein having given great disturbance to the country. This was the last military achievement he performed during the Civil War. On the 24th of December following, the parliament ordered five hundred pounds to be paid to him for disbanding some forces. When the parliament voted that no further addresses should be made to the king, Blake, as Governor of Taunton, joined in an address of thanks to the House of Commons for having taken this step.

It is not easy to guess what induced the parliament to make choice of Blake, who had always served as a horse-officer, to take the supreme command of the fleet, but on February 12th, 1648-9, he was appointed one of the commissioners of the navy, and upon the 21st an Act was passed, appointing him, in conjunction with Deane and Popham, to command the fleet. His first service was driving Prince Rupert's fleet from the Irish coast, and then following him into the Mediterranean. This gave his masters high satisfaction, for it not only put an end to the piratical war in which the prince was engaged, and which did so much damage to trade, but also inspired respect among the powers of Europe for the young Commonwealth of England.

In the month of February, 1651, Blake, on his return homewards, fell in with a French man-of-war of forty guns; when a characteristic incident occurred which certainly deserves to be particularly mentioned. The admiral commanded the French captain on board him, and asked him if he was willing to lay down his sword? He answered that he was not; upon which, Blake generously bade him return to his ship and fight it out as long as he was able. The captain took him at his word, fought him bravely for about two hours, and then submitting, went again on board Blake's ship, first kissed him and then presented his sword to him upon his knees. This ship, with four more, the admiral sent into England; and not long after arriving at Plymouth with his squadron, there received the thanks of the parliament for his vigilance and valour, and was constituted one of the lords-wardens of the Cinque Ports.

In the March following, Colonel Blake, Colonels Popham and Deane, or any two of them, were again appointed by act of parliament to be admirals and generals of the fleet for the year ensuing; in which year Blake reduced the islands of Scilly, Guernsey, and Jersey to the obedience of the parliament; and, as a new mark of honour, was, on November 25th, elected one of the council of state. When the necessity of a Dutch war became apparent, the parliament gave the highest testimony of their sense of his merit and of their entire confidence in his conduct by constituting him, in March 1652, sole general of the fleet.

The story of the Dutch war is told in a separate chapter, where justice is done to Blake's prowess as admiral, and it is only necessary here to give such incidents as bring out his qualities as a man.

Just before the first battle in the Downs, which took place on May

19th, 1652, Blake observed that Van Tromp, the Dutch admiral, bore nearer to his fleet than he had any occasion to do, and so saluted him with two guns without ball, to put him in mind of striking sail; upon which the Dutchman, in contempt, fired on the contrary side. Blake then fired a second and a third gun, which Van Tromp answered with a broadside, and the English admiral perceiving his intention to fight, detached himself from the rest of the fleet to treat with him upon the point of honour, to prevent unnecessary effusion of blood and a national quarrel.

As Blake approached nearer to the Dutchman, Van Tromp, and the rest of his fleet, contrary to the law of nations, fired on him with whole broadsides. Blake was in his cabin drinking with some officers, little expecting to be thus saluted, when the shot broke the windows of the ship and shattered the stern; which put him into a vehement passion, so that curling his whiskers, as he used to do whenever he was angry, he commanded his men to answer the Dutch in their kind, saying, when his heat was somewhat over, "he took it very ill of Van Tromp that he should take his ship for a disorderly house, and break his windows." Blake singly sustained the shock of the Dutch fleet for some time, till his own ships and the squadron under Major Bourne joined him; and then the engagement grew hot on both sides, and bloody on the side of the enemy, till night put an end to it.

After this battle Blake lay in the Downs for a considerable time, which he spent in repairing and augmenting his fleet, and in detaching small squadrons to cruise against the enemy. About the beginning of June, finding he had force enough to undertake any service, he caused a solemn fast to be held on board his ships, to implore the blessing of God upon their arms, and encouraged his seamen by the example of his zeal on this occasion, as much as he had ever done by his personal bravery in a time of action. In the course of this month he sent forty rich prizes into the river, and so effectually ruined the Dutch trade, and broke the spirits of such as were appointed to support it, that most of their vessels declined coming through the Channel, even under convoy; choosing rather to put into French ports, land their cargoes there, and afterwards transport them to Holland, by land or water, as they could.

In the beginning of July, finding Sir George Ayscue returned from Barbadoes, with a force sufficient to guard the Downs, he resolved to sail northwards, to execute a design he had long meditated, of destroying the herring-fishery; which he thought would have put an immediate end to the war by convincing the Dutch of the folly of disputing our sovereignty in our own seas. This appears to have been the most judicious scheme laid down through the whole war; because it tended to clear the ground of the quarrel and to show the Dutch their error in disputing with a nation who had it in their power to distress them at any time in the tenderest part—that which afforded a subsistence to many and was the main source of wealth to all.

On July 2nd Blake bore away to the north, and quickly fell in with the Dutch fishing vessels, which were there in great numbers under the protection of twelve men-of-war. Blake attacked their convoy, and they, knowing the importance of their charge, and having taken on board a great supply of fresh men from the vessels under their care, fought bravely and sold their freedom dearly; but at last were all taken, which left the fishery entirely at the admiral's mercy, who upon this occasion showed the rectitude of his heart and the solidity of his understanding; for having first threatened these busses with utter destruction if ever they were found there again without leave, he afterwards freely permitted them to complete their ladings, on their paying the tenth herring as tribute to the Commonwealth.

During all the changes that happened in the government, Blake impressed his men with the conviction that it was his and their business to act faithfully in their respective stations, and to do their duty to their country, whatever irregularities there might be in the councils at home; and would often say among his officers that state affairs were not their province, but that they were bound to keep foreigners from fooling us. These principles rendered him agreeable to all parties, and gained him so generally the reputation of a patriot, that when Cromwell, in his new model of a parliament, left the populous town of Bridgewater the choice of one representative only, they elected Blake. He was also very acceptable to Cromwell, who knew that Blake's concern for the glory of England would influence him to do all, and even more than any other man could be excited to do by views of interest and ambition.

In 1654 he sailed into the Mediterranean, and came in the month of December into the road of Cadiz, where he was received with great respect and civility by the Spaniards, and indeed by all nations as well as the English, who were then in port. A Dutch admiral would not wear his flag while the English admiral was in the harbour; one of the victuallers attending his fleet, being separated from the rest, fell in with the French admiral and seven men-of-war near the Straits mouth. The captain of the victualling-sloop was ordered on board the admiral, who inquired of him where Blake was, drank his health with five guns, and so wished the captain a good voyage. The Algerines stood in such awe of him that they were wont to stop the Sallee rovers; and, in case they had any prisoners on board, took them out, and sent them to Blake, in hopes thereby of obtaining his favour.

He next sailed from Cadiz to Malaga; and while he lay in that road some of his seamen, going ashore, met the Host as it was being carried to some sick person, and not only paid no respect to it, but laughed at those who did. The priest who accompanied it highly resented this, and stirred up the people to revenge the indignity; upon which they fell upon the sailors and beat some of them very severely. When they returned on board the men complained of their ill usage, and the admiral instantly sent a trumpet to the viceroy, to demand the surrender of the priest who was the author of the insult. The viceroy answered that he had no authority over priests, and therefore could not send him.

Upon this Blake sent a second message to the effect that he would not enter into the question as to who had power to send him, but that, if he was not sent within three hours, he would burn the town about their ears. The inhabitants, to save themselves, obliged the viceroy to send the priest; who, when he came on board, excused himself to the admiral on account of the behaviour of the sailors. Blake with much calmness and composure told him that if he had complained to him of this outrage he would have punished the men severely; for he would not suffer any of his men to affront the established religion of any place that he might visit; but he blamed him for setting on a mob of Spaniards to beat them, adding, that "he would have him and the whole world know that none but an Englishman should chastise an Englishman."

In 1655 Blake proceeded to Algiers, where he arrived on March 10th, and anchored without the mole, sending an officer to the *dey* to demand satisfaction for the piracies that had been formerly committed on the English, and the immediate release of all captives belonging to his nation. The *dey* answered very modestly, that as for the ships and slaves they were now the property of private persons, from whom he could not take them with safety to himself; but that he would make it his care they should be speedily redeemed upon easy terms, and would make a treaty with him to prevent any hostilities being committed on the English for the future.

The admiral left the port upon this and sailed to Tunis, where he sent the like message on shore; but received a very different answer, *viz.*, "Here are our castles of Guletta and Porto Farino: you may do your worst; we do not fear you." Blake entered the bay of Porto Farino, and came within musket-shot of the castle and line, upon both which he played so warmly that they were soon in a defenceless condition. There were then nine ships in the road, which the admiral resolved to burn; and with this view ordered every captain to man his long-boat with choice men, and directed these to enter the harbour and fire the ships of Tunis; while he and his fleet covered them from the castle by playing continually on it with their cannon.

The seamen in their boats boldly assaulted the *corsairs* and burnt all their ships, with the loss of twenty-five men killed and forty-eight wounded. This daring action spread the terror of his name, which had long been formidable in Europe, through Africa and Asia. From Tunis he sailed to Tripoli, and concluded a peace with that government. Thence he returned to Tunis, and granted a peace on terms honourable to himself and profitable to his country.

In 1655 the protector sent Mr. Montague with a small squadron of men-of-war into the Mediterranean to join Blake and to carry him fresh instructions; one of which was to block up the port of Cadiz, in which there was a fleet of forty sail, intended to secure the flota expected from the Indies, and, at the same time, to prevent the flota from coming in without sharing in the riches that were on board. Blake and Montague executed their orders with equal skill and industry, taking care to obtain a supply of fresh provisions and water, as often as they had occasion, from the coast of Portugal. Thither, for that purpose, they had sailed with the greatest part of the fleet, when the squadron from the Indies approached Cadiz. Rear-Admiral Stayner, with seven frigates, plied to and fro, till eight large ships came in view, which he presently recognised as the flota for which he was looking out; whereas the Spaniards took his vessels, because they lay very low in the water, for fishermen. This gave him an opportunity of coming up with and fighting them, though the weather hindered four of his frigates from acting. Yet with the *Speaker*, the *Bridgewater*, and the *Plymouth* he did his business; and, after an obstinate engagement, sunk two, ran two more aground, and took two of the Spanish vessels; so that two only escaped.

In one of those that were destroyed was the Marquis of Badajoz, of the family of Lopez, who had been Governor of Peru for the King of Spain, who thus perished with the marchioness, his wife, and their daughter. The eldest son and his brother were saved and brought safely to the generals with the prize, wherein were two millions of pieces of eight. Soon after, General Montague, with the young Marquis of Badajoz, and part of the fleet to escort the silver, returned to England, delivered the bullion into the mint, after which the young marquis was set at liberty. For this success, a thanksgiving, with a narrative to be read thereon, was appointed by the parliament, who issued their declaration of war against Spain.

Admiral Blake continued to cruise before the haven of Cadiz and in the Straits till the month of April, 1657; and having then information of another Plate fleet, which had put into the haven of Santa-Cruz in the island of Teneriffe, he immediately sailed thither, and arrived before the town on April 20th. Here he found the flota, consisting of six galleons very richly laden, and ten other vessels. The latter lay within the port, with a strong barricade before them; the galleons without the boom, because they drew too much water to lay within it. The port itself was strongly fortified, having on the north a large castle well supplied with artillery, and seven forts united by a line communication, well lined with musketeers. The Spanish governor thought the place so secure, and his own dispositions so well made, that when the master of a Dutch ship desired leave to sail, because he apprehended Blake would presently attack the ships in the harbour, the Spaniard answered tartly, "Get you gone, if you will, and let Blake come, if he dares."

The admiral, after viewing the enemy's preparations, called a council of war, wherein it was resolved to attempt destroying the enemy's ships; for it was impossible to bring them off: and to this end he sent Captain Stayner with a squadron to attack them. Stayner soon forced his passage into the bay, while other frigates played on the forts and line, and hindered them from giving the ships much disturbance. Stayner's squadron was quickly supported by Blake with the whole fleet, who boarded the Spanish galleons, and in a few hours made himself master of them all, and then set them on fire; so that the whole Spanish fleet was burnt down to the water's edge, except two ships which sank outright; and then, the wind veering to south-west, he passed with his fleet safe out of the port again, losing in this dangerous attempt no more than forty-eight men killed, and having about one hundred and twenty wounded. It was without question the boldest undertaking of its kind that had ever been performed; and the Spaniards, who are romantic enough in their own conduct, were so much astonished at his, that they quite lost their spirits, and thenceforward never thought themselves safe either from numbers or fortifications.

When the Protector received the news of this glorious success, he immediately sent it by his secretary, Thurloe, to the parliament then sitting; and they, on hearing the particulars, ordered a day to be set apart for a thanksgiving; a ring of the value of five hundred pounds to be given to the general as a testimony of his country's gratitude; a present of one hundred to the captain who brought the news; and their thanks to all the officers and soldiers concerned in the action. Captain Richard Stayner, returning soon after, was knighted by the Protector; nor was it long before Blake and the fleet returned, which put an end to the Spanish war by sea; for the Protector had lately entered into a closer conjunction with France; and, in consequence thereof, sent over a body of land-forces into Flanders, where they assisted in taking the fortress and port of Dunkirk, which was delivered into the hands of the English, who kept it till after the Restoration.

Another characteristic incident, and one which shows the probity and integrity of Blake, deserves mention. His brother, Captain Benjamin Blake, for whom he had a very tender affection, having been guilty of some misdemeanour or misbehaviour in the action at Santa-Cruz, was, by sentence from Blake, removed from his ship, and the command of it given to another. This was such an instance of disinterested discipline as must have had a very strong effect on the minds of all who served under him; and we need not wonder that such extraordinary things were performed by men so perfectly disciplined.

In a short time after the destruction of the enemy's fleet at Teneriffe we find Blake cruising again off the harbour of Cadiz; where, perceiving his ships had become foul, and that his own health and spirits hourly wore away, he resolved to sail for England. His distemper was a complication of dropsy and scurvy, brought upon him by being for three years together at sea, and wanting all that time the conveniences requisite for the cure of his disease. In his passage home it increased upon him, and he became so sensible of his approaching end, that he frequently inquired for land; which, however, he did not live to see, dying as his ship the *St. George* entered Plymouth Sound, on August 17th, 1657, at about fifty-nine years of age. His body was the next day embalmed and wrapped in lead, and, by order of the Protector, conveyed by water to Greenwich.

On September 4th, after the body had lain several days in state, it was carried from Greenwich in a magnificent barge, overed with velvet, adorned with escutcheons and pendants, and accompanied by his brothers, remoter relations, and their servants, in mourning; by Oliver's privy council, the commissioners of the admiralty and navy, the lord-mayor and aldermen of London, the field-officers of the army, and many other persons of honour and quality, in a great number of barges and wherries covered with mourning, marshalled and ordered by the heralds-at-arms, who directed and attended the solemnity. Thus they passed to Westminster Bridge; and, at their landing, proceeded in the same manner, through a guard of several regiments of foot, to the abbey. The funeral procession over, the body was interred in a vault, built on purpose, in the chapel of Henry VII.

Sometime after the Restoration an order was sent to the dean and chapter of Westminster, directing them to cause such bodies as had been interred in that church during the troubles to be removed; and on September 12th, 1661, the body of Blake was removed from the abbey and buried in the churchyard.

Though Blake was upon principle a supporter of the Commonwealth, his character was such that he won from the royalists some of the warmest tributes he received.

Dr. Bates, in drawing his character, says, "He was a man deserving praise, even from an enemy. Being advanced to a command at sea, he subdued the Scilly Islands, near home; and having attained the office and title of an admiral, performed things worthy of immortal memory abroad. For he humbled the pride of France; reduced Portugal to reason; broke the naval force of Holland, and drove them to the shelter of their ports; suppressed the rovers of Barbary, and twice triumphed over Spain. Alone blamable in this, that he complied with the parricides." In the words of Anthony Wood, "He was a man wholly devoted to his country's service; resolute in his undertakings, and most faithful in the performance of them. With him, valour seldom missed its reward, nor cowardice its punishment."

THE DEFEAT OF SIR ANDREW BARTON

The Story of the First Dutch War
By John Campbell

The causes of this war are differently stated, according to the humours and opinions of different writers. The parliament, on the one side, was jealous of its newly-acquired sovereignty, and expected extraordinary marks of defference from the powers with which it corresponded. The Dutch, on the other hand, were extremely alarmed when they found the English Commonwealth insisting upon the sovereignty of the sea, the right of fishing, and of licensing to fish, and disposed to carry the point of saluting by the flag to the utmost limit. Under these conditions of excitement and tension, anxiety led to watchfulness and proximity to rupture.

It was in the spring of the year 1652 that the war broke out; but it was warmly disputed then, and has not been fully settled since, who were the actual aggressors. It is clear, however, that the Dutch had secretly made great preparations for war, and had actually one hundred and fifty ships of force at sea; whereas the English parliament had equipped no more than the usual squadron for guarding the narrow seas, which was a fleet of twenty-five ships under the command of Admiral Blake.

The first blood drawn in this quarrel was occasioned by Commodore Young, who fired upon a Dutch man-of-war upon the captain's refusing him the honour of the flag. This was on May 14th, 1652, and would have attracted much more public attention if an engagement of greater consequence had not happened immediately after.

Admiral Van Tromp was at sea with a fleet of upwards of forty sail, to protect, as was given out, the Dutch trade. This fleet coming into the Downs on May the 18th, met with a small squadron under the command of Major Bourne, to whom the admiral sent word that he was forced in by stress of weather; Bourne answered roundly, that the truth of this would best appear by the shortness of his stay, and immediately sent advice of it to his admiral. The next day, Van Tromp, with his fleet, bore down upon Blake in Dover road, and on his coming near him Blake fired thrice at his flag; upon which the Dutch admiral returned a broadside. For nearly four hours Blake was engaged almost alone with the Dutch squadron; but, by degrees, the weather permitted his fleet to come in to his assistance. Towards the close of the engagement, which lasted from four in the afternoon till nine at night, Bourne joined him with his eight ships, upon which the enemy bore away.

In this battle the victory was clearly on the side of the English, as the Dutch writers themselves confess, there being two Dutch ships taken and one disabled; whereas the English lost none: and yet the forces were very unequal; for the Dutch fleet consisted of forty-two ships and Blake's at first only of fifteen; and even at the end of the fight of no more than twenty-three. Each of the admirals wrote an account of this affair to their respective masters, wherein they plainly contradict each other: but with this difference, that there is no disproving any one fact mentioned in Blake's letter; whereas there are several inaccuracies in that of Van Tromp. The states themselves were so sensible of being in the wrong, and at the same time so mortified that their fleet, notwithstanding its superiority, had been beaten, that they apologised for it, and sent over another ambassador, Adrian Paauw, to proceed with the treaty. But the demands of the parliament were, in their opinion, too high; so all thoughts of peace were dismissed on both sides, and war was proclaimed in Holland on July 8th.

The English in the meantime, in virtue of the act of navigation, and by way of reprisal for the late damages, affronts, and hostilities, received from the states-general and their subjects, took many Dutch ships. On June 11th Blake brought in eleven merchant ships with their convoy coming from Nantes. On June 12th Captains Taylor and Peacock, in two English frigates, engaged two Dutch men-of-war on the coast of Flanders, for refusing to strike; one of which was taken and the other stranded: and, on the 13th of the same month, Blake took twenty-six merchant ships, with their convoys, homeward bound from France. On July 4th Vice-Admiral Ayscue, who, on his late return from the reduction of Barbadoes, had taken ten merchant ships and four men-of-war, attacked the St. Ubes fleet of about forty sail, of which nearly thirty were taken, burnt or stranded, and plundered, on the French coast.

After this, while the states with the utmost diligence were getting ready a fleet of seventy men-of-war, under the command of Admiral Van Tromp, Blake, with about sixty, received orders to sail to the north to disturb and distress the Dutch fishery. Sir George Ayscue, who, since the destruction of the St. Ubes fleet, had taken five Dutch merchant ships, was left with the remainder of the English fleet, consisting of no more than seven men-of-war, in the Downs. While Blake triumphed in the north, Tromp, with his great fleet, came into the mouth of the Thames, in the hope of either surprising Ayscue or of insulting the coast. Failing in this, he sailed northward to intercept Blake; but his ships being dispersed by a storm, he was disappointed in that scheme also, and lost five or six frigates, which fell into the hands of Blake on his return towards the south.

The people of Holland were very much dissatisfied with the conduct of Admiral Van Tromp, who, first justifying himself to the states, laid down his commission to gratify the people. The main objection against him was his being no great seaman; and this engaged the states to cast their eyes upon De Ruyter, the ablest man among them in his profession. He accepted the command, but accepted it unwillingly; for he saw that as things then stood the English were superior. The parliament, in the meantime, took care to strengthen Sir George Ayscue's fleet, so that it increased to thirty-eight sail; of which only two were large ships, and the rest frigates and fire-ships. With these he put to sea in search of the Dutch, took many rich prizes, and at last met with De Ruyter, who, with a fleet equal to his own, was convoying home between fifty and sixty merchantmen.

This was on August 16th, 1652, and as our admiral was cruising off Plymouth. It was about one in the afternoon when the fleets came in sight. De Ruyter took twenty of the merchant ships into his line of battle, and was then very ready to engage. The fight began about four, when the English admiral, with nine others, charged through the Dutch fleet, and having thus gained the weather-gauge, attacked them again, and continued fighting till night parted them; the rest of Sir George's fleet having very little to do in the action. The rear admiral, Peck, lost his leg, and soon afterwards died; and most of the captains who did their duty were wounded. One fire-ship was lost. On the other side the Dutch were miserably torn, so that many of their best ships were scarcely able to keep the sea. Sir George Ayscue followed them for some time the next day, and then returned into Plymouth Sound to refresh his men and to repair his ships.

Admiral Blake, who was now in the Channel, did infinite damage to the enemy; and, some hostilities having been committed upon the coast of Newfoundland by the French, he attacked a strong squadron of their ships going to the relief of Dunkirk, and took or destroyed them all, by which means this important place fell into the hands of the Spaniards. The Dutch, seeing their trade thus ruined, and apprehensive of still worse consequences, fitted out another fleet under the command of De Witte, and sent it to join De Ruyter, who was appointed to bring home a large number of merchantmen. After the junction of these fleets, and the sending of their convoy into Holland, the admirals showed a design of attacking the English navy, and Blake gave them a fair opportunity of executing their intention. But when it came to the point the Dutch fleet covered themselves behind a sandbank to avoid action.

Blake, however, engaged them on September the 28th, dividing his fleet into three squadrons; the first commanded by himself, the second by Vice-Admiral Penn, and the third by Rear-Admiral Bourne. It was about three when the engagement began, and the English quickly discovered their rashness in attacking an enemy under such disadvantages; for the *Sovereign*, a new ship, struck immediately on the sands, and so did several others; but, getting off again, the English fleet stood aloof till De Witte came freely from his advantages to a fair engagement, which was boldly begun by Bourne and gallantly seconded by the rest of the fleet. A Dutch man-of-war, attempting to board the *Sovereign*, was sunk by her side, and this by the first discharge she made. Soon after, a Dutch rear-Admiral was taken by Captain Mildmay, and two other men-of-war sunk, a third blowing up before the end of the fight. De Witte was then glad to retire, and was pursued by the English fleet as long as it was light. The next day they continued the chase till they were within twelve leagues of the Dutch shore, and then, seeing the Dutch fleet entering into the Goree, Blake returned in triumph to the Downs, and thence into port, having lost about three hundred men, and having as many wounded. For the reception of the wounded the parliament took care to provide hospitals near Dover and Deal, and on the return of the fleet sent their thanks to the admiral and his officers.

It being now the beginning of November, Blake, who thought the season of action over, detached twenty of his ships for the security of the Newcastle colliers; twelve more were sent to Plymouth, and fifteen had retired into the river, in order to repair the damage which they had received in a storm. Admiral Tromp, who had again taken command, having intelligence of this, and that Blake had with him no more than thirty-seven ships, and many of these but thinly manned, resolved to attack him in the Downs, not far from the place where they had fought before. On November the 29th he presented himself before the English fleet, and Blake, after holding a council of war, resolved to engage notwithstanding the great superiority of the enemy; but the wind rising they were obliged to defer fighting until the next day, and that night our fleet rode a little above Dover road. In the morning, both fleets plied westward, Blake having the weather-gauge.

About eleven the battle began with great fury; but, very unluckily for the English, half of their small fleet could not engage. The *Triumph*, in which Blake was in person, the *Victory* and the *Vanguard* bore almost the whole stress of the fight, having twenty Dutch men-of-war upon them at once; and yet they fought it out till it was dark. Late in the evening, the *Garland*, commanded by Captain Batten, and the *Bonaventure*, Captain Hookston, clapped Von Tromp aboard, killed his secretary and purser by his side, and would certainly have taken his ship if they had not been boarded by two Dutch flag-ships, by whom, after their captains were killed, both these ships were taken. Blake, who saw this with indignation, pushed so far to their relief that he was very near sharing the same fate, if the *Vanguard* and *Sapphire* had not stood by him with the utmost resolution and at last brought him off. The *Hercules* was run ashore in the retreat, and if the night had not sheltered them most of the ships that were engaged must have been lost; but they took the advantage of its obscurity, and retired first to Dover and then into the river.

Admiral Tromp continued a day or two in the Downs, sailed from thence towards Calais, took part of the Barbadoes fleet, and some other prizes, and then sailed to the Isle of Rhé with a broom at his top-mast head, intimating that he would sweep the narrow seas of English ships. There appears, however, no such reason for boasting as the Dutch writers suggest: their fleet had indeed many advantages; yet they bought their success very dear, one of their best ships being blown up and two disabled.

The parliament showed their steadiness by caressing Blake after his defeat, and naming him, in conjunction with Deane and Monk, their generals at sea for another year. In order to more speedy manning the navy, they issued a proclamation, offering considerable rewards to such as entered themselves within the term of forty days; they also raised the sailors' pay from nineteen to twenty-four shillings a month: and this had so good an effect that in six weeks' time they had a fleet of sixty men-of-war ready to put to sea; forty under Blake in the river, and twenty more at Portsmouth. On February 11th both fleets joined near Beachy Head, and thence Admiral Blake sailed over against Portland, where he lay across the Channel, in order to welcome Tromp on his return. This was a surprise to the Dutch admiral, who did not think it possible, after the late defeat, for the parliament to fit out, in so short a period, a fleet capable of facing him again. He had between two and three hundred merchant ships under convoy, and was therefore much amazed when, sailing up the Channel, he found Blake so stationed that it was impossible to avoid fighting. English and Dutch authors vary pretty much as to the strength of their respective fleets; but, on comparing the admirals' letters, they appear to have been nearly equal, each having about seventy sail.

The Generals Blake and Deane were both on board the *Triumph*, and with twelve stout ships led their fleet, and fell in first with the Dutch on February the 18th, 1653, about eight in the morning. They were roughly treated before the rest of the fleet came up, though gallantly seconded by Lawson in the *Fairfax*, and Captain Mildmay in the *Vanguard*. In the *Triumph* Blake was wounded in the thigh by a piece of iron which a shot had driven, the same piece of iron tearing General Deane's coat and breeches. Captain Ball, who commanded the ship, was shot dead and fell at Blake's feet; his secretary, Mr. Sparrow, was likewise killed while receiving his orders: besides whom he lost a hundred seamen, the rest being most of them wounded and the ship so miserably shattered that it had little share in the next two days' fights.

In the *Fairfax* there were a hundred men killed, the ship being wretchedly mauled; the *Vanguard* lost her captain and a large number of men. The *Prosperous*, a ship of forty-four guns, was boarded by De Ruyter and taken; but, De Ruyter's ship being at that instant boarded by an English man-of-war, Captain Vesey, in the *Merlin* frigate, entered the *Prosperous*, and retook her. The *Assistance*, vice-Admiral of the blue squadron, was disabled in the beginning of the fight and brought off to Portsmouth, whither the *Advice* quickly followed her, being no longer able to keep the sea. Tromp, who was long engaged with Blake, lost most of his officers and had his ship disabled; De Ruyter lost his main and foretop mast, and very narrowly escaped being taken. One Dutch man-of-war was blown up; six more were either sunk or taken.

Friday night was spent in repairing the damage and making the necessary dispositions for a second engagement. On Saturday morning the enemy was seen again seven leagues off Weymouth, whither the English plied, and came up with them in the afternoon, about three leagues to the north-west of the Isle of Wight. Tromp had again drawn his fleet together, and ranged it in the form of a half-moon, enclosing the merchant ships within a semi-circle; and in that posture he maintained a retreating fight. The English made several desperate attacks, striving to break through to the merchant ships; during which De Ruyter's ship was again so roughly treated that she was towed out of the fleet. At last the merchantmen, finding they could be no longer protected, began to shift for themselves, throwing part of their goods overboard for the greater expedition. According to Blake's own letter, eight men-of-war and fourteen or sixteen merchant ships were taken, and the fight continued all night.

On Sunday morning the Dutch were near Boulogne, where the fight was renewed, but with little effect. Tromp had slipped away in the dark with his merchantmen to Calais sands, where he anchored that day with forty sail; the wind favouring him, he thence tided it home, our fleet pursuing but slowly; for Blake, though he feared not Dutchmen, yet dreaded their shallow coasts: however, the Captains Lawson, Martin, and Graver, took each a Dutch man-of-war, and Penn picked up many of their merchantmen. On the whole, the Dutch had the better of the fight the first day, lost ground the second, and were clearly beaten the third. They lost eleven men-of-war—their own accounts say but nine—thirty merchantmen, fifteen hundred men killed, and as many wounded. As for the English, they lost only the *Sampson*, which Captain Batten, finding disabled, sank of his own accord; though it is certain our loss in killed and wounded was little inferior to that of the Dutch.

Van Tromp now convoyed a great fleet of merchantmen by the north, trying that route to escape the difficulties of the channel; whereupon our navy followed him to Aberdeen, yet to no purpose: for he escaped them both going and coming back, which gave him an opportunity of coming into the Downs, making some prizes, and battering Dover Castle. This scene of triumph lasted but a week; for on May 31st Tromp had intelligence that Monk and Deane, who commanded the English fleet, were approaching, and that their whole fleet consisted of ninety-five sail of men-of-war and five fire-ships. The Dutch had ninety-eight men-of-war and six fire-ships, and both fleets were commanded by men the most remarkable for courage and conduct in either nation; so that it was generally conceived this battle would prove decisive.

On June 2nd, in the morning, the English fleet discovered the enemy, whom they immediately attacked with great vigour. The action began about eleven o'clock, and the first broadside from the enemy carried off the brave Admiral Deane, whose body was almost cut in two by a chain-shot. Monk, with much presence of mind, covered his body with his cloak: and here appeared the wisdom of having both admirals on board the same ship; for as no flag was taken in the fleet had no notice of the accident, and the fight continued with the same warmth as if it had not happened. The blue squadron charged through the enemy, and Rear-Admiral Lawson bid fair for taking De Ruyter; and after he was obliged to leave his ship, sank another of forty-two guns commanded by Captain Buller.

The fight continued very hot till three o'clock, when the Dutch fell into great confusion, and Tromp saw himself obliged to make a kind of running fight till nine in the evening, when a stout ship, commanded by Cornelius van Velsen, blew up. This increased the consternation in which they were before; and though Tromp used every method in his power to oblige the officers to do their duty, and even fired upon such ships as drew out of the line, yet it was to no purpose, but rather served to increase their misfortune. In the night Blake arrived in the English fleet with a squadron of eighteen ships, and so had his share in the second day's engagement.

Tromp did all that was consistent with his honour to avoid fighting the next day; but he would not do more, so that the English fleet came up with him again by eight in the morning and engaged with the utmost fury; the battle continued very hot for about four hours, and Vice-Admiral Penn boarded Tromp twice, and had taken him, if he had not been seasonably relieved by De Witte and De Ruyter. At last the Dutch fell again into confusion, which was so great, that a plain flight quickly followed; and, instead of trusting to their arms, they sought shelter on the flat coast of Newport, from whence, with difficulty enough, they escaped to Zealand. Our writers agree that the Dutch had six of their best ships sunk, two blown up, and eleven taken; six of their principal captains were made prisoners, and upwards of fifteen hundred men.

Among the ships before-mentioned, one was a vice-Admiral and two were rear-Admirals. The Dutch historians, indeed, confess the loss of but eight men-of-war. On our side, Admiral Deane and one captain were all the persons of note killed; of private men there were but few, and not a ship was missing; so that a more signal victory could scarcely have been obtained, or, indeed, desired. After this victory the Dutch sent ambassadors to England to negotiate a peace almost on any terms.

The states were, however, far from trusting entirely to negotiations, but, at the time they treated, laboured with the utmost diligence to repair their past losses and to fit out a new fleet. This was a very difficult task; and, in order to effect it, they were forced to raise the seamen's wages, though their trade was at a full stop; they came down in person to their ports, and saw their men embarked, and advanced them wages beforehand, and promised them if they would fight once more they would never ask them to fight again.

Yet all this would hardly have sufficed if the industry of De Witte, in equipping their new-built ships, and the care and skill of Van Tromp in refitting their old ones, and encouraging the seamen, had not succeeded in equipping a fresh fleet, of upwards of ninety ships, by the latter end of July, a thing admired then, and scarcely credible now. These were victualled for five months; and the scheme laid down by the states was to force the English fleet to leave their ports by coming to block up ours. But first it was resolved Van Tromp should sail to the mouth of the Texel, where De Ruyter, with twenty-five sail of stout ships, was kept in by the English fleet, in order to try if they might not be provoked to leave their station, and thereby give the Dutch squadron an opportunity of coming out.

On July 29th, 1653, the Dutch fleet appeared in sight of the English, upon which the latter did their utmost to engage them; but Van Tromp, having in view the release of De Witte, rather than fighting, kept off; so that it was seven at night before General Monk in the *Resolution*, with about thirty ships, great and small, came up with him and charged through his fleet. It growing dark soon after nothing more passed that night, Monk sailing to the south and Van Tromp to the northward, by which, unsuspected by the English, he both joined De Witte's squadron and gained the weather-gauge. The next day proving very foul and windy, the sea ran so high that it was impossible for the fleets to engage, the English particularly finding it hard enough to avoid running upon the enemy's coasts.

On Sunday, July 31st, the weather having become favourable, both fleets engaged with terrible fury. The battle lasted at least eight hours, and was the most hard fought fight of any that happened during the war. The Dutch fire-ships being managed with great dexterity, many of the large vessels in the English fleet were in the utmost danger of perishing by them, and the *Triumph* was so effectually fired, that most of her crew threw themselves into the sea; and yet the few who stayed behind succeeded in extinguishing the flames. Lawson engaged De Ruyter briskly, killed and wounded more than half his men, and so disabled his ship that it was towed out of the fleet; whereupon the admiral, returning in a *galiot*, went on board another ship.

About noon, Van Tromp was shot through the body with a musket-ball, as he was giving orders. This effectually discouraged his countrymen, so that by two they began to retreat in great confusion, having but one flag standing among them. The lightest frigates in the English fleet pursued them closely, till the Dutch admiral, perceiving they were but small and of no great strength, turned his helm and resolved to engage them; but some larger ships coming to their assistance, the Dutchman was taken. It was night by the time their scattered fleet reached the Texel, while the English, fearing their flats, rode warily about six leagues off.

This was a terrible blow to the Dutch, who, according to Monk's letter, lost no less than thirty ships; but from better intelligence it appeared that four of these had escaped, two into a port of Zealand, and two into Hamburg. Their loss, however, was very great; five captains were taken prisoners, between four and five thousand men killed, and twenty-six ships of war either burnt or sunk. On the side of the English there were two ships only, *viz.*, the *Oak* and the *Hunter* frigate burnt, six captains killed, and upwards of five hundred seamen. There were also six captains wounded and about eight hundred private men.

The parliament then sitting ordered gold chains to be sent to the Generals Blake and Monk, and likewise to Vice-Admiral Penn and Rear-Admiral Lawson; they sent also chains to the rest of the flag-officers, and medals to the captains. August 25th was appointed for a day of solemn thanksgiving; and, General Monk being then in town, Cromwell, at a great feast in the city, put the gold chain about his neck, and obliged him to wear it all dinner-time. As for the states, they supported their loss with inexpressible courage and constancy, and buried Tromp with great magnificence at the public expense.

Hostilities between the two states had not continued quite two years, and yet, in that time, the English took no less than one thousand seven hundred prizes, valued by the Dutch themselves at sixty-two millions of *guilders*, or nearly six millions sterling. On the contrary, those taken by the Dutch did not amount to a fourth part either in number or value. Within that period the English were victorious in no less than five general battles, some of which were of several days' duration; whereas the Hollanders cannot justly boast of having gained one; for the action between De Ruyter and Ayscue, in which they pretended some advantage, was no general fight; and the advantage gained by Tromp in the Downs is owned to have been gained over a part only of the English fleet. Short as this quarrel was, it brought the Dutch to greater extremities than their eighty years of war with Spain.

Stories of the Second Dutch War
By John Campbell.

1. THE DEFEAT OF THE DUTCH OFF HARWICH

The second Dutch war was declared in Holland in January and in England in February, 1665. It arose out of the conflicts of the rival companies of Dutch and English merchants in the East and West Indies and in Africa, and the refusal of Charles II. to remedy a condition of things which had become unendurable.

In 1664 the Dutch sent an embassy to the English court, to complain of the depredations from which they suffered at the hands of the Anglo-African company, of which the king's brother, the Duke of York, was then governor; but the king replied that he had received no particular information of the affairs in question and that the rival companies must settle their differences among themselves. On the other hand, the English merchants appealed to him with so much persistence, that he finally demanded satisfaction of the Dutch.

The first action of consequence that happened after the war actually broke out was an attack made upon a Dutch fleet coming richly laden from Smyrna upon the Spanish coast near Cadiz. This consisted of forty merchant ships, some of them very large, and well provided with ordnance; and their convoy was composed of four third-rate men-of-war. Sir Thomas Allen, who commanded the English squadron, had with him about nine ships. With these he attacked the enemy so successfully, that having killed their commodore, Brackel, and taken or sunk four of their richest ships, he drove the rest into the Bay of Cadiz, where for some time he blocked them up. A misfortune of the same kind befell the Dutch Bourdeaux fleet, out of which about one hundred and thirty ships were taken.

These heavy misfortunes obliged the Dutch to lay an immediate embargo on all vessels in their ports; by which their fisheries and their annual commerce were stopped for that season. They likewise settled a fund of fourteen millions of *guilders* for the support of the war; and, in order to show that there ought to be some difference between such wars as are made by trading nations, and those entered into by arbitrary princes, for the mere thirst of dominion, they ordered about fifty English and Scotch vessels, which had been seized in their harbours, to be set at liberty; and, on the arrival of these ships in England, the civility was returned by a like release of all the Dutch ships that had been stopped here.

The English fleet, which was the first ready, consisted of one hundred and fourteen sail of men-of-war and frigates, twenty-eight fire-ships and ketches, having about twenty-two thousand seamen and soldiers on board. The whole was commanded by the Duke of York, as Lord High-Admiral; Prince Rupert was admiral of the white; and the Earl of Sandwich who, as Captain Montague had won distinction under Blake, was admiral of the blue. On April 21st, 1665, the English sailed for the Dutch coast, and on the 28th sent in a squadron so near the shore and harbour of the Texel that the country was exceedingly alarmed. After remaining there a month, however, the fleet was so ruffled by a storm, that it was found necessary to retire towards our own shore.

This opportunity the Dutch took of sending out their fleet, which, by the latter end of May, appeared about the Dogger Sands. It was divided into seven squadrons, the first under Admiral Opdam, consisting of fourteen men-of-war and two fire-ships; the second under John Everts, of the like force; the third commanded by Admiral Cortenaer, consisting of fourteen men-of-war and one fire-ship; the fourth under Stillingwert, composed likewise of fourteen men-of-war and a fire-ship; the fifth conducted by Van Tromp, the son of the famous old admiral, who fought with Blake, made up of sixteen men-of-war and two fire-ships; the sixth under Cornelius Everts, consisting of fourteen men-of-war and a fire-ship; the seventh commanded by Schram, comprising sixteen men-of-war and two fire-ships—in all, a hundred and three men-of-war, eleven fire-ships, and seven yachts. A mighty fleet indeed!

The Duke of York having retired with our navy from the Dutch coast when they came out, afforded them the opportunity to fall upon our Hamburg fleet, which they did not neglect; capturing the greater part of it, whereby our merchants suffered a loss of nearly two hundred thousand pounds. This exceedingly exasperated the English, and, at the same time, gave great encouragement to the Dutch.

Admiral Opdam, who commanded the latter, was a prudent as well as a truly gallant commander, but he was not allowed the liberty of action absolutely necessary at such a crisis. No sooner was he out at sea than he received a letter from the states directing him to fight at all events; and this order he resolved to obey, though contrary to the advice of most of his officers and to his own opinion. "I am," said he, addressing the council of war, "entirely in your sentiments: but here are my orders. Tomorrow my head shall be bound with laurel or with cypress." On June 3rd the English and Dutch navies engaged about three in the morning off Lowestoft; when the English had the weather-gauge—an advantage they knew how to use as well as keep.

Things went at first very equally on both sides; several squadrons charging through and through, without any remarkable advantage. But about noon, the Earl of Sandwich, with the blue squadron, fell into the centre of the Dutch fleet, and divided it into two parts, thus beginning the confusion which ended in their defeat. The Duke of York in the *Royal Charles*, a ship of eighty guns, and Admiral Opdam in the *Eendracht*, of eighty-four, were closely engaged. The fight continued for some hours with great obstinacy, and the duke was often in the utmost danger. Several persons of distinction were killed on board his ship, particularly the Earl of Falmouth, the king's favourite, Lord Muskerry and Mr. Boyle, son to the Earl of Corke, with one ball, and so near the duke that he was covered with their blood and brains; nay, a splinter from the last-mentioned gentleman's skull razed his hand. About one, the Dutch admiral blew up, with a prodigious noise; but how the accident occurred is not known. In this vessel, together with Admiral Opdam, perished five hundred men, only five of the whole crew escaping; many of those lost being volunteers, of the best families of Holland, and not a few Frenchmen, who had taken this opportunity of being present in a sea-fight.

A little after this unlucky blow, the Dutch received a greater. Four fine ships, the largest of sixty, the least of forty guns, ran foul of each other, and were burnt by one fire-ship, and soon after, three larger vessels, by the same accident, shared the same fate. The *Orange*, a ship of seventy-five guns, after a most gallant defence was also burnt; and thus, towards four in the afternoon, all fell into confusion. Vice-Admiral Stillingwert was shot through the middle by a cannon-ball; and Vice-Admiral Cortenaer received a shot in his thigh, of which he instantly died. Their ships bearing out of the line on the death of their commanders, without striking their flags, drew many after them; so that, by eight at night, Tromp, who held out bravely to the last, and fought retreating, had not more than thirty ships left with him.

According to English accounts, the Dutch had eighteen ships taken, and fourteen sunk in this action, besides such as were burnt or blown up. Yet their accounts admit of no more than nine ships taken, one, their admiral, blown up, and eight burnt. The English lost the *Charity*, a ship of forty-six guns, with most of her men, in the beginning of the fight; about two hundred and fifty men killed, and three hundred and forty wounded; on the other side, they lost at least six thousand men, including two thousand three hundred taken prisoners.

There is very little room for doubt that if there had not been some mismanagement on the side of the English, this, which was the first, might also have been the last action in this war; for the Dutch fleet fled in great confusion, and if the English had pressed them vigorously, as they might have done, having the wind, so many ships might have been either sunk, disabled, or taken as must have forced a peace; in favour of which there was a very strong party in Holland, who did not like the domination of the pensionary De Witte and the dependence in which he held the states, who seldom ventured to do anything of importance when he was absent. This great opportunity was lost through the English fleet's slacking sail in the night, contrary, it is said, to the express directions of His Royal Highness the duke before retiring to rest.

It is far from being an easy matter to determine how this came to pass. But the circumstances appear to have been as follows. The duke, as lord high-Admiral, had two captains on board his ship—Sir William Penn, who had the rank of a vice-Admiral, and Captain, afterwards Sir, John Harman. Sir William had retired as well as the duke, so that the command remained with Captain Harman, who was himself at the helm, when one Mr. Brounker, who was of the duke's bed-chamber, came and told him that "he ought to consider how much His Royal Highness's person had been already exposed in the action, and how much greater risk he might run if their ship, which was the headmost of the fleet, should fall in single with those of the enemy upon their own coasts." Harman heard him, but answered like an honest brave man as he was that he could do nothing without orders. Brounker upon this went to the duke's cabin and returned with orders, in His Royal Highness's name, to make less sail; these Captain Harman, without the least scruple, obeyed, though it caused some confusion in the fleet, several ships coming very near to running foul of each other.

In the morning the duke expressed surprise and resentment at finding the fleet at such a distance from the Dutch, that there was no longer any hope of coming up with them. It then appeared that either through cowardice, or something worse, Brounker had carried Captain Harman orders which he never received. However, this was concealed from His Royal Highness at the time, and other excuses made, such as a brisk wind from shore and their fire-ships being all spent. The truth, however, was very soon whispered about, though the duke was not acquainted with it for more than six months after; upon which he discharged Brounker his service, and would have done more, if the celebrated Duchess of Cleveland, then Countess of Castlemain, with whom he was a favourite, had not by her interest with the king protected him. However, at the end of the war when the House of Commons was out of humour, the matter was mentioned and inquired into; upon which Brounker, who was a member, was expelled the house and ordered to be impeached, but was never prosecuted.

2. The Capture of Dutch Convoys by the Earl of Sandwich

After the defeat of the Dutch off Harwich, the Duke of York returned to England to report himself to the king; and the command of the fleet now lying in Southwold Bay fell upon the Earl of Sandwich, who had contributed so much to the late victory. While here news reached the earl that two rich Dutch squadrons had put to sea; whereupon he immediately prepared to follow them with Sir George Ayscue as vice-Admiral, and Sir Thomas Tyddiman as admiral of the rear, determined either to intercept De Ruyter, the Dutch admiral, on his return, or to take and burn the Turkey and East India fleets of which they had news.

Both these schemes were doomed to failure. De Ruyter returned unexpectedly by the north of Scotland and arrived safely in Holland, where he was immediately promoted to the chief command of the fleet. The Turkey and India fleet—consisting of twenty sail under the command of Commodore Bitter—took the same route; but having intelligence of the approach of the English, took shelter in the port of Bergen in Norway.

Here the Danish governor promised them all the assistance he could give, and to strengthen his hands the Dutch landed forty-one pieces of cannon, which he disposed in a line in front of the port, the Dutch forming another line of their largest ships across the bay, and then waiting the arrival of the English fleet. Bergen, being a neutral port, ought to have been an asylum of safety for these Dutch merchantmen, but the King of Denmark, hoping to share the plunder, showed himself willing to treat with the Earl of Sandwich for liberty to attack the convoy in port. The earl, however, had no desire to share the spoil, and, impatient of delay, ordered Sir Thomas Tyddiman with fourteen sail of men-of-war and three fire-ships to enter the bay and cut out the Dutch squadron. This he attempted with great courage; though the wind was against him and he had to face a fierce fire from the castle, the line of guns, and the Dutch ships. Eventually, he was compelled to bear out of the bay, which he succeeded in doing without the loss of a ship; though five or six of his squadron were very much damaged.

To relieve the Dutch squadron—now practically prisoners in the port of Bergen—the Dutch manned a stout fleet, which put to sea under the command of Admiral Ruyter, who was accompanied by De Witte, appointed, with two other deputies by the states, to attend upon the admiral. After meeting with many difficulties, the Dutch fleet succeeded in eluding that of the English, and arrived safely before Bergen, where, in the meantime, their friends had found a new enemy in their old defender. The Danish governor had modestly desired a hundred thousand crowns for the assistance he had given them in the late affair with the English, and had threatened to sink them without ceremony if they offered to stir out of the port before they had complied with his demand. The arrival of De Ruyter's fleet made him change his tone, and he allowed them to sail without paying the money, but kept the cannon they had put ashore.

Thus far, the Dutch were very successful; but on their return home the fleet was scattered by a storm, in which they lost two fire-ships and some of the merchantmen. The vice-Admiral and rear-Admiral of the East India fleet, ships of very great value, with four men-of-war, were taken by five English frigates, which the same storm had separated from their fleet; and soon after four of their men-of-war, two fire-ships, and thirty merchantmen joined our fleet instead of their own, and through this mistake were all taken prisoners. This ended the operations of the year 1665.

3. The Four Days' Fight in the Channel

The year 1666 opened upon a new condition of affairs. The French having declared in favour of the Dutch, Charles II. recalled his ambassador, Lord Holles, from the French court, and sent the Earl of Sandwich as ambassador to Spain; placing the fleet under the command of Prince Rupert and the Duke of Albemarle, who had won distinction as General Monk, the former to look after the French, who began to talk very high, and the latter to act against the Dutch.

Prince Rupert and the Duke of Albemarle went on board the fleet on April 23rd, 1666, and sailed with it in the beginning of May. Towards the latter end of the month a rumour reached the English court that the French fleet, under the command of the Duke of Beaufort, was coming out to the assistance of the Dutch; and orders were immediately despatched to Prince Rupert to sail with the white squadron to engage it; which order he proceeded to obey.

As Prince Rupert sailed from the Downs, the Dutch with their whole force put to sea, the wind at north-east, and blowing a fresh gale. This brought the Dutch fleet on to the coast of Dunkirk, and carried away His Highness towards the Isle of Wight; but the wind suddenly shifting to the south-west, and blowing hard, brought both the Dutch and the Duke of Albemarle with his two squadrons to an anchor. Captain Bacon in the *Bristol* first discovered the enemy, and, by firing his guns, gave notice of it to the English fleet.

The departure of Prince Rupert had left the Duke of Albemarle with but sixty sail; whereas the Dutch fleet consisted of ninety-one men-of-war, carrying four thousand seven hundred and sixteen guns, and twenty-two thousand four hundred and sixty-two men. But a council of war was called; wherein, without much debate, it was resolved to fight the enemy, notwithstanding their great superiority.

It was the 1st of June when the Dutch fleet was discovered, and the duke was so warm for engaging, that he attacked the enemy without giving them time to weigh anchor; as De Ruyter himself says in his letter, compelling them to cut their cables to make ready for the fight. In the same letter De Ruyter says, that to the last the English were the aggressors, notwithstanding their inferiority of force. The English fleet had the weather-gauge, but the wind bowed their ships so much that they could not use their lowest tier. Sir William Berkley's squadron led the van. The Duke of Albemarle, when he came on the coast of Dunkirk, to avoid running full on the sand, made a sudden tack, and this brought his top-mast by the board, which compelled him to lie by four or five hours till another could be set up. The blue squadron, knowing nothing of this, sailed on, charging through the Dutch fleet, though they were five to one.

In this engagement fell the brave Sir William Berkley, and his ship, the *Swiftsure*, a second-rate, was taken; so was the *Essex*, a third-rate; and Sir John Harman, in the *Henry*, had the whole Zealand squadron to deal with. His ship being disabled, the Dutch admiral, Cornelius Evertz, called to Sir John, and offered him quarter, who answered, "No, sir! it is not come to that yet," and immediately discharged a broadside, by which Evertz was killed and several of his ships damaged. This so discouraged their captains that they quitted the *Henry*, and sent three fire-ships to burn her. The first grappled on her starboard quarters, and there began to raise so thick a smoke that it was impossible to perceive where the irons were fixed. At last, when the ship began to blaze, the boatswain of the *Henry* threw himself on board her, and having, by her own light, discovered and removed the grappling irons, in the same instant jumped back on board his own ship.

He had scarcely done this before another fire-ship was fixed on the larboard, which did its business so effectually that the sails, being quickly on fire, frightened the chaplain and fifty men overboard. Upon this, Sir John drew his sword, and threatened to kill any man who should attempt to provide for his own safety by leaving the ship. This obliged them to endeavour to put out the fire, which in a short time they did; but the cordage being burnt, the cross-beam fell and broke Sir John's leg, at which instant the third fire-ship bore down upon him; but four pieces of cannon loaded with chain-shot disabled her: so that, after all, Sir John brought his ship into Harwich, where he repaired her as well as he could, and, notwithstanding his broken leg, put to sea again to seek the Dutch. The battle ended on the first day about ten in the evening.

The following night was spent in repairing the damage suffered on both sides, and next morning the attack was renewed by the English with fresh vigour. Admiral Van Tromp, with Vice-Admiral Vander Hulst, being on board one ship, rashly engaged it among the English, and their vessel was in the utmost danger of being either taken or burnt. The Dutch affairs, according to their own account, were now in a desperate condition; but Admiral De Ruyter at last disengaged them, though not till his ship was disabled and Vice-Admiral Vander Hulst killed. This only changed the scene; for De Ruyter was now as hard pressed as Tromp had been before. However, a reinforcement arriving preserved him also; and so the second day's fight ended earlier than the first.

The third day the Duke of Albemarle found it necessary to retreat; and he performed it with wonderful courage and skill. He first burnt three ships that were absolutely disabled; he next caused such as were most torn to sail before, and, with twenty-eight men-of-war that were in a pretty good condition, brought up the rear. Sir John Harman, indeed, says he had but sixteen ships that were able to fight. Yet, in the evening, his grace, discovering the white squadron coming to his assistance, resolved to engage the enemy again. In joining Prince Rupert a very unlucky accident happened; for Sir George Ayscue, who was on board the *Royal Prince*, the largest and heaviest ship in the whole fleet, ran upon the *Galloper*, and being there in danger of burning, and past all hope of relief, was forced to surrender; and then night falling ended this day's engagement.

On June the 4th, the Dutch, who were still considerably stronger than the English, were almost out of sight; but the Duke of Albemarle, having prevailed upon the prince to follow them, about eight in the morning they engaged again, and the English fleet charged five times through the Dutch; till Prince Rupert's ship being disabled, and that of the Duke of Albemarle very roughly handled, about seven in the evening the fleets separated, each side being willing enough to retire. In this day's engagement fell that gallant admiral, Sir Christopher Myngs, who, having a shot in the neck, remained upon deck and gave orders, keeping the blood from flowing with his fingers for above an hour, till another shot pierced his throat and put an end to his pain.

This was the most terrible battle fought in this war. De Witte said roundly upon this occasion, "If the English were beaten, their defeat did them more honour than all their former victories; and all the Dutch had discovered was that Englishmen might be killed and English ships burnt, but that English courage was invincible."

After all, it is by no means easy to say who were victors upon the whole, or what was the loss of the vanquished. Some Dutch writers talk of thirty-five ships, and between five and six thousand men lost by the English; which is more than half their fleet, and very little less than all their seamen. Other authorities, however, compute our loss at sixteen men-of-war, of which ten were sunk and six taken. Our writers say the Dutch lost fifteen men-of-war, twenty-one captains, and five thousand men, and they themselves own to the loss of nine ships and a prodigious slaughter of their seamen.

4. The Defence of the Thames

After the four days' fight the Dutch had once more the credit of appearing at sea before the English, their ships having suffered less in that protracted conflict. It was not long, however, before the English fleet appeared. It consisted of eighty men-of-war, great and small, and nineteen fire-ships, divided into three squadrons: the red, under Prince Rupert and the Duke of Albemarle, who were on board the same ship with Sir Joseph Jordan for their vice-Admiral and Sir Robert Holmes for their rear-Admiral. Sir Thomas Allen was admiral of the white, and had under him Sir Thomas Tyddiman and Rear-Admiral Utburt. Sir Jeremiah Smith carried the blue flag, and his officers were Sir Edward Spragge and Rear-Admiral Kempthorne. The Dutch, according to their own accounts, had eighty-eight men-of-war and twenty fire-ships, divided also into three squadrons, under Lieutenant-Admiral De Ruyter, John Evertz, brother to the admiral who was killed in the former engagement, and Van Tromp.

On July the 25th, about noon, the English came up with the enemy off the North Foreland. Sir Thomas Allen, with the white squadron, began the battle by attacking Evertz. Prince Rupert and the duke, about one in the afternoon, made a desperate attack upon De Ruyter, whose squadron was in the centre of the Dutch fleet; but, after fighting about three hours, were obliged to go on board another ship. In this interim the white squadron had entirely defeated their enemies; Admiral John Evertz, his vice-Admiral, De Vries, and his rear-Admiral, Koenders, being all killed, the vice-Admiral of Zealand taken, and another ship of fifty guns burnt. The prince and duke fought De Ruyter ship to ship, disabled the *Guelderland*, of sixty-six guns, which was one of his seconds, killed the captain of another, and mortally wounded two more; upon which some of the Dutch ships began to retreat. However, Vice-Admiral Van Nes stood bravely by De Ruyter, and his ship received great damage; yet, being at last deserted by all but seven ships, they yielded to necessity, and followed the rest of their fleet to sea.

This was the clearest victory gained during the whole war; the Dutch lost twenty ships; four admirals were killed and a great many captains; as to private men, there might be about four thousand slain and three thousand wounded. The English had only the *Resolution* burnt, three captains killed, and about three hundred private men.

By the end of the year 1666, however, both nations had become weary of the war, and the King of Sweden having offered his mediation, it was readily accepted by both sides. Negotiations were immediately set on foot which ultimately resulted in the treaty of Breda;

but in the meantime the Dutch rather increased than relaxed their efforts to strengthen their navy, hoping thereby to influence the terms of the treaty in process of negotiation. Having previously sounded the mouth of the Thames to ascertain how far it might be practicable to attempt to enter it with large ships, and having thereby discovered the facility with which such a project could be carried out, De Witte determined to make the attempt without delay.

The Dutch fleet being ready, sailed over to the English coast, where it was joined by Van Ghent, and formed a fleet of seventy men-of-war, besides fire-ships. On June 7th they attacked Sheerness, which was at that time unfinished and in no state of defence, and captured fifteen iron guns and a considerable quantity of naval stores. The Duke of Albemarle, Sir Edward Spragge, and other officers had made all imaginable provision for the defence of the River Medway, by sinking ships in the passage, throwing a chain across it, and placing three large vessels, which had been taken from the Dutch, behind the chain. The Dutch, however, had the advantage of a strong easterly wind, which encouraged them to make an attempt upon our ships at Chatham, in spite of the precautions taken to preserve them.

It was on June the 12th that they executed this design; which, however, would have miscarried at last, if one Captain Brakell, who was a prisoner on board their fleet for some misdemeanour, had not offered to wipe out the memory of his former mistake by breaking the chain, a service which he gallantly performed. Captain Brakell also with great bravery boarded and took one of the English frigates which guarded the passage; and soon after, the *Matthias*, the *Unity*, and the *Charles the Fifth*, the ships which had been taken from the Dutch, were set on fire. The next day, the advantage of wind and tide continuing, the Dutch advanced with six men-of-war and five fire-ships as high as Upnore Castle; but were so warmly received that they were obliged to return. However, as they came back, they burnt the *Royal Oak*, a very fine ship, and in her Captain Douglas, who chose to be burnt with her rather than live to be reproached with having deserted his command.

On the 14th they carried off the hull of the *Royal Charles*, notwithstanding all the English could do to prevent it; a project which they had dearly at heart. On their return, two Dutch men-of-war ran ashore in the Medway and were burnt, which, with eight fire-ships consumed in the action and one hundred and fifty men killed, is all the loss acknowledged by the Dutch writers; though it is not improbable that they really suffered much more.

De Ruyter, highly pleased with what he had performed, left Admiral Van Nes with part of his fleet in the mouth of the Thames, and sailed with the rest to Portsmouth, in the hope of burning the ships there. Failing in this design, he sailed westward to Torbay, where he was likewise repulsed. Then he returned back again to the mouth of the Thames and with twenty-five sail came as high as the Hope, where our squadron lay under the command of Sir Edward Spragge. This consisted of eighteen sail; yet, the admiral not being on board when the enemy began the attack, the English fleet suffered at first from their fire-ships; but Sir Edward repairing to his command, and being joined by Sir Joseph Jordan with a few small ships, quickly forced the Dutch to retire. The like success attended their attack on Landguard Fort, which was performed by sixteen hundred men, commanded by Colonel Doleman, a republican, under the fire of their whole fleet: but Governor Darrel, an old cavalier, beat them off with great loss. On the 23rd Van Nes sailed again up the river as far as the Hope, where he engaged Sir Edward Spragge, who had with him five frigates and seventeen fire-ships. This proved a very sharp action, at least between the fire-ships, of which the Dutch writers themselves confess they spent eleven to our eight.

The next day the English attacked the Dutch in their turn, and, notwithstanding their superiority, forced them to retire and to burn the only fire-ship they had left, to prevent her being taken. On the 25th they bore out of the river with all the sail they could make, followed at a distance by Sir Edward Spragge and his remaining fire-ships. On the 26th, in the mouth of the river, they were met by another English squadron from Harwich, consisting of five men-of-war and fourteen fire-ships. These boldly attacked the Dutch, and grappled the vice-Admiral of Zealand and another large ship; but were not able to fire them, though they frightened a hundred of their men into the sea. In this struggle the rear-Admiral of Zealand was forced on shore, and so much damaged thereby as to be obliged to return home.

While the whole Dutch fleet was employed in alarming our coasts, Sir Jeremiah Smith was sent with a small squadron northwards; with which, and the assistance of a numerous fleet of privateers, already abroad for their own profit, the Dutch commerce to the Baltic was in a manner ruined, and multitudes of rich prizes were daily brought into English ports. Thus it may be truly said that the nations at this time changed characters. The Dutch preferred the insult at Chatham, which, all things considered, was of little or no consequence to them, to the preservation of their trade; and the English endeavoured to make themselves amends for this unexpected loss of a few men-of-war by taking numbers of merchantmen.

The English, in the West Indies, took the island of St. Eustatia, Saba, St. Martin, Buen Ayre, the island of Tobago, and other places from the Dutch. On the contrary, the Dutch, under the conduct of Commodore Krynsen, made themselves masters of Surinam; and the French, assisted by the Dutch, almost deprived the English of their half of the island of St. Christopher, after several obstinate disputes and the death of their commander Le Salles. Six frigates and some other small vessels from Barbadoes, sailing from thence to repair this loss, were so ill-treated by a violent storm that they were put out of a condition to execute their design, and two or three of the most disabled ships fell into the hands of the enemy; though, before their misfortune, they had burnt two Dutch ships richly laden in the harbour of Los Santos.

There were three distinct treaties of peace signed at Breda respectively, with the Dutch, the French, and the Danes, and these were ratified on August 24th, 1667. The terms upon which this peace was made were safe and honourable at least, though not so glorious and beneficial as might have been expected after such a war. By it the honour of the flag was secured; and the island of Poleron, to prevent further disputes, was yielded to the Dutch. In the West Indies we kept all that we had taken, except Surinam; and the French were obliged to restore what they had taken from us.

The Destruction of the Algerine Navy

On the conclusion of the Dutch war it became necessary to restore order on the high seas by destroying the pirates who had taken advantage of the disturbed condition of things to prey upon English and Dutch commerce; and with this view Charles II. sent Sir Thomas Allen with a stout squadron into the Mediterranean to repress the Algerines, and the Dutch sent Admiral Van Ghent with a squadron to secure their trade. Van Ghent having engaged six *corsairs*, forced them to fly to their own coasts, where probably they would have escaped if Commodore Beach with four English frigates had not fallen upon them, and, after a close chase, obliged them to run aground. In this situation they were attacked by the English and Dutch in their boats; and, being abandoned by their respective crews, were all taken, and a great number of Christian slaves of different nations released.

The English commodore presented sixteen Dutch slaves to Admiral Van Ghent, and received from him twenty English by way of exchange; but the Algerine ships being leaky, they were burnt. The same year some of our frigates attacked seven of the enemy's best ships near Cape Gaeta. The admiral and vice-Admiral of the Algerines carried fifty-six guns each; their rear-Admiral, the biggest ship in the squadron, carried sixty, and the least forty. Yet after a sharp engagement the vice-Admiral sank, and the rest were forced to retire, most of them miserably disabled. At the close of the year 1669 Captain Kempthorne, afterwards Sir John, in the *Mary Rose*, a small frigate, engaged seven Algerine men-of-war; and, after a very warm action, forced them to sheer off, being in no condition to continue the fight any longer.

It is somewhat extraordinary that, considering the Dutch, as well as the English, were concerned in attacking these pirates, we have no better account of the war that was carried on against them, or of the force they employed, than we are left to collect as we can, from scattered accounts of particular engagements. In 1668 their navy only consisted of twenty-four ships, great and small—that is, from about fifty to twenty guns: and they had likewise six new ships of force upon the stocks. Yet this pitiful enemy continued to disturb, and even to distress the commerce of both the maritime powers for several years.

At last Sir Edward Spragge was sent with a strong squadron of men-of-war and frigates to put an end to the war.

Spragge sailed from England, on this expedition, in the spring of the year 1671, with five frigates and three fire-ships, uniting his fleet with a squadron of as many more ships already at sea; so that, in all, his fleet consisted of about twelve sail. In the latter end of the month of April he had intelligence that there were several Algerine men-of-war in Bugia Bay; on which he called a council of war, when it was resolved that he ought immediately to attack them. In pursuance of this resolution he sailed thither, but, in his passage, had the misfortune to have the *Eagle* fire-ship disabled by a storm; and soon after, one of his ships springing her main mast, was obliged to bear away for the Spanish shore. Sir Edward, however, persisted in his design, refitted the *Eagle*, and bore into the bay of Bugia with a brisk gale, not doubting that he should be able to fire the ships; but by the time they got within half-shot of the castle and forts it fell a dead calm, and when the wind rose again it proved contrary.

On May 2nd they were able to do nothing for the same reason, the wind changing every half hour; upon which, Sir Edward resolved to make an attempt upon them in the night with his boats and the smallest of his fire-ships, which rowed as well as a long-boat. About twelve o'clock that night he executed his project, sending in all his boats, and the *Eagle* fire-ship, under the command of his eldest lieutenant, Mr. Nugent; but the night proving very dark, and the high land obscuring the ships as they drew near them, they passed by; and Lieutenant Nugent leaving one of the boats with the fire-ships, besides her own, rowed in to discover the enemy leaving orders with the captain of the fire-ship to come to an anchor in case he found shoal water. The lieutenant had not left them a minute before he perceived himself within pistol-shot of the ships; and, concluding the business now as good as done, steered off again to find the fire-ship, and, to his amazement, saw her in flames.

The enemy taking the alarm at this, the lieutenant was forced to retire with his boats; and so this promising enterprise, which had given hopes of burning the Algerine men-of-war, without the loss of a man, miscarried. The next day the enemy unrigged all their ships and made a strong boom with their yards, top masts, and cables, buoyed up with casks, for which they had all the leisure and convenience they could wish, the wind hindering the English from doing anything; and, to try the admiral's patience to the very utmost, it so fell out that a drunken gunner firing a pistol, his other small fire-ship was destroyed; so that he had now none left but the *Little Victory*, which drew too much water to enter that part of the bay where the Algerines lay.

On Monday, May 8th, 1671, there appeared a considerable body of horse and foot in the neighbourhood of the bay, and this was soon after discovered to be an escort to a very large convoy of ammunition sent from Algiers to the ships; on the safe arrival of which they fired all their cannon, to testify their joy. Sir Edward Spragge considering this, and not knowing what future reinforcements they might receive, resolved to take the earliest opportunity of making his last and utmost effort; and, in order thereto, directed the *Victory* to be lightened, so that she might not draw above eight feet. About noon there sprang up a fine breeze to the east; upon which the admiral gave the signal for the men-of-war to draw into a line and bear up into the bay; but immediately after the wind sank again, and they began to despair of doing anything.

About two the gale sprang up again, and the ships bore in as they were directed. The admiral came to an anchor in four fathom of water, close under the walls of their castle, which fired upon him continually for two hours. In this interim he sent in his own pinnace and those of the *Mary* and the *Dragon*; these cut the boom, though not without considerable loss. The lieutenant who commanded the *Mary's* boat's crew had eight wounded with himself; Lieutenant Pierce of the *Dragon* was also wounded, with ten of his men, and one killed. In the admiral's own pinnace there were seven killed, and all the rest wounded, except Mr. Harman, who commanded it.

The boom being cut, the fire-ship went in, and getting up athwart their bowsprits, their ships being a-ground, and fast to the castles, she burnt very well and destroyed them all. Captain Harris, who commanded her, his master's mate, gunner, and one of his seamen were desperately wounded with small shot, and this at their entrance; so that probably the whole design would have proved abortive if the admiral had not with great prudence commissioned Henry Williams, then one of his master's mates, but who had formerly commanded the *Rose* fire-ship, to take the charge of the vessel in case the captain was disabled; which he did accordingly, and performed all that could be expected from him.

This loss was irreparable to the Algerines, who had picked out the seven men-of-war that were here burnt, on purpose to fight Sir Edward Spragge, and furnished them with their best brass ordnance from on board all the rest of their vessels, and between eighteen and nineteen hundred chosen men double-officered, under the command of old Terkey, their admiral. Of this force between three and four hundred men were killed; the castle and town were miserably shattered; and a vast number of people slain and wounded; and, what much increased the misfortune, all their surgeons' chests were burnt on board their ships, so that numbers died for want of having their wounds dressed. Besides the men-of-war there were burnt a Genoese ship, a small English prize, and a *settee*.

In this engagement Sir Edward Spragge had only seventeen men killed and forty-one wounded. This and other misfortunes caused such a tumult among the Algerines that they murdered their *dey* and chose another, by whom peace was concluded to the satisfaction of the English on December 9th, 1671.

The Story of Sir John Berry
By John Campbell

As an illustration of the way in which a man could rise to the highest honours of the navy in the good old days with no other influence or recommendation than his own merit, the case of Sir John Berry may be instanced here.

John Berry, who was the second son of the Rev. Daniel Berry, Vicar of Knowestone, Devonshire—a clergyman who suffered for his loyalty to the cause of Charles I.—was born at the Vicarage, Knowestone, in the year 1635. His father, after being expelled from his benefice and losing his property by confiscation, died at the early age of forty-five, leaving a widow with nine children, of whom John, aged seventeen, was the second. Thrown entirely upon his own resources, John went to Plymouth, where he bound himself apprentice to Mr. Robert Mering, a merchant and part-owner of several ships. Going to sea in his service, he was extremely unfortunate, being twice taken by the Spaniards, and suffering a long imprisonment, which, however, did him no great harm.

On his return to England, his master, who was suffering from a reverse in circumstances, released him from his indentures, upon which he came up to London; where, by the help of some friends, he was preferred to be boatswain of a ketch belonging to the Royal Navy, called the *Swallow*; which, under the command of Captain Insam, was ordered to the West Indies in company with two of the king's frigates. Both the frigates were lost in the Gulf of Florida; but the *Swallow*, by cutting down her masts and heaving her guns and provisions overboard, got clear, and in the space of sixteen weeks, during which the crew had nothing to eat but the fish they caught, or to drink but rain-water, the survivors arrived at Campeachy. There they furnished themselves with provisions, and then sailed for Jamaica, where they arrived in three weeks.

Sir Thomas Muddiford, a native of Devonshire, was then governor of that island, and he ordered the *Swallow* to be refitted, put eight guns on board her, and having intelligence that a pirate, who had taken one Mr. Peach bound from Southampton to Jamaica, and marooned him and all his crew, was still in those seas, he ordered the *Swallow*, now well victualled and manned, to go in quest of her, and gave his countryman Berry the title of lieutenant.

In three weeks after they sailed from Jamaica they found the pirate at anchor in a bay off the island of Hispaniola. He had a force of about sixty men and twenty guns, whereas the *Swallow* had but forty men and eight small guns. Captain Insam, having considered the enemy's strength and compared it with his own, called up all his men and addressed them in these words: "Gentlemen, the blades we are to attack are men-at-arms, old buccaneers, and superior to us in number and in the force of their ship, and therefore I would have your opinion, whether——"

"Sir," interrupted Lieutenant Berry, "we are men-at arms, too, and what is more, honest men, who fight under the king's commission; and if you have no stomach for fighting, be pleased to walk down into your cabin."

The crew applauded this speech, and declared one and all for Lieutenant Berry, who undertook the affair with all its disadvantages.

The pirate rode at anchor to the windward, by reason of which the *Swallow* was obliged to make two trips under her lee, in which she received two broadsides and two volleys of small shot without returning a gun. Mr. Berry then boarded her on the bow, pouring in his broadside, which killed the pirate and twenty-two men on the spot: they then fought their way to the main mast, soon after which the pirate was taken, having only seven men left, and those all wounded, though they lived long enough to be hanged afterwards in Jamaica; and all this with no other loss than that of the boatswain's mate.

On their return to Jamaica Captain Insam confined his lieutenant and brought him to a court martial; where, on the evidence of the men, the court declared he had done his duty, and ordered the captain to live peaceably with him in their voyage to England, which he did; and Mr. Berry, notwithstanding what was past, behaved towards him with all imaginable modesty and submission.

In a short time after he came home the Dutch war broke out, and Mr. Berry had a sloop given him, the *Maria*, of fourteen guns, with the king's commission. He held this small command for about four months, in which time he took thirty-two prizes; and for his extraordinary diligence had the command given him of the *Coronation*, a ship of fifty-six guns.

In this ship he was soon after sent to the West Indies, where our colonies were in no small danger, having both the French and Dutch upon their hands. On his arrival at Barbadoes the governor bought some large merchant ships, converted them into men-of-war, and having made up nine sail, including the *Coronation*, manned and put them under the command of Commodore Berry. With this little fleet he sailed for Nevis, in order to protect it from the French, who had already made themselves masters of St. Christopher, Antigua, and Montserrat. He had scarcely arrived before he had intelligence that the French were preparing at St. Christopher a very great force, which was intended for the conquest of Nevis. They had twenty-two men-of-war and frigates, six large transport ships of their own, and four Dutch. With these they sailed toward Nevis as to a certain victory.

Commodore Berry sailed with his nine ships to meet them; and, as he turned the point of the island, one of his best ships blew up, which struck his men with astonishment if not dismay. "Now you have seen an English ship blow up," said the commodore, "let us try if we can't blow up a Frenchman. There they are, boys! and if we don't beat them they will beat us." Having said this, he immediately began the fight with the French admiral; and, after an engagement of upwards of thirteen hours, forced this mighty fleet to fly for shelter under the cannon of St. Christopher, whither he pursued them, sent in a fire-ship, and burnt the French admiral. Seeing her in flames, he said to his seamen, "I told you in the morning that we should burn a Frenchman before night; tomorrow we will try what we can do with the rest." While he was refitting his ships the enemy wisely stole away; the French to Martinico, and the Dutch to Virginia.

In the third Dutch war he had the command of the *Resolution*, a seventy-gun ship, in which he was present at the famous action in Southwold Bay, on May 28th, 1672. In this battle, observing that the Duke of York was very hard pressed, he left his station, and came in to his relief, where the service proved so hot that in less than two hours he had no fewer than one hundred and twenty men killed, as many more wounded, and his ship completely disabled: upon this he was towed out of the line, stopped his leaks, and fell into his place again in an hour, and there did such service that when Charles II. came to meet the fleet, and dined on board the *Royal Sovereign* at the Buoy in the Nore, he, of his own thought, called for Captain Berry, and, having knighted him, said very graciously, "As our thoughts have been now upon honour, we will hereafter think of profit; for I would not have so brave a man a poor knight."

In the year 1682 it was thought expedient to send the Duke of York down to Scotland, and for this purpose the *Gloucester* frigate, under the command of Sir John Berry, was ordered to be ready; and accordingly, on April 28th, the Duke of York embarked on board that ship. In their passage Sir John observed, on May 3rd, when in the mouth of the Humber, as he apprehended, an error in the pilot's conduct, though he was looked upon as a man of great ability in his employment. Of this he informed the duke and desired they might lie to, at least for that night, which the pilot opposed; and, being a great favourite of the duke, his advice prevailed.

But His Royal Highness was soon convinced of the superiority of Sir John Berry's judgment; since, in three-quarters of an hour afterwards, the ship was lost, and about three hundred people in her, among whom were some persons of the first rank. The duke himself but narrowly escaped in the long-boat, Sir John Berry standing with his sword drawn in the stern of the boat to hinder people from crowding in, which undoubtedly saved the duke, since a very few more would have overset it.

During the reign of King James II. he was in as high favour as he could desire, the king constantly consulting him in matters relating to the management of the fleet. When it became known that the Dutch meditated an invasion, Sir John Berry was appointed vice-Admiral, and after the landing of the Prince of Orange, when Lord Dartmouth left the fleet, the sole command of it devolved upon him.

The change of the government wrought none in the condition of our admiral. An experienced officer and a man of honour will be a welcome servant to any prince. King William was one who valued abilities and understood them, and therefore he often sent for Sir John Berry to confer with him on naval affairs; and once particularly the king engaged with him in so close and earnest a conversation, that it took up the whole night, and Sir John was not dismissed from the royal closet until it was far advanced in the morning. Yet this favour brought him no accession either for post or profit; he kept what he had, and probably thought that sufficient, being commissioner of the navy, governor of Deal Castle, and captain of an independent company.

In February 1691 he was ordered to Portsmouth to pay off some ships there; and, while thus employed on board one of them, he was taken suddenly ill, and thereupon carried on shore, where it was given out that he died of a fever. A post-mortem revealed that he did not die a natural death, but as the result of poison, though by whom administered, or for what reason, was never made public. His body, according to his own direction, was carried from Portsmouth to London and interred in the chancel of Stepney Church, where a monument is erected to his memory.

The Story of the Third Dutch War
By John Campbel.

THE BATTLE OF SOUTHWOLD BAY.—THE STORY OF THE EARL OF SANDWICH.—THE INVASION OF HOLLAND.

We come now to the story of the third Dutch war, perhaps more frequently called the second, from the fact that it was the second war with Holland in the reign of Charles II.

War was declared by Charles on the 28th of March, 1672; Louis XIV. of France agreeing to join with the English against the Dutch, and sending the Count d'Estrees, Vice-Admiral of France, with a large squadron, to join the English fleet.

The French squadron arrived at St. Helen's on the 3rd of May, and the king immediately went down to Portsmouth; and, to show his confidence in his new ally, went on board the French admiral, where he remained some hours. The English fleet sailed to the Downs, the Duke of York, as high-Admiral, wearing the red, and the Earl of Sandwich, the blue. Here the French squadron joined them, their admiral bearing the white flag; the united fleet consisting of one hundred and one sail of men-of-war, besides fire-ships and tenders. Of these the English had sixty-five ships of war, carrying four thousand and ninety-two pieces of cannon, and twenty-three thousand five hundred and thirty men.

The French squadron consisted of thirty-six sail, on board of which were one thousand nine hundred and twenty-six pieces of cannon, and about eleven thousand men. The Dutch, in the meantime, were at sea with a very considerable fleet, consisting of ninety-one stout men-of-war, fifty-four fire-ships, and twenty-three yachts. On May the 9th they were seen off Dover, and the 13th of the same month a Dutch squadron chased the *Gloucester*, and some other ships, under the cannon of Sheerness.

The English fleet were at anchor in Solebay on May 28th, when the Dutch fell in with them; and, if they had not spent too much time in council, had entirely surprised them. As it was, many of the English captains were forced to cut their cables, in order to get into the line in time for the battle. The engagement began between seven and eight in the morning, when De Ruyter attacked the red squadron in the centre, and engaged the admiral, on board of which was the Duke of York, for two hours, forcing His Highness at last to remove to another ship. The Dutch captain, Van Brakell, attacked the Earl of Sandwich in the *Royal James*; and while they were engaged, almost all the squadron of Van Ghent fell upon the earl's ships. His lordship behaved with amazing intrepidity; killed Admiral Van Ghent with his own hands, sank three fire-ships and a man-of-war, that would have laid him on board; but when he had lost all his officers and two-thirds of his men, his battered ship was grappled and set on fire by a fourth fire-ship.

In this distress, it is said, he might have been relieved by his vice-Admiral, Sir Joseph Jordan, if Sir Joseph had not been more solicitous about assisting the duke. It is said that when the earl saw Sir Joseph sail by, heedless of the condition in which he lay, he said to those about him, "There is nothing left for us now but to defend the ship to the last man," and those who knew him best knew quite well that by the last man he meant himself. When the fourth fire-ship had grappled him, he begged his captain, Sir Richard Haddock, and all his servants, to get into the boat and save themselves, which they did; but many of his men would not leave their admiral, and continued to make fruitless efforts to quench the fire until the ship blew up about noon.

The death of Van Ghent, with the furious attack of part of the blue squadron, coming in, though too late, to the Earl of Sandwich's assistance, threw this part of the Dutch fleet into very great confusion and forced them to stand off. This gave an opportunity for the blue squadron to join the red and to assist the Duke of York, who, deserted by the French, was in the utmost danger of being destroyed by the two squadrons of De Ruyter and Bankert. About this time Cornelius Evertz, Vice-Admiral of Zealand, was killed, and De Ruyter and Allemand narrowly escaped being burnt by fire-ships; but, when the English thought themselves secure of victory, the scattered squadron of Van Ghent came in to the assistance of their countrymen, and again rendered doubtful the fortune of the day.

It is said that all this time the French, who composed the white squadron, instead of seconding the efforts of the English, kept as far out of danger as they could, and left our fleet to sustain the whole force of the enemy at a disadvantage of three to two. But, notwithstanding this inequality of numbers, the fight continued with inexpressible obstinacy till towards the evening, when victory declared for the English. Five or six of the enemy's fire-ships were sunk by an English man-of-war; and Sir Joseph Jordan, of the blue squadron, having the advantage of the wind, pierced the Dutch fleet, and thereby spread through it the utmost confusion; while a fire-ship clapped their admiral, De Ruyter, on board, and was, with the utmost difficulty, repulsed. As it grew dark, De Ruyter, collecting his fleet in the best order he could, fought retreating and steered northwards.

The loss was pretty equal on both sides. The English had four men-of-war sunk or disabled, but they were small ships; whereas the Dutch lost three of the best in their fleet: one sunk, another burnt, and a third taken; a fourth, called the *Great Holland*, commanded by the brave Captain Brakell, was entirely disabled. As for the French, notwithstanding all their caution, they lost two men-of-war and their rear-Admiral, M. de la Rabiniere. Of the English, about two thousand five hundred were killed and as many wounded. The Dutch did not publish any list, though their loss without question must have been as great; since De Ruyter says in his letter, "it was the hardest fought battle that he ever saw."

But though losses were reckoned as pretty equal on either side, the loss of the *Royal James* with its one hundred guns, its eight hundred men, and its admiral, the Earl of Sandwich, who was probably without his equal upon the sea at this time, was loss enough, as the Duke of Buckingham observed, to give the name of victory to the Dutch.

The earl, a son of Sir Sidney Montague, born on July 27th, 1625, had rendered a great deal of distinguished service. On August 20th, 1643, when no more than eighteen years of age, he received a commission to raise and command a regiment in the parliamentary interest in the Civil War. He was present at the storming of Lincoln, on the 6th of May, 1644, which was one of the warmest actions in the course of the war. He was likewise in the battle of Marston Moor, which was fought on July the 2nd, of the same year, where he greatly distinguished himself; insomuch that soon after, when the city of York demanded to capitulate, he was appointed one of the commissioners for settling the articles; which must have been the pure effect of personal ability, since he was then but in his nineteenth year. We find him next in the battle of Naseby; and in the month of July, 1645, he stormed the town of Bridgewater. In September he commanded a brigade in the storming of Bristol, where he performed very remarkable service, and, on September 10th, 1645, subscribed the articles of the capitulation, granted to Prince Rupert on the delivery of that important place to the parliament.

After the first Dutch war was over he was brought into a command of the fleet, and was appointed by the protector to act with Blake in his expedition into the Mediterranean.

In 1657 he was appointed to command the fleet in the Downs, and in the following year, on the death of Oliver, had command of the great fleet sent to the North to preserve the tranquillity of Europe; returning from whence he gave an account of his conduct to parliament, and then retired to his own estate. On the restoration of Charles II. he was made Earl of Sandwich, admiral of the narrow seas, and lieutenant-Admiral to the Duke of York as Lord High-Admiral of England. The story of his career from this time forward has been told in the successive stories of the Dutch wars, and it only remains now to record the last honours done to his remains. His body was found, nearly a fortnight after his death, floating in the sea; and the king testified, by the honours he paid to his remains, how much he admired the man, how sensible he was of his hard fate, and how willing he was to mingle with the dust of his ancestors the ashes of such as died gloriously in their country's service. The facts stand thus recorded in the *Gazette* of June 13th, 1672:—

> Harwich, June 10th.
> This day the body of the Right Honourable Edward, Earl of Sandwich, being, by the order upon his coat, discovered floating on the sea, by one of His Majesty's ketches was taken up and brought into this port; where Sir Charles Littleton, the governor, receiving it, took immediate care for its embalming and honourable disposing, till His Majesty's pleasure should be known concerning it; for the obtaining of which His Majesty was attended at Whitehall, the next day, by the master of the said vessel, who, by Sir Charles Littleton's order, was sent to present His Majesty with the George found about the body of the said earl, who remained, at the time of its taking up, in every part unblemished, saving some impressions made by the fire upon his face and breast: upon which His Majesty, out of his princely regard to the great deservings of the said earl, and

his unexampled performances in this last act of his life, hath resolved to have his body brought up to London, there, at his charge, to receive the rites of funeral due to his great quality and merits.

The Earl of Sandwich's body being taken out of one of his majesty's yachts at Deptford on July 3rd, 1672, and laid in the most solemn manner in a sumptuous barge, proceeded by water to Westminster Bridge, attended by the king's barges, His Royal Highness the Duke of York's, as also with the several barges of the nobility, lord mayor, and the several companies of the city of London, adorned suitable to the melancholy occasion, with trumpets and other music that sounded the deepest notes. On passing by the Tower the great guns there were discharged, as well as at Whitehall; and, about five o'clock in the evening, the body being taken out of the barge at Westminster Bridge, there was a procession to the abbey-church with the highest magnificence. Eight earls were assistant to his son Edward, Earl of Sandwich, chief mourner, and most of the nobility and persons of quality in town gave their assistance to his interment in the Duke of Albemarle's vault, in the north side of King Henry VII.'s chapel, where his remains are deposited.

After the Battle of Solebay the Dutch fleet returned to the coast of Holland, where they were obliged to lay up for the want of powder, all available ammunition being wanted by the land forces to dispute the victorious march of the French.

In their extremity the Dutch sued for peace, and sent four deputies to England and as many to the French king. At both courts they were treated with the same scant courtesy. Charles II., instead of hearing and giving them an answer in person, sent four of his ministers to confer with them, and afterwards sent the Duke of Buckingham, the Earl of Arlington, and Viscount Halifax into Holland to treat with them there. These ambassadors made most extravagant demands; asking ten millions of guilders for the expense of the war, an annual tribute of one hundred thousand for the liberty of fishing, and the perpetual *stadtholdership* for the Prince of Orange and his issue male.

These, however, were moderate articles in comparison with the rest; for they insisted on a share in the Dutch East India trade, the possession of the city of Sluys in Flanders, and the islands of Cadzand, Walcheren, Goree and Voorn. The deputies sent to the French court were answered in the style of a conqueror, and so sent back to spread despair through the country; whereupon the Dutch seeing nothing before them but slavery, resolved to lay aside all treaties and to die free.

In the meantime, the French and English fleets, being perfectly refitted, and the latter having taken on board a large body of land forces, sailed again for the Dutch coasts, with a design to make a descent on Zealand, the only province into which the French had not carried their arms by land. Here they found the Dutch fleet; but, not thinking proper to attack them among the sands, they deferred the execution of their design, and blocked up the Maese and Texel; which De Ruyter, having strict orders to avoid battle, saw with concern, yet wanted power to prevent. The Duke of York now resolved to disembark his troops on the Isle of Texel. The occasion was favourable in all respects; the French and the Bishop of Munster were in the heart of the Dutch territories, so that no great force could be drawn together to resist the English on shore, and the coast was so low and flat that it looked as if nothing could secure the Dutch from invasion.

It was upon July 3rd this resolution was taken; and it was intended that the forces should have landed the next flood. But at this critical juncture wind and wave interposed in favour of a free people, and saved them from a yoke which seemed already to press upon their necks. The ebb continued much longer than usual, and this defeated the intended descent for that time; and the storm, that rose the night following, forced the fleet out to sea, where they struggled for some time with very foul weather, and then returned to the English shore. The Dutch clergy magnified this circumstance into a miracle; and certainly it was a good stroke of policy at such a time to persuade the nation, struggling against superior enemies, that they were particularly favoured by Heaven.

After this disappointment, there was no other action thought of at sea for this year, except the sending Sir Edward Spragge, with a squadron, to disturb the Dutch herring-fishery; which he performed with a degree of moderation that became so great a man; contenting himself with taking one of their vessels, when he saw that was sufficient to disperse the rest.

All this time affairs in England were getting into very strained conditions. The parliament had never owned the Dutch war, and though they voted liberal supplies to the king, did so without naming the object to which they were to be applied further than to designate them "the king's extraordinary occasions." At this time, too, the Test Act was passed, an Act, which, putting it out of the power of the papists to continue in public offices, compelled Lord Clifford to quit the treasury and the Duke of York to give up the fleet.

Early in the year 1673 it was resolved that Prince Rupert should succeed the Duke of York at the head of the fleet, and by the middle of May he was ready for sea.

The object of the English was to make another attempt to land troops upon the Dutch coast; and, with this view, a considerable number of soldiers was put on board the fleet. Charles II. and the Duke of York visited the navy on May 19th; and, in a council of war held in their presence, it was resolved to attack the enemy even upon their own coast, in case they could not be provoked to put to sea. In pursuance of this determination, Prince Rupert stood over towards the coast of Holland, and found De Ruyter with the Dutch fleet riding within the sands of Schonevelt, in a line between the Rand and the Stony-bank, which was a very advantageous situation.

On the 28th, in the morning about nine o'clock, Prince Rupert sent a detached squadron of thirty-five frigates and thirteen fire-ships to draw the enemy out, which was very easily done; for De Ruyter presently advanced in good order, and, the English light ships retreating, put their own fleet in some disarray. This engagement took place upon very unequal terms: the confederate fleet consisted of eighty-four men of war, besides fire-ships, divided into three squadrons, under the command of Prince Rupert, Count d'Estrees, and Sir Edward Spragge. The Dutch were scarcely seventy men-of-war and frigates, under De Ruyter, Tromp, and Bankert.

The battle was very hard fought on both sides, insomuch that Tromp shifted his flag four times; from the *Golden Lion* to the *Prince on Horseback*, from the *Prince on Horseback* to the *Amsterdam*, and from the *Amsterdam* to the *Comet*, from on board which he dated his letter to the states in the evening. Sir Edward Spragge and the Earl of Ossory distinguished themselves on our side by their extraordinary courage and conduct. Prince Rupert also performed wonders, considering that his ship was in a very bad condition and took in so much water at her ports that she could not fire the guns of her lower tier. The battle lasted till night, and then the Dutch are said to have retired behind their sands.

Both sides, however, claimed the victory: De Ruyter, in his letter to the Prince of Orange, says, "We judge absolutely that the victory is on the side of this state and of your highness."

Prince Rupert, in his letter to the Earl of Arlington, says, "I thought it best to cease the pursuit and anchor where I now am."

As to the slain on both sides in this battle, it is reported the Dutch lost Vice-Admiral Schram, Rear-Admiral Vlugh, and six of their captains, and had one ship disabled, which was lost in her retreat. On our side fell the Captains Fowls, Finch, Tempest, and Worden: Colonel Hamilton had his legs shot off, and we had only two ships disabled, none either sunk or taken.

In one respect, however, the Dutch may certainly be credited with victory; since they prevented a descent intended upon their country, which was the main object of the attack, and for which service, in case of the victory of the English fleet, Count Schomberg, with six thousand men, lay ready at Yarmouth.

The Dutch, being upon their own coast, had the advantage of receiving quick supplies; whereas the wind prevented the English from obtaining succour. Prince Rupert, however, did all in his power to repair his fleet, and believing that the Dutch would not be long before they resumed hostilities, he went on board the *Royal Sovereign* in the evening of June 3rd, "where he went not to bed all night." His foresight was justified by events; for on the 4th, in the morning, the Dutch fleet, by this time at least as strong as the confederates, bore down upon them as fast as the wind would permit. Prince Rupert was so much in earnest that, finding his ship's crew raised his anchors very slowly, he ordered his cables to be cut, that he might make haste to meet the Dutch. Count d'Estrees, with the white squadron, is said to have betrayed no such great willingness to fight, but to have kept as much as might be out of harm's way.

At last, about five in the evening, Spragge and Tromp engaged with great fury. De Ruyter showed at first a design of coming to a close engagement with the prince: but before he came within musket-shot, he tacked and bore away; whence it was concluded that he had suffered some considerable damage. Spragge, in the meantime, had forced Tromp to sheer off. He then fell into Vice-Admiral Sweers's division, which he soon put to confusion, and had a third engagement with Tromp, wherein he shot down his flag. The battle lasted till between ten and eleven at night, and then the Dutch stood to the south-east, and so it ended.

Both sides claimed the victory as before, losses being pretty equal on both sides, though far from considerable on either.

The prince was for attacking the enemy again; but it was carried in a council of war to sail for the English coast, in order to obtain supplies, as well of ammunition as provision; of the want of which a great many captains complained loudly. Besides, the fleet was so poorly manned that if it had not been for the land forces on board they could not have fought at all. On June the 8th the fleet arrived at the Nore, and on the 14th Prince Rupert went to London, to give the king an account of the condition of things and to press for necessary supplies.

About the middle of July Prince Rupert was once more at sea, having on board the troops intended for a descent upon the Dutch coast. His Highness arrived off Holland on the 21st of the said month; and, declining an engagement, stood along the shore in order to find an opportunity for disembarking his troops. On August the 9th he took a Dutch East India ship richly laden. This induced De Ruyter to bear down upon the English fleet; upon seeing which, Prince Rupert commanded the French a particular course, and had thereby an opportunity of discerning what he was to expect from them in a time of action. They lay by twice that night; first about eleven o'clock, when the prince sent to Count d'Estrees to order him to make sail, which he did till about one o'clock and then laid his sail to the mast again causing a second stop to the fleet and obliging the prince to send him another message. In those days, when party-spirit ran very high, nobody ever suspected the Count d'Estrees' courage, which was so well known and so thoroughly established as clearly to disclose his orders.

These delays gave the Dutch admiral an opportunity of gaining the wind, which he did not neglect; but, early on August 11th, bore down upon the confederates as if he meant to force them to a battle; upon which His Highness thought fit to tack, and thereby brought the fleet into good order. He put the French in the van, himself in the centre, and Sir Edward Spragge in the rear; and in this disposition the French lay fair to get the wind of the enemy, which, however, they neglected. The English fleet consisted of about sixty men-of-war and frigates, the French of thirty, and the Dutch of seventy or thereabouts; so that the royal fleets were indisputably superior to that of the republic.

De Ruyter, bearing down with his fleet in three squadrons, prepared to attack the prince himself, while Tromp engaged Spragge and the blue squadron, in which the English admiral obliged him, by laying his fore-top sail to his mast, in order to stay for him, contrary to the express order of the prince. This fondness for a point of honour proved fatal to himself as well as disadvantageous to the fleet. Bankert, with his Zeeland squadron, should have engaged the white, commanded by D'Estrees; but it seems the Dutch understood the temper of the French better than to give themselves much trouble about them; for Bankert contented himself with sending eight men-of-war and three fire-ships to attack the rear-Admiral, De Martel, who seemed to be the only man that had any real design to fight; and then the rest of the Zeeland squadron united themselves to De Ruyter, and fell together upon Prince Rupert.

The battle between De Ruyter and the red squadron began about eight o'clock in the morning, and a multitude of circumstances concurred to threaten the English admiral with inevitable ruin. Sir Edward Spragge, intent on his personal quarrel with Van Tromp, had fallen to the leeward several leagues with the blue squadron; and to complete Prince Rupert's misfortune, the enemy found means to intercept his own rear-Admiral, Sir John Chichele, with his division; so that by noon His Highness was wholly surrounded by the Dutch, being pressed by De Ruyter and his division on his lee-quarter, an admiral with two flags more on his weather-quarter, and the Zeeland squadron on his broadside to windward.

His Highness, in the midst of these disappointments, behaved with such intrepidity, and encouraged all his officers so effectually by his own example that, by degrees, he cleared himself of his enemies, rejoined Sir John Chichele, and by two o'clock had time to think of the blue squadron, which was now at three leagues' distance; and, not hearing their guns well plied, he made all the sail he could towards them, in order to unite with and relieve them. De Ruyter, perceiving His Highness's design, left firing and bore away also with his whole force to the assistance of Tromp; so that both fleets ran down side by side within range of cannon-shot, and yet without firing on either part. About four the prince joined the blue squadron, which he found in a very tattered condition.

At the beginning of the fight, Tromp in the *Golden Lion*, and Sir Edward Spragge in the *Royal Prince*, fought ship to ship. The Dutch admiral, however, would not come to a close fight, which gave him a great advantage; for Spragge, who had more than his complement on board, suffered much by the enemy's cannon, and, having the wind and smoke in his face, could not make such good use of his own as he would otherwise have done. After three hours' warm fighting the *Royal Prince* was so disabled that Sir Edward was forced to go on board the *St. George*; and Tromp quitted his *Golden Lion* to hoist his flag on board the *Comet*, when the battle was renewed with incredible fury.

The great aim of the Dutch admiral was to take or sink the *Royal Prince*; but the Earl of Ossory and Sir John Kempthorne, together with Spragge himself, so effectually protected the disabled vessel that none of the enemy's fire-ships could come near her, though they often attempted it. At last, the *St. George* being terribly torn and disabled Sir Edward Spragge designed to go on board a third ship, the *Royal Charles*; but, before he had got ten boats' length, a shot, which passed through the *St. George*, took his boat, and though they immediately rowed back, before they could get within reach of the ropes that were thrown out from the *St. George*, the boat sank, and Sir Edward was drowned.

When Prince Rupert drew near the blue squadron he found the admiral disabled, the vice-Admiral lying to the windward, mending his sails and rigging, the rear-Admiral astern of the *Royal Prince*, between her and the enemy, bending his new sails and mending his rigging. The first thing His Highness did was to send two frigates to take the *Royal Prince* in tow. He then steered in between the enemy and the lame ships, and perceiving that Tromp had tacked and was coming down again upon the blue squadron, he made a signal for all the ships of that squadron to join him: but it was in vain; for, except the two flags, Sir John Kempthorne and the Earl of Ossory, there was not one in a condition to move.

The French still continued to look on with all the coolness imaginable; and notwithstanding the prince put out the blue flag upon the mizen-peak, which was the signal to attack set down in the general instructions for fighting, and known not only to all the English captains but also to those of the white squadron, yet they remained, as before, wholly inactive. But, to give some kind of colour to this conduct, the Count d'Estrees, after the battle was in a manner over, sent to know what this signal meant. An officer who wrote an account of this engagement, says:

> The sending to inquire the meaning of the signal was cunningly done: but one of De Ruyter's sailors seems to have had as much penetration as the French ministry had artifice; for, upon one of his companions asking him what the French meant by keeping at such a distance, 'Why, you fool,' said he, 'they have hired the English to fight for them; and all their business here is to see that they earn their wages.'

About five in the evening, De Ruyter, with all his flags and fleet, came close up with the prince, and then began a very sharp engagement. His Highness had none to second him but the vice-Admiral and rear-Admiral of the blue, Sir John Harman, Captain Davis, and Captain Stout, of his own division, Sir John Holmes in the *Rupert*, Captain Legge in the *Royal Katharine*, Sir John Berry in the *Resolution*, Sir John Ernle in the *Henry*, Sir Roger Strickland in the *Mary*, and Captain Carter in the *Crown*; in all about thirteen ships. The engagement was very close and bloody till about seven o'clock, when His Highness forced the Dutch fleet into great disorder and sent in two fire-ships amongst them to increase it, at the same time making a signal for the French to bear down; which, even then, if they had done, a total defeat must have followed: but, as they took no notice of it and the prince saw that most of his ships were not in any condition to keep the sea long, he wisely provided for their safety by making with an easy sail toward our own coasts.

This battle ended as doubtfully as any of the rest; for the Dutch very loudly claimed the victory now, as they did before, and with fully as much reason. The truth is, it seems to have been a drawn battle; since the Dutch, notwithstanding all their advantages, did not take or sink a single English man-of-war, and killed but two captains, Sir William Reeves and Captain Havard, besides our gallant admiral, Sir Edward Spragge, and no great number of private men. On their side they lost two vice-Admirals, Sweers and Liefde, three captains, and about one thousand private men.

Soon after this battle the English fleet came into the Thames, and Prince Rupert returned to court, where he joined his representations to those of others who were desirous for peace, the result of which was that a treaty of peace was signed in London on February 9th, 1674, whereby all differences were adjusted. The limits of the British seas were particularly defined; and the states undertook that not only separate ships, but whole fleets should strike their sails to any fleet or single ship carrying the king's flag, as the custom was in the days of his ancestors.

The East India trade was likewise settled so as to prevent subsequent debates, and not leave either party at liberty to encroach upon the other. Places taken on both sides were by this treaty to be restored; and the states-general were to pay His Majesty eight hundred thousand *patacoons* at four payments; the first, immediately after the ratification of this treaty, and the other three by annual payments.

Thus ended the third of our Dutch wars; which, though made against the interest and will of the people, terminated to their advantage; whereas the former war, begun at the instance of the nation, ended but indifferently; so little correspondence is there between the grounds and issues of things.

The Battle of Beachy Head

There was little to record to the honour of the navy in the reign of James II. As Duke of York he had held the office of Lord High-Admiral for years, and he doubtless knew as much about the navy as any man of his time. This knowledge he is said to have employed as soon as he came into power to bring the navy into a state of efficiency, and yet, when in November 1688 the Prince of Orange sailed for England, he was able to effect his passage and land his army at Torbay without any opposition from the fleet.

During the first year of the reign of William and Mary the navy did some service in Ireland, Admiral Herbert engaging the French in Bantry Bay without much success, and Commodore Rooke effecting the relief of Londonderry. The former engagement was virtually a defeat for the English, as the French effected their purpose by landing their supplies and making good their retreat. William III., however, willing to put the best possible construction upon the event, and desirous of conciliating the navy, created Admiral Herbert Earl of Torrington, and knighted Captains John Ashby and Cloudesley Shovel.

As to the remaining naval transactions of this year, they were neither many nor great, but they included the taking of two celebrated sea-officers of the French service, the Chevalier Fourbin and John du Bart. These gentlemen commanded two small frigates, and had under their convoy six rich merchantmen, homeward-bound. Near the Isle of Wight they were chased by two of our fifty-gun ships, which they engaged very bravely, though they saw that it was impossible for them to avoid being taken. All they aimed at was to give their merchantmen time to escape, and in this they succeeded; for, while they fought desperately, the vessels under their convoy got safely into Rochelle. As for the Chevalier Fourbin and Captain Bart, they were carried prisoners into Plymouth, from whence not long after they found means to escape, and got safely over to Calais. For this gallant and generous action the French king rewarded each of them with the command of a man-of-war.

In 1690, however, the fleet was called upon to face a far more formidable encounter. The French, who had for years been paying increased attention to naval affairs, and who had made use of the recent Dutch wars, first on one side and then on the other, to obtain knowledge and experience of maritime affairs, now despatched their fleet with a considerable body of troops to make a descent upon England in the interests of James II., while the Jacobins in London made active preparations for a simultaneous rising.

On June 12th the French fleet put to sea in three squadrons, each squadron being divided into three divisions. Of these the white and blue squadrons, commanded by Count d'Estrees, on board the *Le Grand*, a ship of eighty-six guns, formed the vanguard, consisting of twenty-six men-of-war. The main body was composed of the white squadron, which consisted likewise of twenty-six sail, commanded by the Admiral Count Tourville in the *Royal Sun*, a ship of one hundred guns; while the blue squadron, commanded by M. d'Amfreville in the *Magnificent*, a ship of eighty guns, comprised twenty-five sail and formed the rear-guard. In all there were seventy-eight men-of-war and twenty-two fire-ships, and the whole fleet carried upwards of four thousand seven hundred pieces of cannon. On June the 13th they steered for the English coast, and on the 20th arrived off the Lizard. The next day the admiral took some English fishing-boats; and, after having paid the people who were on board for their fish, set them at liberty again. These men were the first to bring the news of the arrival of the French fleet on our coast, while our own fleet was lying idle in the Downs.

Under the arrangement of the conspirators the French fleet was to enter the Thames, and the Jacobins in London were to rise, seize the queen and her principal ministers, and proclaim James once more king, whereupon James was to leave Ireland to the care of Lauzun and Tyrconnel, return to England and take the head of the revolution, while the French landed troops at Torbay and intercepted the return of William from Ireland.

The Earl of Torrington was at St. Helen's when he received the news of the arrival of the French fleet, which must have surprised him very much, since he was so far from expecting the French in that quarter that he had no scouts to the westward. He put to sea, however, with such ships as he had, and stood to the south-east, leaving orders that all the English and Dutch ships which could have notice should follow him. In the evening he was joined by several more ships, and the next morning he found himself within sight of the enemy. The French landed and made some prisoners on shore; and by them sent a letter from Sir William Jennings, an officer in the navy, who had followed the fortunes of King James and served now as third captain on board the admiral, promising pardon to all such captains as would now adhere to that prince. The next day Torrington received another reinforcement of seven Dutch men-of-war, under the command of Admiral Evertzen, and for some time the English fleet lay off Ventnor, while the French fleet stood off the Needles. It is certain that the Earl of Torrington did not think himself strong enough to venture on an engagement, and in all probability the rest of the admirals agreed with him.

His whole strength consisted of about thirty-four men-of-war of several sizes, and the three Dutch admirals had under their command twenty-two large ships. Outnumbered by more than twenty sail it was perhaps but natural that he should seek to avoid hostilities.

In London, where the Jacobin plot was known, the utmost excitement prevailed. The rival fleets were known to be in sight of each other, and it was clear that the English admiral was reluctant to engage. Under these circumstances the queen, fearful of the consequences of continued tension, by the advice of the privy council sent the earl orders to fight at all costs and compel the French fleet to withdraw. In obedience to this order, as soon as it was light, on June 30th, the admiral threw out the signal for drawing into line and bore down upon the enemy, while they were under sail, with their heads to the northward.

The signal for battle was made about eight, when the French braced their head sails to their masts, in order to lie by. The action began about nine, when the Dutch squadron, which made the van of the united fleets, fell in with the van of the French, and put them into some disorder. About half an hour after our blue squadron engaged their rear very warmly; but the red, commanded by the Earl of Torrington in person, which made the centre of our fleet, could not come up till about ten; and this occasioned a great opening between them and the Dutch. The French, making use of this advantage, weathered, and of course surrounded the Dutch, who defended themselves very gallantly, though they suffered extremely from so unequal a fight. The admiral, seeing their distress, endeavoured to relieve them; and while they dropped their anchors, the only method they had left to preserve themselves, he drove with his own ship and several others between them and the enemy, and in that situation anchored about five in the afternoon, when it grew calm; but discerning how much the Dutch had suffered, and how little probability there was of regaining anything by renewing the fight, he weighed about nine at night, and retired eastward with the tide of flood.

The next day it was resolved in a council of war, held in the afternoon, to preserve the fleet by retreating, and rather to destroy the disabled ships, if they should be pressed by the enemy, than to hazard another engagement by endeavouring to protect them. This resolution was executed with as much success as could be expected, which, however, was chiefly owing to want of experience in the French admirals; for, by not anchoring when the English did, they were driven to a great distance; and, by continuing to chase in a line of battle, instead of leaving every ship at liberty to do her utmost, they could never recover what they lost by their first mistake.

But, notwithstanding all this, they pressed on their pursuit as far as Rye Bay; and forcing the *Anne*, of seventy guns, which had lost all her masts, on shore near Winchelsea, they sent in two ships to burn her, which the captain prevented by setting fire to her himself. The body of the French fleet stood in and out of the bays of Bourne and Pevensey, in Sussex, while about fourteen of their ships anchored near the shore. Some of these attempted to burn a Dutch ship of sixty-four guns, which at low water lay dry; but her commander defended her so stoutly every high water, that they were at length forced to desist, and the captain carried her safe into Holland.

Our loss in this unlucky affair, if we except reputation, was not so great as might have been expected; not more than two ships, two sea captains, two captains of marines, and three hundred and fifty private men. The Dutch were much more unfortunate, because they were more thoroughly engaged. Besides three ships sunk in the fight, they were obliged to set fire to three more that were stranded on the coast of Sussex, losing in all six ships of the line. They likewise lost many gallant officers; particularly their rear-Admirals, Dick and Brakel, and Captain Nordel, with a great number of inferior officers and seamen.

After the engagement our fleet retreated towards the River Thames; and the Earl of Torrington, going on shore, left the command to Sir John Ashby. On July 8th the French fleet stood toward their own coast, but were seen, upon the 27th, off the Berry Head, a little to the eastward of Dartmouth, and then, the wind taking them short, they put into Torbay. There they lay but a short time; for they were discovered on the 29th near Plymouth, at which place the necessary preparations were made by platforms and other works to give them a warm reception. On August 5th they appeared again off the Rame Head, in number between sixty and seventy, when, standing westward, they were no more seen in the Channel during 1690.

The earl was tried by court martial on the charge of having from treachery or cowardice misbehaved in his office, drawn dishonour on the English nation and sacrificed our good allies the Dutch. He defended himself with dignity and eloquence, affirming that he fought under orders, against his own judgment and that of his staff, against superior forces without any probability of success; that the Dutch suffered for their own rashness, and that if he had sustained them in the manner they expected, the whole fleet must have been surrounded and destroyed. In the end the earl was acquitted, but the day after the trial he was superseded.

The Victory of La Hogue
By John Campbell

On the dismissal of the Earl of Torrington from the command of the navy, Edward Russel was appointed admiral and commander-in-chief; but twelve months elapsed before an opportunity occurred for wiping out the dishonour of the engagement off Beachy Head.

As soon as Louis XIV. perceived that it was impossible to support the war in Ireland any longer to advantage, he resolved to employ the forces still left with King James to serve his purpose in another way. With this view, he concerted with the malcontents in England an invasion of the coast of Sussex; and though for this design it was necessary to draw together a large number of transports, as well as a very considerable body of troops, he had both in readiness before his purpose was so much as suspected here.

The land forces consisted of fourteen battalions of English and Irish troops, and about nine thousand French soldiers, commanded by Marshal de Belfondes; so that in all there were not less than twenty thousand men. The fleet of transports consisted of three hundred sail, and was well provided with everything necessary for the invasion. In short, nothing was wanting to the execution of this design in the beginning of April but the arrival of Count d'Estrees' squadron of twelve men-of-war, which was to escort the embarkation; while the Count de Tourville cruised in the Channel with the grand fleet, ready to put to sea but detained by contrary winds. Things being in this position, King James sent over Colonel Parker and some other agents to give his friends intelligence of his motions; and some of these people, in hopes of reward, gave the first clear account of the whole design to the English government; upon which, order after order was sent to Admiral Russel to hasten out to sea in whatever condition the fleet might be.

There were at this very critical juncture two considerable squadrons at sea; one under the command of Sir Ralph Delaval, sent to bring home a fleet of merchantmen from the Mediterranean; the other under Rear-Admiral Carter, near the French coast. It was apprehended that the French would have endeavoured to intercept the former; and therefore, on the last of February, orders were sent by the *Groin* packet-boat to Vice-Admiral Delaval, to avoid coming near Cape St. Vincent, but rather to sail to Dingle Bay, the mouth of the Shannon, or some other port thereabouts. But, for fear these orders might not reach him soon enough at Cadiz, an advice-boat was ordered to cruise for him off Cape Clear, with instructions to put into Cork or Kingsale. However, both these orders missed him, and he was so fortunate as to arrive in the beginning of March, 1692, safe in the Downs.

Rear-Admiral Carter was ordered to continue cruising with his squadron of eighteen sail as near the French coast as possible, in order to be the better and earlier informed of the movements of the enemy. King William, as soon as he arrived in Holland, took care to hasten the naval preparations with unusual diligence; so that the fleet was ready to put to sea much sooner than had been expected, or at least much sooner than it had done the year before, and was also in a much better condition. Admiral Russel went on board in the beginning of May, and soon after received orders to cruise between Cape la Hogue and the Isle of Wight till the squadrons should join him, though he had proposed the junction should be made off Beachy Head. However, he obeyed his orders as soon as he received them, and plied down through the sands with a very scanty wind, contrary to the opinion of many of his officers and all the pilots, who were against hazarding so great a fleet in so dangerous an attempt; and yet to this bold stroke of the admiral's was due his subsequent success.

On May the 8th the fleet came safe off Rye, and that night the admiral sent to the Dutch admiral to weigh and make sail after him, that no time might be lost. He also sent a squadron of small ships to look for Sir Ralph Delaval, being in great anxiety until the whole confederate fleet was collected in one body. On May 11th he sailed from Rye Bay for St. Helen's; where in two days' time he was joined by Sir Ralph Delaval and Rear-Admiral Carter with their squadrons. While here, the admiral received a letter from the Earl of Nottingham, as secretary of state, written by Queen Mary's direction, wherein he was informed that a scandalous and malicious report had been spread with regard to some of the officers of the fleet, to the effect that they were disaffected or not hearty in the service, and that Her Majesty had thereupon been pressed to discharge many of them from their employment; but Her Majesty charged the admiral to acquaint his officers that she was satisfied this report was raised by the enemies of the government, and that she reposed so entire a confidence in their fidelity that she had resolved not to displace so much as one of them. Upon this the flag-officers and captains drew up a very dutiful and loyal address, dated from on board the *Britannia* at St. Helen's, May 15th, 1692, which was the same day transmitted to court, and on the next presented by the lords of the Admiralty to Her Majesty, who was pleased to make the following wise and gracious answer, which was published that night in the *Gazette*:

> I always had this opinion of the commanders; but I am glad this is come to satisfy others.

When all the ships, English and Dutch, were assembled the admiral proposed that a small detachment of six or eight frigates might be sent to hover about the coast of Normandy, and that the grand fleet should lie westward of that place, in order to protect them from the enemy. This proposition being in part approved, he detached six light ships to gain intelligence, and sailed on May 18th for the coast of France. The next day, about three in the morning, the scouts westward of the fleet fired swivel-guns, and made the signal of discovering the enemy. Immediately orders were given for drawing into a line of battle; and the signal was made for the rear of the fleet to tack, in order to engage the sooner if the French stood to the northward. A little after four, the sun dispersing the fog, the enemy were seen standing southward. The admiral upon this caused the signal for the rear to tack to be taken in, and bore away with his ship to leeward, that each ship in the fleet might fetch his wake and then be brought to and lay by, with his fore-top sail to the mast; that so others might have the better opportunity of placing themselves according to the manner formerly directed for such an occasion.

The confederate fleet was in good order by eight, having the Dutch squadron in the van, the red in the centre, and the blue in the rear. About ten the French fleet bore down upon them with great resolution. About half-past eleven Count Tourville in the *Royal Sun* brought to and began the fight with Admiral Russel, being within three-quarters musket-shot. He plied his guns very warmly till one, but then began to tow off in great disorder; his rigging, sails, and topsail yards being very much injured. About two the wind shifted; so that five of the enemy's blue squadron posted themselves, three ahead and two astern of their admiral, and fired very briskly till after three. The admiral and his two seconds, Mr. Churchil and Mr. Aylmer, had all these ships to deal with. The fog was so thick about four that the enemy could not be seen; and, as soon as it cleared up, the French admiral was discovered towing away northward; upon which the admiral followed him and made the signal for chasing.

While this passed between the admirals, Sir Cloudesley Shovel got to the windward of Count Tourville's squadron and engaged them; but the fog growing darker than before, they were forced to anchor. The weather clearing up a little, the French followed their flying admiral, and the English chased the best they could. About eight in the evening it grew foggy again, and part of the English blue squadron, having fallen in with the enemy, engaged about half an hour, till, having lost four ships, they bore away for Conquet road. In this short action Rear-Admiral Carter was killed.

The 20th of May proved so dark and foggy, that it was eight o'clock before the Dutch discovered the enemy; and then the whole fleet began to chase, the French crowding away westward. About four in the afternoon both fleets anchored; about ten they weighed again, and about twelve Admiral Russel's foretop mast came by the board.

On the 22nd, about seven in the morning, the English fleet continued the chase with all the success they could desire; about eleven the French admiral ran ashore and cut her masts away; upon which her two seconds plied up to her and other ships began to hover about them; and the English admiral ordered Sir Ralph Delaval, who was in the rear, to keep with him a strength sufficient to destroy these ships, and to send the rest, under his command, to join the body of the fleet. In the evening a great number of the enemy's ships were seen going into La Hogue. On the 23rd the admiral sent in Sir George Rooke with several men-of-war, fire-ships, and all the boats of the fleet, to destroy these ships in the bay. On their entering it was perceived that there were thirteen sail; but they were got up so high that none but the small frigates could reach them.

Sir George, however, was resolved to execute his orders; and therefore, having manned his boats, he went in person to encourage the attempt, burnt six of them that night, and the other seven the next morning, together with a great number of transport ships, and other vessels laden with ammunition. This remarkable piece of service, the greatest that happened during the whole affair, was performed under a prodigious fire from the enemy's battery on shore, and within sight of the Irish camp, with the loss only of ten men.

Sir John Ashby, with his own squadron and some Dutch ships, pursued the rest of the French fleet till they ran through the Race of Alderney, among such rocks and shoals that our pilots were absolutely against following them; for which the admiral was censured, though some of the ablest seamen in England were of opinion that there could not be a more desperate undertaking than the flight of the French ships through that passage. Though despair might justify the French in making the attempt, clearly prudence forbade the English from following them.

The Story of Sir George Rooke
By John Campbell.

THE LOSS OF THE SMYRNA FLEET OFF ST. VINCENT.—THE DEFEAT OF THE FRENCH AT VIGO.—THE STORMING OF GIBRALTAR.—THE BATTLE OFF MALAGA.

Sir George Rooke was the son of Sir William Rooke, Knt., of an ancient and honourable family in the county of Kent, where he was born in the year 1650.

Originally intended for another profession, his passion for the sea was not to be denied, and Sir William, after a fruitless struggle with his son's bent for the navy, at last gave way and suffered him to go to sea. His first station in the navy was that of a volunteer, then styled a reformade, in which he distinguished himself by his courage and application. This soon secured him the post of lieutenant, from which he rose to that of captain before he was thirty; promotion then thought very extraordinary. Admiral Herbert distinguished him early, by sending him, in the year 1689, as commodore, with a squadron to the coast of Ireland, where he concurred with Major-general Kirke in the relief of Londonderry, assisting in person in taking the island in the Lake, which opened a passage for the relief of the town.

In the year 1690 he was appointed rear-Admiral of the red; and, in that station, served in the fight off Beachy Head, where, notwithstanding the misfortune of our arms, indisputably the greatest we ever met with at sea, Admiral Rooke was allowed to have done his duty with much resolution. In the spring of 1691 he was promoted to the rank of vice-Admiral of the blue, in which station he served in the famous battle of La Hogue, on May the 22nd, 1692, and contributed no small share to the victory. For this service, an account of which will be found in the story of *The Victory of La Hogue*, he was knighted in the following year.

The direction of the fleet being now put in commission, Sir George Rooke was entrusted with the command of the squadron appointed to escort the Smyrna fleet, and the joint admirals received orders to accompany him as far to sea as they thought proper; after which his instructions were to take the best care of the fleet he could, and, in case of any misfortune, to retire into some of the Spanish ports and put himself under the protection of their guns.

The combined fleet had not proceeded far before the accompanying admirals signified their intention to return, and Sir George Rooke, who had good reason to believe that the French squadron had gone to Toulon with a view to intercepting the ships under his convoy, had to content himself with protesting against the withdrawal of the grand fleet so early in the voyage, and proceeding upon the journey alone. On June the 15th, being about sixty leagues short of Cape St. Vincent, he ordered the *Lark* to stretch ahead of his scouts into Lagos Bay; and on the following day, having confirmed advice of danger, from the close proximity of the enemy, proposed in a council of war to keep the wind or lie by during the night, with a view to discovering the enemy's strength in the morning. In this he was over-ruled, for it was urged that the wind being fresh northerly, it gave the fleet a fair opportunity of pushing for Cadiz; with which view he ran along the shore all night with a pressed sail, forcing several of the enemy's ships to cut from their anchors in Lagos Bay.

The next day, when off Villa Nova, it fell calm, and a little after daybreak ten sail of the enemy's men-of-war and several small ships were seen in the offing. The French no sooner discovered Sir George Rooke than they stood away with their boats ahead, setting fire to some, and sinking others of their small craft, to save them from falling into his hands. The crew of a fire-ship which fell in with our fleet in the night, being carried on board the flag ship and examined by the admiral, told him that the French squadron consisted of only fifteen ships of the line, notwithstanding there were three flags, and had with them forty-six merchantmen and store-ships, bound either for Toulon or to join M. d'Estrees. They said also that the squadron had been becalmed off the Cape, and that, having watered in the bay, were bound directly into the Straits, without any intention of following our fleet.

This story, consistent with the hasty retreat of their men-of-war in the morning and their desertion and destruction of their small vessels, completely deceived the admiral and the rest of the officers; though afterwards it appeared that they made this retreat with a view to drawing the English squadron more completely into their power. About noon the sea breeze sprang up and the admiral bore away along shore upon the enemy, discovering their real strength as he came nearer to them, until at last he sighted about eighty sail.

About three in the afternoon the Dutch vice-Admiral sent Sir George Rooke word that, in his judgment, the best course would be to avoid fighting. Sir George differed with him upon the point and had actually made his arrangements for engaging the enemy; but reflecting that he should take upon himself the whole blame of the consequences if he fought contrary to the Dutch admiral's advice, he brought to and then stood off with an easy sail, at the same time despatching the *Sheerness* with orders to the small ships that were on the coast to endeavour to get along shore in the night and save themselves in the Spanish ports; this, happily, many of them succeeded in doing.

Sir George Rooke's whole squadron consisted of no more than twenty-three ships of war; of these, thirteen only were English, eight Dutch, and two Hamburgers. The fleet of merchantmen under his convoy numbered four hundred sail of all nations, though the greater part of them were English ships. The fleet under M. Tourville consisted of one hundred and twenty sail, of which sixty-four were of the line, and eighteen three-deck ships; yet Sir George Rooke saved all his men-of-war and no less than sixty merchantmen, and was said by the Dutch gazettes to have gained more reputation by his escape than the French had by their victory.

Early in the year 1697 Sir George Rooke was appointed admiral and commander-in-chief of the fleet, and put to sea towards the latter end of June. As the French avoided fighting Sir George found it impossible to do anything with them; but while cruising off the French coast he met with a large fleet of Swedish merchantmen, and having obliged them to bring to and submit to be searched, found just grounds for believing that most of their cargoes belonged to French merchants: upon which he sent them under the convoy of some frigates into Plymouth. This caused a great deal of excitement, the Swedish minister interposing, and some of our statesmen being inclined to disapprove the admiral's conduct.

Upon this Sir George insisted that the matter should be brought to trial before the court of admiralty, where, upon the clearest evidence, it was shown that these Swedish ships were freighted by French merchants, partly with French goods, but chiefly with Indian merchandise, which had been taken out of English and Dutch ships; and that the

Swedes had no further concern therein than receiving two per cent. for lending their names, procuring passes, and taking other necessary precautions for screening the effects of the French merchants; so that the whole of this rich fleet was adjudged to be good prize, and the clamour that had been raised against Sir George Rooke was converted into general applause!

The following year he was elected member of parliament for Portsmouth, where, voting mostly with the Tories, the Whigs tried to ruin him in the king's favour; but, to the honour of King William be it said, that when pressed to remove Sir George Rooke from his seat at the Admiralty-board, he answered plainly "Sir George Rooke has served me faithfully at sea, and I will never displace him for acting as he thinks most for the service of his country in the House of Commons."

Upon the accession of Queen Anne, in 1702, Sir George was constituted vice-Admiral and lieutenant of the Admiralty of England, as also lieutenant of the fleets and seas of this kingdom; and, upon the declaration of war with France, it was resolved that Sir George Rooke should command the grand fleet sent against Cadiz, the Duke of Ormond having the command-in-chief of the land forces.

When it was found impracticable for the land forces to make themselves masters of Cadiz, Sir George Rooke proposed bombarding it, but this suggestion meeting with opposition the admiral decided to return home.

On September 19th, 1702, the fleet sailed homeward bound, but on October 6th the admiral received information from Captain Hardy that a number of galleons under the escort of a strong French squadron had entered the harbour of Vigo; upon which Sir George called a council of war composed of English and Dutch flag-officers, by whom it was resolved to sail to Vigo as expeditiously as possible, and attack the enemy.

The passage into the harbour was not more than three-quarters of a mile across, and was defended on the north side by a battery of eight brass and twelve iron guns; and on the south by a platform of twenty brass and twenty iron guns, also a stone fort, with a breast-work and deep trench before it, mounting ten guns and manned by five hundred men. There was, from one side of the harbour to the other, a strong boom composed of ships-yards and top masts, fastened together with three-inch rope, and underneath with hawsers and cables. The top-chain at each end was moored to a seventy-gun ship; one the *Hope*, which had been taken from the English, and the other the *Bourbon*. Within the boom were moored five ships, of between sixty and seventy guns each, with their broadsides fronting the entrance of the passage, so as to command any ship that came near the boom, forts, and platform.

The admirals removed their flags from the great ships into third-rates, the first- and second-rates being all too big to go in. Sir George Rooke went out of the *Royal Sovereign* into the *Somerset*; Admiral Hopson out of the *Prince George* into the *Torbay*; Admiral Fairbourne out of the *St. George* into the *Essex*; and Admiral Graydon out of the *Triumph* into the *Northumberland*. A detachment of fifteen English and ten Dutch men-of-war, with all their fire-ships, frigates, and bomb-vessels, was ordered to go upon the service.

The Duke of Ormond, to facilitate this attack, landed two thousand five hundred men on the south side of the river, at a distance of about six miles from Vigo; and Lord Shannon, at the head of five hundred men, attacked the stone fort at the entrance of the harbour and made himself master of the platform of forty pieces of cannon. The French governor, M. Sozel, ordered the gates of the fort to be thrown open, resolving to force his way through the English troops. But though there was great bravery, there was but very little judgment in this action, for his order was no sooner obeyed than the grenadiers stormed the place, sword in hand, and forced the garrison, consisting of about three hundred and fifty Frenchmen and Spaniards, to surrender as prisoners of war.

As soon as our flag was seen flying from the fort the ships advanced; and Vice-Admiral Hopson in the *Torbay*, crowding all the sail he could, ran directly against the boom, and broke it; upon which the *Kent*, with the rest of the squadron, English and Dutch, entered the harbour. The enemy made a prodigious fire upon them, both from their ships and batteries on shore, until the latter were captured by our grenadiers; who, seeing the execution done by their guns on the fleet, stormed them with incredible resolution. In the meantime, one of the enemy's fire-ships had laid the *Torbay* on board and did her considerable damage. Her foretop mast was shot by the board; most of the sails burnt or scorched; the fore-yard consumed to a cinder; the larboard shrouds, fore and aft, burnt to the dead eyes; several ports blown off the hinges; her larboard side entirely scorched; one hundred and fifteen men killed and drowned, of whom about sixty jumped overboard as soon as they were grappled by the fire-ship.

In the meantime Captain William Bokenham, in the *Association*, a ship of ninety guns, lay with her broadside to the battery, on the left of the harbour, which was soon disabled; and Captain Francis Wyvill, in the *Barfleur*, a ship of the same force, was sent to batter the fort on the other side, which was a very dangerous and troublesome service, since the enemy's shot pierced the ship through and through, and for some time he durst not fire a gun because our troops were between him and the fort; but they soon drove the enemy from their post, and then the struggle was between the French firing their ships and the galleons and our men endeavouring to save them. In this dispute the *Association* had her main-mast shot, and two men killed; the *Kent* had her foremast shot and the boatswain wounded; the *Barfleur* had her main-mast shot, two men killed, and two wounded; the *Mary* had her bowsprit shot. Of the troops there were only two lieutenants and thirty men killed, and four superior officers wounded; a very inconsiderable loss, considering that the enemy had fifteen French men-of-war, two frigates and a fire-ship, burnt, sunk, or taken, besides seventeen galleons.

Six galleons were taken by the English and five by the Dutch, who sank six. As to the wealth on board the galleons we have no exact account. Of the silver fourteen millions of pieces were saved; of the goods about five. Four millions of plate were destroyed with ten millions of merchandise; and about two millions in silver and five in goods were brought away by the English and Dutch.

Sir Cloudesley Shovel arriving on October 16th as the troops were embarking, the admiral left him at Vigo with orders to see that the French men-of-war and the galleons that we had taken, and that were in a condition to be brought to England, were carefully rigged and properly supplied with men. He was likewise directed to burn such as could not be brought home, and to take the best care he could to prevent embezzlements. After appointing a strong squadron for this service, the admiral, with the rest of the fleet and one of the Spanish galleons, sailed home, and arrived in the Downs on November 7th, 1702, whence the great ships were sent round to Chatham.

The year 1703 was barren of naval achievements; but, if one year can be said to make up for another, 1704 was equal to the occasion. On July 17th the fleet being in the road of Tetuan a council of war was called at which Sir George Rooke proposed the attacking of Gibraltar, a proposal which was immediately agreed to and speedily put into execution, as will be seen by the admiral's own account as follows:—

July 17th, the fleet being then about seven leagues to the eastward of Tetuan, a council of war was held on board the *Royal*

Catherine, wherein it was resolved to make a sudden attempt upon Gibraltar. Accordingly the fleet sailed thither, and on the 21st got into the bay. At three o'clock in the afternoon the marines, English and Dutch, to the number of one thousand eight hundred, with the Prince of Hesse at the head of them, were put on shore on the neck of land to the northward of the town to cut off all communication with the country. His Highness, having posted his men there, sent a summons to the governor to surrender the place, which he rejected with great obstinacy. The admiral, on the 22nd in the morning, gave orders that the ships which had been appointed to cannonade the town under the command of Rear-Admiral Byng and Rear-Admiral Vanderdussen, as also of those which were to batter the south mole head, commanded by Captain Hicks of the *Yarmouth*, should range themselves accordingly; but the wind blowing contrary they could not possibly get into their places till the day was spent. In the meantime, to amuse the enemy, Captain Whitaker was sent with some boats, who burnt a French privateer of twelve guns at the mole. The 23rd, soon after break of day, the ships being all placed, the admiral gave the signal for beginning the cannonade, which was performed with very great fury, above fifteen thousand shot being made in five or six hours' time against the town, insomuch that the enemy were soon beat from their guns, especially at the south mole head: whereupon the admiral, considering that by gaining the fortification they should of consequence reduce the town, ordered Captain Whitaker, with all the boats armed, to endeavour to possess himself of it; which he performed with great expedition.

But Captain Hicks and Captain Jumper, who lay next the mole, had pushed on shore with their pinnaces and some other boats before the rest could come up; whereupon the enemy sprang a mine that blew up the fortifications upon the mole, killed two lieutenants and forty men, and wounded about sixty. However, our men kept possession of the great platform which they had made themselves masters of, and Captain Whitaker landed with the rest of the seamen which had been ordered upon this service, who advanced and took a redoubt, or small bastion, halfway between the mole and the town, and possessed themselves of many of the enemy's cannon. The admiral then sent a letter to the governor, and at the same time a message to the Prince of Hesse to send to him a peremptory summons, which His Highness did accordingly; and on the 24th in the morning, the governor, desiring to capitulate, hostages were exchanged, and the capitulation being concluded the prince marched into the town in the evening and took possession of the land and north-mole gates and the out-work.

The town is extremely strong, and had an hundred guns mounted, all facing the sea and the two narrow passes to the land, and was well supplied with ammunition. The officers, who have viewed the fortifications, affirm there never was such an attack as the seamen made; for that fifty men might have defended those works against thousands.

After this remarkable service the Dutch admiral thought of returning home, and actually detached six men-of-war to Lisbon; so little appearance was there of any further engagement. But on August the 9th the French fleet, under the command of the Count de Toulouse, was seen at sea, and appeared to be the strongest fleet that had been equipped during the whole war; the English admiral, however, resolved to do all in his power to force an engagement, which determination resulted in the battle off Malaga, of which the following is Sir George Rooke's own account, as published by authority. It was dated from on board the *Royal Catherine*, off Cape St. Vincent, August 27th, 1704, and addressed to his Royal Highness Prince George of Denmark.

On the 9th instant, returning from watering our ships on the coast of Barbary to Gibraltar, our scouts made the signals of seeing the enemy's fleet; which, according to the account they gave, consisted of sixty-six sail, and were about ten leagues to windward of us. A council of flag-officers was called, wherein it was determined to lie to the eastward of Gibraltar to receive and engage them. But perceiving that night, by the report of their signal guns, that they wrought from us, we followed them in the morning with all the sail we could make.

On the 11th we forced one of the enemy's ships ashore near Fuengorolo; the crew quitted her, set her on fire and she blew up immediately. We continued still pursuing them, and the 12th, not hearing any of their guns all night nor seeing any of their scouts in the morning, our admiral had a jealousy they might make a double, and, by the help of their galleys, slip between us and the shore to the westward: so that it was resolved, that in case we did not see the enemy before night, we should make the best of our way to Gibraltar; but standing in to the shore about noon we discovered the enemy's fleet and galleys to the westward, near Cape Malaga, going very large. We immediately made all the sail we could and continued the chase all night.

On Sunday the 13th, in the morning, we were within three leagues of the enemy, who brought to with their heads to the southward, the wind being easterly, formed their line and lay to to receive us. Their line consisted of fifty-two ships and twenty-four galleys; they were very strong in the centre and weaker in the van and rear, to supply which most of the galleys were divided into those quarters. In the centre was Monsieur de Toulouse with the white squadron; in the van the white and blue, and in the rear the blue. Each admiral had his vice- and rear-Admirals. Our line consisted of fifty-three ships, the admiral, and Rear-Admirals Byng and Dilkes being in the centre; Sir Cloudesley Shovel and Sir John Leake led the van, and the Dutch the rear.

The admiral ordered the *Swallow* and *Panther*, with the *Lark* and *Newport* and two fire-ships, to lie to the windward of us, that, in case the enemy's van should push through our line with their galleys and fire-ships, they might give them some diversion.

We bore down upon the enemy in order of battle a little after ten o'clock, when, being about half gun-shot from them, they set all their sails at once and seemed to intend to stretch ahead and weather us; so that our admiral, after firing a chase-gun at the French admiral to stay for him, of which he took no notice, put the signal out and began the battle, which fell very heavy on the *Royal Catherine, St. George*, and the *Shrewsbury*. About two in the afternoon the enemy's van gave way to ours, and the battle ended with the day, when the enemy went away, by the help of their galleys, to the leeward. In the night the wind shifted to the northward, and in the morning to the westward, which gave the enemy the wind of us. We lay by all day, within three leagues one of another; repairing our defects; and at night they filled and stood to the northward.

On the 15th, in the morning, the enemy was four or five leagues to the westward of us; but a little before noon we had a breeze of wind easterly, with which we bore down on them till four o'clock in the afternoon: it being too late to engage, we brought to and lay by with our heads to the northward all night.

On the 16th, in the morning, the wind being still easterly, hazy weather, and having no sight of the enemy or their scouts, we filled and bore away to the westward, supposing they would have gone away for Cadiz; but being advised from Gibraltar and the coast of Barbary that they did not pass the Straits, we concluded they had been so severely treated as to oblige them to return to Toulon.

The admiral says he must do the officers the justice to say that every man in the line did his duty, without giving the least umbrage for censure or reflection, and that he never observed the true English spirit so apparent and prevalent in our seamen as on this occasion.

This battle is so much the more glorious to Her Majesty's arms because the enemy had a superiority of six hundred great guns, and likewise the advantage of cleaner ships, being lately come out of port, not to mention the great use of their galleys in towing on or off their great ships and in supplying them with fresh men as often as they had any killed or disabled. But all these disadvantages were surmounted by the bravery and good conduct of our officers and the undaunted courage of our seamen.

In this fierce engagement neither side lost a ship, but the carnage was very great, the English killed and wounded numbering three thousand and the French nearly four thousand. The French claimed it as a victory but showed no disposition to follow it up.

Upon his return to England Sir George found himself the subject of much party strife, and, as perceiving that as he rose in credit with his country he lost his interest in those at the helm, resolved to retire from public service and prevent the affairs of the nation from receiving any disturbance upon his account. Retiring to his seat in Kent he spent the rest of his life in rest and peace, dying of the gout on January 24th, 1708-9 in the fifty-eighth year of his age.

A good husband and a kind master, he lived hospitably with his neighbours and left behind him a moderate fortune. "I do not leave much," said he, "but what I leave was honestly gotten; it never cost a sailor a tear or the nation a farthing." After he was laid aside a privy seal was offered him for passing his accounts; but he refused it, and made them up in the ordinary way and with all the exactness imagi-

The Spanish Armada.

nable.

Off Gibraltar

It is not to be supposed that our enemies quietly accepted the conquest of Gibraltar by Sir George Rooke as final; indeed, a very short time elapsed before they began to make efforts to regain it.

The Spaniards, who were the best judges, found our possession of the great fortress so great a thorn in their sides that they prevailed upon the French to hazard an engagement at sea to facilitate their retaking it, and afterwards obtained a squadron of French ships, under the command of Monsieur de Pointis, to assist them in carrying on a siege. The Prince of Hesse having sent early advice of this to Lisbon, Sir John Leake, in the beginning of the month of October, 1704, proceeded with his squadron to the relief of the garrison, and actually landed several gunners, carpenters, and engineers, with a body of four hundred marines; but receiving intelligence that the French were approaching with a force much superior to his own, he found it necessary to return to Lisbon.

He did this with a view only to refit and to be in a better condition to supply and assist the garrison in a second expedition, for which he had very prudently directed preparations to be made in his absence. This enabled him to put to sea again on October 25th, and on the 29th he entered the Bay of Gibraltar at a very critical juncture; for that very night the enemy intended to storm the town on all sides, and had procured two hundred boats from Cadiz in order to land three thousand men near the new mole. Sir John Leake entered so suddenly that he surprised two frigates in the bay, one of forty-two and the other of twenty-four guns, a *brigantine* of fourteen, a fire-ship of sixteen, a store-ship full of bombs, and two English prizes; while a *tartane* and a frigate of thirty guns, which had just left the bay, were taken by an English ship that followed him.

The enemy, notwithstanding these discouragements, continued the siege in expectation of strong naval succours from France, and therefore Sir John Leake resolved to land as many men as he could spare to reinforce the garrison. This he performed on the 2nd, 3rd, and 4th of November, and continued still on the coast in order to alarm and distress the enemy. On the 19th and 20th he ordered his smallest frigates as near the shore as possible, and then manned his boats as if he intended a descent.

This was done so slowly that the Spanish general had time to draw down a great body of cavalry, upon which the admiral put his design in execution and saluted them in such a manner with his great and small arms that they scampered back to their camp with great precipitation. The *Centurion* arrived on November 22nd, and brought in with her a French prize from Martinico, very richly laden; and, at the same time, gave the admiral intelligence that he had discovered a very strong squadron in the Bay of Cadiz, which he apprehended would soon be in a condition to sail. Upon this Sir John Leake resolved to put to sea, and to stand with his fleet to the eastward of Gibraltar, that he might be the better able to take such measures as should be found necessary, as well for the preservation of the place as for securing the succours that were expected from Lisbon.

On December 7th the *Antelope* arrived with nine transports under her convoy, and two days afterwards the *Newcastle* with seven more, having on board nearly two thousand land troops. These escaped the French fleet very luckily; for when they were off Cape Spartel they had sight of Monsieur Pointis's squadron, consisting of twenty-four sail of men-of-war sailing under English and Dutch colours. As they expected to meet the confederate fleet under Sir John Leake and Rear-Admiral Vanderdussen thereabouts they were readily deceived and did their utmost to join their enemies. Being becalmed they put their boats to sea on both sides to tow the ships; but, observing that the men-of-war stretched themselves and endeavoured to make a half-moon to surround them, they made a private signal which Sir John Leake would have understood. This betrayed the French, who, finding themselves discovered, put up their colours and endeavoured to fall upon the transports; which, however, escaped by means of their oars, and night coming on got away by favour of a small breeze from the south-west.

By the arrival of these succours the garrison of Gibraltar was increased to upwards of three thousand men; and having already obtained many advantages over the enemy, it was no longer thought requisite to keep the fleet, which by long service was now but in an indifferent condition, either in the bay or on the coast; whereupon it was unanimously resolved to sail with all convenient speed to Lisbon in order to refit and to provide further supplies for the garrison, in case, as the Spaniards gave out, they should receive such reinforcements from King Louis and King Philip as would enable them to renew the siege both by land and sea. This resolution was as speedily executed as wisely taken, and the fleet arrived at Lisbon in the latter end of 1704.

Four years later fortune favoured Sir John Leake in these waters once again.

Upon receiving advice from Colonel Elliot, governor of Gibraltar, in April 1708, that some French ships of war were seen cruising off the Straits mouth the admiral sailed from the river of Lisbon on the 28th, and, in his passage up the Straits on May 11th, when about twelve leagues from Alicante, sighted several vessels which he took to be fishing-boats. Sir John had previously detached some light frigates to give notice of the approach of his fleet, and one of them had had the good luck to take a French frigate of twenty-four guns, from which he obtained an account of a convoy that was expected. Upon this the captains of our frigates made the necessary dispositions for intercepting it. The next day the French convoy appeared in sight, consisting of three men of war, one of forty-four, another of forty, and the third of thirty-two guns, with ninety *settees* and *tartanes* laden with wheat, barley, and oil for the use of the Duke of Orleans' army, and bound for Peniscola, near the mouth of the Ebro.

The British frigates bore down immediately upon the enemy's men-of-war, who, however, abandoning their barques and endeavouring to make their escape, came in view of the main fleet, upon which Sir John Leake made signal to give chase. As our great ships could not follow them near the coast, the French made their escape in the night; but the vice-Admiral of the white, perceiving the *barques* near the coast, sent his long-boats and small ships in and took several of them. The next morning others were captured, and some barques of Catalonia, coming out of their harbours to secure a share in the booty, sixty-nine of them were taken and the rest dispersed.

The Story of Admiral Benbow
By John Campbell

Admiral Benbow was descended from the ancient and honourable family of the Benbows in the county of Salop; a family that suffered for their loyalty to the cause of Charles I.

When the Civil War broke out, the king, relying upon the loyalty of the inhabitants of this county, repaired in person to Shrewsbury, on September 20th, 1642; whereupon the Lords Newport and Littleton, with many of the gentry of the county, came in and offered His Majesty their services; among these were Thomas Benbow and John Benbow, Esquires, both men of estates, and both colonels in the king's service, of whom the latter was the father of our admiral.

After the execution of Charles I. his followers retired into the country and lived as privately as they could. But though their interests were much reduced and their fortunes in a great measure ruined, their spirits remained unbroken, and when the time came they acted as cheerfully for the service of King Charles II. as if they had never suffered in the cause of his father. When, therefore, Charles II. marched from Scotland towards Worcester, the two Benbows, among other gentlemen of the county of Salop, went to attend him; and after fighting bravely in his support were both taken prisoners by the parliamentary forces.

After the Battle of Worcester, which was fought September 3rd, 1651, a court martial was appointed to sit at Chester, whereby ten gentlemen, of the first families in England, were sentenced to death for complicity with His Majesty, and five of them were executed. They then proceeded to try Sir Timothy Featherstonhaugh, Colonel Thomas Benbow and the Earl of Derby for being in his service. They were all condemned, and, in order to strike the greater terror in different parts of the county, the Earl of Derby was adjudged to suffer death on October 15th, at Bolton; Sir Timothy to be beheaded on the 17th, at Chester; and Colonel Thomas Benbow to be shot on the 19th, at Shrewsbury; all these sentences were severally put in execution.

As for Colonel John Benbow, he made his escape after a short imprisonment, and lived privately in his own county till after the Restoration, when he was far advanced in years; and yet was so hard pressed for a livelihood that he was glad to accept a small office belonging to the ordnance in the Tower, which brought him an income just sufficient to keep him and his family from starving. He was found in this situation when, a little before the breaking out of the first Dutch war, Charles II. came to the Tower to examine the magazines. The king, whose memory was as quick as his eye, knew him at first sight, and immediately came up and embraced him.

"My old friend, Colonel Benbow," said he, "what do you here?"

"I have," returned the colonel, "a place of fourscore pounds a year, in which I serve Your Majesty as cheerfully as if it brought me in four thousand."

"Alas!" said the king, "is that all that could be found for an old friend at Worcester? Colonel Legge, bring this gentleman to me tomorrow, and I will provide for him and his family as it becomes me."

But the poor old colonel did not live to receive, or so much as to claim, the effects of this gracious promise; for his feelings so overcame him, that, sitting down on a bench, he breathed his last before the king was well out of the Tower. Thus both brothers fell martyrs to the royal cause, one in grief, and the other in joy.

John, the subject of this sketch, who was then about fifteen, had been bred to the sea; probably in some lowly capacity, although even in Charles II.'s reign he was owner and commander of a ship called the *Benbow* frigate, and made as respectable a figure as any man concerned in the trade to the Mediterranean. He was always considered by the merchants as a bold, brave, and active commander; one who took care of his seamen, and was therefore cheerfully obeyed by them, though he maintained strict discipline.

In the year 1686 Captain Benbow in his own vessel, the *Benbow* frigate, was attacked in his passage to Cadiz by a Sallee rover, against which, though greatly outnumbered, he defended himself with the utmost bravery. At last the Moors boarded him, but were quickly beaten back, with the loss of thirteen men, whose heads Captain Benbow ordered to be cut off and thrown into a tub of pork-pickle. Arrived at Cadiz, he went ashore and ordered a negro servant to follow him with the Moors' heads in a sack. He had scarcely landed before the officers of the revenue inquired of his servant what he had in his sack? The captain answered salt provisions for his own use.

"That may be," answered the officers, "but we must insist upon seeing them."

Captain Benbow alleged that he was no stranger there, and pretended to take it very ill that he was suspected. The officers told him that the magistrates were sitting not far off and that if they were satisfied with his word his servant might carry the provisions where he pleased; but that otherwise it was not in their power to grant any such dispensation.

The captain consented to the proposal; and away they marched to the custom-house, Mr. Benbow in the front, his man in the centre and the officers in the rear. The magistrates, when he came before them, treated him with great civility; told him they were sorry to make a point of such a trifle, but that, since he had refused to show the contents of his sack to their officers they were obliged to demand a sight of them; and that if they were salt provisions the showing of them could be of no great consequence either way.

"I told you," said the captain sternly, "they were salt provisions for my own use. Cæsar, throw them down upon the table; and, gentlemen, if you like them, they are at your service." The Spaniards were exceedingly struck at the sight of the Moors' heads, and no less astonished at the account of the captain's adventure, who, with so small a force, had been able to defeat such a number of barbarians. They sent an account of the whole matter to the court of Madrid; and Charles II. of Spain was so pleased with it that he must needs see the English captain, who made a journey to court, where he was received with great show of respect and dismissed with a handsome present. His Majesty also wrote a letter on his behalf to King James, who, upon the captain's return, gave him a ship; which was Captain Benbow's introduction to the Royal Navy.

After the Revolution, Benbow distinguished himself by several successful cruises in the Channel, where he was employed at the request of the merchants in protecting trade, and was very successful, and where his diligence and activity recommended him to the favour of William III., to whose personal kindness he owed his early promotion to a flag. After this he was generally employed as the most experienced seaman in the navy to watch the movements of the French at Dunkirk, and to prevent, as far as it was possible, the depredations of Du Bart; in which he showed such diligence and did such signal service that he escaped the slightest censure at a time when libels flew about against almost every other officer of rank in the fleet. The truth was, the seamen generally looked upon Rear-Admiral Benbow as their greatest patron; one who not only used them well while under his care, but was always ready to interpose in their favour when they were ill-treated by others.

Admiral Benbow's next employment was in the West Indies, where he met with many difficulties and rendered valuable service, receiving on his return home unmistakable marks of royal favour. Shortly after his return it became necessary to send another expedition to the same place, and when the subject of leadership was discussed the ministers suggested Admiral Benbow. This, however, the king, who seems to have had some affection for our admiral, would not hear of. "Benbow," he said, "had but just come home from thence, where he had met with nothing but difficulties; and it was but fair that some other officer should take his turn."

One or two were named and consulted, but excused themselves upon various grounds; upon which the king said merrily, alluding to the dress and appearance of these gentlemen, "Well then, I find we must spare our *beaux* and send honest Benbow."

William, accordingly, sent for our admiral and asked him whether he was willing to go to the West Indies, assuring him, if he was not, he would not take it amiss if he desired to be excused. Mr. Benbow answered bluntly, "That he did not understand such compliments; that he thought he had no right to choose his station; and that if His Majesty thought fit to send him to the East or West Indies, or anywhere else, he would cheerfully execute his orders as became him." Thus the matter was settled in very few words, and the command of the West India squadron conferred on Vice-Admiral Benbow.

He arrived at Barbadoes on November 3rd, 1701, from whence he sailed to examine the state of the French and of our own Leeward Islands. He found the former in some confusion, and the latter in so good a state of defence, that he saw no necessity of remaining, and therefore sailed to Jamaica. Here he received advice of two French squadrons having arrived in the West Indies, much to the alarm of the inhabitants of Jamaica and of Barbadoes. After arranging for the safety of both places as far as his strength would permit, he formed a design of attacking Petit Goave; but before he could execute it, received intelligence that Monsieur Du Casse was in the neighbourhood of

Hispaniola with a squadron of French ships, to settle the *assiento* in favour of the French and to destroy the English and Dutch trade for negroes.

After alarming Petit Goave, which he found it inexpedient to attack, the admiral sailed for Donna Maria Bay, where he continued until August 10th; when, having received advice that Monsieur Du Casse had sailed for Carthagena, and from thence was to sail to Portobello, he resolved to follow him, and accordingly sailed for the Spanish coast of Santa-Martha.

On August the 19th, in the evening, he discovered ten sail of tall ships to the westward. Standing towards them he found the best part of them to be French men-of-war; upon which he made the usual signal for a line of battle, going away with an easy sail, that his sternmost ships might come up and join him, the French steering along-shore under their top sails. Their squadron consisted of four ships, from sixty to seventy guns, with one great Dutch-built ship of about thirty or forty, and there was another full of soldiers; the rest small ones, and a sloop. Our frigates astern were a long time in coming up, and the night advancing, the admiral steered alongside of the French, endeavouring to near them, yet intending to avoid attack until the *Defiance* was abreast of the headmost.

Before he could reach that station the *Falmouth*, which was in the rear, attempted the Dutch ship, and the *Windsor* the ship abreast of her, as did also the *Defiance*; and soon after the vice-Admiral himself was engaged. But the *Defiance* and the *Windsor* stood no more than two or three broadsides before they luffed out of gun-shot, whereupon the two sternmost ships of the enemy lay upon the admiral and galled him very much; nor did the ships in the rear come up to his assistance with due diligence. From four o'clock until night the fight continued, and though the French then left off firing, our admiral still kept them company.

On the 20th, at daybreak, the admiral found himself very near the enemy with only the *Ruby* to assist him, the rest of the ships lying three, four, or five miles astern. About two in the afternoon the sea-breeze began to blow, and then the enemy got into a line, making what sail they could; and the rest of his ships not coming up, the admiral and the *Ruby* plied them with chase-guns and kept them company all the next night.

On the 21st the admiral was on the quarter of the second ship of the enemy's line, within point-blank shot; but the *Ruby* being ahead of the same ship was attacked by two of the enemy's line. The *Breda*, which carried the admiral, engaged the ship that first attacked the *Ruby*, and plied her so warmly that she was forced to tow off. The admiral would have followed her, but the *Ruby* was in such a condition that he could not leave her. During this engagement the rear ship of the enemy's was abreast of the *Defiance* and *Windsor*, but neither of those ships fired a single shot. On the 22nd, at daybreak, the *Greenwich* was five leagues astern, though the signal for battle was never struck night or day; about three in the afternoon the wind came southerly, which gave the enemy the weather-gauge.

On the 23rd the enemy was six leagues ahead and the great Dutch ship separated from them. At ten the enemy tacked with the wind at east-north-east, the vice-Admiral fetched point-blank within a shot or two of them, and each gave the other his broadside. About noon they recovered from the enemy a small English ship called the *Anne* galley, which they had taken off the rock of Lisbon. The *Ruby* being disabled, the admiral ordered her for Port Royal. The rest of the squadron now came up, and the enemy being but two miles off, the brave admiral was in hopes of doing something at last, and therefore continued to steer after them; but his ships, except the *Falmouth*, were soon astern again. At twelve the enemy began to separate.

On the 24th, about two in the morning, they came up within call of the sternmost, there being then very little wind. The admiral fired a broadside with double round below, and round and cartridge aloft. At three o'clock the admiral's right leg was shattered to pieces by a chain-shot, and he was carried below; but he presently ordered his cradle to be carried to the quarter-deck, and continued the fight till day. Then appeared the ruins of the enemy's ship of about seventy guns; her main yard down and shot to pieces, her foretop-sail yard shot away, her mizen-mast shot by the board, all her rigging gone, and her sides bored to pieces. The admiral soon after discovered the enemy standing toward him with a strong gale of wind. The *Windsor*, *Pendennis*, and *Greenwich*, ahead of the enemy, came to the leeward of the disabled ship, fired their broadsides, passed her, and stood to the southward; then came the *Defiance*, fired part of her broadside, when the disabled ship returning about twenty guns, the *Defiance* put her helm a-weather, and ran away right before the wind, lowered both her top-sails, and ran to the leeward of the *Falmouth* without any regard to the signal of battle.

The enemy seeing the other two ships stand to the southward, expected they would have tacked and stood towards them, and therefore they brought their heads to the northward. But when they saw these ships did not tack, they immediately bore down upon the admiral, and ran between their disabled ship and him, and poured in all their shot, by which they brought down his maintop-sail yard, and shattered his rigging very much; none of the other ships being near him or taking the least notice of his signals, though Captain Fog ordered two guns to be fired at the ships ahead in order to put them in mind of their duty.

The French, seeing things in this confusion, brought to and lay by their own disabled ship, remanned and took her into tow. The *Breda's* rigging being much shattered she was forced to lie by till ten o'clock; and, being by that time refitted, the admiral ordered his captain to pursue the enemy, then about three miles to the leeward, his line-of-battle signal out all the while; and Captain Fog, by the admiral's orders, sent to the other captains, to order them to keep the line and behave like men. Upon this Captain Kirby came on board the admiral, and told him that "he had better desist; that the French were very strong; and that from what was past he might guess he could make nothing of it."

The brave Admiral Benbow, more surprised at this language than he would have been at the sight of another French squadron, sent for the rest of the captains on board in order to ask their opinion. They obeyed him indeed, but were most of them in Captain Kirby's way of thinking; which satisfied the admiral that they were not inclined to fight; and that, as Kirby phrased it, *there was nothing to be done*, though there was the fairest opportunity that had yet offered. Our strength was, at this time, one ship of seventy guns, one of sixty-four, one of sixty, and three of fifty; their masts, yards, and all things else in as good condition as could be expected, and not above eight men killed, except in the vice-Admiral's own ship, nor was there any want of ammunition; whereas the enemy had now no more than four ships, from sixty to seventy guns, and one of them disabled and in tow. The vice-Admiral thought proper upon this to return to Jamaica, where he arrived with his squadron, very weak with a fever induced by his wounds, and was soon after joined by Rear-Admiral Whetstone, with the ships under his command.

As soon as he conveniently could, Vice-Admiral Benbow issued a commission to Rear-Admiral Whetstone and to several captains to hold a court martial for the trial of several offenders. On October 6th,

1702, the court sat at Port Royal, when Captain Kirby, of the *Defiance*, was put upon his trial. He was accused of cowardice, breach of orders and neglect of duty; which crimes were proved upon oath, by the admiral himself, ten commissioned, and eleven warrant officers; by whose evidence it appeared that the admiral boarded Du Casse in person three times, and received a large wound in his face, and another in his arm before his leg was shot off; that Kirby, after two or three broadsides, kept always out of gun-shot, and by his behaviour created such a fear of his desertion as greatly discouraged the English in the engagement; that he kept two or three miles astern all the second day, though commanded again and again to keep his station; that the third day he did not fire a gun though he saw the admiral in the deepest distress, having two or three French men-of-war upon him at a time; and that he threatened to kill his boatswain for repeating the admiral's command to fire. He had very little to say for himself, and therefore was most deservedly sentenced to be shot.

The same day Captain Constable, of the *Windsor*, was tried; his own officers vindicated him from cowardice, but the rest of the charge being clearly proved he was sentenced to be cashiered and to be imprisoned during Her Majesty's pleasure. The next day Captain Wade was tried, and the charge being fully proved by sixteen commissioned and warrant officers on board his own ship, as also that he was drunk during the whole time of the engagement, he, making little or no defence, had the same sentence with Kirby. As for Captain Hudson, he died a few days before his trial should have come on, and thereby avoided dying as Kirby and Wade did; for his case was exactly the same with theirs.

The reflections he made on this unhappy business threw the brave admiral into a deep melancholy, which soon brought him to his end; for he died on November 4th, 1702, of a fever engendered by his wounds and worries. The condemned captains were sent home from Jamaica on board Her Majesty's ship the *Bristol*, and arrived at Plymouth on April 16th, 1703, where, as in all the western ports, there lay a warrant for their immediate execution, and they were shot on board the ship that brought them home.

The mortification felt by the admiral at the failure of his officers is indicated in the answer he gave to one of his lieutenants who expressed sorrow for the fact that the admiral had lost his leg. "Why, yes," said the fine old sailor, "I am sorry for it too, but I would rather have lost them both than have seen this dishonour brought upon the

English nation."

The French accounts of this engagement represent the whole affair to their own advantage; but M. Du Casse, who was a brave man, and withal by far the best judge of the circumstances, has put the matter out of dispute by the following short letter, written by him immediately after his arrival at Carthagena; the original of which is said to be still in the hands of Admiral Benbow's family.

> Sir,—I had little hopes, on Monday last, but to have supped in your cabin; but it pleased God to order it otherwise; I am thankful for it. As for those cowardly captains who deserted you, hang them up; for, by God, they deserve it.
>
> Yours,
>
> Du Casse.

Defeat of the Spanish Fleet in the Faro off Messina
By John Campbell.

Early in the year 1718 the activity of the naval preparations in England, rendered necessary by the disturbed condition of Europe, excited considerable anxiety and comment.

M. de Monteleone, the Spanish minister here, a man of foresight and intrigue, taking alarm, in a memorial dated March 18th, 1718, represented "That so powerful an armament in time of peace could not but cause umbrage to the king his master and alter the good intelligence that reigned between the two crowns."

To which King George I. replied, "That it was not his intention to conceal the object of the armament; and that he designed soon to send Admiral Byng with a powerful squadron into the Mediterranean, in order to maintain the neutrality of Italy against those who should seek to disturb it." The reasons assigned for acting with so much vigour were the preparations made in Spain for attacking the island of Sicily and the hardships suffered by British merchants.

In the month of March, 1718, Sir George Byng was appointed admiral and commander-in-chief of the squadron intended for the Mediterranean; and in the May following he received his instructions as follows: "That he should, upon his arrival in the Mediterranean, acquaint the King of Spain, and likewise the Viceroy of Naples and Governor of Milan, he was sent into that sea in order to promote all measures that might best contribute to the composing the differences arisen between the two crowns, and for preventing any further violation of the neutrality of Italy, which he was to see preserved. That he was to make instances to both parties to forbear all acts of hostility, in order to the setting on foot and concluding the proper negotiations of peace. But, in case the Spaniards should still persist to attack the emperor's territory in Italy, or to land in any part of Italy for that purpose, or should endeavour to make themselves masters of the island of Sicily, which must be with a design to invade the kingdom of Naples, he was then, with all his power, to hinder and obstruct the same; but, if they were already landed, he was to endeavour amicably to dissuade them from persevering in such an attempt, and to offer them his assistance to withdraw their troops and put an end to all farther acts of hostility; but if his friendly endeavours should prove ineffectual he was then to defend the territories attacked, by keeping company with, or intercepting their ships, convoys, or (if necessary) by opposing them openly."

The admiral sailed from Spithead on June 15th, 1718, with twenty ships of the line-of-battle, two fire-ships, two bomb-vessels, a hospital-ship, and a store-ship. Arriving on the 30th off Cape St. Vincent he despatched the *Superbe* to Cadiz, with a letter to Colonel Stanhope, the king's envoy at Madrid, desiring him to inform the King of Spain of his arrival in those parts on his way to the Mediterranean, and to lay before him the instructions he had received.

The envoy showed the letter to Cardinal Alberoni, who, upon reading it, told him with some warmth, that "his master would run all hazards, rather than recall his troops or consent to any suspension of arms;" adding, that "the Spaniards were not to be frightened, and that he was so well convinced of their fleets doing their duty that if the admiral should think fit to attack them he should be in no pain for the success." Mr. Stanhope having in his hand a list of the British squadron, desired his eminence to peruse it, and to compare its strength with that of their own squadron; this the cardinal took and threw on the ground with much passion.

All that the cardinal could be brought to promise was to lay the admiral's letter before the king, and to let the envoy know his resolution upon it in two days; but it was nine before he could obtain and send it away. The answer was written under the admiral's letter in these words:—

His Catholic Majesty has done me the honour to tell me that the Chevalier Byng may execute the orders which he has from the king his master.
The Cardinal Alberoni.

Escurial, July 15th, 1718.

The admiral, pursuing his voyage with unfavourable winds, reached the Bay of Naples on August the 1st, and on the 9th anchored in view of the Faro of Messina. The Spanish army, having taken the city of Messina, were now encamped before the citadel which the troops under Sir George Byng's convoy were intended to relieve. From these strained conditions hostilities seemed imminent, and the desire of the English was that the Spaniards should take the responsibility and the blame of striking the first blow.

Under these circumstances Sir George Byng sent Captain Saunders with a letter to the Marquis de Lede, in which he acquainted him with the instructions under which he was acting, and proposed to him to come to a cessation of arms in Sicily for two months, in order to give time for the several courts to conclude on such resolutions as might restore a lasting peace: but added that "if he was not so happy as to succeed in this offer of service, nor to be instrumental in bringing about so desirable a work, he then hoped to merit His Excellency's esteem in the execution of the other part of his orders, which were, to use all his force to prevent farther attempts to disturb the dominions his master stood engaged to defend."

The next morning the captain returned with the general's answer, "That as he had no powers to treat he could not of consequence agree to any suspension of arms, but should follow his orders, which directed him to seize on Sicily for his master the King of Spain." Upon receiving this answer Admiral Byng immediately weighed, with the intention of coming with his squadron before Messina, in order to encourage and support the garrison and the citadel. In executing this manoeuvre he sighted two Spanish scouts in the Faro; whereupon he altered his design, and stood through the Faro with all the sail he could, following the scouts, imagining they would lead him to the fleet, which they did. About noon he came in view of their whole Spanish fleet, lying by and drawn into a line of battle, consisting of twenty-seven sail of men-of-war small and great, besides two fire-ships, four bomb-vessels, seven galleys, and several ships laden with stores and provisions, commanded by the Admiral Don Antonio de Casteneta and four rear-Admirals, who, sighting the English squadron, stood away large but in good order of battle.

The admiral followed them all the rest of that day and the succeeding night, and the next morning early, the English having approached near to them, the Marquis de Mari, rear-Admiral, with six Spanish men-of-war and all the galleys, fire-ships, bomb-vessels and store-ships, separated from the main fleet and stood in for the Sicilian shore; upon which Admiral Byng detached Captain Walton in the *Canterbury* with five other ships to follow them.

The admiral pursuing the main body of the Spanish fleet, the *Orford*, Captain Falkingham, and the *Grafton*, Captain Haddock, came up first with them, about ten o'clock, the Spaniards firing their stern-chase guns. The Spaniards repeating their fire, the *Orford* attacked the *Santa Rosa*, of sixty-four guns, and took her. The *St. Carlos*, of sixty guns, struck next, without much opposition to the *Kent*, Captain Matthews. The *Grafton* attacked warmly the *Prince of Asturias*, of seventy guns, formerly called the *Cumberland*, in which was Rear-Admiral Chacon; but the *Breda* and *Captain* coming up, Captain Haddock left that ship, much shattered, for them to take, and stretched ahead after another ship of sixty guns, which had kept firing on his starboard bow during his engagement with the *Prince of Asturias*.

About one o'clock the *Kent*, and soon after the *Superbe*, Captain Master, came up with and engaged the Spanish admiral of seventy-four guns, who, with two ships more, fired on them and made a running fight till about three; and then the *Kent*, bearing down under his stern, gave him her broadside and fell to leeward afterwards; the *Superbe*, putting forward to lay the admiral aboard, fell on his weather-quarter; upon which, the Spanish admiral shifting his helm, the *Superbe* ranged under his lee-quarter; on which he struck to her. At the same time the *Barfleur*, which carried the English admiral, being astern of the Spanish admiral, within shot, and inclining on his weather-quarter, Rear-Admiral Guevara and another sixty-gun ship, which were to windward, bore down upon him, and gave him their broadsides, and then clapped upon a wind, standing in for land. The admiral immediately tacked and stood after them until it was almost night; but there being little wind, and the enemy hauling away out of his reach, he left pursuing them and rejoined the fleet two hours after night.

The *Essex* took the *Juno* of thirty-six guns, the *Montague* and *Rupert* took the *Volante* of forty-four guns, and Rear-Admiral Delaval, in the *Dorsetshire*, took the *Isabella* of sixty guns. The action happened off Cape Passaro, at about six leagues' distance from the shore. The English received but little damage: the ship that suffered most was the *Grafton*, for, being a good sailer, her captain engaged several ships in succession, always pursuing the headmost and leaving the ships he had disabled or damaged to be taken by those that followed him. The admiral lay by for some days at sea to refit the rigging of his ships and to repair the damages which the prizes had sustained, and on the 18th received a letter from Captain Walton, who had been sent in pursuit of the Spanish ships which had made for the Sicilian shore under the Marquis de Mari. The letter is singular enough to deserve notice. It ran thus:—

> Sir,—We have taken and destroyed all the Spanish ships and vessels which were upon the coast, the number as *per* margin.
>
> I am, etc.,
>
> George Walton.

Canterbury, off Syracuse, August 16th, 1718.

The ships that Captain Walton thrust into his margin would have furnished matter for some pages in a French relation of the engagement; for, from the account they referred to, it appeared that he had taken four Spanish men-of-war—one of sixty guns, commanded by Rear-Admiral Mari, one of fifty-four, one of forty, and one of twenty-four guns with a bomb-vessel and a ship laden with arms—and burnt four men-of-war, one of fifty-four guns, two of forty, and one of thirty guns, with a fire-ship and a bomb-vessel.

The Story of Captain Hornby and the French Privateer

The difficulties under which merchantmen carried on their trade with foreign countries before the navy had reduced to order the highway of the seas, is well illustrated in many a narrative of adventure with pirates and fights with privateers, which equal in the heroism and daring they display the proudest stories of naval conquest. The following story taken from Young's *History of Whitby* is a case in point.

Mr. Richard Hornby, of Stokesley, was master of a merchant ship, the *Isabella*, of Sunderland, in which he sailed from the coast of Norfolk for the Hague, June 1st, 1744, in company with three smaller vessels recommended to his care. Next day they made Gravesant steeple in the Hague; but while they were steering for their port, a French privateer, that lay concealed among the Dutch fishing-boats, suddenly came against them, singling out the *Isabella* as the object of attack, while the rest dispersed and escaped.

The conquest was very unequal, for the *Isabella* mounted only four carriage guns and two swivels, and her crew consisted of only five men and three boys, besides the captain; while the privateer, the *Marquis de Brancas*, commanded by Captain André, had ten carriage guns and eight swivels, with seventy-five men and three hundred small arms.

Yet Captain Hornby, after consulting his mate and gaining the consent of his crew, whom he animated by an appropriate address, hoisted the British colours, and with his two swivel guns returned the fire of the enemy's chase guns. The Frenchmen, in abusive terms, commanded him to strike, to which he returned an answer of defiance. Upon this the privateer advanced, and poured in such showers of bullets into the *Isabella* that Captain Hornby found it prudent to order his brave fellows into close quarters. While he lay thus sheltered the enemy twice attempted to board him on the larboard quarter; but by a dexterous turn of the helm he frustrated both attempts, though the Frenchmen kept firing upon him both with their guns and small arms, which fire Captain Hornby returned with his two larboard guns.

At two o'clock, when the action had lasted an hour, the privateer, running furiously in upon the larboard of the *Isabella*, entangled her bowsprit among the main shrouds, and was lashed fast to her; upon which Captain André bawled, in a menacing tone, "You English dog, strike!" but the undaunted Hornby challenged him to come on board and strike his colours, if he dared. The enraged Frenchman took him at his word, and threw in twenty men upon him, who began to hack and hew into his close quarters; but a discharge of blunderbusses made the invaders retreat as fast as their wounds would permit them.

The privateer, being then disengaged from the *Isabella*, turned about, and made another attempt on the starboard side; when Captain Hornby and his valiant mate shot each his man as they were again lashing the ships together.

The Frenchmen once more commanded him to strike, and the brave Briton returning another refusal, twenty fresh men entered, and made a fierce attack on the close quarters with hatchets and pole-axes, with which they had nearly cut their way through in three places, when the constant fire kept up by Captain Hornby and his brave crew obliged them to retreat, carrying their wounded with them, and hauling their dead after them with boat-hooks. The *Isabella* continued lashed to the enemy; the latter, with small arms, fired repeated and terrible volleys into the close quarters, partly from his forecastle and partly from his main deck, bringing forward fresh men to supply the place of the dead and wounded: but the fire was returned with such spirit and effect that the Frenchmen repeatedly gave way.

At length Captain Hornby, seeing them crowding behind their main mast for shelter, aimed a blunderbuss at them, which being by mistake doubly loaded, containing twice twelve balls, burst in the firing, and threw him down to the great consternation of his little crew, who supposed him dead; yet he soon started up again, though greatly bruised, while the enemy, among whom the blunderbusses had made dreadful havoc, disengaged themselves from the *Isabella*, to which they had been lashed an hour and a quarter, and sheered off with precipitation, leaving their grapplings, pole-axes, pistols, and cutlasses behind them.

The gallant Hornby fired his two starboard guns into the enemy's stern; and the indignant Frenchman soon returning, the conflict was renewed, and carried on yard-arm and yard-arm with great fury for two hours together. The *Isabella* was shot through her hull several times, her sails and rigging were torn to pieces, her ensign was dismounted, and every mast and yard wounded; yet she bravely maintained the conflict, and at last by a fortunate shot which struck the *Brancas* between wind and water, obliged her to sheer off and careen. While the enemy were retiring, Hornby and his brave little crew sallied out from their fastness, and erecting their fallen ensign gave three cheers.

By this time both vessels had driven so near the shore that immense crowds, on foot and in coaches, had assembled to be spectators of the action.

The Frenchman, having stopped his leak, returned to the combat, and poured a dreadful volley into the stern of the *Isabella*, when Captain Hornby was wounded in the temples by a musket shot, and bled profusely.

This somewhat disconcerted his companions in valour; but he called to them briskly to take courage and stand to their arms, for his wound was not dangerous; upon which their spirits revived, and again taking post in their close quarters, sustained the shock of another assault, and after receiving three tremendous broadsides, repulsed the foe by another well-aimed shot, which sent the *Brancas* again to careen. The huzzas of the *Isabella's* crew were renewed, and they again set up their shattered ensign, which was shot through and through into honourable rags.

André, who was not deficient in bravery, soon renewed the fight; and having disabled the *Isabella* by five terrible broadsides, once more summoned Hornby, with dreadful menaces, to strike his colours.

Captain Hornby animated his gallant comrades—"Behold," said he, pointing to the shore, "the witnesses of your valour this day!" then finding them determined to stand by him to the last, he hurled his final defiance upon the enemy. The latter immediately ran upon his starboard and lashed close alongside; but his crew murmured, and refused to renew the dangerous task of boarding, and, cutting off the lashings, again retreated. Captain Hornby resolved to salute the privateer with one parting gun; and this last shot, fired into the stern of the *Brancas*, reached the magazine, which blew up with a tremendous explosion, and the vessel instantly foundered.

Out of seventy-five men, thirty-six were killed or wounded in the action, and all the rest, together with the wounded, perished in the deep, except three who were picked up by the Dutch fishing-boats. The horrible catastrophe excited the commiseration of Captain Hornby and his brave men, who could render no assistance to their unfortunate enemies, the *Isabella* having become unmanageable, and her boat being shattered to pieces. The engagement lasted seven hours.

For this singular instance of successful bravery Mr. Hornby received from the king a large gold medal commemorating his heroism. He survived the action seven years, and dying at sea of a lingering illness, was buried at Liverpool, being then fifty-two years of age.

Off Cape Finisterre

Towards the end of the year 1746 the French ministry came to a determination to increase their forces in Canada, and, with the assistance of the native Indians, to extend their territories by encroachments on the neighbouring provinces belonging to Great Britain. At the same time they formed a design against some of our settlements in the East Indies. For these purposes, in the beginning of the year 1747, a considerable armament was prepared at Brest; the squadron destined for America being under the command of Monsieur Jonquiere, and that for the East Indies under that of Monsieur de St. George. For greater security these two fleets were ordered to sail at the same time.

The British ministry, being informed of the strength and destination of these squadrons, sent a superior fleet, commanded by Vice-Admiral Anson, to the coast of France. This fleet sailed from Plymouth on April 9th, 1747, and, cruising off Cape Finisterre, on May 3rd fell in with the French fleet, consisting of thirty-eight sail, nine of which shortened sail and prepared to engage, while the rest bore away with all the sail they could make. Admiral Anson first formed his squadron in line-of-battle; but, perceiving the enemy begin to sheer off, he made a signal for his whole fleet to give chase and engage promiscuously. The *Centurion* came up with the sternmost ship of the enemy about four in the afternoon. She was followed by the *Namur*, *Defiance*, and *Windsor*, who were soon warmly engaged with five of the French squadron. The *Centurion* had her main-top mast shot away early in the action, which obliged her to drop astern; but she was soon repaired.

The battle now became general, and the French maintained this very unequal conflict with great spirit and gallantry till about seven in the evening, when the whole fleet struck their colours. The *Diamant* was the last French ship that submitted, after fighting the *Bristol* for nearly three hours. In justice to our enemy it is necessary to remember that the squadron, commanded by Admiral Anson, consisted of fourteen ships of the line, a frigate, a sloop and a fire-ship, with nine hundred and twenty-two guns, and six thousand two hundred and sixty men on board; and that Monsieur de la Jonquiere had no more than five line-of-battle ships and as many frigates, four hundred and forty-two guns, and three thousand one hundred and seventy-one men.

Admiral Anson in the meantime detached the *Monmouth*, the *Yarmouth*, and the *Nottingham* in pursuit of the convoy, and they returned with the *Vigilant* and *Modeste*, both of twenty-two guns, the rest having made their escape. But though we acknowledge the great superiority of the British squadron, it is necessary to inform the reader that no more than eight English ships were engaged. Captain Grenville, of the *Defiance*, a very gallant officer, lost his life in this engagement. Our number of killed and wounded amounted to five hundred and twenty; that of the enemy to seven hundred. Captain Boscawen was wounded in the shoulder by a musket-ball. Monsieur de la Jonquiere was also wounded in the same part; one French captain was killed and another lost a leg.

Admiral Anson returned to England and brought the captive squadron safe to an anchor at Spithead. He set out immediately for London, where he was graciously received by the king, and afterwards created a peer. Rear-Admiral Warren was made Knight of the Bath. The money taken on board of the French fleet was brought through the city of London in twenty waggons and lodged in the Bank.

About the middle of April Captain Fox in the *Kent*, with the *Hampton Court*, the *Eagle*, the *Lion*, the *Chester*, and the *Hector*, with two fire-ships, sailed on a cruise, designing to intercept a fleet of St. Domingo men under the convoy of four French men-of-war. After cruising a month between Ushant and Cape Finisterre, Captain Fox fell in with this French fleet of one hundred and seventy sail. They were immediately deserted by their men-of-war, and forty-six of them were taken.

The British ministry, having received intelligence that nine French men-of-war of the line had sailed from Brest in order to convoy a large fleet of merchantmen to the West Indies, ordered Rear-Admiral Hawke, with fourteen men-of-war, to sail immediately in quest of them. The admiral, with the fleet under his command, left Plymouth on August 9th. The French fleet, consisting of the above-mentioned men-of-war and two hundred and fifty-two merchant vessels, sailed from the Isle of Aix on October 6th, and on the 14th they had the misfortune to fall in with the British squadron. As soon as the French admiral became sensible of his situation, he made a signal for the trade to make the best of their way with the *Content* and frigates, and for the rest of his squadron to prepare for battle. Admiral Hawke first made a signal to form the line; but finding the French begin to sheer off, he ordered his whole fleet to give chase and engage as they came up with the enemy. The *Lion* and the *Louisa* began the conflict about noon and were soon followed by the *Tilbury*, the *Eagle*, the *Yarmouth*, the *Windsor*, and the *Devonshire*, which ships particularly shared the danger and consequently the glory of the day.

About four o'clock four of the French squadron struck—*viz.*, *Le Neptune*, *Le Monarque*, *Le Fougeux*, and *Le Severn*; at five *Le Trident* followed their example and *Le Terrible* surrendered about seven. Be it, however, remembered, to the credit of their several commanders, that they maintained this unequal conflict with great spirit and resolution, and that they did not submit until they were entirely disabled. Their number of killed and wounded was about eight hundred, and of prisoners three thousand three hundred men. M. Fromentierre, who commanded *Le Neptune*, was among the slain, and their commander-in-chief was wounded in the leg and in the shoulder. The English had one hundred and fifty-four killed and five hundred and fifty-eight wounded. Captain Saumarez, of the *Nottingham*, was among the former. We lost no other officer of distinction. On the last day of October Admiral Hawke brought these six French men-of-war to Portsmouth in triumph, and, in reward for his services, was soon after honoured with the Order of the Bath.

During this year the English took from the French and Spaniards six hundred and forty-four prizes, among which were one Spanish and seventeen French men-of-war. The English vessels, including one man-of-war and a fire-ship, taken by the French and Spaniards, amounted to five hundred and fifty-one. The Royal Navy of Spain was now reduced to twenty-two ships of the line, and that of France to thirty-one; whilst the navy of Britain amounted to one hundred and twenty-six sail of the line besides seventy-five frigates.

The Loss of H.M.S. "Namur"
By James Alms

On July 15th, 1747, Captain Boscawen was made rear admiral of the blue, and placed at the head of a large military and naval expedition dispatched to the East Indies. In 1749 soon after the peace of Aix-la-Chapelle had put an end to hostilities.

The fleet was lying in the road of Fort St. David, when on the 12th of April it began to blow most violently from the north-north-west. The following day the fleet encountered a terrible storm in which the flag-ship the *Namur*, seventy-four guns, foundered; the admiral, captain, and several of the officers being fortunately on shore. The *Pembroke*, of sixty guns, was also lost in this storm.

Mr. Alms, of the *Namur*, gives the following account of the loss of that ship, in a letter to Mr. Ives:—

> We were at anchor in the *Namur*, in Fort St. David's road, Thursday, April 13th, 1749. In the morning it blew fresh, wind north-east. At noon we veered away to a half cable on the small bower. From one to four o'clock we were employed in setting up the lower rigging. Hard gales and squally, with a very great sea. At six o'clock the ship rode very well, but half an hour afterwards had four feet of water in her hold. We immediately cut the small bower cable, and stood to sea under our courses. Our mate, who cut the cable, was up to his waist in water at the bitts.
>
> At half-past seven we had six feet of water in the hold, when we hauled up our courses and heaved overboard most of our upper-deck and all the quarter-deck guns to the leeward. By three-quarters after eight the water was up to our orlop gratings, and there was a great quantity between decks so that the ship was water logged; when we cut away all the masts, by

which she righted. At the same time we manned the pumps and baled, and soon perceived that we gained upon the ship, which put us in great spirits. A little after nine we sounded, and found ourselves in nine fathoms of water: the master called, 'Cut away the sheet-anchor!' which was done immediately, and we veered away to a little better than a cable; but, before the ship came head to the sea, she parted at the chesstree. By this time it blew a hurricane. It is easier to conceive than to describe what a dismal, melancholy scene now presented itself—the shrieking cries, lamentations, ravings, despair, of above five hundred poor wretches verging on the brink of eternity!

I had, however, presence of mind to consider that the Almighty was at the same time all-merciful, and experienced consolation in the reflection that I had ever put my whole trust in Him. In a short prayer I then implored His protection, and jumped overboard. The water, at that time, was up to the gratings of the poop, from which I leaped. The first thing I grappled was a capstan-bar, by means of which, in company with seven more, I got to the davit; but, in less than an hour, I had the melancholy experience of seeing them all washed away, and finding myself upon it alone, and almost exhausted. I had now been above two hours in the water, when, to my unspeakable joy, I saw a large raft with a great many men driving towards me. When it came near I quitted the davit, and with great difficulty swam to the raft, upon which I got, with the assistance of one of our quarter-gunners. The raft proved to be the *Namur's* booms. As soon as we were able we lashed the booms close together, fastened a plank across them, and by these means made a good catamaran.

It was by this time one o'clock in the morning; soon afterwards the seas became so mountainous that they turned our machine upside down, but providentially, with the loss of only one man. About four, we struck ground with the booms, and, in a very short time, all the survivors reached the shore. After having returned thanks to God for His almost miraculous goodness towards us, we took each other by the hand, for it was not yet day, and still trusting to the Divine Providence for protection, we walked forward in search of some place to shelter ourselves from the inclemency of the weather; for the spot where we landed offered nothing but sand.

When we had walked about for a whole hour, but to no manner of purpose, we returned to the place where we had left our catamaran, and to our no small uneasiness found that it was gone. Daylight appearing, we found ourselves on a sandy bank, a little to the southward of Porto Novo, from which we were divided by a river that we were under the necessity of fording, soon after which we arrived at the Dutch settlement where we were received with much hospitality. From our first landing till our arrival at Porto Novo we lost four of our company, two at the place where we were driven ashore, and two in crossing the river.

After we had sufficiently refreshed ourselves at Porto Novo, the chief there was so obliging as to accommodate me with clothes, a horse and a guide to carry me to Fort St. David, where I arrived about noon the following day, and immediately waited on the admiral, who received me very kindly indeed; but so excessive was the concern of that great and good man for the loss of so many poor souls, that he could not find utterance for those questions he appeared desirous of asking me concerning the particulars of our disaster.

"Till I reached Porto Novo, you beheld me shipwrecked and naked; I must again repeat it, that the Dutch received, refreshed, and kindly conveyed me to my truly honourable patron, through whose kindness and humanity I am not only well clothed and comforted, but am also made lieutenant of the *Syren*, from which ship I date this letter. I am, etc.,

James Alms.

P.S.—There were only twenty-three of us saved on the wreck; twenty of whom came ashore on the booms.

The Loss of H.M.S. "Pembroke"
By Master Cambridge

The melancholy fate of the *Namur*, which was lost at the same time and place as the *Pembroke*, has already been related. The calamity which befell the latter was, if possible, still more deplorable. Out of her whole crew, only twelve persons were saved; her commander, Captain Fincher, and about three hundred and thirty men were drowned, among whom were all the officers excepting a captain of marines. The following particulars of this disaster are given by an eyewitness, Mr. Cambridge, the master.

> About ten o'clock in the morning of April 13th, 1749, it blew fresh, the wind at north-east by east and a great sea began to come in: we having then a cable out the captain ordered half a cable more to be veered away. At one in the afternoon it blew very hard, the wind at north-east. His Majesty's ship *Namur*, lying about a cable's length within us and abaft our beam, I went to the captain, as did likewise the lieutenants, and desired him to go to sea. He replied, he could not answer to go to sea unless the *Namur* did (on board which Rear-Admiral Boscawen's flag was flying), but ordered all our ports to be barred in and well secured.
>
> At three o'clock I went to the captain, who was sick and in his cabin, and again desired him to go to sea. He seemed angry, and said he could not, giving the same reason as before, nor would he suffer any more cable to be veered away. At the same time the ship rode hard, strained much, and made water.
>
> "At five, the sea increasing, our cable parted, and we cast our head off to the sea; otherwise we should have fallen on board the *Namur*. We immediately set the fore and mizen sails, got on board the main-tack, and set our main sail, fore and mizen stay-

sails; at the same time some of our people were employed in heaving in the cable, for the captain would not have it cut. This took up some time; it blew so very hard that the ship would not bear any more sail.

At six, there being a great head sea, we made very little way, and were obliged to set both pumps to work. At half-past six our main sail split in pieces; we got down the yard in order to bend a new sail; but it blowing hard, the ship lay down so much that we could not get the sail to the yard. At eight the carpenter sent word to the captain that the ship gained upon them much, and had four feet of water in her hold.

At half-past eight our tiller broke short off at the rudder-head, and we likewise found one of the rudder chains broken: the sails we had now set were our fore sail, mizen, and fore-stay sails. The sea made a free passage over us, and the ship being water logged, we hauled up our fore sail to ease her, but expected to go down every minute. In hauling down our fore-stay sail it split; and as I looked aft from the forecastle, I saw the main and mizen masts had gone, though I never heard them go. By this time the ship righted much, and in about seven minutes the foremast went by the board, but the bowsprit held fast. Our pumps were kept continually working. The third lieutenant being on the quarter-deck, sent forward to me to clear and let go the small bower anchor, which was immediately done. We found the ship drove to shore very fast.

At half-past ten, we had eight feet of water in the hold, and kept all the pumps working. About eleven we found the ship settle; the depth of water twelve or fourteen fathoms. The anchor then brought the ship up, but the cable parted in a few minutes: then we let go the sheet anchor, which was all we had. The sea now making a free passage over us again, broke and tore away our boats and booms. The sheet cable tore out with such violence that no person could venture near it till the clench brought up the ship: but the sea came with such force and was so very high that in the hollow of the sea the ship struck, and the cable immediately parted.

It was now near twelve o'clock; the ship struck fore and aft, but abaft very hard. The third lieutenant was near me when the ship first struck, but I saw no more of him afterwards. I kept the forecastle accompanied by the boatswain, cook, and about eight more men. I got myself lashed to the bitts before the ship took heel, but shifted myself over to windward when she began to heel, and lashed myself as before: the sea continually beating over us. About two I saw the captain's cabin washed away, and the ship almost on her broadside.

When daylight came, we were sixteen men on the forecastle and four hanging abaft to the timber heads; but three of the latter got upon a piece of the wreck which was loose, and drove away; the other was drowned. All this time the sea came over us in a dreadful manner, so that we could scarcely take breath.

About eight o'clock nine men were washed off the forecastle. We could not now see the trees on shore between the seas. At nine, the boatswain and cook were washed away from each side of me, on which I removed to the cat-head, as did likewise another man. About ten all our men were washed away, excepting those who were lashed to the cat-head. We judged that we were about two miles off the shore: we continued there all the day; the sea beating over us incessantly, so that we had little time to fetch breath or speak to one another.

At noon we found the sea to come every way upon us, and could perceive that the wind having shifted was the cause of it. This part of the wreck kept together, but night coming on, we had a dismal prospect before us, without any hopes of relief. About midnight the sea abated, so that we could speak to one another for the space of two or three minutes together; but I found myself so weak, having been sick ever since we arrived in the country, that when the sea washed me on one side in my lashing, I was not able to help myself up, but was obliged to get my companion to assist me.

At daylight I found myself much weaker and very thirsty. The sea at this time came over us once in a quarter of an hour. We found the wreck much nearer the shore than yesterday. About noon we found the sea much abated, so that it seldom came over us, and the weather began to be fine, but I felt extremely faint. About two or three o'clock we saw two paddy boats coming along shore, about a mile away from us. We spread out a handkerchief, which I had about my neck, that the boats might see us. One of them seemed to edge towards us for some minutes, but hauled off again. We then saw several catamarans near the shore, which we judged to be fishing. We spread abroad the handkerchief again, but none of them approached us. Soon afterwards we saw several people gather together on shore; the sun began to grow low, so that we judged it to be about five o'clock. At last we saw two of the catamarans above mentioned coming towards us, with three black men on each, who took us off the wreck and carried us on shore.

As soon as we were landed, we found ourselves surrounded by about three hundred armed men. My companion told me we had fallen into the hands of the Mahrattas, who were at this time at war with the English. They ordered us to come off the catamarans. I strove to rise, but I found myself so weak and my legs so terribly bruised that I could not get up; on which some of them came and lifted me off, and laid me on the sand, for I was unable to stand. I made a signal to them that I wanted some water to drink, but they gave me none, and only laughed at our condition. Their commander ordered them to strip us, which they did quite naked.

As I was not able to walk, they led us part of the way to Cavecotta, a fort belonging to them, and there put us into a canoe, and carried us up a river to the walls of the fort. About ten that night they put us within the walls and laid us on the ground, where we had nothing to cover us but the heavens, and about eleven brought us a little rice with some water. Great numbers of people gathered round us, laughing at us and expressing great contempt and derision.

The country people flocked daily to the fort to see us, but none of them showed us the least pity; on the contrary, they laughed and threatened us with death. We slept very little the first night on account of the cold and the risk we ran of our lives, these barbarians having signified that they would cut us in pieces with their sabres. When daylight appeared and the gates were opened, I was very ill. I had dysentery, and my legs were so much swelled that I concluded I had not long to live, at least if I did not receive some relief. I acquainted my comrade with my situation, and begged him, if he ever should be so fortunate as to return to England, to inform my friends in what manner I had terminated my career. Some days we received rice and others we had none. On the seventh day they gave me some lamp oil, with which I fomented my legs, and this simple application afforded me considerable relief.

Our lodging place was between the gate-ways; and when we had been there fourteen days they carried us into the country. Though my legs were much better, yet still I could not walk; and my companion was extremely weak, which I believe was owing to the want of more victuals. So they put us into *dooleys* or cradles, fastened together with ropes, which they got from the wreck.

About four o'clock on the fifteenth day they carried us about twelve miles to their king, who was encamped against our company's troops. That prince examined us a long time, and inquired whether we were officers: I replied in the negative, conceiving that an acknowledgment of that kind would render our escape much more difficult. He was desirous that we should enter into his service, but we told him by means of the interpreters, who were three Dutchmen, that we could not consent to it. He promised we should want for nothing if we would accept his offers; but we persisted in replying that we were too ill to be capable of serving. He ordered refreshment to be given to us, of which we stood in great need, having scarcely taken any nourishment since the day we fell into the hands of his subjects. The interpreters asked us whether we chose to enter into the king's service or to go to prison; to which we answered that we could not resolve to fight against our countrymen.

At sunset we departed. Our conductors having halted till three o'clock in the morning, we again set out and continued our march till noon, when they again stopped two hours to take some refreshment, and afterwards directed their course to the south-west. We arrived that night at a fort and were immediately put into a dungeon. There we found two other prisoners, one of them our shipmate and the other a deserter from the company's troops.

The next morning they opened the gates and made signs to us to come out. My companions complied, but I chose rather to stay where I was as I found myself extremely weak and my legs were covered with ulcers. I begged them to give me a little lamp oil to foment them, which they did. Our only nourishment was water and a quart of rice a day, though there were four of us, and a small pot of grease instead of butter. I rubbed my legs with oil and grease, and on the fourth day found myself much better, which gave me fresh spirits. We were permitted to walk morning and evening before the dungeon.

In about three weeks my legs were almost well, so that I was able to walk. We began to entertain some hopes of making our escape, and taking an opportunity, I, with some difficulty, got high enough upon the wall to look over it, and found it was very lofty and surrounded with a wide moat or ditch; but there was a path between the wall and the ditch, so that we might choose our place to swim over, if it proved deep. We got, several times, some strands of rope off the *dooleys* which they had carried us in, as they happened to be left within the bounds of our liberty; and in a few days collected so many pieces that when knotted together they made several fathoms.

After some consultation, we resolved to undermine the foundation of the dungeon at the farthest part from the guards, and on May 27th began to work. On June 1st we came to the foundation, being six feet deep, and the wall thirty inches through. In two days' time we had worked upwards, on the other side, so far that the light began to appear through the surface, so that we let everything remain till night. At seven it beginning to grow dark they put us into the dungeon as usual, and soon afterwards we worked ourselves quite out. Without being discovered we got over the wall by the help of our rope, and in less than half an hour had crossed the moat, though very wide and deep. We travelled all night, we judged about sixteen miles, and in the day hid ourselves among the bushes.

The second night we travelled as before, to the south-east, and day coming on, we concealed ourselves among some rushes. About three in the afternoon we were discovered, which obliged us to go on; but we were not molested. We proceeded till about midnight, and then lay down till daybreak. I had a fever and was extremely weak for want of food. This day, which was the third, we resolved to travel till noon, and to plunder the first house we might chance to meet with. But Providence was more favourable to us than we could have expected; for about ten o'clock we met a *cooley* who told us he would show us to Caracal. About noon we arrived there, and were received with great humanity; but my fever was no better.

The next morning the governor sent to Mr. Boscawen to let him know we were there, and by the return of the messenger the admiral desired we might be furnished with what money we wanted. In about twelve days we found ourselves well recovered, and went to Tranquebar, a place belonging to the Danes, where we stayed three days, and got a passage for Fort St. David where we arrived on June 23rd.

The Story of Admiral the Honourable John Byng

The honourable John Byng was the fourth son of George Viscount Torrington, and was born at his father's seat at Southill, in Bedfordshire, in the year 1704. Showing a strong inclination for the navy, his father took him to sea with him when he was only thirteen years old; and so rapid was his promotion, that at twenty-three he was made captain of the *Gibraltar* frigate, then stationed in the Mediterranean. These were, comparatively speaking, peaceable times, and the record of the next twenty-five years was one of routine service, honourably performed and rewarded by steady promotion.

Towards the end of the year 1755 the British Government received intelligence that a powerful armament was equipping in Toulon, which was intended to act against Fort St. Philip. Though the case was urgent, the government took no notice of repeated warnings until at last, on the strong and positive representation of General Blakeney that his garrison must be reinforced if the ministry wished to retain it, they made a tardy and inadequate arrangement to relieve the garrison and protect the Island of Minorca.

To effect this purpose it was necessary to send out a fleet and a reinforcement of troops. The command of this fleet they gave to Admiral Byng, whom they promoted to the rank of admiral of the blue. The ministers were blamed at the time for appointing Admiral Byng to this command. The service was one of the greatest importance; it required not only great personal courage and professional skill and experience, but also a comprehensive judgment and great activity and zeal, and Admiral Byng, whatever talents he possessed, had never had an opportunity of displaying them; he was, in fact, without that degree of experience which ought to have been regarded as an indispensable requisite in the person entrusted with this command. Moreover, the force placed under his command was inadequate to the service; it consisted only of ten sail of the line, several of which were not in a proper condition either for fighting or going to sea; and most of them were either short of their complement of men, or manned by crews consisting of young and inexperienced seamen.

On April 7th, 1756, Admiral Byng sailed from St. Helen's, and on May 2nd he arrived at Gibraltar. From this place he wrote a letter to the Admiralty, which is supposed, by reflecting on the conduct of ministers, to have irritated them against him. On May 8th he sailed for Minorca, but having contrary winds, did not make that island until the morning of the 19th, when he saw the English flag still flying on the castle of St. Philip, and several bomb-batteries playing upon it from the enemy's works. Early in the morning the admiral despatched Captain Hervey, in the *Phœnix*, with the *Chesterfield* and *Dolphin*, with orders to reconnoitre the entrance into the harbour, and, if possible, to convey a letter to General Blakeney. Captain Hervey got round the Laire, and made signals to the garrison for a boat to come off, but without effect; and the admiral, about this time discovering the French fleet, ordered him to return.

At two o'clock on the following day Admiral Byng made a signal to bear away two points from the wind and engage. Rear-Admiral West was then at too great a distance to comply with both these orders; he therefore bore away seven points from the wind, and with his whole division attacked the enemy with such impetuosity that several of their ships were soon obliged to quit the line. Had Admiral Byng been equally alert, it is most probable that the French fleet would have been defeated and Minorca saved; but the enemy's centre keeping their station, and Byng's division not advancing, Admiral West was prevented from pursuing his advantage by the danger of being separated from the rest of the fleet.

After engaging about a quarter of an hour, the *Intrepid*, the sternmost ship of the van, lost her foretop mast, which, according to Byng's account of the action, obliged his whole division to back their sails to prevent their falling foul of each other. But when this matter came to be examined by the court martial, it appeared that immediately after the signal for engaging, while the van were bearing down upon the enemy, Admiral Byng, in the *Ramillies*, edged away some points, by which means the *Trident* and *Louisa* got to windward of him, and that, in order to bring them again into their stations, he backed his mizen-top sail, and endeavoured to back his main-top sail. This manoeuvre necessarily retarded all the ships in his division and gave the enemy time to escape. M. Galissoniere seized the opportunity, and, his ships being clean, he was soon out of danger.

The English had in this engagement forty-two men killed and one hundred and sixty-eight wounded; the French one hundred and forty-five wounded and twenty-six killed. The next morning the admiral, finding that three of his squadron were damaged in their masts, called a council of war, which decided to proceed to Gibraltar.

Admiral Byng wrote an account of this engagement, which he sent to the Admiralty who, after some delay, published it with excisions which materially affected the impression it was likely to produce.

Not only were parts of Admiral Byng's letter withheld from the public, but the letter itself, though said to have been received on June 16th, was not inserted in the *Gazette* till the 26th of that month. The hired writers in the pay of the ministry were instantly set to work to censure his conduct in the most violent and inflammatory language. One fact was particularly pointed out and most strenuously insisted upon as a proof of personal cowardice; from the returns of the killed and wounded on board of the different ships it appeared that on board the *Ramillies*, Admiral Byng's own ship, there was not one man either killed or wounded.

Sir Edward Hawke and Admiral Saunders were ordered to supersede Mr. Byng, whom they were instructed to send home under arrest. By this time the popular clamour and indignation were so extremely violent that government were afraid some of it would be directed against themselves unless they placed it beyond doubt that they were resolved to proceed against Mr. Byng without the least delay, and in the most rigorous manner.

The admiral landed at Portsmouth. At every place that he passed through he was hooted by the mob. On the road to Greenwich Hospital, where he was to remain until his trial, he was guarded as if he had been guilty of the most heinous crime, while that part of the hospital where he was confined was most scrupulously and carefully fortified, the government taking care that all their precautions to prevent his escape should be made known.

On December 27th, 1756, the court martial assembled on board the *St. George* in Portsmouth Harbour, and on January 15th, 1757, the evidence concluded. The opinion of the court was that "the admiral did not do his utmost to relieve the garrison of St. Philip, and that during the engagement he did not do his utmost to take, seize, and destroy the ships of the French king, and assist such of his own ships as were engaged." They therefore came to the following resolution:—

> That the admiral appears to fall under the following part of the twelfth article of the articles of war, *viz.*—'or shall not do his utmost to take or destroy every ship which it shall be his duty to engage, and to assist and relieve all and every of His Majesty's ships which it shall be his duty to assist and relieve': and as that article positively prescribes death, without any alternative left to the discretion of the court, under any variation of circumstances, resolved that he be adjudged to be shot to death at such time, and on board such ship, as the lords commissioners of the Admiralty shall direct; but as it appears by the evidence of Lord Robert Bertie, Lieutenant-colonel Smith, Captain Gardiner, and other officers of the ship, who were near the person of the admiral, that they did not perceive any backwardness in him during the action, or any marks of fear or confusion, either from his countenance or behaviour, but that he seemed to give his orders coolly and distinctly and did not seem wanting in personal courage, and from other circumstances the court do not believe that his misconduct arose either from cowardice or disaffection, and do therefore unanimously think it their duty most earnestly to recommend him as a proper object of mercy.

Not only in their resolution did the court martial recommend him to mercy, but in the letter which accompanied a copy of their proceedings to the board of Admiralty they expressed themselves strongly to the same effect.

Notwithstanding these repeated, strong, and earnest representations of the opinion and wishes of the court martial, the lords of the Admiralty contented themselves, when they laid before His Majesty a copy of the proceedings, with transmitting the letters of the court martial; hinting, indeed, a doubt respecting the legality of the sentence, because the crime of negligence, for which alone Admiral Byng was condemned, did not appear in any part of the proceedings. When the sentence was known, George, Lord Viscount Torrington, a near relation of the admiral's, presented two petitions to His Majesty; and his other friends interested themselves in his behalf: but the people were so clamorous and violent that it would scarcely have been safe to have pardoned him; however, in consequence of the representation of the lords of the Admiralty respecting the doubtful legality of the sentence, His Majesty referred it to the twelve judges, who were unanimous in their opinion that it was legal. The next step was to transmit this opinion to the lords of the Admiralty, in order that they might sign the warrant for the execution. All the lords signed it, except Admiral Forbes, who entered his reasons for his refusal.

Admiral Forbes was not the only naval officer who resolutely honourably stood forward and protested against the sentence passed upon Admiral Byng. Mr. West, who had been second in command under him in the Mediterranean, and who on his return was appointed one of the lords commissioners of the Admiralty, and soon afterwards commander-in-chief of a squadron destined for a secret expedition, on the very day sentence was passed on Admiral Byng wrote official and private letters, declining these appointments on account of the treatment of Admiral Byng.

When the warrant was signed, Mr. Keppel, one of the members of the court martial, rose in his place in the House of Commons, and prayed, on behalf of himself and some other members of the court, that they might be released from their oath of secrecy, in order to disclose the reasons which had induced them to pass sentence of death upon Admiral Byng; as, probably, by this disclosure, some circumstances might come out that would prove the sentence to be illegal. To this the Commons agreed, and an order was sent down to Portsmouth to respite the execution of the admiral until March 14th. The House of Lords, however, after interrogating the members of the court martial who were responsible for the bill, unanimously rejected it.

On his way to receive sentence on board the *St. George* Admiral Byng told some of his friends that he expected to be reprimanded, and possibly he might be cashiered; "because," added he, "there must have been several controverted points: the court martial has been shut up a long time, and almost all the questions proposed by the court have tended much more to pick out faults in my conduct than to get a true state of the circumstances; but I profess I cannot conceive what they will fix upon."

When he arrived on board the *St. George*, and as he was walking on the quarter-deck, a member of the court martial came out and told one of his relations that they had found the admiral capitally guilty, and requested him to prepare him for his sentence. The gentleman to whom this communication was made went up to him immediately, but was unable to address him for some time; his countenance, however, and the embarrassment of his manner, led the admiral to suspect that he had some unpleasant intelligence to communicate; and he said to him, "What is the matter? have they broke me?" The gentleman, perceiving from this question that he was totally unprepared for his sentence, hesitated still more: upon which the countenance of the admiral changed a little, and he added, "Well, I understand—if nothing but my blood will satisfy, let them take it."

A few minutes afterwards one of his friends endeavoured to support and reconcile him to his fate by observing that a sentence without guilt could be no stain; and adding that it was extremely unlikely that the sentence would be carried into execution, begged him to indulge the hope of obtaining a pardon; he replied, "What will that signify to me? What satisfaction can I receive from the liberty to crawl a few years longer on the earth with the infamous load of a pardon at my back? I despise life upon such terms, and would rather have them take it."

When the respite for fourteen days came down to Portsmouth, his friends endeavoured to encourage the expectation that he would be honourably pardoned, and dwelt upon every circumstance which gave countenance and probability to this idea; to them he replied, in a calm and unembarrassed manner, "I am glad *you* think so, because it makes you easy and happy; but I think it has now become an affair merely political, without any relation to right or wrong, justice or injustice; and therefore I differ in opinion from you."

Immediately after he received his sentence he was put on board the *Monarque*, a third-rate man-of-war, lying at anchor in the harbour of Portsmouth, under a strong guard, in the custody of the marshal of the Admiralty. On Sunday morning, March 13th, Captain Montague, who had received the warrant from Admiral Boscawen for his execution next day, gave it to the admiral for him to read; he read it over without the slightest sign of perturbation, and then remarked with some warmth that "the place named in the warrant for his execution was upon the forecastle." A circumstance which evidently filled his mind with indignation.

His friends endeavoured to turn his thoughts from this idea; they could not indeed hold out to him the expectation that the place would be changed, because the warrant expressly named it: they coincided with him in the opinion that it ought not to have been so; but they trusted, at this awful and important moment, he would deem such a circumstance beneath his notice, and not suffer it to break in upon the tranquillity of his mind. On this he composed his thoughts and feelings, and replied, "It is very true, the place or manner is of no great importance to me; but I think living admirals should consult the dignity of the rank for their own sakes. I cannot plead a precedent; there is no precedent of an admiral, or a general officer in the army, being shot. They make a precedent of me, such as admirals hereafter may feel the effects of."

During the time he was at dinner no alteration in his manner was observable; he was cheerful and polite, helping his friends and drinking their healths; but he did not continue long at table. After dinner he conversed a good deal respecting his approaching execution; and the indignation and uneasiness he had before felt about the place appointed for it recurred with considerable force in his thoughts. His friends were extremely desirous of conversing on other subjects; and at length, perceiving this, he remarked, "I like to talk upon the subject; it is not to be supposed I do not think of it; why then should it be more improper to talk of it?" He frequently noticed how the wind was; and on his friends inquiring the reason of his anxiety on this subject, he said he hoped it might continue westerly long enough for the members of the court martial (who were just about to sail) to be present when his sentence was put in execution.

About six o'clock, according to his usual custom, he ordered tea; and while he and his friends were at it his conversation was easy and cheerful. Perceiving that his friends were astonished at this circumstance, "I have observed," said he "that persons condemned to die have generally had something to be sorry for that they have expressed concern for having committed; and though I do not pretend to be exempt from human frailties, yet it is my consolation to have no remorse for any transaction in my public character during the whole series of my long services."

On one of his friends observing that no man was exempt from human frailties, and that what came under that denomination were not crimes cognisable here, or supposed to be so hereafter, he replied, "I am conscious of no crimes, and am particularly happy in not dying the mean, despicable, ignominious wretch my enemies would have the world to believe me. I hope I am not supposed so now; the court martial has acquitted me of everything criminal or ignominious." One of his friends assured him that none called or thought him so but persons who were obstinately prejudiced against him, and his enemies, whose interest and design it was to deceive the nation; and it was vain to expect that they would be induced to change their opinion or do him justice by any reasoning or statement. This observation seemed to please him much.

In the evening he ordered a small bowl of punch to be made; and as all his friends were seated round the table, taking his own glass with a little punch in it, after having helped his friends, he said, "My friends, here is all your healths, and God bless you; I am pleased to find I have some friends still, notwithstanding my misfortunes." After drinking his glass, he added, "I am to die tomorrow, and as my country requires my life, I am ready to resign it, though I do not as yet know what my crime is. I think my judges, in justice to posterity, to officers who come after us, should have explained my crime a little more and pointed out the way to avoid falling into the same errors I did. As the sentence and resolutions stand now, I am persuaded no admiral will be wiser hereafter by them, or know better how to conduct himself on the like occasion." Observing one or his friends with his eyes attentively fixed upon him while he was speaking: "My friend," said he, "I understand reproof in that grave look. It is a long time since I have spoken so much upon the subject, and you now think I say too much; perhaps I do so."

"Far from presuming to mean any reproof," replied his friend, "I am all attention to what you say, sir; and though all of us here are satisfied of these truths, yet we must be pleased to hear you make them plainer."

The admiral was always watched in the great cabin during the night by officers who relieved one another at twelve at night and at four o'clock in the morning. At these hours he was seldom found awake; but the night before his execution at both hours he was found in a tranquil and profound sleep.

He had always been in the habit of rising very early; and while he was on board the *Monarque* he used to banter the marshal for not being up so soon as he was. On Monday morning, the day of his execution, he was up by five o'clock: the marshal did not make his appearance till six; and when he saw him, "Well," said he, "I think I have beat you at rising this morning." Soon afterwards, when he was shifting, as he regularly did every morning, "Here," said he to his valet, "take these sleeve-buttons and wear them for my sake; yours will do to be buried with."

As soon as he was dressed he returned to the state-room by himself, where he spent some time; on coming out he sat down to breakfast with the marshal as composedly as usual. He was dressed in a light grey coat, white waistcoat and white stockings, and a large white wig. These clothes he had regularly worn since he received the intelligence of his suspension at Gibraltar; for after having read the order he stripped off his uniform and threw it into the sea.

About nine o'clock his friends came on board the *Monarque*; he received them in an easy, familiar manner, took each of them by the hand and inquired after their health. They informed him that the place of his execution was changed; that it was not to take place on the forecastle, but on the quarter-deck. This intelligence seemed to give him great satisfaction. He had constantly declared his resolution to die with his face uncovered, and to give the word of command to the platoon of marines himself; saying, "As it is my fate I can look at it and receive it." His friends were grieved at this determination and endeavoured to dissuade him from it; sometimes he seemed disposed to comply with their wishes, but at other times he replied, "No, it cannot be; I cannot bear it; I must look and receive my fate."

His friends, however, persevered in representing to him that, considering his rank, it was impossible the marines could receive the word of command from him, or look in his face and see him looking at them without being intimidated and awed; they hinted, also, at the consequences which might result; that he might be wounded only and mangled. By arguments and entreaties they at length prevailed upon him to have a bandage over his eyes, and to make a signal by dropping a handkerchief.

He then requested to be made acquainted with all the particulars of the form, in order that he might conduct himself strictly according to them, remarking that he had never been present at an execution.

As soon as the admiral had agreed upon the signal he was to make, it was communicated to the commanding officer of the marines, in order that he might instruct his men accordingly; and he was also desired to tell them that they should have ten guineas if they conducted themselves properly. The marines were drawn up, under arms, upon the poop, along the gangways, in the waist, and on one side of the quarter-deck. A heap of sawdust was thrown on the other side of the quarter-deck, and a cushion placed upon it; in the middle, upon the gratings, a platoon of nine marines were drawn up in three lines, three in each: the two foremost lines, which were intended to fire, had their bayonets fixed, as is customary on such occasions.

Orders had been given for all the men-of-war at Spithead to send their boats, with the captains and all the officers of each ship, accompanied by a party of marines under arms, to attend the execution. In compliance with these orders they rowed from Spithead and made the harbour a little after eleven o'clock; but with great difficulty and danger, as it blew a dreadful gale at west-north-west and the tide was ebbing. Notwithstanding the state of the weather, there was a prodigious number of other boats present.

About eleven o'clock Admiral Byng, walking across his cabin, and observing the crowd of boats out of one of the cabin windows, took up a glass to view them more distinctly. The decks, shrouds, and yards of all the ships that lay near were crowded with men; upon which he remarked, "Curiosity is strong; it draws a great number of people together; but their curiosity will be disappointed: where they are, they may hear, but they cannot see." A gentleman said to him, "To see you so easy and composed, sir, gives me as much pleasure as I can have on this occasion; but I expected no less from the whole of your conduct heretofore; and the last actions of a man mark his character more than all the actions of his life." "I am sensible they do, sir," replied he, "and am obliged to you for putting me in mind. I find innocence is the best foundation for firmness of mind."

He continued to walk about in the cabin for some time; inquired what time it would be high water; observed that the tide would not suit to carry his body ashore after dark; expressed some apprehensions that his body might be insulted if it were carried ashore in the daytime, on account of the prejudices of the people against him: but his friends assuring him that there was no such disposition among the inhabitants of Portsmouth, he appeared very well satisfied.

He walked out of the great cabin to the quarter-deck, accompanied by a clergyman, who had attended him during his confinement, and two gentlemen, his relations. One of these went with him to the cushion and offered to tie the bandage over his eyes; but he, having a white handkerchief ready folded in his hand, replied, with a smile on his countenance, "I am obliged to you, sir; I thank God I can do it myself; I think I can; I am sure I can;" and tied it behind his head himself.

He continued upon his knees rather more than a minute, much composed, and apparently recommending himself to the Almighty, and then dropped his handkerchief, the signal agreed upon, a few minutes before twelve o'clock. On this a volley was fired from the six marines, five of whose bullets went through him, and he was in an instant no more: the sixth bullet went over his head. The spectators were amazed at the intrepidity of his behaviour, and scarcely could refrain from tears. One of the common seamen, who had stood all the time full of attention, with his arms across, cried out with enthusiasm, when he saw him fall, "There lies the bravest and best officer of the navy."

A few minutes before his execution he delivered to the marshal of the Admiralty the following paper, addressing himself to him in these words:—

> Sir, these are my thoughts on this occasion. I give them to you that you may authenticate them and prevent anything spurious being published that might tend to defame me. I have given a copy to one of my relations.
>
> A few moments will now deliver me from the virulent persecutions and frustrate the farther malice of my enemies: nor need I envy them a life subject to the sensations my injuries and the injustice done me must create. Persuaded, I am, justice will be done to my reputation hereafter: the manner and cause of raising and keeping up the popular clamour and prejudice against me will be seen through. I shall be considered (as I now perceive myself) a victim destined to divert the indignation and resentment of an injured and deluded people from the proper objects.
>
> My enemies themselves must now think me innocent. Happy for me, at this my last moment, that I know my own innocence, and am conscious that no part of my country's misfortunes can be owing to me. I heartily wish the shedding my blood may contribute to the happiness and service of my country; but cannot resign my just claim to a faithful discharge of my duty according to the best of my judgment and the utmost exertion of my ability for His Majesty's honour and my country's service. I am sorry that my endeavours were not attended with more success, and that the armament under my command proved too weak to succeed in an expedition of such moment.
>
> Truth has prevailed over calumny and falsehood; and justice has wiped off the ignominious stain of my supposed want of personal courage or disaffection. My heart acquits me of these crimes. But who can be presumptuously sure of his own judgment? If my crime is an error of judgment, or differing in opin-

ion from my judges, and if yet the error in judgment should be on their side, God forgive them, as I do; and may the distress of their minds and uneasiness of their consciences, which in justice to me they have represented, be believed and subside, as my resentment has done.

The supreme Judge sees all hearts and motives, and to Him I must submit the justice of my cause.

J. Byng.

On board His Majesty's ship *Monarque*, in Portsmouth Harbour, March 14th, 1757.

In his parish church, at Southill, is the following inscription to the memory of this unfortunate officer:—

TO THE PERPETUAL DISGRACE OF
PUBLIC JUSTICE,
THE HONOURABLE JOHN BYNG,
VICE-Admiral OF THE BLUE,
FELL A MARTYR TO
POLITICAL PERSECUTION
ON MARCH 14, IN THE YEAR 1757:
WHEN BRAVERY AND LOYALTY
WERE INSUFFICIENT SECURITIES
FOR THE LIFE AND HONOUR
OF A NAVAL OFFICER.

In Indian Seas
1758-9

Though the great achievements of large fleets are apt to monopolise fame, it often happens in the story of our English navy that small squadrons in out-of-the-way places show equal heroism in achieving less important results. Of such services the following are illustrations.

Captain Forrest, of the *Augusta*, having sailed from Port Royal in Jamaica, in 1758, proceeded to cruise off Cape Francis, a harbour in the island of St. Domingo; he was accompanied by Captains Suckling and Langdon, commanding the *Dreadnought* and *Edinburgh*. There lay at that time, at the Cape, a French squadron of four ships of the line and three stout frigates, which the French commodore, piqued at seeing the coast insulted by Forrest's little squadron, reinforced with several store-ships, which he mounted with cannon and supplied with seamen from the merchant vessels and with soldiers from the garrison. Thus prepared, he weighed anchor and stood out for sea.

When Forrest perceived the approach of the French ships, he called his two captains. "Gentlemen," said he, "you know our own strength and see that of the enemy. Shall we give them battle?" Being answered in the affirmative, he bore down on the French fleet, and between three and four in the afternoon came to action. The French attacked with great impetuosity, and displayed uncommon spirit in the sight of their own coast. But, after an engagement of more than two hours, their commodore found his ship so much shattered that he was obliged to make a signal for his frigates to tow him out of the line. The rest of the squadron followed his example, and availed themselves of the land breeze to escape in the night from the three British ships, which were too much damaged in their sails and rigging to pursue their victory.

Captain Forrest signalised his courage in this engagement; but he displayed equal courage and still more uncommon conduct and sagacity in a subsequent adventure near the western coast of Hispaniola. Having received intelligence that there was a considerable French fleet at Port au Prince, a harbour on that coast, ready to sail for Europe, he proceeded from Jamaica to cruise between Hispaniola and the little island Goave. He disguised his ship with tarpaulins, hoisted Dutch colours, and, in order to avoid discovery, allowed several small vessels to pass without giving them chase.

The second day after his arrival in these parts he perceived a fleet of seven sail steering to the westward. He kept from them to prevent suspicion, but, at the approach of night, pursued them with all the sail he could crowd. About ten in the evening he came up with two vessels of the chase, one of which fired a gun and the other sheered off. The ship which had fired no sooner discovered her enemy than she submitted. Forrest manned her with thirty-five of his own crew, and now perceiving eight sail to leeward, near the harbour of Petit Goave, ordered them to stand for that place, and to intercept any vessels that attempted to reach it. He himself, in the *Augusta*, sailed directly for the French fleet, and, coming up with them by daybreak, engaged them all by turns as he could bring his guns to bear. The *Solide*, the *Theodore*, and the *Marguerite* returned his fire; but, having soon struck their colours, they were immediately secured, and then employed in taking the other vessels, of which none had the fortune to escape. The nine sail, which, by this well-conducted stratagem, had fallen into the power of one ship, and that even in the sight of their own harbours, were safely conducted to Jamaica, where the sale of their rich cargoes rewarded the merit of the captors.

While Forrest acquired wealth and glory by protecting the trade of Jamaica, the vigilance of Captain Tyrrel secured the English navigation to Antigua. In the month of March 1758 this enterprising and judicious commander demolished a fort on the island of Martinico, and destroyed four privateers riding under its protection. In November of the same year, he, in his own ship, the *Buckingham*, of sixty-four guns, accompanied by the *Weazle* sloop, commanded by Captain Boles, discovered, between the islands of Guadaloupe and Montserrat, a fleet of nineteen sail under convoy of the *Florissant*, a French man-of-war of seventy-four guns, and two frigates of which the largest carried thirty-eight, and the other twenty-six guns.

Captain Tyrrel, regardless of the great inequality of force, immediately gave chase in the *Buckingham*; and the *Weazle*, running close to the enemy, received a whole broadside from the *Florissant*. Though she sustained it without much damage, Mr. Tyrrel ordered Captain Boles to keep aloof, as his vessel could not be supposed to bear the shock of heavy metal; and he alone prepared for the engagement. The *Florissant*, instead of lying to for him, made a running fight with her stern chase, while the two frigates annoyed the *Buckingham* in her pursuit. At length, however, she came within pistol-shot of the *Florissant*, and poured in a broadside which did great execution. The salutation was returned with spirit and the battle became close and obstinate. Mr. Tyrrel, being wounded, was obliged to leave the deck, and the command devolved upon Mr. Marshall, his first lieutenant, who fell in the arms of victory. The second lieutenant took the command, and finally silenced the enemy's fire.

On board the *Florissant* one hundred and eighty men were slain and three hundred wounded. She was so much disabled in her hull that she could hardly be kept afloat. The largest frigate received equal damage. The *Buckingham* had only seven men killed and seventeen dangerously wounded; she had suffered much, however, in her masts and rigging, which was the only circumstance that prevented her from adding profit to glory by making prizes of the French fleet under so powerful a convoy.

In the East Indies the French squadron was commanded by M. d'Aché, and the English by Admiral Pocock, who had succeeded Admiral Watson. The former was reinforced by a considerable armament under the command of General Lally, an adventurer of Irish extraction in the French service. The English admiral was also reinforced March 24th, 1758, by four ships of the line; and, being soon after apprised of Lally's arrival, hoisted his flag on board the *Yarmouth*, a ship of sixty-four guns, and sailed in quest of the enemy. He made the height of Negapatam on March 28th, and the day following discovered the enemy's fleet in the road of Fort St. David. It consisted of eight ships of the line and a frigate, which immediately stood out to sea and formed the line-of-battle. Pocock's squadron consisted only of seven ships; with which he formed the line, and, bearing down upon M. d'Aché, began the engagement.

The French commodore, having sustained a warm action for about two hours in which one of his largest ships was disabled, sheered off with his whole fleet. Being afterwards joined by two more ships of war, he again formed the line-of-battle to leeward. Admiral Pocock, though his own ship and several others were considerably damaged, and though three of his captains had misbehaved in the engagement, prepared again for the attack. But the manoeuvres of the French fleet seem to have been intended merely to amuse him; for they neither showed lights nor gave any signal in the night, and next morning the smallest trace of them could not be observed.

Admiral Pocock made various attempts to bring the French squadron to a second engagement. These, however, proved ineffectual till August 3rd, when he perceived the enemy's fleet, consisting of eight ships of the line and a frigate, standing to sea off the road of Pondicherry. They would have gladly eluded his pursuit, but he obtained the weather-gauge, and sailed down upon them in order of battle. As it was now impossible to escape without coming to action the French prepared for the engagement, and fired on the *Elizabeth*, which happened to be within musket-shot of the ship in their van. But this spirited attack was not seconded with equal perseverance. In little more than ten minutes after Admiral Pocock had displayed the signal for battle, M. d'Aché set his fore-sail, and bore away, maintaining a running fight in a very irregular line for nearly an hour. The whole squadron immediately followed his example; and at two o'clock they cut away their boats, crowded sail and put before the wind. They escaped by favour of the night into the road of Pondicherry; but their fleet was so much damaged that, in the beginning of September, their commodore sailed for the Isle of Bourbon in order to refit, thus leaving the English admiral, whose squadron had always been inferior to that of the French in number of ships and men as well as in weight of metal, sovereign of the Indian seas.

In the glorious '59 the French fleet, under M. d'Aché, was augmented to eleven sail of the line, besides frigates and store-ships, an armament hitherto unknown in the Indian seas. The English commander, however, no sooner had intelligence of their arrival than he sailed to the coast of Coromandel, and determined to pursue and give them battle, notwithstanding the fact that the French had a superiority of one hundred and ninety-two guns and two thousand three hundred and sixty-five men, besides a great advantage in the size of their ships. On the morning of September 2nd the French fleet were descried from the mast-head. Admiral Pocock immediately threw out the signal for a general chase; but, the wind abating, he could not approach near enough to engage, though he crowded all the sail he could carry.

At length they totally disappeared, and the admiral stood for Pondicherry on a supposition that they intended to sail thither. His conjecture was well founded; for on September 8th he observed them standing to the southward, and on the 10th, about two in the afternoon, M. d'Aché, seeing no possibility of escaping, made the signal for battle. The cannonading began without farther delay, and both squadrons engaged with equal impetuosity; but the French directing their cannon at the masts and rigging, while the English fired only at the hulls of the ships, the former sustained such a loss of men, and found their vessels in so shattered a condition that they were glad to sheer off with all their canvas set.

The loss on the side of the English was not inconsiderable, there being five hundred and sixty-nine men killed and wounded; that on the side of the French must have been far greater, as their ships could hardly keep the sea, and they were obliged to make the best of their way to the Island of Mauritius in order to be refitted. Soon after this engagement Admiral Cornish arrived from England with four ships of the line, and confirmed the dominion of the English over the Indian seas.

The Story of the "Glorious Fifty-Nine" and the Battle of Quiberon Bay

The year 1759 has been described as one of the most glorious years in the history of England, a year during which "it was necessary to ask every morning what new victory there was, for fear of missing one." The early part of the year was, indeed, one of "magnanimous fear"—as Pitt called it—for the French were known to be making unparalleled efforts for the invasion of England with the proud hope of entire conquest, and in Germany, in America, and in India, England was at war. Hostile fleets were assembled at Havre, Brest, Dunkirk, and Toulon. The fleet at Havre was an immediate menace to the English coasts; the Brest squadron was destined for the invasion of Ireland, the ships at Dunkirk were commissioned to harass Scotland, while it was hoped that the Toulon fleet would supply reinforcements wherever needed. In France this naval combination was regarded as irresistible.

But Pitt had aroused the national spirit, and aggressive reprisals were adopted with enthusiasm. Admiral Rodney was entrusted with an attack upon Havre, where a vast number of flat-bottomed boats with a quantity of military stores of all kinds had been prepared to assist in the projected invasion. On July 3rd he anchored in Havre roads. The French commander had been forewarned of the English approach, and had made ample preparations for resistance. Powerful batteries had been erected all along the shore, and on both sides of the river's mouth; these were garrisoned with several thousand men, who opened a heavy fire on the squadron the moment it came within gunshot. The pilots proved wholly ignorant of the place, but some of Rodney's captains worked all night in taking soundings. The bombardment was continued without intermission for two days and two nights. Nearly all the French transports and boats were burnt, with all the warehouses containing the stores; and Havre itself was so disabled as to be valueless as an arsenal during the remainder of the war.

In August the Toulon fleet slipped through the Straits of Gibraltar, with the intention of reinforcing the Brest fleet; only, however, to be vigorously attacked and decisively defeated by Admiral Boscawen, who gave battle in Lagos Bay off the south coast of Portugal; meanwhile the ships at Dunkirk were blockaded by Admiral Boyce.

In May, Admiral (afterwards Lord) Hawke was ordered to blockade the Brest fleet. For six months the blockade lasted. The gales and the difficulty of victualling the fleet governed the situation. When a westerly gale sprang up, the French could not get out to sea from Brest; but there was the great danger of some of the English ships being driven on shore, and the question was "How to get the fleet into a place of safety, like Plymouth or Torbay, and out again before the wind changed and allowed the French to sail." It was like "a cat watching a mouse." The difficulties of the commissariat may be estimated by a letter in which Hawke wrote to the responsible officer at Plymouth:

> The beer brewed at your port is so excessively bad that it employs the whole of the time of the squadron in surveying it and throwing it overboard.... A quantity of bread will be returned to you; though not altogether unfit for use, yet so full of weevils and maggots that it would have infected all the bread come on board this day.

The fierce gales of November made Hawke's task of keeping a large fleet in the Bay of Biscay one of supreme difficulty, and unusually wild weather compelled him to run for shelter in Torbay. On the 14th the storm abated, and De Conflans, seeing the coast clear, put to sea. The same day Hawke left the shelter of the English coast; on the 16th he was off Ushant. Dr. John Campbell writes:

> On that afternoon several English transports returning from Quiberon Bay passed through the fleet, and informed the admiral that they had seen the French squadron on the preceding day, standing to the south-east, and distant about twenty-three leagues from Belle-Isle.

The intelligence was received by the whole British fleet with acclamations, and every ship prepared for action. The wind also became favourable and every sail was spread to catch the gale.

On the 20th, about half an hour after eight o'clock in the morning, the *Maidstone* frigate let fly her top-gallant sails, which was a signal for discovering a fleet. About nine, Lord Howe, in the *Magnanime*, made signal that they were enemies. Sir Edward Hawke immediately told his officers that he did not intend to trouble himself with forming lines, but would attack them in the old way, to make downright work with them; and accordingly he threw out a signal for seven of his ships to chase, in order to allure the enemy to fight.

As the British neared the French, the weather became squally and rough; but Conflans in a very gallant style seemed to offer battle: his courage, however, soon cooled, and long before the fleets were within the range of shot, he changed his plan, and stood right before the wind toward the shore. It was two in the afternoon before our headmost ships could get up with his rear; but at that time the *Warspite* and *Dorsetshire* began to fire.

The imagination can conceive nothing more sublime than the spectacle which the hostile squadrons presented at this moment. A dreadful storm darkened the face of the heavens; the sea was rolling in tremendous waves which on all sides were dashing themselves into foam on treacherous rocks and shallows unknown to the English pilots. In the midst of these terrible circumstances, calculated, from the very majesty of the physical power in action, to awe and intimidate, two adverse navies, the greatest that had been employed in one of the greatest wars in the annals of Europe, freighted with the fate, and worthy of being intrusted with the glory of the rival nations, were preparing for battle.

It was a moment as if nature had resolved to contrast the tameness of physical terror with the grandeur of heroism, and to show how much more sublime are the moral sentiments of a collected mind than all the awful phenomena of the heavens darkened, and the ocean agitated by a tempest, with the multifarious dangers of secret rocks and unknown shallows.

In the open sea Conflans might have hazarded a battle without the imputation of temerity, as his fleet was equal in force to that of Hawke, but like a prudent commander he endeavoured to avail himself of all the advantages arising from the local knowledge of his pilots, who were well acquainted with the navigation of the shallows. He directed them to steer in such a manner as to decoy the English among the rocks. But the very execution of this proceeding, which at the time was thought disreputable to his character as a commander, required more time in execution than the occasion allowed, and the British ships came up with the French before they were well prepared for action.

At half an hour after two o'clock the British van opened fire on the French rear. The *Formidable*, a French man-of-war, commanded by Admiral de Verger, a man of great courage and noble determination, behaved in the most heroic manner; broadside after broadside were poured into her by the British as they sailed successively past towards the van of the enemy; and she returned their fire with a promptitude that excited the admiration of friends and foes.

In the meantime, the *Royal George*, with Hawke on board, was approaching the *Soleil Royal*, which bore the flag of Conflans. Intent, as it were, only on her prey, she passed on without heeding the shot of the other ships. The sea was dashing over her bows, and as she came rapidly nearer, she appeared as if she had been actuated by the furiousness of rage. Her pilot, seeing the breakers foaming on every side, told the admiral that he could not go farther, without the most imminent danger from the shoals. "You have done your duty in pointing out the danger," said Hawke, "but lay me alongside of the *Soleil Royal*." The pilot bowed in obedience, and gave the necessary orders.

The *Superbe*, a French ship of seventy guns, perceiving what was intended by the movements of the English admiral, generously interposed between her commander and received the whole fatal broadside which the *Royal George* had intended for Monsieur Conflans. The thunder of the explosion was succeeded by a wild shriek from all on board. The British sailors gave a shout of triumph, which was instantly checked by a far other feeling; for the smoke clearing away, only the masts of the *Superbe*, with her colours still flying, were seen above the water, and in a moment they were covered by a roll of the sea, and seen no more; but the *Soleil Royal* was spared; she escaped to the shore, where she was afterwards burnt with disgrace.

About four in the afternoon, the *Formidable*, which had maintained the whole battle with such heroic determination, struck her colours; but not until after all her officers had been killed. The *Héros*, a seventy-four, also struck, and the *Thésée*, of seventy guns, was sunk like the *Superbe*.

Darkness coming on, the remainder of the enemy's fleet fled; seven ships of the line hove their guns overboard, and ran into the River Villaine; about as many more, in a shattered condition, escaped to other ports. The wind blowing strong in shore, Hawke made the signal for anchoring to the westward of the small island of Durnel. Here the fleet remained during the night, and as the tempest continued to increase, the darkness was occasionally broken by the flashes of cannon and the howl of the wind; and the roar of the breakers was augmented in horror by the sound of guns of distress. "This action, more memorable on account of the terrific circumstances in which it was fought, than any other of equal magnitude in the annals of heroic achievement," put an end to the naval power of France for many years, and therefore, to all fear of invasion. It, moreover, indicated the overwhelming superiority of the English marine.

The capture of Goree in January, and of Guadaloupe in June, the victory of Minden in August, and of Lagos in September, the capture of Quebec in October, and the crowning victory of Quiberon Bay in November have immortalised "the glorious fifty-nine" in English history.

The Story of Lord Rodney
By John Campbell

George Brydges Rodney was born at Walton-on-Thames in the year 1718. His father, Henry Rodney, was at the time of his son's birth commander of the yacht in which the king, attended by the Duke of Chandos, used to pass to and from Hanover; hence he was christened George and Brydges after the king and the duke, who stood godfathers to him. He entered the navy at fourteen years of age, and obtained command of a ship at twenty-four. He was made governor of Newfoundland in 1749, and in 1759 admiral of the blue. This same year he distinguished himself by destroying the stores prepared for the invasion of England at Havre de Grace.

In 1761 he served in the West Indies and was made a baronet. In 1768 he was elected member of parliament for Northampton; but the cost of his election ruined him and he was obliged to seek a temporary asylum on the Continent. While here he received overtures from the French government, which he rejected; upon which the English government gave him command of the Mediterranean squadron. The two principal victories of his life were gained over the Spanish and French fleets in 1780 and 1782, in connection with his appointment to the West Indian squadron.

There were two naval objects which demanded the attention of the ministry at the commencement of the year 1780, the relief of Gibraltar and the protection of the West Indies. To secure both these Admiral Rodney was appointed to command a fleet in the West Indies, and *en route* to convoy a large supply of provisions and stores to Gibraltar. The admiral had been but a very few days at sea when he fell in with a Spanish fleet, bound from St. Sebastian to Cadiz: it consisted of fifteen sail of merchantmen under the protection of a fine new sixty-four gun ship, four frigates, mounting from twenty-six to thirty-two guns, and two smaller vessels; these ships of war belonged to the Royal Company of the Caraccas, and had been assigned to the others as a convoy. The whole fleet were captured; and on examining the cargoes of the merchantmen, the capture was ascertained to be extremely fortunate, as the greater part of them were laden with wheat, flour, and other stores, which the admiral of course destined for Gibraltar.

On January 16th, about a week after this capture, he fell in with another Spanish squadron, consisting of eleven ships of the line, under the command of Don Juan Langara, off Cape St. Vincent. As the Spaniards, being inferior in force and favoured by the wind, endeavoured to escape, the British admiral changed the signal for a line of battle abreast to that for a general chase, with orders to engage as the ships came up. Night came on, but the pursuit was still continued, though the dangers of a dark and tempestuous night were increased by the vicinity of the shoals of St. Lucar. About four o'clock the headmost ships began to engage. Early in the action the Spanish ship *St. Domingo*, of seventy guns and seven hundred men, blew up, and all on board perished; the English ship opposed to her nearly suffering the same fate.

The engagement did not terminate till two in the morning, when the *Monarca*, the headmost of the enemy's fleet, struck to the *Sandwich*, Admiral Rodney's own ship. Three others were also taken and carried safely into port; among these was the *Phœnix*, of eighty guns, Don Langara's ship. Two others had struck, but after the officers had been taken out, they were driven on shore by the tempestuous weather, and one of them was entirely lost. Two frigates and four ships of the line escaped; of the latter, two were much damaged in the action. Our loss amounted to thirty-two killed and one hundred and two wounded.

The convoy having been conducted safely to Gibraltar, and the provisions and stores having been landed there, Admiral Digby, taking under his charge the Spanish prizes and homeward bound transports, sailed for England on February 15th, 1780; and Admiral Rodney, with the remainder, proceeded to his station in the West Indies.

The great object of the French and Spanish forces in the West Islands at this time was the reduction of Jamaica. Hitherto foiled in attaining this object, they were in great hopes of being more successful in 1782. In order to frustrate their design, soon after his arrival in England, in the fall of the year 1781, Admiral Rodney was sent back to resume his command in the West Indies, with a reinforcement of twelve sail of the line. He sailed from the Channel in the month of January, 1782, and arrived off the island of Barbadoes on the 19th of the following month. Having formed a junction with Sir Samuel Hood he resolved to proceed with his whole fleet to St. Lucia; the most convenient station for watching the motions of the enemy. As soon as he arrived off this island he ordered some of his frigates to cruise, for the purpose of giving him the earliest intelligence of the movements of the enemy; and in the meantime took on board provisions and water sufficient to last him for five months.

The first object which Admiral Rodney had in view was to prevent, if possible, the junction of the French and Spanish fleets, as he had reason to believe that, if this junction were effected, Jamaica would fall a prey to the enemy. The Spanish fleet at this time were to leeward of the French.

On April 5th Admiral Rodney was informed that the French were embarking troops on board their ships of war; and on the 8th of the same month, at break of day, a signal was made from the *Andromache* that their fleet was coming out of Fort Royal and standing to the north-west. Admiral Rodney immediately made the necessary signal for weighing anchor and getting under weigh, and this was obeyed with so much promptitude and alacrity that the whole British fleet, consisting of thirty-six sail of the line, was clear off Grosislet Bay before noon. They proceeded, under as much sail as they could carry, in pursuit of the enemy, so that before daylight the next morning the French fleet was discovered under the island of Dominica. At this time both fleets were becalmed; the enemy got the breeze first, and taking advantage of it stood towards Guadaloupe.

The breeze next favoured the van of the English fleet, under the command of Sir Samuel Hood, who stood after them with a press of sail; all this while the rear and the centre of Admiral Rodney's fleet were still becalmed. This circumstance, which to all appearance was unfavourable to the English, proved in the issue highly advantageous to them; for the Count de Grasse, who had determined to avoid an engagement, and to press forward in order to effect a junction with the Spanish fleet, perceiving the van of the English at a distance from, and unsupported by, the rear and centre, was tempted to engage; so as soon as Sir Samuel Hood's division came near enough the Count de Grasse bore down upon him with his whole force.

Sir Samuel Hood was not dispirited; though at one period of this very unequal engagement his own ship, the *Barfleur*, had seven of the enemy's ships firing upon her, and during the greatest part of the action not less than three. The example of the *Barfleur* was followed by all the rest of the division, so that no advantage could be obtained over them. At length part of the centre got near enough to engage; and the breeze soon afterwards reaching the rear of the British fleet, the Count de Grasse withdrew his ships, and having the advantage of the wind was enabled to decline any further contest, notwithstanding all the endeavours of Admiral Rodney to continue it. During this partial engagement the *Royal Oak* and the *Montague*, the leading ships of the van, sustained considerable damage. Captain Boyne of the *Alfred* was killed. Two of the French ships were so disabled as to be obliged to take shelter in Guadaloupe.

The British fleet lay to all the night after the action for the purpose of repairing their damages, but the next morning made sail to the windward in pursuit of the enemy. But the pursuit seemed in vain, for on the morning of the 11th the French fleet had got so far to windward that some of their ships were scarcely visible.

About noon on April 11th one of the enemy's ships was seen in a disabled state, a great way to windward; Admiral Rodney now entertained hopes that he should either be able to capture her or to bring on a general engagement, if the Count de Grasse bore down to her support; he therefore ordered a general chase. Towards evening, one of the leading ships of the British approached so near the disabled ship of the enemy, that her capture was inevitable if she were not assisted. The Count de Grasse, perceiving her danger, bore down with his whole fleet for her protection. Admiral Rodney had now gained his object; for by nightfall the two fleets were very near each other: it was necessary, however, to put off the engagement till the next day, April 12th. Still, however, as during the night the French admiral might have drawn off his fleet, Admiral Rodney took such measures as effectually prevented this from taking place; so that when daylight broke he had the satisfaction to perceive that the Count de Grasse, even if so inclined, could not avoid a general engagement.

The action was begun about half-past seven in the morning of the 12th by Captain Penny, of the *Marlborough*, the leading ship of the British van. The two fleets met on opposite tacks; the British ranging slowly along—there being but little wind—and close under the lee of the enemy's line, continuing a most tremendous fire, which the French received and returned with the utmost firmness. About noon, Sir George Rodney in the *Formidable*, having passed the *Ville de Paris*, the French admiral's ship, and her second—and during her passage directing against them a most tremendous and effective fire—stood athwart the line of the enemy, between the second and third ship astern of the *Ville de Paris*; she was immediately followed and supported by the *Duke*, *Namur*, and *Canada*; and the rest imitated their example. As soon as the *Formidable* had broken the line she wore round; and a signal being made for the van division to tack, the British fleet thus gained the wind and stood upon the same tack with the enemy. By this bold and masterly manoeuvre the French line was completely broken and the whole thrown into confusion; the consequences were decisively advantageous and glorious to the British; for though the enemy still continued to fight with great gallantry, it was evident that the victory was with Admiral Rodney.

The action hitherto had been chiefly supported by the van and centre of the British; for the rear under Sir Samuel Hood being becalmed, did not for some time get into the engagement; and when the breeze did spring up, it was so trifling that Sir Samuel Hood, in the *Barfleur*, took an hour and a half to reach that part of the enemy's line where it had been broken through by the *Formidable*. During all this time, however, he kept up a tremendous and well-directed fire.

As the French ships always carry a much larger complement of men than the British, and as, moreover, at this time they had on board a great number of troops, the carnage was extreme; notwithstanding this, however, and the certainty that they must ultimately be beaten, the Count de Grasse in the *Ville de Paris* and the other ships in the centre, withstood till the evening all the efforts of the various ships that attacked him. Nor was the gallantry of the British inferior to that of the French. Captain Cornwallis, of the *Canada*, especially distinguished himself; for, having obliged the *Hector*, a ship of the same force as his own, to strike her colours, he did not lose time by taking possession of her, but leaving her in charge of a frigate pushed on to the *Ville de Paris*, which he engaged for the space of two hours, notwithstanding her great superiority, and left her a complete wreck.

The Count de Grasse, however, refused to surrender; and as it was supposed that he would not yield to any vessel that did not carry an admiral's flag, towards sunset Sir Samuel Hood poured from the *Barfleur* a most dreadful fire into the *Ville de Paris*. The Count de Grasse bore it for about ten minutes, when he surrendered: at this time there were only three men alive and unhurt on the upper deck, and of this number the count himself was one. Besides the *Ville de Paris* and the *Hector*, the *Ardent*, of sixty-four guns, which had been captured in the British Channel, was retaken; the *Cæsar* and the *Glorieux*, of seventy-four guns each, also surrendered after they were made complete wrecks. The *Diadem*, early in the engagement, bore up to assist in protecting the *Ville de Paris* from the *Formidable*, but by a single broadside from the latter she was sunk.

Night, which must have been ardently wished for by the French, now came on; when the British admiral made the signal for his fleet to bring to, in order that he might secure his prizes. In the course of this night the *Cæsar*, one of the prizes, blew up by accident; and a British lieutenant and fifty seamen, with about four hundred prisoners, perished.

The *Ville de Paris* was the most important of the prizes; she was the largest ship in the French king's service. She had been a present from the city of Paris to Louis XV., and no expense had been spared to render the gift worthy of the city and of the monarch; the expense of building her and fitting her for sea is said to have been one hundred and fifty-six thousand pounds. On board of her there were, at the time of her capture, thirty-six chests of money, intended for the pay and subsistence of the men who were to have been employed in the expedition against Jamaica: in the other captured ships the whole train of artillery and the battering cannon, and travelling carriages meant for that expedition, were also found.

The loss of men in the British fleet in both actions, on April the 9th and 12th, was very small, amounting only to two hundred and thirty-seven killed and seven hundred and seventy-six wounded. The loss of the French is computed to have been three thousand slain and more than double that number wounded. In the *Ville de Paris* alone upwards of three hundred men were killed; and several other of the captured ships lost between two or three hundred.

Two sail of the line and three frigates were captured the following day, so that the total loss of the enemy amounted to eight sail of the line and two frigates; six of which were in possession of the British, one sunk and another blown up. The Count de Grasse was sent prisoner to England.

After his success, Sir Samuel Hood joined Admiral Rodney, who proceeded to Jamaica with his prizes; leaving Sir Samuel with twenty-five sail of the line to keep the sea and watch the motions of the enemy.

Admiral Pigot, having arrived from England to succeed Sir George Rodney on the West India station, the latter sailed from Jamaica in the beginning of August. The news of his victory gave great and universal joy in Great Britain, and the admiral was created an English peer, and a pension of £2,000 a year was conferred upon him. Sir Samuel Hood was created an Irish peer.

Lord Rodney died in 1792, and a memorial was erected to his memory in St. Paul's Cathedral by public subscription.

ADMIRAL DUNCAN ADDRESSING HIS CREW AFTER THE MUTINY AT THE NORE

The Loss of the "Ramilies"
By G. H. Walker

Admiral (afterwards Lord) Graves having requested leave to return to England in 1782, was appointed by Lord Rodney to command the convoy sent home with a numerous fleet of merchantmen from the West Indies in the month of July. He accordingly hoisted the flag on board the *Ramilies*, of seventy-four guns, and sailed on the 25th from Bluefields, having under his orders the *Canada* and *Centaur*, of seventy-four guns each, with the *Pallas* frigate of thirty-six guns, and the following French ships taken by Lord Rodney and Sir Samuel Hood, out of the armament commanded by the Count de Grasse, viz., the *Ville de Paris*, of one hundred and ten guns; the *Glorieux* and *Hector*, of seventy-four guns each; the *Ardent*, *Caton*, and *Jason*, of sixty-four guns each. These were originally British ships and had been in so many actions and so long absent from England, as to have become extremely out of condition, while that of the prizes was still more deplorable; and the following authentic account of the various disasters which attended this distressed convoy will be found equally melancholy and interesting.

Soon after the fleet had sailed, the officers of the *Ardent* united in signing such a representation of her miserable plight as induced Admiral Graves to order her back to Port Royal; and the *Jason* by not putting to sea with the convoy, from the want of water, never joined him at all. The rest proceeded, and after the vessels that were bound for New York had separated, the whole convoy was reduced to ninety-two or three sail.

On September 8th, the *Caton* springing a leak, made such alarming complaints, that the admiral directed her and the *Pallas*, which had also become leaky, to bear away immediately and keep company together, making for Halifax, which then bore north-north-west and was about eighty-seven leagues distant.

The afternoon of September 16th, showing indications of a gale and foul weather from the south-east quarter, every preparation was made on board the flag ship for such an event, not only on account of her own safety, but also by way of example to the rest of the fleet. The admiral collected the ships about six o'clock, and brought to under his main sail on the larboard tack, having all his other sails furled, and his top-gallant yards and masts lowered down.

The wind soon increasing, blew strongly from the east-south-east with a very heavy sea, and about three o'clock in the morning of the 17th flew suddenly round to the contrary point, blowing most tremendously, and accompanied with rain, thunder, and lightning; the *Ramilies* was taken by the lee, her main sail thrown aback, her main mast went by the board, and her mizen mast half way up; the foretop mast fell over the starboard bow, the foreyard broke in the slings, the tiller snapped in two, and the rudder was nearly torn off. Thus was this capital ship, from being in perfect order, reduced within a few minutes to a mere wreck, by the fury of the blast and the violence of the sea, which acted in opposition to each other. The ship was pooped, the cabin, where the admiral lay, was flooded, his cot bed jerked down by the violence of the shock and the ship's instantaneous revulsion, so that he was obliged to pull on his boots half-leg deep in water, without any stockings, to huddle on his wet clothes, and repair upon deck.

On his first coming hither, he ordered two of the lieutenants to examine into the state of the affairs below, and to keep a sufficient number of people at the pumps, while he himself and the captain kept the deck, to encourage the men to clear away the wreck, which by its constant swinging backwards and forwards by every wave against the body of the ship, had beaten off much of the copper from the starboard side, and exposed the seams so much to the sea that the decayed oakum washed out, and the whole frame became at once exceedingly porous and leaky.

At dawn of day they perceived a large ship under their lee, lying upon her side, water-logged, her hands attempting to wear her by first cutting away the mizen mast, and then main mast: hoisting her ensign, with the union downwards, in order to draw the attention of the fleet; but to no purpose, for no succour could be given, and she very soon went down head foremost, the fly of her ensign being the last thing visible. This was the *Dutton*, formerly an Indiaman, and then a store ship, commanded by a lieutenant of the navy, who in his agitation leaped from her deck into the sea; but, as might be expected, was very soon overwhelmed by the billows. Twelve or thirteen of the crew contrived, however, to slip off with one of the boats, and running with the wind, endeavoured to reach a large ship before them, failing in which, however, and afraid of filling if they attempted to haul up for that purpose, they made up for another ship more to the leeward, who, fortunately descrying them, threw a number of ropes, by the help of which these desperate fellows scrambled up her sides and fortunately saved their lives.

Out of ninety-four or ninety-five sail seen the day before scarcely twenty could now be counted; of the ships of war there were discovered the *Canada* half hull down upon the lee quarter, having her main-top mast and mizen mast gone, the main top damaged, the main yard aloft, and the main sail furled. The *Centaur* was far to windward, without masts, bowsprit or rudder; and the *Glorieux* without fore mast, bowsprit, or main-top mast. Of these the two latter perished with all their crews, excepting the captain of the *Centaur* and a few of his people, who contrived to slip off her stern into one of the boats unnoticed, and thus escaped the fate of the rest.

The *Ville de Paris* appeared to have received no injury, and was commanded by a most experienced seaman, who had made twenty-four voyages to and from the West Indies, and had, therefore, been pitched upon to lead the ship through the Gulf; nevertheless, she was afterwards buried in the ocean with all on board her, consisting of above eight hundred people. Of the convoy, besides the *Dutton* before mentioned and the *British Queen*, seven others were discovered without mast or bowsprit; eighteen lost masts, and several others had actually foundered.

In the course of this day the *Canada* crossed upon and passed the *Ramilies*. Some of the trade attempted to follow the *Canada*, but she ran at such a rate that they soon found it to be in vain, and then returned to the flag ship. The *Ramilies* had at this time six feet of water in her hold, and the pumps would not free her, the water having worked out the oakum, and her beams amid ship being almost drawn from her clamps.

The admiral therefore gave orders for all the buckets to be manned, and every officer to help towards freeing the ship; the mizen-top sail was set upon the foremast, the main top-gallant sail on the stump of the mizen mast, and the tiller shipped. In this condition, by bearing away, she scudded on at so good a rate that she held pace with some of the merchantmen.

The day having been spent in baling and pumping, with materially gaining on the water, the captain, in the name of the officers, represented to the admiral the necessity of parting with the guns for the relief of the ship; but he objected that there would then be left no protection for the convoy. At length, however, he consented to their disposing of the forecastle and aftermost quarter-deck guns, together with some of the shot, and other articles of very great weight. The ensuing night was employed in baling and endeavouring to make the pumps useful, for the ballast, by getting into the well, had choked and rendered them useless, and the chains had broken as often as they were repaired. The water had risen to seven feet in the hold. The wind from the eastward drove a vast sea before it, and the ship, being old, strained most violently.

On the morning of the 18th nothing could be seen of the *Canada*, she having pushed on at her greatest speed for England. The frame of the *Ramilies* having opened during the night, the admiral was prevailed upon, by the renewed and pressing remonstrances of his officers, although with great reluctance, to let six of the forwardmost and four of the aftermost guns of the main deck be thrown overboard, together with the remainder of those on the quarter-deck; and the ships still continuing to open very much, he ordered tarred canvas and hides to be nailed fore and aft from under the sills of the ports on the main deck under the fifth plank above, or within the water ways; and the crew, without orders, did the same on the lower deck. Her increasing complaints required still more to be done.

The admiral directed all the guns on the upper deck, the shot, both on that and the lower deck, and various heavy stores, to be thrown overboard; a leakage in the light-room of the grand magazine having almost filled the ship forward, and there being eight feet of water in the magazine, every gentleman was compelled to take his turn at the whips or in handing the buckets. The ship was besides frapped from the foremast to the main mast.

Notwithstanding their utmost efforts the water still gained on them the succeeding night, and the wind blowing very hard, with extremely heavy squalls, a part of the orlop deck fell into the hold: the ship herself seemed to work excessively, and to settle forward.

On the morning of the 19th, under these very alarming circumstances, the admiral commanded both the bower anchors to be cut away, all the junk to be flung overboard, one sheet and one bower cable to be reduced to junk and served the same way, together with every remaining ponderous store that could be got at, and all the powder in the grand magazine (it being damaged); the cutter and pinnace to be broken up and tossed overboard, the skids having already worked off the side. Every soul on board was now employed in baling. One of the pumps was got up; but to no purpose, for the shot lockers being broken down, some of the shot, as well as the ballast, had fallen into the well; and as the weather moderated a little everything was made ready for heaving the lower-deck guns into the sea, the admiral being anxious to leave nothing undone for the relief of the ship.

When evening approached, there being twenty merchant ships in sight, the officers united in beseeching him to go into one of them; but this he positively refused to do, deeming it, as he declared, unpardonable in a commander-in-chief to desert his garrison in distress; that his living a few years longer was of very little consequence, but that, by leaving his ship at such a time, he should discourage and slacken the exertions of the people by setting them a very bad example. The wind lulling somewhat during the night, all hands baled the water, which, at this time, was six feet fore and aft.

On the morning of the 20th the admiral ordered the square and stream-anchors to be cut away, and within the course of the day all the lower-deck guns to be thrown overboard. When evening came the spirits of the people in general, and even of the most courageous, began to fail, and they openly expressed the utmost despair, together with the most earnest desire of quitting the ship, lest they should founder in her.

The admiral hereupon advanced and told them that he and their officers had an equal regard for their own lives, that the officers had no intention of deserting either them or the ship, that, for his part, he was determined to try one night more in her; he therefore hoped and entreated they would do so too, for there was still room to imagine that one fair day, with a moderate sea, might enable them, by united exertion, to clear and secure the well against the encroaching ballast which washed into it; that if this could be done they might be able to restore the chains to the pumps and use them, and that then hands enough might be spared to raise jury masts, with which they might carry the ship into Ireland; that her appearance alone, while she could swim, would be sufficient to protect the remaining part of her convoy; above all, that as everything that could be thought of had now been done for her relief, it would be but reasonable to wait the effect. He concluded with assuring them that he would make the signal directly for the trade to lie by them during the night, which he doubted not they would comply with.

This temperate speech had the desired effect; the firmness and confidence with which he spoke, and their reliance on his seamanship and judgment, as well as his constant presence and attention to every accident, had a wonderful effect upon them; they became pacified, returning to their duty and their labours. Since the first disaster, the admiral had, in fact, scarcely ever quitted the deck; this they had all observed, together with his diligence in personally inspecting every circumstance of distress. Knowing his skill and experience, they placed great confidence in them; and he instantly made, according to his promise, a signal for all the merchantmen.

At this period, it must be confessed, there was great reason for alarm, and but little for hope; for all the anchors and guns, excepting one, together with every other matter of weight, had been thrown overboard, and yet the ship did not seem to be at all relieved. The strength of the people was likewise so nearly exhausted, having had no sleep since the first fatal stroke, that one half of the crew were ordered to bale, and the other to repose; so that, although the wind was much abated, the water still gained upon them, in spite of all their efforts, and the ship rolled and worked prodigiously in a most unquiet sea.

At three in the morning of the 21st, being the fourth night, the well being broken in, the casks, ballast, and remaining shot rushed together and destroyed the cylinder of the pumps; the frame and carcase of the ship began to give way in every part, and the whole crew exclaimed that it was impossible to keep her any longer above water.

In this extremity the admiral resolved within himself not to lose a moment in removing the people whenever daylight should arrive; but told the captain not to communicate any more of his design than that he intended to remove the sick and lame at daybreak, and for this purpose he should call on board all the boats of the merchantmen. He, nevertheless gave private orders to the captain, while this was doing, to have all the bread brought upon the quarter-deck, with a quantity of beef, pork, and flour, to settle the best distributing of the people according to the number of trade ships that should obey their signal, and to allow an officer to each division of them; to have the remaining boats launched, and as soon as the sick were disposed of, to begin to remove the whole of the crew, with the utmost dispatch, but without risking too many in a boat.

Accordingly, at dawn, the signal was made for the boats of the merchantmen, but nobody suspected what was to follow, until the bread was entirely removed and the sick gone. About six o'clock the rest of the crew were permitted to go off, and between nine and ten, there being nothing farther to direct and regulate, the admiral himself, after shaking hands with every officer, and leaving his barge for their better accommodation and transport, quitted forever the *Ramilies* which had then nine feet of water in her hold. He went into a small leaky boat, loaded with bread, out of which both himself and the surgeon who accompanied him were obliged to bale the water all the way. He was in his boots, with his surtout over his uniform, and his countenance as calm and composed as ever. He had, at the going off, desired a cloak, a cask of flour, and a cask of water, but could get only the flour; and he left behind all his stock, wines, furniture, books, charts, etc., which had cost him upwards of one thousand pounds, being unwilling to employ even a single servant in saving or packing up what belonged to himself alone, in a time of such general calamity, or to appear to fare better in that respect than any of the crew.

The admiral rowed for the *Belle*, Captain Forster, being the first of the traders that had borne up to the *Ramilies* the preceding night in her imminent distress, and by his anxious humanity set such an example to his brother-traders as had a powerful influence upon them—an influence that was generally followed by sixteen others.

By three o'clock most of the crew were taken out, at which time the *Ramilies* had thirteen feet of water in her hold, and was evidently foundering in every part. At half-past four the captain and first and third lieutenants left her, with every soul excepting the fourth lieutenant, who stayed behind only to execute the admiral's orders for setting fire to her wreck when finally deserted. The carcase burned rapidly, and the flame quickly reaching the powder, which was filled in the after magazine, and had been lodged very high, in thirty-five minutes the decks and upper works blew up with a horrid explosion and cloud of smoke, while the lower part of the hull was precipitated to the bottom of the ocean.

At this time the admiral, in the *Belle*, stood for the wreck to see his last orders executed, as well as to succour any boats that might be too full of men, the swell of the sea being prodigious, although the weather had been moderate ever since noon of the foregoing day. There were, however, at intervals, some squalls, with threats of the weather soon becoming violent. It was not long before they were realised, for within two hours after the last of the crew were put on board their respective ships, the wind rose to a great height, and so continued, without intermission, for six or seven successive days, so that no boat could, during that time, have lived in the water. On such a small interval depended the salvation of more than six hundred lives!

Upon their separation taking place, the officers who were distributed with portions of the crew among the *Jamaica* men, had orders respectively to deliver them to the first man of war or tender they should meet with, and to acquaint the Secretary of the Admiralty by the earliest opportunity of their proceedings. A pendant was hoisted on board the *Belle*, by way of distinction that she might, if possible, lead the rest. Some of the traders kept with her, and others made the best of their way, apprehensive lest they should soon fall short of provisions, as they had so many more to feed.

The *Silver Eel* transport, which had sailed from Bluefields with the invalids of Sir George Rodney's fleet, and was under the command of a lieutenant of the navy, had been ordered to keep near the *Ramilies*. That ship was accordingly at hand on September 21st, the day of her destruction, and in consequence of several deaths on the passage, had room enough for the reception of all those that were now ailing or maimed, and was consequently charged with them, being first properly fitted for their accommodation.

The *Silver Eel* parted from the admiral in latitude 42° 48′ N. and longitude 45° 19′ W.; after seeing the *Ramilies* demolished, and being ordered to make for the first port, ran into Falmouth, October 6th, on the afternoon of which day one of the trade ships, with a midshipman and sixteen of the crew of the *Ramilies*, reached Plymouth Sound. Another of the same convoy having on board another portion of the crew, with the captain and first lieutenant, anchored in the same place before daylight the next morning. The *Canada*, however, having exerted her utmost speed, had, prior to all these, on the 4th of the same month got to Portsmouth, where she spread the news of the dispersion of this miserable fleet, which being conveyed to France, her privateers immediately put to sea in hopes of making prize of them.

Some of the *Jamaica* men, with part of the crew of the *Ramilies*, fell in consequence into their hands; two of the *West India* men were captured in sight of the *Belle*, but she herself, with the admiral and thirty-three of his crew, arrived safe, though singly, on October 10th, in Cork Harbour, where was the *Myrmidon* frigate. The admiral immediately hoisted his flag on board the latter, and sailing with the first fair wind, arrived, on the 17th, in Plymouth Sound.

The Loss of H.M.S. "Centaur"
By Captain Inglefield

The storm which proved fatal to the *Ramilies* was responsible for the loss of many other ships in the same convoy, among which was the *Centaur* of seventy-four guns, whose commander, Captain Inglefield, with the master and ten of the crew, providentially escaped the general fate. The captain's narrative affords the best explanation of the manner and means by which this signal deliverance was effected. Captain Inglefield says:

The *Centaur* left Jamaica in rather a leaky condition, keeping two hand pumps going, and, when it blew fresh, sometimes a spell with a chain pump was necessary. But I had no apprehension that the ship was not able to encounter a common gale of wind.

In the evening of September 16th, when the fatal gale came on, the ship was prepared for the worst weather usually met in those latitudes, the main sail was reefed and set, the top-gallant masts struck, and the mizen yard lowered down, though at that time it did not blow very strong. Towards midnight it blew a gale of wind, and the ship made so much water that I was obliged to turn all hands up to spell the pumps. The leak still increasing, I had thoughts to try the ship before the sea. Happy I should have been, perhaps, had I in this been determined. The impropriety of leaving the convoy, except in the last extremity, and the hopes of the weather growing moderate, weighed against the opinion that it was right.

About two in the morning the wind lulled, and we flattered ourselves the gale was breaking. Soon after we had much thunder and lightning from the south-east, with rain, when it began to blow strong in gusts of wind, which obliged me to haul the main sail up, the ship being then under bare poles. This was scarcely done, when a gust of wind, exceeding in violence anything of the kind I had ever seen or had any conception of, laid the ship on her beam ends. The water forsook the hold and appeared between decks, so as to fill the men's hammocks to leeward: the ship lay motionless, and to all appearance irrecoverably overset. The water increasing fast, forced through the cells of the ports, and scuttled in the ports from the pressure of the ship.

I gave immediate directions to cut away the main and mizen mast, hoping when the ship righted to wear her. The main mast went first, upon cutting one or two of the lanyards, without the smallest effect on the ship; the mizen mast followed, upon cutting the lanyard of one shroud; and I had the disappointment to see the foremast and bowsprit follow. The ship upon this immediately righted, but with great violence; and the motion was so quick, that it was difficult for the people to work the pumps. Three guns broke loose upon the main deck, and it was some time before they were secured. Several men being maimed in this attempt, everything movable was destroyed, either from the shot thrown loose from the lockers, or the wreck of the deck. The officers, who had left their beds naked, when the ship overset in the morning, had not an article of clothes to put on, nor could their friends supply them.

The masts had not been over the sides ten minutes before I was informed the tiller was broken short in the rudder head; and before the chocks could be placed the rudder itself was gone. Thus we were as much disastered as it was possible, lying at the mercy of the wind and sea; yet I had one comfort, that the pumps, if anything, reduced the water in the hold; and as the morning came on (the 17th) the weather grew more moderate, the wind having shifted in the gale to north-west.

At daylight I saw two line-of-battle ships to leeward; one had lost her foremast and bowsprit, the other her main mast. It was the general opinion on board the *Centaur* that the former was the *Canada*, the other the *Glorieux*. The *Ramilies* was not in sight, nor more than fifteen sail of merchant ships.

About seven in the morning I saw another line-of-battle ship ahead of us, which I soon distinguished to be the *Ville de Paris*, with all her masts standing. I immediately gave orders to make the signal of distress, hoisting the ensign on the stump of the mizen mast, union downwards, and firing one of the forecastle guns. The ensign blew away soon after it was hoisted, and it was the only one we had; but I had the satisfaction to see the *Ville de Paris* wear and stand towards us. Several of the merchant ships also approached us, and those that could hailed, and offered their assistance; but depending upon the king's ship, I only thanked them, desiring, if they joined Admiral Graves, to acquaint him of our condition.

I had not the smallest doubt but the *Ville de Paris* was coming to us, as she appeared to us to have suffered the least by the storm, and having seen her wear, we knew she was under government of her helm; at this time, also, it was so moderate that the merchantmen set their top-sails; but approaching within two miles she passed us to windward: this being observed by one of the merchant ships she wore and came under our stern, offering to carry any message to her. I desired the master would acquaint Captain Wilkinson that the *Centaur* had lost her rudder as well as her masts, that she made a great deal of water, and that I desired he would remain with her until the weather grew moderate.

I saw this merchantman approach afterwards near enough to speak to the *Ville de Paris*, but am afraid that her condition was much worse than it appeared to be, as she continued upon the tack. In the meantime all the quarter-deck guns were thrown overboard, and all but six which had overset on the main deck. The ship, lying in the trough of the sea, laboured prodigiously. I got over one of the small anchors, with a boom and several gun carriages, veering out from the head door by a large hawser, to keep the ship's bow to the sea; but this, with a top-gallant sail upon the stump of the mizen mast, had not the desired effect.

As the evening came on it grew hazy, and blew strong in squalls. We lost sight of the *Ville de Paris*, but I thought it a certainty that we should see her the next morning. The night was passed in constant labour at the pumps. Sometimes the wind lulled, the water diminished; when it blew strong again, the sea rising, the water again increased.

Towards the morning of the 18th I was informed there was seven feet water upon the kelson; that one of the winches was broken, that the two spare ones would not fit, and that the hand pumps were choked. These circumstances were sufficiently alarming; but upon opening the after hold, to get some rum up for the people, we found our condition much more so.

It will be necessary to mention that the *Centaur's* after hold was inclosed by a bulk head at the after part of the well: here all the dry provisions and the ship's rum were stowed upon twenty chaldron of coals, which unfortunately had been started on this part of the ship, and by them the pumps were continually choked. The chain pumps were so much worn as to be of little use; and the leathers, which, had the well been clear, would have lasted twenty days or more, were all consumed in eight. At this time it was observed that the water had not a passage to the well, for here there was so much that it washed against the orlop deck.

All the rum—twenty-six puncheons—all the provisions, of which there was sufficient for two months, in casks, were staved, having floated with violence from side to side until there was not a whole cask remaining; even the staves that were found upon clearing the hold were most of them broken in two or three pieces. In the fore hold we had a prospect of perishing; should the ship swim, we had no water but what remained in the ground tier, and over this all the wet provisions and butts filled with salt water were floating, and with so much motion that no man could with safety go into the hold. There was nothing left for us to try but baling with buckets at the fore hatchway and fish-room; and twelve large canvas buckets were immediately employed at each.

On opening the fish-room, we were so fortunate as to discover that two puncheons of rum, which belonged to me, had escaped. They were immediately got up and served out at times in drams; and had it not been for this relief, and some lime juice, the people would have dropped.

We soon found our account in baling; the spare pump had been put down the fore hatchway, and a pump shifted to the fish-room; but the motion of the ship had washed the coals so small that they reached every part of the ship, and the pumps were soon choked. However, the water by noon had considerably diminished by working the buckets; but there appeared no prospect of saving the ship if the gale continued. The labour was too great to hold out without water: yet the people worked without a murmur, and indeed with cheerfulness.

At this time the weather was more moderate, and a couple of spars were got ready for shears to set up a jury foremast; but as the evening came on the gale again increased. We had seen nothing this day but the ship that had lost her main mast, and she appeared to be as much in want of assistance as ourselves, having fired guns of distress; and before night I was told her foremast was gone.

The *Centaur* laboured so much that I had scarcely a hope she could swim till morning. However, by great exertion with the chain pumps and baling, we held our own; but our sufferings for want of water were very great, and many of the people could not be restrained from drinking salt water.

"At daylight (the 11th) there was no vessel in sight; and flashes from guns having been seen in the night, we feared the ship we had seen the preceding day had foundered. Towards ten o'clock in the forenoon the weather grew more moderate, the water diminished in the hold, and the people were encouraged to redouble their efforts to get the water low enough to break a cask of fresh water out of the ground tier; and some of the most resolute of the seamen were employed in the attempt. At noon we succeeded with one cask, which, though little, was a seasonable relief.

All the officers, passengers, and boys, who were not of the profession of seamen, had been employed in thrumming a sail, which was passed under the ship's bottom, and I thought had some effect. The shears were raised for the foremast; the weather looked promising, the sea fell, and at night we were able to relieve at the pumps and baling every two hours. By the morning of the 20th the fore hold was cleared of the water, and we had the comfortable promise of a fine day. It proved so, and I was determined to make use of it with all possible exertion. I divided the ship's company, with officers attending them, into parties, to raise the jury fore-mast; to heave over the lower-deck guns; to clear the wreck of the fore and after holds; to prepare the machine for steering the ship, and to work the pumps.

By night the after hold was as clear as when the ship was launched; for, to our astonishment, there was not a shovel of coals remaining, twenty chaldrons having been pumped out since the commencement of the gale. What I have called the wreck of the hold was the bulkheads of the after hold, fish-room, and spirit-rooms. The standards of the cockpit, an immense quantity of staves and wood, and part of the lining of the ship were thrown overboard, that if the water should again appear in the hold we might have no impediment in baling. All the guns were overboard, the fore mast secured, and the machine, which was to be similar to that with which the *Ipswich* was steered, was in great forwardness; so that I was in hopes, the moderate weather continuing, that I should be able to steer the ship by noon the following day, and at least save the people on some of the western islands. Had we had any other ship in company with us, I should have thought it my duty to have quitted the *Centaur* this day.

This night the people got some rest by relieving the watches; but in the morning of the 21st we had the mortification to find that the weather again threatened, and by noon it blew a storm. The ship laboured greatly and the water appeared in the fore and after hold, and increased. The carpenter also informed me that the leathers were nearly consumed; and likewise, that the chains of the pumps, by constant exertion and the friction of the coals, were considered as nearly useless.

As we had now no other resource but baling, I gave orders that scuttles should be cut through the deck to introduce more buckets into the hold, and all the sail-makers were employed, night and day, in making canvas buckets; and the orlop deck having fallen in on the larboard side, I ordered the sheet cable to be tossed overboard. The wind at this time was at west, and being on the larboard tack, many schemes had been practised to wear the ship, that we might drive into a less boisterous latitude, as well as approach the western islands; but none succeeded; and having a weak carpenter's crew they were hardly sufficient to attend the pumps, so that we could not make any progress with the steering machine.

Another sail had been thrummed and got over, but we did not find its use; indeed, there was no prospect but in a change of weather. A large leak had been discovered and stopped in the fore hold, but the ship appeared so weak from her labouring that it was clear she could not last long. The after cockpit had fallen in, the fore cockpit the same, with all the store-rooms down: the stern post was so loose that, as the ship rolled, the water rushed in on either side in great streams, which we could not stop.

Night came on, with the same dreary prospect as that of the preceding day, and was passed in continual labour. Morning came (the 22nd) without our seeing anything, or any change of weather, and the day was spent with the same struggles to keep the ship above water, pumping and baling at the hatchways and scuttles. Towards night another of the chain pumps was rendered quite useless, by one of the rollers being displaced at the bottom of the pump, and this was without remedy, there being too much water in the well to get to it; we also had but six leathers remaining, so that the fate of the ship was not far off. Still the labour went on without any apparent despair, every officer taking his share of it, and the people always cheerful and obedient.

During the night the water increased, but about seven in the morning of the 23rd I was informed that an unusual quantity of water appeared, all at once, in the fire hold, which, upon my going forward to be convinced, I found but too true; the stowage of the hold ground tier was all in motion, so that in a short time there was not a whole cask to be seen. We were convinced the ship had sprung a fresh leak. Another sail had been thrumming all night, and I was giving directions to place it over the bows, when I perceived the ship settling by the head, the lower-deck bow ports being even with the water.

At this period the carpenter acquainted me the well was staved in, destroyed by the wreck of the hold, and the chain pumps displaced and totally useless. There was nothing left but to redouble our efforts in baling, but it became difficult to fill the buckets, from the quantity of staves, planks, anchor stocks, and yard-arm pieces which were now washed from the wings and floating from side to side with the motion of the ship. The people, till this period, had laboured, as if determined to conquer their difficulties, without a murmur or without a tear; but now, seeing their efforts useless, many of them burst into tears, and wept like children.

I gave orders for the anchors, of which we had two remaining, to be thrown overboard, one of which (the spare anchor) had been most surprisingly hove in upon the forecastle and midships when the ship had been upon her beam-ends, and gone through the deck.

Every time that I visited the hatchway I observed the water increased, and at noon washed even with the orlop deck; the carpenter assured me the ship could not swim long, and proposed making rafts to float the ship's company, whom it was not in my power to encourage any longer with a prospect of their safety. Some appeared perfectly resigned, went to their hammocks, and desired their messmates to lash them in; others were lashing themselves to gratings and small rafts: but the most predominant idea was that of putting on their best and cleanest clothes.

"The weather, about noon, had been something moderate, and as rafts had been mentioned by the carpenter, I thought it right to make the attempt, though I knew our booms could not float half the ship's company in fine weather; but we were in a situation to catch at a straw. I therefore called the ship's company together, told them my intention, recommending them to remain regular and obedient to their officers. Preparations were immediately made for this purpose; the booms were cleared; the boats, of which we had three, *viz.*, cutter, pinnace, and five-oared yawl, were got over the side; a bag of bread was ordered to be put in each, and any liquors that could be got at, for the purpose of supplying the rafts.

I had intended myself to go in the five-oared yawl, and the coxswain was desired to get anything from my steward that might be useful. Two men, captains of the tops of the forecastle, or quarter-masters, were placed in each of them, to prevent any person from forcing the boats or getting into them till an arrangement was made. While these preparations were making, the ship was gradually sinking, the orlop decks having been blown up by the water in the hold, and the cables floated to the gun-deck. The men had for some time quitted their employment of baling, and the ship was left to her fate.

In the afternoon the weather again threatened, and blew strong in squalls, the sea ran high, and one of the boats (the yawl) was staved alongside and sunk. As the evening approached the ship appeared little more than suspended in water. There was no certainty that she would swim from one minute to another; and the love of life began now to level all distinctions. It was impossible, indeed, for any man to deceive himself with a hope of being saved upon a raft in such a sea; besides that, the ship in sinking, it was probable, would carry everything down with her in a vortex, to a certain destruction.

It was near five o'clock, when, coming from my cabin, I observed a number of people looking very anxiously over the side, and looking myself, I saw that several men had forced the pinnace and that more were attempting to get in. I had immediate thoughts of securing this boat before she might be sunk by numbers. There appeared not more than a moment for consideration; to remain and perish with the ship's company, to whom I could not be of use any longer, or seize the opportunity, which was the only way of escaping, and leave the people, with whom I had been so well satisfied on a variety of occasions that I thought I could give my life to preserve them—this, indeed, was a painful conflict, such as, I believe, no man can describe, nor any have a just idea of who have not been in a similar situation.

The love of life prevailed. I called to Mr. Rainy, the master, the only officer upon deck, desired him to follow me, and immediately descended into the boat, at the after-part of the chains; but not without great difficulty got the boat clear of the ship, twice the number that the boat would carry pushing to get in, and many jumping into the water. Mr. Baylis, a young gentleman fifteen years of age, leaped from the chains after the boat had got off, and was taken in. The boat falling astern, became exposed to the sea, and we endeavoured to pull her bow round to keep her to the break of the sea, and to pass to windward of the ship; but in the attempts she was nearly filled, the sea ran too high, and the only probability of living was keeping her before the wind.

It was then that I became sensible how little, if any, better our condition was than that of those who remained in the ship; at best, it appeared to be only a prolongation of a miserable existence. We were, all together, twelve in number, in a leaky boat, with one of the gunwales staved, in nearly the middle of the Western Ocean, without a compass, without quadrant, without sail, without great-coat or cloak, all very thinly clothed, in a gale of wind, with a great sea running! It was now five o'clock in the evening, and in half an hour we lost sight of the ship. Before it was dark a blanket was discovered in the boat.

This was immediately bent to one of the stretchers, and under it, as a sail, we scudded all night, in expectation of being swallowed up by every wave, it being with great difficulty that we could sometimes clear the boat of the water before the return of the next great sea; all of us half drowned, and sitting, except those who baled, at the bottom of the boat; and without having really perished, I am sure no people ever endured more. In the morning the weather grew moderate, the wind having shifted to the southward, as we discovered by the sun. Having survived the night, we began to recollect ourselves, and to think of our future preservation.

When we quitted the ship the wind was at north-west or north-north-west. Fayal had borne east-south-east two hundred and fifty or two hundred and sixty leagues. Had the wind continued for five or six days, there was a probability that running before the sea we might have fallen in with some of the Western Islands. The change of wind was death to these hopes; for, should it come to blow, we knew there would be no preserving life but by running before the sea, which would carry us again to the northward, where we must soon afterwards perish.

Upon examining what we had to subsist on, I found a bag of bread, a small ham, a single piece of pork, two quart bottles of water, and a few of French cordials. The wind continued to be southward for eight or nine days, and providentially never blew so strong but that we could keep the side of the boat to the sea; but we were always most miserably wet and cold. We kept a sort of reckoning, but the sun and stars being somewhat hidden from us, for twenty-four hours we had no very correct idea of our navigation. We judged, at this period, that we had made nearly an east-north-east course since the first night's run, which had carried us to the southeast, and expected to see the island of Corvo. In this, however, we were disappointed, and we feared that the southerly wind had driven us far to the northward.

Our prayers were now for a northerly wind. Our condition began to be truly miserable, both from hunger and cold; for on the fifth we had discovered that our bread was nearly all spoiled by salt water, and it was necessary to go on allowance. One biscuit divided into twelve morsels for breakfast, and the same for dinner; the neck of a bottle broken off, with the cork in, served for a glass, and this filled with water was the allowance of twenty-four hours for each man. This was done without any sort of partiality or distinction; but we must have perished ere this, had we not caught six quarts of rain water; and this we could not have been blessed with, had we not found in the boat a pair of sheets, which by accident had been put there. These were spread when it rained, and when thoroughly wet wrung into the kid with which we baled the boat. With this short allowance, which was rather tantalising than sustaining in our comfortless condition, we began to grow very feeble, and our clothes being continually wet, our bodies were in many places chafed into sores.

On the 13th day it fell calm, and soon after a breeze of wind sprang up from the south-south-west and blew to a gale, so that we ran before the sea at the rate of five or six miles an hour under our blanket, till we judged we were to the southward of Fayal and to the westward sixty leagues; but the wind blowing strong we could not attempt to steer for it. Our wishes were now for the wind to shift to the westward. This was the fifteenth day we had been in the boat, and we had only one day's bread and one bottle of water remaining of a second supply of rain. Our sufferings were now as great as human strength could bear, but we were convinced that good spirits were a better support than any great bodily strength; for on this day Thomas Matthews, quartermaster, the stoutest man in the boat, perished from hunger and cold; on the day before he complained of want of strength in his throat, as he expressed it, to swallow his morsel, and in the night drank salt water, grew delirious and died without a groan.

As it became next to a certainty that we should all perish in the same manner in a day or two, it was somewhat comfortable to reflect that dying of hunger was not so dreadful as our imagination had represented. Others had complained of these symptoms in their throats; some had drunk their own urine; and all but myself had drunk salt water.

As yet despair and gloom had been successfully prohibited; and as the evenings closed in, the men had been encouraged by turns to sing a song, or relate a story, instead of supper; but this evening I found it impossible to raise either. As the night came on it fell calm, and about midnight a breeze of wind sprang up, we guessed from the westward by the swell, but there not being a star to be seen, we were afraid of running out of the way, and waited impatiently for the rising sun to be our compass.

As soon as the dawn appeared we found the wind to be exactly as we had wished, at west-south-west, and immediately spread our sail, running before the sea at the rate of four miles an hour. Our last breakfast had been served with the bread and water remaining, when John Gregory, quarter-master, declared with much confidence that he saw land in the south-east. We had so often seen fogbanks, which had the appearance of land, that I did not trust myself to believe it, and cautioned the people (who were extravagantly elated) that they might not feel the effects of disappointment, till at length one of them broke out into a most immoderate fit of joy, which I could not restrain, and declared he had never seen land in his life if what he now saw was not land.

We immediately shaped our course for it, though on my part with very little faith. The wind freshened, and the boat went through the water at the rate of five or six miles an hour; and in two hours' time the land was plainly seen by every man in the boat, at a very great distance, so that we did not reach it till ten at night. It was at least twenty leagues from us when first discovered; and I cannot help remarking, with much thankfulness, the providential favour shown to us in this instance.

In every part of the horizon, except where the land was discovered, there was so thick a haze that we could not have seen anything for more than three or four leagues. Fayal, by our reckoning, bore east by north, which course we were steering, and in a few hours, had not the sky opened for our preservation, we should have increased our distance from the land, got to the eastward, and of course missed all the island. As we approached the land our belief was strengthened that it was Fayal. The island of Pico, which might have revealed it to us, had the weather been perfectly clear, was at this time capped with clouds, and it was some time before we were quite satisfied, having traversed for two hours a great part of the island, where the steep and rocky shore refused us a landing.

This circumstance was borne with much impatience, for we had flattered ourselves that we should meet with fresh water at the first part of the land we might approach; and being disappointed, the thirst of some had increased anxiety almost to a degree of madness, so that we were near making the attempt to land in some places where the boat must have been dashed to pieces by the surf. At length we discovered a fishing canoe, which conducted us into the road of Fayal about midnight, but where the regulation of the port did not permit us to land till examined by the health officers; however, I did not think much of sleeping this night in the boat, our pilot having brought us some refreshments of bread, wine, and water.

In the morning we were visited by Mr. Graham, the English consul, whose humane attention made very ample amends for the formality of the Portuguese. Indeed, I can never sufficiently express the sense I have of his kindness and humanity both to myself and people; for I believe it was the whole of his employment for several days to contrive the best means of restoring us to health and strength. It is true, I believe, there never were more pitiable objects. Some of the stoutest men belonging to the *Centaur* were obliged to be supported through the streets of Fayal. Mr. Rainy, the master, and myself, were, I think, in better health than the rest; but I could not walk without being supported; and for several days, with the best and most comfortable provisions of diet and lodgings, we grew rather worse than better.

The Loss of the "Royal George"
By G. H. Walker.

When the brave die in battle, the ardour which impels them to glory and renders them insensible of their danger leaves a brilliance behind, which mitigates, in a great degree, the grief of their relatives and friends. But nothing can be more distressing than to behold a multitude of gallant men in a moment of inactivity, perhaps in the midst of amusements and the height of enjoyment, anchored on their own coast, and riding in smooth water, overwhelmed in a moment in the liquid abyss, and precipitated into an awful eternity. Such was the fate of the crew of the *Royal George*.

The *Royal George*, one hundred and eight guns, the flag ship of Admiral Kempenfeldt and one of the best ships in the navy, had just returned from a cruise in which she had sprung a leak which demanded attention. The carpenter and others, after a strict survey, finding that the leak was not more than two feet below the water-mark, and supposing it to be occasioned by the rubbing off the copper sheathing, it was resolved, in order to save time, instead of sending her into dock to give her a slight careen, or in the language of the seamen, "a parliament heel"—that is, to lay her to a certain degree upon her side while her defects were examined and repaired at Spithead. It was meanwhile discovered that the pipe, for the occasional admission of water to cleanse and sweeten the ship, was out of repair, and that it was necessary to replace it with a new one.

As the ship required to be heeled very much for this purpose, the greater part of the guns were removed from one side to the other; but the vessel heeling more than was intended and the crew having neglected to stop the scuppers of the lower decks, the water came in and for some time she stole down imperceptibly. During this time many of the crew were at dinner; but as soon as they discovered their dangerous condition they beat to arms to right the ship. They were, however, too late, and all their efforts were in vain, for in a few minutes the *Royal George* fell flat on one side, filled with water, and the guns, shot, etc., falling to the underside, she went to the bottom, August 29th, 1782, before any signal of distress could be made.

At this fatal moment there were nearly twelve hundred persons on board, including about two hundred and fifty women and several children, chiefly belonging to the seamen, who had been permitted to go on board when the ship cast anchor at Spithead and to remain there until the order for sailing arrived.

The people who were on watch upon deck, to the number of two hundred and thirty, were mostly saved by the boats, which were manned with the utmost expedition by the ships near the *Royal George* when they observed that the vessel was going down. Their assistance was, however, delayed for some time by the swell occasioned by the sinking of such a large body, which produced a temporary whirlpool in the water. About seventy others, who rose after the ship disappeared, were also picked up; among these were four lieutenants, eleven women, and the rest seamen.

One of the officers thus rescued was Lieutenant Durham, who fortunately was the officer of the watch and upon deck when he observed the vessel going down. He had just time to throw off his coat and scramble on the beam from which, as the ship sank, he was soon washed and left floating about among men and hammocks. A drowning marine caught him by the waistcoat and held him fast, so that he was several times drawn under water. It was in vain to reason with the man: he therefore clung with his legs round a hammock, with one hand unbuttoned his waistcoat, and, sloping his shoulders, committed it, together with the unfortunate marine, to the waves. He then got to some of the top rigging; a boat came to him, but he nobly declined the assistance offered by those on board her, pointing out to them where Captain Waghorne was in great danger, and desiring them to go to his relief, after which the gallant youth was taken up and brought in safety to the shore.

Mr. Henry Bishop, a young man about nineteen years of age, experienced a very extraordinary preservation. Being on the lower deck at the time of the fatal accident, as the vessel filled the force of the water hurried him almost insensibly up the hatchway, when at that instant he was met by one of the guns which had fallen from the middle deck. Striking him on his left hand it broke three of his fingers; he, however, found himself a few seconds later floating on the surface of the water, where he was ultimately taken up by a boat.

By this sudden and dreadful catastrophe nearly nine hundred persons perished. Among the rest, the loss of Admiral Kempenfeldt, whose flag was then flying on board the *Royal George*, was universally lamented. He was the son of Lieutenant-Colonel Kempenfeldt, a native of Sweden, whose character is preserved in the *Spectator*, under the name of Captain Sentry. He entered very early into the service of the navy, for which profession he soon discovered uncommon talents. In the year 1757 he was appointed captain of the *Elizabeth*, and proceeded with Commodore Stevens to the East Indies, where he distinguished himself in three several actions against the French squadron, being always opposed to a ship of superior force. His skill was of the utmost importance during the blockade of Pondicherry as well as at the subsequent reduction of Manilla by Admiral Cornish in 1761.

After serving a considerable time in the West Indies he obtained leave to return to England. During the peace he constantly spent part of the year in France, not in the pursuit of pleasure, but in search of professional knowledge, in which, if he did not excel, he at least equalled any naval officer in Europe. At the commencement of the American war he was appointed to the *Buckingham*, and served as first captain under the Admirals Hardy, Geary, and Darby; and his gallant conduct contributed in no small degree to the capture of the convoy under M. Guichen. His character in private life rendered his acquaintance an enviable acquisition, and as an officer his death was a very severe loss to his country.

The *Lark* sloop victualler, which was lying alongside the *Royal George*, was swallowed up in the vortex occasioned by the sinking of the vessel, and several of the people on board her perished.

The *Royal George* was the oldest first-rate in the service. She was built at Woolwich; her keel was laid down in 1751 and she was hauled out of the dock in July 1755, it being unusual, at that time, to build such large ships on slips to launch. She was pierced for one hundred guns, but having recently had two additional ports, including the carronades, mounted one hundred and eight guns; she was rather short and high, like all the old first-rates, but sailed so well that she had more flags on board her than any vessel then in the service. Lord Anson, Admiral Boscawen, Lord Hawke, Lord Rodney, Lord Howe, and several other principal officers, repeatedly commanded in her. She carried the tallest masts and squarest canvas of any English built ship in the navy, and originally the heaviest metal—namely, fifty-two, forty, and twenty-eight pounders—but they had been changed, on account of her age, to forty, thirty-two and eighteen pounders.

The Mutiny of the "Bounty"

The circumstances detailed in the following narrative are altogether of so singular and romantic a character that but for the undeniable authenticity of every particular, the whole might be considered as the production of the ingenious brain of a Defoe. Some of the incidents indeed surpass in impressive interest anything to be met with in the fictitious history of Alexander Selkirk's solitary existence and adventure.

In December 1787 the *Bounty* sailed from Spithead for Otaheite under the command of Lieutenant Bligh, who had previously accompanied Captain Cook in his exploiting voyages in the Pacific Ocean. The object of the present expedition was to convey from Otaheite to our West Indian colonies the plants of the bread-fruit tree which Dampier, Cook, and other voyagers had observed to grow with the most prolific luxuriance in the South Sea Islands, and which furnished the natives with a perpetual and wholesome subsistence without even the trouble of cultivation.

The crew of the *Bounty* consisted of forty-five individuals, including the commander and two skilful gardeners to take charge of the plants, for the removal of which every accommodation had been provided on board, under the superintendence of Sir Joseph Banks who had personally visited Otaheite with Captain Wallis. After a most distressing voyage, in which, after reaching Cape Horn, they were compelled to put the helm a-weather and take the route by Van Diemen's Land, the voyagers anchored in Matavia Bay, Otaheite, on October 26th, 1788, having run over, by the log, since leaving England, a space of 27,086 miles, or an average of one hundred and eight miles in twenty-four hours.

The simple natives, who had experienced much kindness from Captain Cook, testified great joy on the arrival of the strangers, and loaded them with presents of provisions of every sort. The character, condition, and habits of the islanders, as described to us even by their early visitors, present a most extraordinary contrast to the usual features of savage life. They were a kind, mild-tempered, social, and affectionate race, living in the utmost harmony amongst themselves, their whole lives being one unvaried round of cheerful contentment, luxurious ease, and healthful exercise and amusements.

Bligh appears to have been tempted to remain at this luxurious spot much longer than was either proper or necessary, as the bread-fruit plants, and provisions of hogs, fowls, fish, and vegetables of every description were amply supplied him by the kind natives. The liberty which he gave his crew to go on shore and enjoy all the indulgences which the place afforded, was extremely imprudent; and this, together with the capricious harshness and unjustifiable insult with which he occasionally treated everyone on board—officers as well as men—appears to have been the sole cause of the unfortunate occurrence that afterwards took place. The *Bounty* which, as we have mentioned, arrived October 20th, 1788, did not sail till April 4th, 1789, when she departed loaded with presents, and amid the tears and regrets of the natives. They continued till the 27th amongst the islands of that archipelago, touching many of them, bartering and interchanging presents with the natives, many of whom remembered Bligh when he accompanied Cook in the *Resolution*.

It was on the night of the 27th that the mutiny broke out. The affair, as far as can ever be learned by the strictest investigation, was entirely unpremeditated, and resulted entirely from the commander's giving way to one of those furious and ungovernable fits of passion which he from time to time exhibited. On the day previous (the 26th), Bligh, having missed some of the cocoanuts that were piled up on deck, ordered a search to be made; but none being discovered, he burst into a paroxysm of passion, calling them all scoundrels and thieves alike, swearing he would make the half of them jump overboard before they got through Endeavour Straits, and ordering the villains' (officers) grog to be stopped and gave them half a pound of yams for dinner.

The officer of the watch, a young man of respectable family, named Fletcher Christian, who was master's mate, and had been two voyages with Bligh, incurred the greatest share of abuse, the latter cursing him for a hound, and accusing him of having stolen the cocoanuts for his own use. Christian, who was a fiery-spirited young man, appears to have become exasperated at this ignominious treatment, to much of the same kind of which he had been subjected for some time previous; so much so, indeed, that he declared to some of his messmates that he had been in hell for the last fortnight, on account of Bligh's usage of him, and expressed his determination to leave the ship in a raft on the first opportunity, and commit himself to the waves rather than remain on board. During the night of the 28th he accordingly began to prepare his raft; and while so employed, one of the crew unfortunately suggested that it would be better for him to seize the ship at once. The idea which Christian does not seem to have thought of till that moment, was instantly caught at, and a few whispers amongst the crew showed that the majority were quite ready for the scheme, which was forthwith put into execution.

About sunrise on Tuesday, April 28th, Christian, with three of the crew, entered Bligh's cabin and secured him in bed, tied his hands behind his back, and hurried him on deck. Their companions had in the meanwhile secured those who were suspected to be disinclined to the mutiny; among whom was Mr. Peter Heywood (afterwards so much distinguished in the royal navy service), and two other midshipmen, who were detained (contrary to their express wishes) to assist the mutineers in managing the vessel. Several other of the crew, likewise, who disclaimed all share in the mutiny, were thus forcibly detained. A boat was then hoisted alongside, and Bligh, with eighteen unfortunate companions, was forced into it. Some provisions, clothes, and four cutlasses were given them, and they were cast adrift in the open ocean. Twenty-five remained on board, the ablest of the ship's company. As the boat put off, "Huzza for Otaheite!" was shouted by the mutineers, thus indicating the destination of their further proceedings.

Being near the island of Tofoa, the castaways rowed towards it for the purpose of obtaining some bread-fruit and water, with which the natives at first seemed very willing to supply them, until Bligh imprudently advised his men to say, in answer to the queries put them about the ship, that it had overset and sunk. The consequence was, that the natives attacked them, stoned one man to death, and it was with difficulty that the remainder escaped. Bligh's companions then entreated him to steer for home at all risks and hazards; and on being told that no hope of relief could be entertained till they reached Timor, off the coast of New Holland, a distance fully twelve hundred leagues, they readily agreed to be content with an allowance, which, on calculation, was found would not exceed an ounce of bread and a quarter of a pint of water per day for each man.

After taking them, bound by a solemn promise to this effect, these unfortunate men boldly bore away, on May 2nd, across a sea where the navigation was little, in an open boat twenty-three feet long and deep, laden with eighteen men. It is not our purpose here to detail the particulars of this adventurous voyage. Suffice it to say that, after enduring the most horrible distresses from cold, thirst, famine, and running a distance by the log of more than three hundred miles, the whole reached the island of Timor alive on June 14th, but so much spent as more to resemble spectres than men. They were treated with great kindness by the inhabitants, but, notwithstanding every attention, four or five of them here died; the rest proceeded to Batavia, whence they obtained passages to England, where Bligh arrived in March, 1790.

The intelligence of the mutiny, and the sufferings of Bligh and his companions, naturally excited a great sensation in England. Bligh was immediately promoted to the rank of commander, and Captain Edwards was despatched to Otaheite in the *Pandora* frigate, with instructions to search for the *Bounty* and her mutinous crew, and bring them to England. The *Pandora* reached Matavia Bay on March 23rd, 1791; and even before she had come to anchor, Joseph Coleman, formerly armourer of the *Bounty*, pushed off from shore in a canoe, and came on board. He frankly told who he was, and professed his readiness to give every information that might be required of him.

Scarcely had the ship anchored, when Messrs. Heywood and Stewart, late midshipmen of the *Bounty*, also came on board; and in the course of two days afterwards, the whole of the remainder of the *Bounty's* crew (in number sixteen) then on the island surrendered themselves, with the exception of two, who fled to the mountains, where, as it afterwards appeared, they were murdered by the natives.

From his prisoners, and the journals kept by one or two of them, Captain Edwards learnt the proceedings of Christian and his associates after turning Bligh and his companions adrift in the boat. It appears that they steered in the first instance to the island of Toobouai, where they intended to form a settlement; but the opposition of the natives, and want of many necessary materials, determined them to return in the meantime to Otaheite, where they arrived on May 25th, 1789. In answer to the inquiries of Tinah, the king, about Bligh and the rest of the crew, the mutineers stated that they had fallen in with Captain Cook, who was forming a settlement in a neighbouring island, and had retained Bligh and the others to assist him, while they themselves had been despatched to Otaheite for an additional supply of hogs, goats, fowls, bread-fruit and various other articles.

Overjoyed at hearing their old friend Cook was alive, and about to settle so near them, the humane and unsuspicious islanders set about actively to procure the supplies wanted, that in a few days the *Bounty* received on board three hundred and twelve hogs, thirty-eight goats, eight dozen of fowls, a bull and a cow, and a large quantity of breadfruit, plantains, bananas, and other fruits. The mutineers also took with them eight men, nine women, and seven boys, with all of whom they arrived a second time at Toobouai on June 26th, where they warped the ship up the harbour, landed the live stock, and set about building a fort fifty yards square. Quarrels and disappointments, however, soon broke out among them. The poor natives were treated like slaves, and upon attempting to retaliate, were mercilessly put to death.

Christian, finding his authority almost entirely disregarded, called a consultation as to what steps were next to be taken, when it was agreed that Toobouai should be abandoned; that the ship should once more be taken to Otaheite, where those who might choose it would be put ashore, while the rest who preferred remaining in the vessel might proceed wherever they had a mind. This was accordingly done: sixteen of the crew went on shore at Matavia (fourteen of whom, as already stated, were received on board the *Pandora*, and two were murdered), while Christian with his eight comrades, and taking with them seven Otaheitan men and twelve women, finally sailed from Matavia on September 21st, 1789, from which time they had never been more heard of.

Captain Edwards instituted a strict search after the fugitives amongst the various groups of islands in the Pacific, but finding no trace of them, he set sail, after three months' investigation, for the east coast of New Holland. Here, by some mismanagement, the *Pandora* struck upon the singular coral reef that runs along that coast, called the Barrier Reef, and filled so fast that scarcely were the boats got out when she foundered and went down, thirty-four of the crew and four of the prisoners perishing in her. It is painful to record anything to the discredit of that service which has proved the pride and safeguard of Great Britain, and made her the acknowledged sovereign of the sea. But the concurring testimony of the unfortunate prisoners exhibits the conduct of Captain Edwards towards them in colours which are shocking to contemplate. They were confined in a small round house, built on the after deck on purpose, which could only be entered by a scuttle in the top, about eighteen inches square.

From this narrow prison they were never allowed to stir, and they were, over and above, heavily loaded with irons both at the wrists and ankles. When the *Pandora* went down, no attempt was made to save them, and the ten survivors escaped almost in a state of complete nudity. After reaching a low, sandy, desert island, or rather quay, as such are nautically termed, Captain Edwards caused his men to form tents out of the sails they had saved, under which he and his men reposed in comparative comfort; but he refused the same indulgence to his miserable captives, whose only refuge, therefore, from the scorching rays of the sun, was by burying themselves up to the neck amongst the burning sand, so that their bodies were blistered as if they had been scalded with boiling water. But we refrain from dwelling on facts so disreputable to the character of a British sailor.

The *Pandora's* survivors reached Batavia in their boats, whence they obtained passages to England in Dutch vessels. A court martial was soon after held (September, 1792), when six of the ten mutineers were found guilty and condemned to death—the other four were acquitted. Only three of the six, however, were executed. Mr. Heywood, who was amongst the condemned (chiefly by the perverted and prejudiced evidence of Captain Bligh and a fellow-midshipman), was afterwards pardoned upon the strong recommendation of the court, who, notwithstanding the vindictive evidence against him, were perfectly convinced of his innocence. His subsequent honourable career proved him fully deserving the favourable opinion of his judges, as well as of the promotion he obtained.

Nearly twenty years elapsed after the period of the above occurrences, and all recollection of the *Bounty* and her wretched crew had passed away, when an accidental discovery, as interesting as unexpected, once more recalled public attention to that event. The captain of an American schooner having in 1808 accidentally touched at an island, up to that time supposed to be uninhabited, called Pitcairn's Island, found a community, speaking English, who represented themselves as the descendants of the mutineers of the *Bounty*, of whom there was still one man, of the name of Alexander Smith, alive amongst them. Intelligence of this singular circumstance was sent by the American captain (Folger) to Sir Sydney Smith at Valparaiso, and by him transmitted to the Lords of the Admiralty. But the government was at that time perhaps too much engaged in the events of the continental war to attend to the information, nor was anything further heard of this interesting little society until 1814.

In that year two British men-of-war cruising in the Pacific, made an island, which they could not at first believe to be Pitcairn's Island, as it was more than three degrees out of the longitude assigned it by Captain Carteret, who first discovered it in 1797. They were confirmed in this opinion by observing symptoms of cultivation, and, on nearing the shore, saw plantations regularly and orderly laid out. Soon afterwards they observed a few natives coming down a steep descent with their canoes on their shoulders, and in a few minutes perceived one of these little vessels darting through a heavy surf, and paddling off towards the ships. But their astonishment may be imagined, when, on coming along side, they were hailed in good English with—"Won't you heave us a rope now?" This being done, a young man sprang up the side with extraordinary activity, and stood on the deck before them.

In answer to the question, "Who are you?" he replied that his name was Thursday October Christian, son of the late Fletcher Christian by an Otaheitan mother; that he was the first born on the island, and was so named because he was born on a Thursday in October. All this sounded singular and miraculous in the ears of the British captains, Sir Thomas Staines and Mr. Pipon, but they were soon satisfied of its truth. Young Christian was at this time about twenty-four years old, a tall, handsome youth fully six feet high, with black hair, and an open, interesting English countenance. As he wore no clothes except a piece of cloth round his loins, and a straw hat ornamented with black cock's feathers, his fine figure and well-shaped muscular limbs were displayed to great advantage, and attracted general admiration. His body was much tanned by exposure to the weather; but although his complexion was somewhat brown, it wanted that tinge of red peculiar to the natives of the Pacific. He spoke English correctly both in grammar and pronunciation; and his frank and ingenuous deportment excited in every one the liveliest feelings of compassion and interest. His companion was a fine, handsome youth, of seventeen or eighteen years of age, named George Young, son of one of the *Bounty's* midshipmen.

The youths expressed great surprise at everything they saw, especially a cow, which they supposed to be either a huge goat or a horned sow, having never seen any other quadruped. When questioned concerning the *Bounty*, they referred the captains to an old man on shore, the only surviving Englishman, whose name they said was John Adams, but who proved to be the identical Alexander Smith before mentioned, having changed his name from some caprice or other. The officers went ashore with the youths, and were received by old Adams, as we shall now call him, who conducted them to his house, and treated them to an elegant repast of eggs, fowls, yams, plaintains, bread-fruit, etc. They now learned from him an account of the fate of his companions, who, with himself, preferred accompanying Christian in the *Bounty* to remaining at Otaheite—which account agreed with that he afterwards gave at greater length to Captain Beechey in 1825. Our limit will not permit us to detail all the interesting particulars at length, as we could have wished, but they are in substance as follows:—

It was Christian's object, in order to avoid the vengeance of the British law, to proceed to some unknown and uninhabited island, and the Marquesas Islands were first fixed upon. But Christian, on reading Captain Carteret's account of Pitcairn's Island, thought it better adapted for the purpose, and shaped his course thither, Having landed and traversed it, they found it every way suitable to their wishes, possessing water, wood, a good soil, and some fruits. The anchorage in the offing was extremely dangerous for ships, and it was scarcely possible for boats to get through the surf that broke on the shore. The mountains were so difficult of access, and the passes so narrow, that they might be maintained by a few persons against an army, and there were several caves, to which, in case of necessity, they could retreat, and where, as long as their provisions lasted, they might bid defiance to all pursuit.

Having ascertained all this, they returned on board, and having landed their hogs, goats, and poultry, and gutted the ship of everything that could be useful to them, they set fire to her, and destroyed every vestige that might lead to the discovery of their retreat. This was on January 23rd, 1790. The island was then divided into nine equal portions amongst them, a suitable spot of neutral ground being reserved for a village. The poor Otaheitans now found themselves reduced to the condition of mere slaves; but they patiently submitted, and everything went on peaceably for two years.

About that time, Williams, one of the seamen, having the misfortune to lose his wife, forcibly took the wife of one of the Otaheitans, which, together with their continued ill-usage, so exasperated the latter that they formed a plan for murdering the whole of their oppressors. The plot, however, was discovered and revealed by the Englishmen's wives, and two of the Otaheitans were put to death. But the surviving natives soon afterwards matured a more successful conspiracy, and in one day murdered five of the Englishmen, including Christian. Adams and Young were spared at the intercession of their wives, and the remaining two, M'Koy and Quintal (two desperate ruffians), escaped to the mountains, whence, however, they soon rejoined their companions.

But the further career of these villains was short. M'Koy having been brought up in a Scotch distillery, succeeded in extracting a bottle of ardent spirits from the tea root; from which time he and Quintal were never sober, until the former became delirious, and committed suicide by jumping over a cliff. Quintal being likewise almost insane with drinking, made repeated attempts to murder Adams and Young, until they were absolutely compelled, for their own safety, to put him to death, which they did by felling him with a hatchet.

Adams and Young were at length the only surviving males who had landed on the island, and being both of a serious turn of mind, and having time for reflection and repentance, they became extremely devout. Having saved a Bible and prayer-book from the *Bounty*, they now performed family worship morning and evening, and addressed themselves to training up their own children, and those of their unfortunate companions, in piety and virtue. Young, however, was soon carried off by an asthmatic complaint, and Adams was thus left to continue his pious labours alone.

At the time Captain Staines and Pipon visited the island, this interesting little colony consisted of about forty-six persons, mostly grown-up young people, and all living in harmony and happiness together; and not only professing, but fully understanding and practising, the precepts and principles of the Christian religion. Adams had instituted the ceremony of marriage, and he assured his visitors that not one instance of debauchery or immoral conduct had occurred amongst them.

The visitors having supplied these interesting people with some tools, kettles, and other articles, took their leave. The account which they transmitted home of this newly-discovered colony, was, strange to say, as little attended to by government as that of Captain Folger, and nothing more was heard of Adams and his family for nearly twelve years, when in 1825, Captain Beechey, in the *Blossom*, bound on a voyage of discovery to Behring's Straits, touched at Pitcairn's Island. On the approach of the *Blossom* a boat came off under all sail towards the ship, containing old Adams and ten of the young men of the island. After requesting and obtaining leave to come on board, the young men sprang up the side, and shook every officer cordially by the hand. Adams, who was grown very corpulent, followed more leisurely. He was now dressed in a sailor's shirt and trousers, with a low-crowned hat, which he held in his hand in sailor fashion, while he smoothed down his bald forehead when addressed by the officers of the *Blossom*.

It was the first time he had been on board a British vessel since the destruction of the *Bounty*, now thirty-five years ago; and it was evident his mind recurred to the events of that period. Captain Beechey procured from Adams a detailed narrative of the whole transaction of the mutiny and subsequent events, which has since been published by that gentleman, and of which we have already given an abstract. The little colony had now increased to about sixty-six, including an English sailor of the name of John Buffet, who at his own earnest desire had been left by a whaler. In this man, the society luckily found an able and willing schoolmaster. He instructed the children in reading, writing, and arithmetic, and devoutly co-operated with old Adams in affording religious instruction to the community. The officers of the *Blossom* went ashore, and were entertained with a sumptuous repast at young Christian's, the table being spread with plates, knives, and forks. Buffet said grace in an emphatic manner, and so strict were they in this respect, that it was not deemed proper to touch a morsel of bread without saying grace both before and after it. The officers slept in the house all night, their bed-clothing and sheets consisting of the native cloth made of the native mulberry-tree.

The only interruption to their repose was the melody of the evening hymn, which was chanted together by the whole family after the lights were put out; and they were awakened at early dawn by the same devotional ceremony. On Sabbath the utmost decorum was attended to, and the day was passed in regular religious observances. All that remains to be said of these excellent people, concludes Beechey, is, that they appear to live together in perfect harmony and contentment; to be virtuous, religious, cheerful, and hospitable beyond the limits of prudence; to be patterns of conjugal and parental affection, and to have very few vices. We remained with them many days, and their unreserved manners gave us the fullest opportunity of becoming acquainted with any faults they might have possessed.

In consequence of a representation made by Captain Beechey, the British government sent out Captain Waldegrave in 1830, in the *Seringapatam*, with a supply of sailors' blue jackets and trousers, flannels, stockings and shoes, women's dresses, spades, mattocks, shovels, pickaxes, trowels, rakes, etc. He found their community increased to about seventy-nine, all exhibiting the same unsophisticated and amiable characteristics as we have before described. Other two Englishmen had settled amongst them; one of them, called Nobbs, a self-constituted missionary, who was endeavouring to supersede Buffet in his office of religious instructor.

The patriarch Adams, it was found, had died in March, 1826, aged sixty-five. While on his death-bed he had called the heads of families together, and urged upon them to elect a chief, which, however, they had not yet done; but the greatest harmony still prevailed amongst them, notwithstanding Nobb's exertions to form a party of his own. Captain Waldegrave thought that the island, which is about four miles square, might be able to support a thousand persons, upon reaching which number they would naturally emigrate to other islands.

Such is the account of this most singular colony, originating in crime and bloodshed. Of all the repentant criminals on record, the most interesting, perhaps, is John Adams. Nor do we know where to find a more beautiful example of the value of early instruction than in the history of this man, who, having run a full career of most kinds of vice, was checked by an interval of leisure and reflection, and a sense of new duties awakened by the power of natural affection.

The Story of Lord Exmouth
(Sir Edward Pellew)

Edward Pellew, afterwards Viscount Exmouth, was born at Dover in 1757. At thirteen years of age he went to sea on board the *Juno* frigate as midshipman, and later served in the *Blonde* frigate on Lake Champlain during the American War. While here, in command of the *Pelican* in 1782, he defeated three French privateers. Attracting the attention of his superiors by his cool and intrepid daring, he was sent home with despatches and strongly recommended for promotion.

On the outbreak of war with France in 1793 he was made captain of the *Nymph*, a thirty-six gun frigate, which he manned chiefly with Cornish miners, signalising his appointment by capturing the *Cleopatra* of forty guns—"a crack ship of France"—after a brief and brilliant encounter on the morning of June 18th. The captain of the French frigate was killed and three lieutenants wounded, besides which she lost sixty of her men, one hundred and fifty being taken prisoners. Captain Pellew lost twenty-three men killed and twenty-seven wounded. This being the first capture after the outbreak of the war, Captain Pellew received the honour of knighthood. His next appointment was to the *Arethusa*, of forty-four guns, in which he distinguished himself on many occasions while serving in the Channel with Sir J. B. Warren's squadron.

Sir Edward Pellew was, however, distinguished not only for his military skill and prowess but for his heroic humanity. The story of the shipwreck of the *Dutton* and of Sir Edward Pellew's gallant rescue of her crew and passengers has been often told, and we are glad to be able to quote the description given by his biographer.

In January, 1796, Sir Edward's ship the *Indefatigable* was refitting in Plymouth Harbour, and on the 26th Sir Edward and Lady Pellew were driving to a dinner party when they learned that there was a wreck off the shore, upon which Sir Edward left the carriage and proceeded to the Hoe.

Arrived at the beach, he saw at once that the loss of nearly all on board, between five hundred and six hundred, was inevitable, without someone to direct them. The principal officers of the ship had abandoned their charge and got on shore just as he arrived on the beach. Having urged them, but without success, to return to their duty, and vainly offered rewards to pilots and others belonging to the port to board the wreck—for all thought it too hazardous to be attempted—he exclaimed, 'Then I will go myself!' A single rope, by which *the officers* and a few others had landed, formed the only communication with the ship, and by this he was hauled on board through the surf. The danger was greatly increased by the wreck of the masts which had fallen towards the shore, and he received an injury in the back which confined him to his bed for a week, in consequence of being dragged under the main mast. But, disregarding this at the time, he reached the deck, declared himself and assumed the command. He assured the people that everyone would be saved if they quietly obeyed his orders; that he himself would be the last to quit the wreck, but that he would run any one through who disobeyed him.

His well-known name, with the calmness and energy he displayed, gave confidence to the despairing multitude. He was received with three hearty cheers, which were echoed by the multitude on shore, and his promptitude and resource soon enabled him to find and apply the means by which all might be safely landed. His officers, in the meantime, though not knowing that he was on board, were exerting themselves to bring assistance from the *Indefatigable*. Mr. Pellowe, first lieutenant, left the ship in the barge, and Mr. Thomson, acting master, in the launch; but the boats could not be brought alongside the wreck and were obliged to run for the Barbican. A small boat belonging to a merchant vessel was more fortunate.

Mr. Esdell, signal midshipman to the port admiral, and Mr. Coghlan, mate of the (merchant) vessel, succeeded, at the risk of their lives, in bringing her alongside. The ends of two additional hawsers were got on shore, and Sir Edward contrived cradles, to be slung upon them, with travelling ropes to pass forward and backward between the ship and the beach. Each hawser was held on shore by a number of men, who watched the rolling of the wreck, and kept the ropes tight and steady. Meantime a cutter had with great difficulty worked out of Plymouth Pool, and two large boats arrived from the dockyard, under the directions of Mr. Hemmings, the master-attendant, by whose caution and judgment they were enabled to approach the wreck, and received the more helpless of the passengers who were carried to the cutter.

Sir Edward, with his sword drawn, directed the proceedings and preserved order, a task the more difficult as the soldiers had got at the spirits before he came on board and many were drunk. The children, the women and the sick were the first landed. One of them was only three weeks old, and nothing in the whole transaction impressed Sir Edward more strongly than the struggle of the mother's feelings before she would entrust her infant to his care, or afforded him more pleasure than the success of his attempt to save it. Next, the soldiers were got on shore, then the ship's company, and finally Sir Edward himself, who was one of the last to leave her. Everyone was saved, and presently afterwards the wreck went to pieces.

Mr. Giffard says in his *Deeds of Naval Daring*:

> Nothing could equal the lustre of such an action, except the modesty of him who was the hero of it. Indeed, upon all occasions, forward as he was to eulogise the merits of his followers, Sir Edward was reserved, almost to a fault, upon everything connected with his own services. The only notice taken of the *Dutton* in the journal of the *Indefatigable*, is the short sentence, 'Sent two boats to the assistance of a ship on shore in the Sound;' and in his letter to Vice-Admiral Onslow, who had hoisted his flag at Plymouth a day or two before, he throws himself almost out of sight and ascribes the chief merit to the officer who directed the boats:—
>
>> Dear Sir,—I hope it happened to me this afternoon to be serviceable to the unhappy sufferers on board the *Dutton*; and I have much satisfaction in saying that every soul in her was taken out before I left her, except the first mate, boatswain and third mate, who attended the hauling of ropes to the shore, and they eased me on shore by the hawsers. It is not possible to refrain speaking in raptures

of the handsome conduct of Mr. Hemmings, the master-attendant, who, at the imminent risk of his life, saved hundreds. If I had not hurt my leg and been otherwise much bruised, I would have waited on you; but hope this will be a passable excuse.—I am, with respect, sir, your most obedient humble servant,

Ed. Pellew

Services performed in the sight of thousands could not thus be concealed. Praise was lavished upon him from every quarter. The corporation of Plymouth voted him the freedom of the town. The merchants of Liverpool presented him with a valuable service of plate. On the 5th of March following he was created a baronet as Sir Edward Pellew, of Ireverry, and received for an honourable augmentation of his arms a civic wreath, a stranded ship for a crest, and the motto "*Deo adjuvante Fortuna sequatur.*" This motto, so modest, and not less expressive of his own habitual feeling, was chosen by himself, in preference to one proposed which was more personally complimentary.

In 1799 he removed into *L'Impétueux*, of seventy-four guns, and later to *Le Tonnant*, of eighty guns, soon after being raised to the rank of rear-Admiral and placed in command of the fleet in the East Indies, where he exterminated the French cruisers and remained until 1809. After this he served in the North Sea and then in the Mediterranean. His services were rewarded with a peerage, to which he was raised as Baron Exmouth, and a pension of £2,000 a year. In 1816 he proceeded to the Barbary States on a mission to liberate the Christian slaves; but finding on his return that his treaties were disregarded, he returned to Algiers and bombarded the town, reducing the enemy to submission, for which service he was made a viscount. In 1817 he was appointed to the chief command at Plymouth, and in 1821 he returned from active service, but was made Vice-Admiral of England in 1832.

Says a biographer:

Few men in the naval service of this country—eminently distinguished as many have been—ever bore so prominent a part, or evinced more determined courage and coolness in the discharge of their arduous duties than did this gallant, humane and active officer. He seemed to be a very *beau idéal* of a British sailor; his undaunted courage and enterprise was strikingly shown in his manly aspect, and though a perfect disciplinarian, his hearty and encouraging words produced a magic effect on his officers and men, while they always felt the fullest confidence in his skill and intrepidity. He died in January 1833.

The Glorious First of June

On January 21st, 1793, Louis XVI. of France was guillotined, and in the following month the French Republic declared war against England. Fully sensible of their inability to cope with the English in regular naval warfare the French contented themselves for some time with sending out cruisers and small squadrons and even single ships; and these were so successful that in the month of May, 1794, ninety-nine ships were taken by the French, whereas only one, a frigate of thirty-eight guns, was captured by the English.

At length the French government were compelled to attempt a naval armament on a larger scale, for their harvest failed them, and in dread of famine they were compelled to look abroad for sources of supply. The stability of their own government depended upon the success with which they dealt with this difficulty, for it was not to be expected that a new government, deriving its power and authority from the people, would be able to continue if the nation became irritated and excited by the pressure of famine. And yet the difficulties that beset their path were all but insurmountable. The nations of Europe were almost without exception hostile to them, and America was almost the only country to which they could look for help, and the task of convoying supplies from America while the English were masters of the sea was one attended with very great difficulty and risk.

The French Government, however, had only a choice of difficulties. If they sent their fleet to sea it must encounter the English fleet; if they did not send a fleet to sea they were sure to lose their convoy of provisions and worse disasters would follow. There can be no doubt, however, that, under the circumstances, the utter destruction even of the whole fleet would have been a much less serious evil than the loss of the provision convoy, for the fleet might, in the course of time, be replaced, but if the provisions were taken France would either be actually starved or the people, under the apprehension of starvation, would rise against the government.

It was therefore resolved to send the French fleet to sea; and about the middle of May a fleet, under the command of Rear-Admiral Villaret, sailed from Brest; Jean Bon St. Andre, one of the representatives of the people, sailing on board the admiral's ship to stimulate and encourage the expedition.

Lord Howe, aware of the expected convoy, proceeded to sea early in the same month with twenty-six sail of the line in the hope of intercepting it. On the 19th as he was cruising off Brest, he received information that the enemy's fleet had put to sea, and on the same evening he received despatches from Rear-Admiral Montague, who was also cruising in the Channel, which induced him to attempt a junction of the two fleets. Had this been effected Lord Howe would have had a very great superiority over the French fleet; but in the meantime he learnt that the French were but a few leagues to the westward, and he was consequently obliged to alter his course to go in quest of them.

Early in the morning of May 28th the advanced English frigates discovered the French fleet far on the weather bow of the English admiral's ship. At first the enemy did not appear to see the English, for they came down for some time in very loose order; but when they came nearer they hauled to the wind. They were, however, very slow in completely forming in regular order of battle, occupying indeed several hours in the operation. This circumstance was of great consequence to Lord Howe, as it afforded time for the detached part of the British fleet, commanded by Rear-Admiral Pasley, to be placed advantageously for effecting an impression on their rear; and in the meantime the whole of the English fleet was making a nearer approach.

In the French official report of the engagement given by Jean Bon St. Andre, he observes that while the two fleets continued manoeuvring, one of the ships, *La Révolutionnaire*, from motives not understood by the rest of the fleet, slackened its sails on the approach of the English; and that Admiral Pasley taking advantage of this circumstance, led on his division and attacked this vessel. In the conflict the British rear-Admiral had his top mast disabled; assistance was therefore immediately ordered, and Lord Hugh Seymour, in the *Leviathan*, pushed up also to attack the *Révolutionnaire*, and was supported by Captain Parker, of the *Audacious*. The captain of the *Révolutionnaire* was killed and the vessel greatly damaged. English official accounts add that the

Révolutionnaire struck to the *Audacious*. Night, however, put an end to the conflict; and in the morning a French ship fell in with the *Révolutionnaire* and towed her into Rochefort.

During the whole of the night of the 28th the two fleets continued in sight of each other; and on the morning of the following day Lord Howe made the signal for the fleet to tack, with the intention, if possible, of making some further impression on the rear of the enemy. As soon as the French admiral perceived this manoeuvre he also made the signal for his fleet to wear from van to rear, and continued edging down in a line for the purpose of bringing the van of the British fleet to action. Lord Howe upon this made the signal for passing through the enemy's line, and a severe action commenced. The *Cæsar*, which was the leading ship of the British van, did not, however, keep to the wind; and this circumstance appearing likely to prevent the movement of passing the French line from taking its full and proper effect, the admiral immediately tacked, and being followed and supported by the *Bellerophon* and the *Leviathan*, passed through between the fifth and sixth ships of the line of the enemy.

Lord Howe having accomplished this part of his plan, put about again, in preparation for renewing the attack; but after manoeuvring and counter-manoeuvring for some time the French wore round and stood away in order of battle, on the larboard tack, followed by the British fleet in the same order. The fleets then remained separated a few miles; and as there was a very thick fog they were seldom seen by each other. This fog lasted for the greater part of the two following days.

The object of the British admiral, hitherto, had been to obtain the weather-gauge of the enemy, in order that he might not only compel him to fight, but to fight on terms and in a situation comparatively favourable to himself. Having succeeded in this object, an opportunity occurred on June 1st for bringing the French fleet to close and general action. Lord Howe accordingly threw out the signal for his ships to bear up together and come to close action, between seven and eight o'clock in the morning. The French fleet originally consisted of twenty-six sail of the line, and the British of the same force; but on the part of the former the *Révolutionnaire* had been towed into Rochefort; and on the part of the latter the *Audacious* had parted company after her engagement with the *Révolutionnaire*.

The battle immediately commenced and was carried on in a very courageous manner on both sides; but though the revolutionary spirit of the French officers and seamen incited them to fight with more obstinacy than they generally displayed in naval engagements, it could not give them discipline, skill and experience equal to that of the British, and they soon became sensible that the victory could not be with them. Several of the ships on both sides were dismasted, and the carnage was very great. In the French official account of the battle it was stated that the officers and crew of *Le Vengeance*, of seventy-four guns, displayed a true republican spirit; that after the lower decks were under water and destruction inevitable, they continued to fire the upper tier; and that at the moment the ship went to the bottom the air resounded with the cry of "*Vive la république, vive la liberté et la France.*"

Giffard in his *Deeds of Naval Daring* gives several anecdotes of incidents which occurred during this famous day. He says:

> On the morning of June 1st Rear-Admiral Neuilly pointing out to Captain Troubridge, at that time a prisoner on board the *Sans Pareil*, our fleet sailing parallel to them, said, 'Your people are not disposed to fight; they won't venture down.' Troubridge, who had seen the signal flying for breakfast on board the ships of the British fleet, was at the time partaking of the same meal, and, dropping the loaf he held, he placed his hand on the French officer's shoulder, saying, 'Not fight! stop till they have had their breakfasts. I know John Bull well, and when his belly is full, you will get it. Depend on it, they will pay you a visit in half an hour.' In a few minutes after the British fleet bore up to engage.
>
> During the action Troubridge was sent below, where for some time he leaned against the fore-mast. Suddenly he felt the vibration of the mast as it was struck by a shot, and heard it fall over the side, when, grasping the astounded Frenchman appointed to guard him with both hands, he began to caper about with all the gestures of a maniac. Lord Howe, in the *Queen Charlotte*, wished to be placed alongside the *Montagne*, the French admiral's ship, and gave his orders to his master accordingly. As they approached the French line it appeared so compact and close that a doubt was expressed whether they could get through; while closing with the *Montagne*, the master, who held the helm, called out that they would be on board the next ship. 'What's that to you, sir?' said Lord Howe.

Bowen, the master, as bold a man as his admiral, replied coolly in an undertone, 'If you don't care, I am sure I don't. I'll go near enough to singe some of our whiskers.' The *Queen Charlotte* dashed through the line, brushed the ensign of the French admiral's (*Villaret Joyeuse*) flag ship on one side, grazing on the other the *Jacobin's* mizen shrouds with her jibboom, an exploit which has never been equalled, although approached by Collingwood at Trafalgar. The cannonade was tremendous and our gunnery most effective. The broadside poured into the stern of the *Montagne* as the *Queen Charlotte* passed made a hole, said the sailors, large enough to row the admiral's barge through it.

Howe's masts were shot away as the *Montagne* ceased firing; this gave her the opportunity to make off to leeward. The *Queen, Defence, Marlborough, Royal George,* and *Brunswick* were the only ships which, like Howe's, pushed through the enemy's line on that memorable and eventful day. The *Queen*, in which Lord Gardner's flag was flying, was dreadfully cut up; her Captain, Hutt, died of his wounds, and has a monument in St. Paul's. Gardner learned during the engagement that a near relative, to whom he was attached, was killed. He went on giving his orders in an unaltered tone; but as the wind for a moment cleared off the smoke, marks of tears were on his face; they were easily traced, for it was besmeared with smoke and powder.

The *Defence*, Captain Gambier, got into the midst of the French ships, lost her main and mizen masts and behaved in the most gallant manner. Captain Berkeley of the *Marlborough* was carried off deck wounded, and the second lieutenant, Seymour, afterwards Sir Michael, lost an arm. The ship was reduced to a wreck, but was fought to the last by Lieutenant Monckton. While the bowsprit of the *Impétueux* was over the *Marlborough's* quarters, a sailor, leaping over, said he would pay them a visit. He was called to take a sword. 'I'll find one there,' he said, and actually came back with two of the enemy's cutlasses in his hands.

The *Brunswick* had a figure-head of the duke, with a laced cocked-hat on; the hat was shot off. The crew thinking that a prince of that house should not be uncovered in the face of an enemy, sent a request to their captain to supply the loss. He ordered his servant to give them his cocked-hat. The carpenter nailed it on, and there it remained until the battle was over.

These incidents, amidst a terrific fire, paint our sailors as they were and as they are. Harvey, the captain of the *Brunswick*, died of his wounds.

In less than an hour after the engagement had become close and general the French admiral, who had been engaged by Lord Howe's ship, the *Queen Charlotte*, made all sail and crowded off, followed by nearly all the ships in his van that were in a condition to carry sail; ten or twelve of those that were dismasted, or much crippled, were left behind. Had the British fleet not been very much disabled all these must have been captured; but in consequence of their state several of them escaped; two or three, even under a sprit sail singly or a smaller sail, hoisted on the stump of the foremast, were able to get away. Six, however, were secured and captured—*viz.*, *La Juste* of eighty guns; *La Sans Pareille* of eighty guns; *L'Amérique* of seventy-four guns; *L'Achille* of seventy-four guns; *L'Impétueux* of seventy-four guns; and the *Northumberland* of seventy-four guns; these added to *Le Vengeur* and *Le Jacobin*, which were also sunk, made the whole loss of the French amount to eight ships of the line.

The return of those killed on board of the English fleet was two hundred and seventy-two, and of wounded seven hundred and eighty-seven. The loss of the French is not accurately known, but it is believed to have been much greater than that of the English. On board of *La Montagne* the captain was killed and nearly three hundred men were either killed or wounded. In the ships that were taken six hundred and ninety men were killed and five hundred and eighty wounded; besides, it is supposed that three hundred and twenty perished in *Le Vengeur*.

Though this victory was a great triumph to the English and a severe blow to the arms of the Republic, the French can hardly be said to have failed in the object of their expedition; for while Lord Howe was engaged in chasing and fighting the French fleet, the provision convoy, which the French fleet came out to protect, managed to escape him, and one hundred and sixty sail of vessels, valued at five millions sterling, and conveying an immense quantity of provisions and naval stores, arrived from America safe in port a few days after the engagement.

On the Wednesday, Thursday, and Friday immediately following the publication of the *Extraordinary Gazette* which announced Lord Howe's victory there were illuminations in all parts of the metropolis;

a subscription was almost immediately raised at Lloyd's Coffee House for the widows and children of the seamen who fell in the engagement, and the proprietors of Drury Lane Theatre gave a clear benefit, which produced upwards of one thousand three hundred pounds, in aid of the subscription.

In order to show all due honour to the fleet which had achieved such a victory, on Thursday, June 26th, George III. and Queen Charlotte and three of the princesses arrived at Portsmouth; the three younger princesses having come down the day before. The royal party then proceeding in barges in the usual procession, and receiving the customary honours, visited Lord Howe's ship at Spithead. Here His Majesty held a naval *levée*, and presented Lord Howe with a diamond-hilted sword, the value of which was three thousand guineas, and a gold chain, to which a medal was afterwards suspended, to be worn round the neck. After these ceremonies were gone through the royal party dined with Lord Howe on board his ship. His lordship was also raised to the rank of an earl for his glorious services in the battle.

Triumph in Retreat
A Story of "Billy Blue"

After the defeat of the French by Lord Howe on the 1st of June, 1794, the French navy was much too shattered to attempt anything like offensive warfare for some time. Notwithstanding this, however, fortune favoured France with an opportunity of revenge as early as the following year.

In June, 1795, Admiral Cornwallis, known in the fleet as "Billy Blue," was cruising off Belle Isle when on the 7th he fell in with a fleet of merchantmen under the convoy of three ships of the line and six frigates. His own force consisted of five sail of the line and two frigates, with which he made an easy capture of eight of the enemy's ships, the men-of-war effecting their escape. On the 16th, however, came the Frenchman's opportunity of turning the tables; for, as the admiral was standing in towards the land, near the Penmarks, one of his frigates signalled the sighting of the enemy's fleet, which numbered thirteen sail of the line, several frigates, two brigs and a cutter. The wind at first falling calm and afterwards coming round to the north, the enemy's ships were enabled to get to windward, and the next morning by daylight they were seen mooring on both quarters of the British squadron.

During the preceding day and night the admiral himself had led the retreating ships in the *Royal Sovereign*, in order that he might be able to take advantage of any favourable opportunity that might present itself in the night for altering his course and getting away unperceived by the enemy; but with daylight he changed his disposition, ordering the two heavy sailing ships, the *Brunswick* and the *Bellerophon*, to lead, and the *Mars* and *Triumph* to form the rear, while he himself, in the *Royal Sovereign*, formed a connecting link, and was prepared to bear down to the assistance of any of his squadron that might particularly need his help. It was now in the power of the French admiral to have engaged closely, and at about nine o'clock in the morning a line-of-battle ship and a frigate opened their fire upon the *Mars*. From this time a pretty constant cannonade was kept up, the French ships firing at a distance as they came up, and three of the English ships returning it. Such was the bad sailing of the *Brunswick* and *Bellerophon* that their fire was quite lost and they were obliged to keep their course without retaliating; in fact, it became necessary to cut away their anchors and launches, throw overboard part of their ballast, and crowd all the sail they could carry, to enable them to keep their proper place, while the *Mars* and *Triumph* continued under easy sail.

The day had nearly passed over, and there was no serious appearance of attack; but as the afternoon drew on, the enemy, as if ashamed of having yet done nothing effectual to check the progress, or even to ruffle the majestic steadiness of our little line, seemed to be inclined to close upon the rear ship, the *Mars*. Two or three of them had fore-reached upon her beam, and a beautiful eighty-four-gun ship was hauling towards her, as if determined to act as champion, and by arresting one of the ships to bring the matter to an immediate issue, when an incident occurred which completely deceived the enemy.

In the early morning the admiral had called by signal for a boat from the *Phaëton*, and as her young officer, afterwards Admiral Sir Francis Beaufort, K.C.B., was eagerly springing up the *Royal Sovereign's* side, he was stopped by the noble old admiral's foot and the words, "Stop, sir; listen: go back immediately and tell your captain to go ahead of the squadron a long way, and, when far enough off, to make the signals for seeing first one or two strange sail, then more, and then a fleet; in short, to humbug those fellows astern. He will understand me. Go." The *Phaëton* sailed well, but it took a long time to get to the admiral's "far enough," in order to give colour and credibility to her signals.

At length, about three o'clock p.m., she made the signal for a stranger, then two, five, and then for a fleet, which was made by letting fly the top-gallant sheets and firing a lee gun. It was well known that the French had copies of our "Tabular" signals, and by them Captain Stopford announced that the fleet was English; the large recall flag (the Dutch ensign) was then hoisted to bring them into the squadron, and when time had been given for the supposed answer, the *Phaëton* wore round, under easy sail, towards the squadron, thus implying that a fleet of English ships was following her, and, passing under the admiral's stern, gave him three cheers.

By a happy coincidence two or three small distant vessels were at that time actually peeping up on the horizon; but the bait had been fully swallowed; a flood of signals was made by the enemy—their fire became languid—and at half-past six their whole force tacked off to the eastward, leaving our gallant squadron to enjoy the fruit of their bravery and wit.

In the official announcement of this encounter the admiral gives full credit to his gallant companions, as well as to Sir C. Cotton and Sir Erasmus Gower, who, in the *Mars* and *Triumph*, bore the brunt of the fray. Of the officers, seamen and marines, he says that:

> Instead of being cast down at seeing thirty sail of the enemy's ships attacking our little squadron, they were in the highest spirits imaginable, and although circumstanced as we were, we had no great reason to complain of the conduct of the enemy, yet our men could not help repeatedly expressing their contempt of them. Could common prudence have allowed me to let loose their valour I hardly know what might not have been accomplished by such men.

Of the admiral himself we are told that, on the anxious morning he continued the operation of shaving, dressing and powdering with his usual composure, and observed to Captain Whitby, in his customary cool and dry manner, that he had been in similar situations before, and knew very well what they, the French, would do. More than once during the day he repeated that sooner than abandon his comrades in the slow sailers, the *Brunswick* and the *Bellerophon*, the *Royal Sovereign* should go down with her colours flying.

Admiral (then Captain) Cornwallis had previously exhibited great daring in Rodney's celebrated action in 1782, when, in the *Canada*, seventy-four, after having defeated the *Hector*, a ship of equal force, single-handed, he bore down upon the huge *Ville de Paris*, and lay her alongside and commenced a combat which lasted two hours. A point of honour prevented De Grasse striking to anything short of a flag; but when Sir Samuel Hood came up in the *Barfleur* the count surrendered, having only three men, of whom he himself was one, alive and unhurt upon his upper deck. He declared, after the action, that the little red-sided ship (the *Canada*) had done him more harm than all the rest with which he had contended.

The fleet from which Admiral Cornwallis thus escaped were not destined long to boast of their triumph; for on the 22nd of the same month, Lord Bridport, with fourteen sail of the line and eight frigates, fell in with them, and as they indicated no intention to fight him, made the signal for four of his best sailing vessels to chase. As there was very little wind the pursuit continued all that day and during the night.

Early on the morning of the 23rd some of the British ships came up with the enemy; and a little before six o'clock the action began, and continued till three in the afternoon. The French kept as near their own shore as possible; so that only three were captured—the *Alexander*, which had been taken from the British the preceding year, the *Formidable* and the *Tigre*. The rest of the French squadron escaped into *L'Orient*. The loss of the British in this action was thirty-one killed and one hundred and fifteen wounded; the loss of the French was not accurately ascertained.

The Mutiny of 1797

At Spithead, April 15th.—At the Nore, May 22nd

In the course of February and March, 1797, Lord Howe received several anonymous letters, enclosing petitions from the ships' companies of a number of vessels of the Channel fleet, asking for increased pay and better provisions. These letters, though coming from different quarters, were apparently written by the same hand, and the authorities judging that they were so, and that they represented an agitation carried on by one person, took but little notice of them.

A word to the wise is sufficient, but governments are not always wise, or the Admiralty would at least have made inquiries as to the justice of the demands made. Of this, however, they can hardly have been unaware, for while the pay of the army and the militia had been increased, the pay of the navy had remained the same from the time of Charles II., and many abuses had sprung up in the administration of the commissariat which bore very hardly upon the men. The greed of purveyors and the corruption of commissioners provided them with food short in quantity and often unfit to eat; while under the system then in vogue the ship's purser was allowed to deduct two ounces in every pound of provisions served out to the men and a similar proportion of grog and beer in lieu of direct wages from the government.

It soon became evident, however, that the disaffection was far more formidable than was at first supposed. On the return of the Channel fleet into port a secret correspondence was arranged between all the ships that composed it; and this ended in a unanimous agreement that no ship should lift an anchor until a redress of grievances was obtained. At this stage it was reported to Lord Spencer, the head of the Admiralty, that a general conspiracy had been entered into to take command of the fleet on April 16th; to test which on the 15th Lord Bridport ordered the signal to prepare for sea. But instead of the men proceeding to weigh anchor, they manned the rigging and gave three cheers, as the signal for mutiny, and every other ship followed the example.

The officers of every ship exerted themselves to their utmost to bring their men back to obedience; but all their endeavours were vain. The fleet being now in the complete possession of the seamen, every ship's company appointed two delegates, and Lord Howe's cabin was fixed upon as their place of consultation. On the 17th an oath was administered to every man in the fleet to support the cause in which they had engaged, and ropes were reeved to the yard arms in every ship as signals of the punishment that would be inflicted on those that betrayed it. Several officers who had made themselves particularly obnoxious to their respective crews were sent ashore.

In the meantime, though the admiral was restricted from putting to sea, he retained the command of the fleet in every other respect; the strictest discipline was maintained and the severest orders and regulations were enacted by the delegates, enjoining the most respectful attention to their officers, and threatening disobedience with rigorous chastisement.

On the 18th two petitions, one to the Admiralty and the other to the House of Commons, were drawn up and signed by the delegates. They were both worded with the highest propriety of expression and respect. The petition to parliament stated that the price of all articles necessary for subsistence having advanced at least thirty *per cent.* since the reign of Charles II., when the seamen's pay was settled as at present, they requested that a proportionate relief might be granted to them. It represented at the same time that, while their loyalty was equal to that of the army, the pensions of Chelsea had been augmented to thirteen pounds a year, but those of Greenwich still remained at seven. The petition to the Admiralty contained a recital of the services rendered by the petitioners and a warm declaration of their readiness to defend their country, and set forth the low rate of their pay, and the insufficiency of their allowance of provisions, demanding increase of both, together with the liberty of going ashore while in harbour and the continuance of pay to wounded seamen till cured and discharged.

Such, in the meanwhile, was the alarm of the public, and particularly of the government, that it was judged necessary to transfer the board of Admiralty to Portsmouth, in order to be nearer at hand to inspect the transactions on board the fleet, and to consult on the readiest and most likely means of quelling the discontent, the consequences of which might prove ruinous to the nation by throwing open the Channel and all the neighbouring seas to the uncontrolled dominion of the French fleets and cruisers.

The first lord of the Admiralty, Lord Spencer, accompanied by Lord Arden and Admiral Young, repaired accordingly to Portsmouth, where they directly proceeded to take into consideration the petition that had been transmitted to the board. They authorised Lord Bridport to inform the ships' companies that they would recommend the king to propose to parliament an augmentation of pay to the seamen in the navy at the rate of four shillings a month to petty officers and able seamen, three shillings to ordinary seamen, and two shillings to landsmen. Seamen wounded in action were also to continue in the receipt of their pay till cured or declared unable to serve, when they should be allowed a pension or admitted into Greenwich Hospital.

To this notification the seamen replied by requesting that the long-established distinctions in the navy, of able and ordinary seamen, should be retained; the pay of the former to be raised to one shilling a day, and that of petty officers and ordinary seamen in the usual proportion; they also requested that the pay of the marines while on board should be the same as of ordinary seamen, and that the pensions of Greenwich Hospital should be increased to ten pounds.

On April 20th the lords of the Admiralty notified to Lord Bridport their compliance with the demands of the seamen, directing him to make it known through the fleet, and to require, in consequence, an immediate return of the people to their duty, on pain of forfeiting their right to smart-money, to pensions from the chest of Chatham, and to an admission into Greenwich Hospital, and of being made responsible for the consequences that might ensue from the continuance of their disobedience. They were informed, at the same time, that an unqualified pardon for all that had taken place would be granted to every ship's company that should, within one hour of these resolutions being communicated to them, submit to their officers and cease to hold farther intercourse with those who remained in a state of mutiny.

On the 21st, Admirals Gardner, Colpoys and Poole went on board the *Royal Charlotte* in order to confer with the delegates, who explicitly informed them that it was the determination of the crews to agree to nothing that should not be sanctioned by parliament and guaranteed by the king's proclamation. Admiral Gardner was so irritated by this declaration that he seized one of the delegates by the collar, and swore he would have them all hanged, with every fifth man throughout the fleet. This behaviour of the admiral so exasperated the ship's company that it was with difficulty he escaped with his life.

The delegates from the *Royal George* returned immediately to their ship and informed their crew of what had happened; after some consultation they resolved to summon all the delegates on board their ship. This was forthwith done by hoisting the red, a signal that struck terror through the fleet, as it was not generally understood; the officers in particular being apprehensive that some fatal designs were in agitation. The crew now proceeded to load their guns, to order the watch to be kept as at sea, and to put everything in a state of defence.

On the following day the ships' crews directed two letters to be written, one to the lords of the Admiralty, to acquaint them with the motives for their conduct on the preceding day, and another to Lord Bridport, in which they styled him their father and their friend, and assured him of their respect and attachment. This induced him to return to his ship the next day, the 23rd, and to rehoist his flag, which he had struck during the confusion on the 21st. After a short and pathetic address to the crew he informed them that he had brought with him a redress of all their grievances and the king's pardon for what had passed. After some deliberation these offers were accepted and every man returned to his duty.

From April 23rd to May 7th the fleet remained in due subordination; but on that day a fresh mutiny broke out. The seamen, from whatever cause it arose, had conceived a mistrust of government, and apprehending a violation of the promises made to them, renewed their former menaces. As soon as this alarming intelligence arrived, government dispatched with all speed a person of the highest weight and authority to quell this unexpected tumult. This was Lord Howe, an officer long held in the first degree of respect and esteem in the British navy, and personally beloved by all that had served under him for his humane disposition as well as for his many great qualities. His presence and exhortations wrought the desired effect, and happily dissipated the suspicions that were beginning to prevail.

Conformably to the expectation of the public, the House of Commons on May 8th took into consideration the estimates laid before it by the ministry, for the purpose of augmenting the pay, and the Bill, as soon as it was framed, went through the necessary formalities without delay, and immediately received the royal assent by commission.

The suppression of the disturbances among the seamen at Portsmouth, without recurring to violent measures, and by granting their petitions, occasioned universal satisfaction, and it was hoped that no farther complaints would arise. These reasonable expectations were, however, wholly disappointed by a fresh mutiny that broke out at the Nore on May 22nd.

The crews on that day took possession of their respective ships, elected delegates to preside over them, and to draw up a statement of their demands and transmit them to the lords of the Admiralty. These demands went much farther than those of the seamen at Portsmouth and Plymouth, and were not met with the same indulgence. On June 6th, in the morning, the fleet at the Nore was joined by the *Agamemnon*, *Leopard*, *Ardent*, and *Isis* men-of-war, together with the *Ranger* sloop, which ships had deserted from the fleet under Admiral Duncan.

The principal person at the head of this mutiny was one Richard Parker, a man of good natural parts and some education, and of a remarkably bold and resolute character. Admiral Buckner, the commanding officer at the Nore, was directed by the lords of the Admiralty to inform the seamen that their demands were totally inconsistent with the good order and regulations necessary to be observed in the navy, and could not for that reason be complied with; but that on returning to their duty they would receive the king's pardon for their breach of obedience. To this offer Parker replied by a declaration that the seamen had unanimously determined to keep possession of the fleet until the lords of the Admiralty had repaired to the Nore and redressed the grievances which had been laid before them.

In order to put an end with all possible expedition to a mutiny that appeared so dangerous, Lord Spencer, Lord Arden and Admiral Young hastened immediately to Sheerness and held a board, at which Parker and the other delegates attended; but their behaviour was so audacious that the lords of the Admiralty returned to town without the least success. The principal article of complaint on the part of the mutineers was the unequal distribution of prize-money, for the omission of which they much blamed their fellow-seamen at Portsmouth. On the return of the lords of the Admiralty from Sheerness a proclamation was issued offering His Majesty's pardon to all such of the mutineers as should immediately return to their duty; intimating at the same time Admiral Buckner was the proper person to be applied to on such an occasion.

All the buoys, by the order of government, were removed from the mouth of the Thames and the neighbouring coast; from which precaution any ships that might attempt to get away would be in danger of running aground. Great preparations were also made at Sheerness against an attack from the mutinous ships, which had manifested some strong indications of an intention to bombard that place; and furnaces and hot balls were kept ready.

Emboldened by the strength of men and shipping in their hands, and resolved to persevere in their demand till they had exhorted a compliance, the mutineers proceeded to secure a sufficiency of provisions for that purpose by seizing two vessels laden with stores, and sent notice ashore that they intended to block up the Thames and cut off all communication between London and the sea in order to force government to a speedy accession to their terms. They began the execution of this menace by mooring four of their vessels across the mouth of the river and stopping several ships that were coming from the metropolis.

These transactions, while they excited the greatest alarm in the nation, were violently reprobated by the seamen belonging to the two divisions of the fleet lying at Portsmouth and at Plymouth. Each of them addressed an admonition to their fellow-seamen at the Nore, warmly condemning their proceedings as a scandal to the name of British seamen, and exhorting them to be content with the indulgence already granted by government, and to return to their duty without insisting on more concessions than had been demanded by the rest of the navy.

But these warnings proved ineffectual. The reinforcement of the four ships lately arrived, and the expectation of being joined by others, induced them to persist in their demands. The committee of delegates on board the *Sandwich* came to a determination to commission Lord Northesk, whom they had kept in confinement in the *Montague*, of which he was commander, to repair to the king in the name of the fleet, and to acquaint him with the conditions on which they were willing to deliver up the ships. The petition which he was charged to lay before the king was highly respectful and loyal to him, but very severe on his ministers, and they required an entire compliance with every one of their demands, threatening on the refusal of any to put immediately to sea. Lord Northesk readily undertook to be the bearer of their petition, but told them that from the unreasonableness of their demands he could not flatter them with the hope of success. Confiding in him, they said, as the seamen's friend, they had entrusted him with this mission on pledging his honour to return with a clear and positive answer within fifty-four hours.

Lord Northesk departed accordingly for London, and was introduced by Lord Spencer to the king. But no answer being returned to the message, and information being brought to the fleet that the nation at large highly disapproved of their proceedings, great divisions took place among the delegates, and several of the ships deserted the others—not, however, without much contest and bloodshed. The mutineers, despairing now of accomplishing their designs, struck the red flag, which they had hoisted as the signals of mutiny, and restored a free passage to the trade of the metropolis. Every ship was now left at its own command, and they all gradually returned to obedience, though on board of some violent struggles happened between the mutineers and the loyal parties.

The principal conductor of the mutiny, Richard Parker, was seized and imprisoned, and after a solemn trial that lasted three days on board of the *Neptune*, was sentenced to death. He suffered with great coolness and intrepidity, acknowledging the justice of his sentence, and expressing his hope that mercy might be extended to his associates. But it was judged necessary to make public examples of the principal and most guilty, who were accordingly tried, and after full proof of their criminality, condemned and executed. Others remained under sentence of death till after the great victory obtained over the Dutch fleet at Camperdown by Admiral Duncan, when His Majesty issued a general pardon.

The Battle of Camperdown

The mutiny at Spithead found the British ministry intent upon blocking up the Dutch fleet in the Texel and Admiral Duncan appointed to the duty. The pacific suppression of that formidable rising left the government free to pursue their policy and Admiral Duncan to carry out his instructions. Early in June, however, the admiral found himself deserted by the *Agamemnon*, the *Leopard*, the *Ardent*, and the *Isis* men-of-war and the *Ranger* sloop, which left him and joined in the mutiny of the Nore on the 6th.

When the admiral found himself deserted by so important a section of his fleet, he called his own ship's crew together and addressed them in the following speech:—

> My Lads,—I once more call you together with a sorrowful heart from what I have lately seen, the disaffection of the fleet. I call it disaffection, for the crews have no grievances. To be deserted by my fleet in the face of an enemy is a disgrace which, I believe, never before happened to a British admiral; nor could I have supposed it possible. My greatest comfort under God is that I have been supported by the officers, seamen, and marines of this ship; for which, with a heart overflowing with gratitude, I request you to accept my sincere thanks. I flatter myself much good may result from your example, by bringing those deluded people to a sense of their duty, which they owe, not only to their king and country, but to themselves.
> The British navy has ever been the support of that liberty which has been handed down to us by our ancestors, and which I trust we shall maintain to the latest posterity; and that can only be done by unanimity and obedience. This ship's company and others, who have distinguished themselves by their loyalty and good order, deserve to be, and doubtless will be, the favourites

of a grateful country. They will also have from their inward feelings a comfort which will be lasting, and not like the floating and false confidence of those who have swerved from their duty.

It has often been my pride with you to look into the Texel and see a foe which dreaded coming out to meet us; my pride is now humbled indeed; my feelings are not easily to be expressed! our cup has overflowed and made us wanton. The all-wise Providence has given us this check as a warning, and I hope we shall improve by it. On Him then let us trust, where our only security can be found. I find there are many good men among us; for my own part, I have had full confidence of all in this ship; and once more beg to express my approbation of your conduct.

May God, who has thus far conducted you, continue to do so; and may the British navy, the glory and support of our country, be restored to its wonted splendour, and be not only the bulwark of Britain, but the terror of the world.

But this can only be effected by a strict adherence to our duty and obedience; and let us pray that the almighty God may keep us in the right way of thinking.

God bless you all.

At an address so unassuming, modest and pious, and so well calculated, from its simplicity and truth, to touch the human heart, the whole ship's crew were dissolved in tears. They declared, by every expression they could devise, their resolution to abide by the admiral in life or death. Their example was followed by all the other ships, besides those already mentioned. And the admiral, notwithstanding the defection of so considerable a part of his squadron, repaired to his station off the coast of Holland to watch the motions of the Dutch fleet, and resolved still to do battle if opportunity served.

While he lay off the Texel the Dutch fleet did not venture out; but on his being driven from his station by a gale of wind they took advantage of his absence and put to sea; they had scarcely cleared the land, however, when they were descried by the British fleet, which had returned from Yarmouth as soon as possible. It was at nine o'clock on the morning of October 12th, 1797, that the two fleets came in sight of each other. Admiral Duncan, having judiciously placed his squadron in such a position that the enemy could not regain the Texel unless they fought their way thither, immediately bore up and made the signal for a general chase. The Dutch at the time were forming in a line on the larboard tack to receive the British, the wind being at north-west.

As soon as the British squadron came near, Admiral Duncan made the signal to shorten sail in order to connect the ships of his squadron: soon after this the land was seen between Camperdown and Egmont, on the coast of Holland. This convinced him that no time was to be lost in making the attack, as otherwise he might get entangled with the shore; he accordingly made the signal to bear up, break the enemy's line and engage them to leeward, each ship her opponent. By this manner he got between them and the land, whither they were fast approaching.

Vice-Admiral Onslow, in obedience to the signal, bore down on the rear of the Dutch fleet in the most gallant manner, his division following the example; and the action commenced about forty minutes after twelve o'clock. Admiral Duncan, in the *Venerable*, soon got through the line of the enemy, and began a close action with his division against their van. The engagement lasted nearly two hours and a half, when the masts of the Dutch admiral's ship were observed to go by the board: even for some time after this, however, she was defended in the most gallant manner; but at last, being overpowered by numbers, her colours were struck, and the Dutch admiral, De Winter, was brought on board the *Venerable*.

About the same time Vice-Admiral Onslow had obliged the ship which carried the Dutch vice-Admiral's flag to strike her colours. Many others had also surrendered. During the action the two fleets had approached so near the coast of Holland, being within five miles of it, that they had only nine fathoms of water. The first thing, therefore, to which Admiral Duncan directed his attention was to get the heads of the disabled ships off shore. This was indeed difficult and dangerous; for the wind continued for some time to blow strong from west-south-west to west-north-west, and consequently directly on the coast of Holland; as soon as it shifted to the north the admiral made the signal to wear, and stood to the westward. On October 14th he succeeded in reaching Orford Ness, the *Venerable* being so leaky that, with all her pumps going, she could be scarcely kept free of water.

During the action one of the enemy's ships caught fire and drove very near the *Venerable*; but no mischief was done. The British squadron suffered much in their masts, rigging, etc. The number of killed and wounded on board of the British ships was very great; but that of the Dutch much greater, five hundred men being killed and wounded on board two of their ships only. Besides the Dutch admiral's ship, eight others of the line and two frigates were captured. The Dutch attributed their defeat to the circumstance that Vice-Admiral Storey fled into the Texel with the greater part of his division soon after the action began.

It was in connection with this engagement that the incident occurred which forms the subject of the illustration on the cover of this volume. The admiral's ship, the *Venerable*, was so hotly pressed that more than once her colours were shot away. On one of these occasions the flag is said to have been rescued and replaced by Jack Crawford, one of the *Venerable's* men, in some such way as is described in the following lines:—

> We had battled all the morning, 'mid the never-ceasing hail
> Of shot and shell and splinter, of cable—shred, and sail;
> We had thrice received their onslaught, which we thrice had driven back,
> And were waiting, calm and ready, for the last forlorn attack;
> When the stainless flag of England, that has braved a thousand years,
> Was shot clean from the masthead; and they gave three hearty cheers.
> 'Twas the purpose of a moment, and the bravest of our tars
> Plunged headlong in the boiling surf, amid the broken spars;
> He snatched the shot-torn colours, and wound them round his arm,
> Then climbed upon the deck again, and there stood safe and calm
> He paused but for a moment—for it was no time to stay—
> Then leaped into the rigging that had yet survived the fray;
> Higher yet he climbed and higher, till he gained a dizzy height,
> And then turned and paused a moment to look down upon the fight.
>
> Whistled wild the shots around him, as a curling, smoky wreath
> Formed a cloudy shroud to hide him from the enemy beneath.
> Beat his heart with proud elation as he firmly fixed his stand,
> And again the colours floated as he held them in his hand.
> Then with pistol deftly wielded, 'mid the battle's ceaseless blast,
> Fastened there the colours firmly, as he nailed them to the mast;
> Then, as if to yield him glory, the smoke-clouds cleared away—
> And we sent him up the loudest cheer that reached his ear that day,
> And, with new-born zeal and courage, dashed more boldly to the fight,
> Till the day of battle ended in the triumph of the night.

Jack Crawford was a native of Sunderland, where he died in 1831.

In 1890 a statue was erected to his memory in his native town by public subscription, and was unveiled on April 8th by Lord Camperdown, a descendant of Admiral Duncan, in whose ship Crawford served.

The Loss of H.M.S. "Repulse"
By G. H. Walker

The *Repulse* was one of the ships belonging to the Channel fleet, under the command of Sir Allen Gardner, but had been detached for the purpose of intercepting provision vessels going into Brest. On the night of March 10th, 1800, she struck upon a sunken rock, supposed to be the Mace, about twenty-five leagues southeast of Ushant. The crew made good a landing on one of the Glenan Islands, about two miles from the continent. Here the captain, and most of the officers, were made prisoners, and sent to Quimper; but Mr. Rother, the first lieutenant, Mr. Gordon, the fifth, Mr. Finn, the master, two midshipmen, and eight seamen, got into the larger cutter; and, on the fourth day after leaving the ship, during which interval they experienced bad weather, and were, at times, near perishing, arrived safe at Guernsey.

The following letter from one of the officers who escaped, to his father, gives a full account of the loss of the *Repulse*, and likewise of the adventures of the boat's crew, from the time of their quitting the ship till their arrival at Guernsey:—

Guernsey, March 13th, 1800.
My dear Father,—I embrace the opportunity of a packet sailing for England, to acquaint you with the unfortunate fate of the *Repulse*. Coming off the Penmarks, in company with the *Agamemnon*, on Saturday, March 9th, it then blowing a very heavy gale of wind, Captain Alms was thrown down the companion ladder by the rolling of the ship, by which accident some of his ribs were broken and he was much bruised. The same day, we parted company with the *Agamemnon*, in chase of a strange sail to leeward; and, about six in the evening, we came up with and recaptured the *Princess Royal* packet, from the West Indies.
Next morning, Captain Alms, finding himself much worse, re-

solved to put into Torbay. We accordingly bore up and shaped a course, which, if our reckoning had been correct, would have carried us far enough to the westward of Ushant. But, unfortunately, owing to the thickness of the weather (not having had an observation for some days), and to the different set of the tides, which are very strong on this coast, the ship had got nearly three degrees to the east of her reckoning; and at twelve o'clock the same night going under an easy sail, that the prize might be able to keep up, breakers were discovered ahead.

It was extremely foggy, and the ship was going at the rate of about seven knots, with the wind almost right aft, so that our endeavours to clear the danger were ineffectual. In a moment the ship struck with great violence and was instantly so completely surrounded with rocks, that we could not even see the opening which we had entered. In this dreadful situation we continued nearly three quarters of an hour, the ship, from the great surf that ran among the rocks, striking so violently, that we every moment expected she would go to pieces.

I shall not attempt to describe the appearance of so many men, with certain and almost instant death staring them in the face: but I cannot forbear observing, that those whom I ever considered the greatest reprobates now became the greatest cowards, and were so overcome by their awful situation, that they were totally unable to exert themselves for their own preservation. We had no hopes of deliverance. The prize was, indeed, in company, and we kept firing guns to inform her of our danger. It was, however, absolutely impossible for us to receive any assistance from that quarter; and if our firing enabled her to escape herself it was as much as we could expect. That nothing on our part might be left untried, the sails were hove aback, and, with the Divine assistance, the ship backed astern, clear of the danger.

Our joy on this occasion was, however, of short duration, for the ship made so much water, that in half an hour it reached as high as the orlop deck; and the rudder having lost all command, there appeared to be no other chance of saving our lives than by running for the coast of France. Accordingly, having got her head round to the eastward, we made all the sail we could. We had now sufficient employment for all hands, some were busy at the pumps, others were engaged in throwing the guns overboard, and otherwise lightening the ship; while others, again, were employed in lining a sail with beds, blankets, etc., which being got over the bows, and bowsed taut up to the ship's bottom, was of very great service. The water being considerably above the orlop deck, we were enabled to bale at the hatchway; by which, and the wonderful exertions of men actuated by the fear of death, we were enabled to keep her afloat till five o'clock, when, to our inexpressible joy, the echo of the report of one of our guns announced our being near the land, the fog being so thick that we could not see the length of the ship.

But judge what must have been our sensations when we found ourselves within half a ship's length of a lee shore, bounded by a precipice as high as our mast head, against which the sea broke with excessive violence, and on which we were running with great rapidity. The only chance of preservation we now had, was by letting go an anchor, which, however, did not bring us up. At the moment when we expected to be dashed to pieces, our jib-boom almost touching the precipice, Providence again interposed in our behalf, and the eddy wind, reverberating from the rock, took the sail aback, and most miraculously saved us from destruction.

We now cut the cable, and the ship drifted along the shore, till we cleared a rugged point a quarter of a mile to the leeward of us, when she filled and ran up under a weather shore, which, being very high, sheltered us a good deal. Here we grounded; but, from the heavy surf, the ship continued striking with such violence that we were afraid she would go to pieces before we could leave her. We therefore made what haste we could in getting the boat out, and then cut away the masts, when she lay tolerably easy.

As I had early in the morning resolved within myself to attempt escaping in one of the boats, rather than be made prisoner, I mentioned my design to Mr. Gordon, fifth lieutenant, who readily agreed to accompany me. The eight-oared cutter being hoisted, I got into her, as she was the best boat for the purpose, under pretence of seeking a landing place; and having taken on board as many men as she could conveniently carry, I landed them to the leeward of the point about a mile from the ship, and then returned for another cargo. Having disclosed my plan to the boat's crew, I sent one of them on board the ship for a compass, boat's mast, sails, etc., but, to my infinite mortification, he could only get a compass, the boat's sail being down in the store-room. The pilot now came into my boat to go on shore. I thought if I could secure him, it would be a great point, and I was glad to obtain his concurrence.

I had made four or five more trips between the ship and the shore, when Mr. Rothery, the first lieutenant, called me to take him on board, which I did, and was agreeably surprised to find that Mr. Gordon had acquainted him with our secret, that he was resolved to go with us, and had made some provision for the voyage. It consisted of some pieces of hung beef, which, though raw, was better than nothing, a small quantity of bread, and half a dozen of brandy, as he imagined, but which afterwards proved to be wine. When I mentioned our want of sail, he replied that we must make shift to supply that deficiency with some table-cloths and sheets he had brought with him.

We still continued going and returning, till almost all the people were landed, and on our way had fortunately picked up the jolly-boat's mast and sails, and the masts and yards belonging to several other boats, so that the only article we now wanted was water. I recollected the fire cask in the mizen chains, which we desired a man to push overboard. Having picked it up and taken it in, with Mr. Gordon, we again committed ourselves to the mercy of the waves and the care of Providence.

But before I leave the ship, it will be proper to mention the number of lives that were lost. When we first struck upon the rock, five of the crew, whose apprehensions were too powerful for any other consideration, got into a boat that was hung over the quarter, and in their hurry to escape, cut one of the tackles by which the boat was suspended, while they kept the other fast. The boat, consequently, hung by one end, and they were all thrown out and drowned.

I forgot to mention that, while the boats were employed in landing the people, those on board had thrown the ends of several hawsers on shore, which the peasantry made fast to the rock, and which being hauled taut on board, they could go on shore upon them with great ease. Two men, however, being intoxicated, fell off the hawsers into the water, and perished. These, together with four marines, who lay upon deck dead-drunk at the time we came away, and who, I believe, were not afterwards carried on shore, are, as far as I know, all that suffered on this occasion.

Having a fair wind, we set the jolly-boat's sail for a fore sail, then made a sparing breakfast and thought to recruit our spirits with a dram, when, to our great disappointment, we found we had nothing but wine. This was not the greatest of our misfortune, for, upon broaching our water, we found it so strongly impregnated with the varnish with which the cask had been so frequently laid over, that it was scarcely drinkable, and even made some of us sick.

One of the men having, fortunately, some sail needles in his pocket, all hands turned to sail-making, some sewing, others unlaying rope, and making it into twine. A table-cloth and a sheet sewed together made an excellent main sail; and out of a piece of canvas we happened to have in the boat we contrived to make a mizen sail, so that in a couple of hours we had a complete suit.

About twelve o'clock we were much alarmed by being becalmed among the Penmark rocks, and they were obliged to pull hard to avoid being dashed to pieces against them. We soon afterwards had a fine breeze, and about five found ourselves close in with the land, a few miles to the southward of Cape Roz. The wind was so scant that we could barely lie along shore, and were obliged to pass several signal posts, at each of which the enemy had a gun, so that we every moment expected to be fired at. I believe by our being so badly rigged, and white sail, they took us for Frenchmen.

About dusk, we had another narrow escape among a reef of rocks, which lay off Cape Roz, and upon which we were set by a very heavy swell and a strong tide. It was now nearly dark, and, as it had every appearance of blowing hard, we ran down into a deep bay, a little to the southward of Brest Harbour, purposing to come to an anchor till the morning; but in luffing up round a point, under which we intended to take shelter, we were much surprised by the appearance of something like a fort, and soon found our fears realised when the sentinel hailed us in French, which he did twice. We now bore up, and made sail from it as fast as we could, and I fancy were out of reach before they could get a gun ready, as we saw a number of lights moving about.

Some of the boat's crew now thought our undertaking so desperate that they proposed to surrender rather than run any further risk. It was, however, agreed to wait till daylight, and we accordingly came to an anchor in the middle of the bay, not daring to trust ourselves any more in shore. About eleven, the wind having moderated, and the moon shining bright, we got under weigh, and ran between the Saints and the main, which is a very dangerous passage. By two o'clock next morning we were clean off Ushant, having also passed between that and the main. We were now in high spirits to think we had got clear of the coast of France, and regaled ourselves with an additional glass of wine; having also a fair wind for England, which continued all that day till four in the afternoon, when, to our great distress, it fell calm, at a time when, by the distance we had to run, we computed ourselves at no more than eight leagues from Plymouth.

At seven, a breeze sprang up from the northward, and at eight it blew extremely violent, with a heavy sea. The gale continued to increase till eleven, when our situation became very alarming, exposed to a heavy gale of wind, in the middle of the English Channel, in an open boat, with the sea breaking over us in such a manner that we expected each succeeding wave would overwhelm the boat and terminate our existence.

The pilot, after some consideration, proposed to us, as the only chance we had remaining, to bear up for the island of Guernsey or Jersey. To this proposal we all would readily have acceded, but were of opinion that if he once put the boat before the sea she would immediately fill. During our consultation a singular circumstance occurred, which determined us to follow the pilot's advice. Three distinct flashes of lightning were perceived, at regular intervals, in the southeast which was exactly the direction the islands bore from us. This the superstition of the boat's crew interpreted as a signal from heaven. We accordingly bore up, and stood in the same direction in which we had observed the lightning.

Next morning the gale rather abated; and about two o'clock in the afternoon, to our inexpressible joy, we discovered the island of Guernsey; but the wind failing, we did not make the land till late the following morning.

The "Victory" at Portsmouth

The Story of Nelson's Boyhood
By Robert Southey

Horatio Nelson, son of Edmund and Catherine Nelson, was born September 29th, 1758, in the Rectory of Burnham Thorpe, a village in the county of Norfolk, of which his father was rector. The maiden name of his mother was Suckling: her grandmother was an elder sister of Sir Robert Walpole, and Horatio was named after his godfather, the first Lord Walpole. Mrs. Nelson died in 1767, leaving eight, out of eleven, children. Her brother, Captain Maurice Suckling, of the navy, visited the widower upon this event, and promised to take care of one of the boys. Three years afterwards, when Horatio was only twelve years of age, being at home during the Christmas holidays, he read in the county newspaper that his uncle was appointed to the *Raisonnable*, of sixty-four guns. "Do, William," said he to a brother who was a year and a half older than himself, "write to my father, and tell him that I should like to go to sea with Uncle Maurice."

Mr. Nelson was then at Bath, whither he had gone for the recovery of his health; his circumstances were straitened, and he had no prospect of ever seeing them bettered: he knew that it was the wish of providing for himself by which Horatio was chiefly actuated, and did not oppose his resolution: he understood also the boy's character, and had always said, that in whatever station he might be placed, he would climb, if possible, to the very top of the tree. Accordingly, Captain Suckling was written to. "What," said he in his answer, "has poor Horatio, who is so weak, done, that he above all the rest should be sent to rough it out at sea? But let him come, and the first time we go into action, a cannon ball may knock off his head, and provide for him at once."

It is manifest from these words that Horatio was not the boy whom his uncle would have chosen to bring up in his own profession. He was never of a strong body; and the ague, which at that time was one of the most common diseases in England, had greatly reduced his strength; yet he had already given proofs of that resolute heart and nobleness of mind, which, during his whole career of labour and of glory, so eminently distinguished him. When a mere child, he strayed a-bird's-nesting from his grandmother's house in company with a cow-boy: the dinner hour elapsed; he was absent, and could not be found, and the alarm of the family became very great, for they apprehended that he might have been carried off by gipsies. At length, after search had been made for him in various directions, he was discovered alone, sitting composedly by the side of a brook which he could not get over.

"I wonder, child," said the old lady when she saw him, "that hunger and fear did not drive you home."

"Fear! grandmamma," replied the future hero, "I never saw fear: what is it?"

Once, after the winter holidays, when he and his brother William had set off on horseback to return to school, they came back because there had been a fall of snow; and William, who did not much like the journey, said it was too deep for them to venture on.

"If that be the case," said the father, "you certainly shall not go: but make another attempt, and I will leave it to your honour. If the road is dangerous, you may return; but remember, boys, I leave it to your honour."

The snow was deep enough to have afforded them a reasonable excuse; but Horatio was not to be prevailed upon to turn back. "We must go on," said he; "remember, brother, it was left to our honour!"

There were some fine pears growing in the schoolmaster's garden, which the boys regarded as lawful booty, and in the highest degree tempting; but the boldest among them were afraid to venture for the prize. Horatio volunteered upon this service: he was lowered down at night from the bedroom window by some sheets, plundered the tree, was drawn up with the pears, and then distributed them among his schoolfellows without reserving any for himself. "He only took them," he said, "because every other boy was afraid."

Early on a cold and dark spring morning Mr. Nelson's servant arrived at this school at North Walsham, with the expected summons for Horatio to join his ship. The parting from his brother William, who had been for so many years his playmate and bed-fellow, was a painful effort, and was the beginning of those privations which are the sailors' lot through life. He accompanied his father to London. The

Raisonnable was lying in the Medway. He was put into the Chatham stage, and on its arrival was set down with the rest of the passengers and left to find his way on board as best he could. After wandering about in the cold without being able to reach the ship, an officer observed the forlorn appearance of the boy, questioned him, and, happening to be acquainted with his uncle, took him home and gave him some refreshments. When he got on board, Captain Suckling was not in the ship, nor had any person been apprised of the boy's coming. He paced the deck the whole remainder of the day without being noticed by any one, and it was not till the second day that somebody, as he expressed it, "took compassion on him."

The *Raisonnable* having been commissioned on account of the dispute respecting the Falkland Islands, was paid off as soon as the difference with the court of Spain was accommodated, and Captain Suckling was removed to the *Triumph*, seventy-four, then stationed as a guardship in the Thames. This was considered as too inactive a life for a boy, and Nelson was therefore sent on a voyage to the West Indies in a merchant ship, commanded by Mr. John Rathbone, an excellent seaman, who had served as master's mate under Captain Suckling in the *Dreadnought*. He returned a practical seaman, but with a hatred of the king's service, and a saying then common among the sailors—"*Aft the most honour; forward the better man.*"

Rathbone had probably been disappointed and disgusted in the navy; and, with no unfriendly intentions, warned Nelson against a profession which he himself had found hopeless. His uncle received him on board the *Triumph* on his return, but he had not been many months on board when his love of enterprise was excited by hearing that two ships were fitting out for a voyage of discovery towards the North Pole. In consequence of the difficulties which were expected on such a service, these vessels were to take out effective men instead of the usual number of boys. This, however, did not deter him from soliciting to be received, and by his uncle's interest he was admitted as coxswain under Captain Lutwidge, second in command.

They sailed from the Nore on June 4th; on the 6th of the following month they were in latitude 79° 56′ 39″, longitude 9° 43′ 30″ E. The next day, about the place where most of the old discoverers had been stopped, the *Racehorse* was beset with ice; but they hove her through with ice anchors. Captain Phipps continued ranging along the ice, northward and westward, till the 24th; he then tried to the eastward. On the 30th he was in latitude 80° 13′, longitude 18° 48′

E., among the islands and in the ice, with no appearance of an opening for the ships. The weather was exceedingly fine, mild, and unusually clear. Here they were becalmed in a large bay, with three apparent openings between the islands which formed it; but everywhere, as far as they could see, surrounded with ice.

There was not a breath of air, the water was perfectly smooth, the ice covered with snow, low and even, except a few broken pieces near the edge, and the pools of water in the middle of the ice fields just crusted over with young ice. On the next day the ice closed upon them, and no opening was to be seen anywhere, except a hole or lake, as it might be called, of about a mile and a half in circumference, where the ships lay fast to the ice with their ice anchors. They filled their casks with water from these ice-fields, which was very pure and soft. The men were playing on the ice all day; but the Greenland pilots, who were further than they had ever been before and considered that the season was far advancing, were alarmed at being thus beset.

The next day there was not the smallest opening, the ships were within less than two lengths of each other, separated by ice, and neither having room to turn. The ice, which the day before had been flat and almost level with the water's edge, was now in many places forced higher than the mainyard by the pieces squeezing together. A day of thick fog followed: it was succeeded by clear weather, but the passage by which the ships had entered from the westward was closed, and no open water was in sight, either in that or any other quarter. By the pilots' advice the men were set to cut a passage and warp through the small openings to the westward. They sawed through pieces of ice twelve feet thick; and this labour continued the whole day, during which their utmost efforts did not move the ships above three hundred yards, while they were driven, together with the ice, far to the north-east and east by the current.

Young as he was, Nelson was appointed to command one of the boats which were sent out to explore a passage into the open water. It was the means of saving a boat belonging to the *Racehorse* from a singular but imminent danger. Some of the officers had fired at, and wounded, a walrus. The wounded animal dived immediately and brought up a number of its companions, and they all joined in an attack upon the boat. They wrested an oar from one of the men; and it was with the utmost difficulty that the crew could prevent them from staving or upsetting her, till the *Carcass's* boat came up, and the walruses, finding their enemies thus reinforced, dispersed. Young Nelson exposed himself in a more daring manner.

One night, during the mid-watch, he stole from the ship with one of his comrades, taking advantage of a rising fog, and set out over the ice in pursuit of a bear. It was not long before they were missed. The fog thickened, and Captain Lutwidge and his officers became exceedingly alarmed for their safety. Between three and four in the morning the weather cleared, and the two adventurers were seen at a considerable distance from the ship, attacking a huge bear. The signal for them to return was immediately made: Nelson's comrade called upon him to obey it, but in vain; his musket had flashed in the pan, their ammunition was expended, and a chasm in the ice, which divided him from the bear, probably preserved his life. "Never mind," he cried; "do but let me get a blow at this devil with the butt-end of my musket, and we shall have him."

Captain Lutwidge, however, seeing his danger, fired a gun, which had the desired effect of frightening the beast; and the boy returned. The captain reprimanded him sternly for conduct so unworthy of the office which he filled, and desired to know what motive he could have for hunting a bear. "Sir," said he, pouting his lip, as he was wont to do when agitated, "I wished to kill the bear that I might carry the skin to my father."

A party were now sent to an island about twelve miles off (named Walden's Island in the chart, from the midshipman who was entrusted with this service) to see where the open water lay. They came back with information that the ice, though close all about them, was open to the westward, round the point by which they came in. They said also, that upon the island they had had a fresh east wind. This intelligence considerably abated the hopes of the crew: for where they lay it had been almost calm, and their main dependence had been upon the effect of an easterly wind in clearing the bay. There was but one alternative, either to wait the event of the weather upon the ships, or to betake themselves to the boats. No time was to be lost; the ships had driven into shoal water, having but fourteen fathoms. Should they, or the ice to which they were fast, take the ground, they must inevitably be lost, and at this time they were driving fast towards some rocks on the north-east.

Captain Phipps had sent for the officers of both ships and told them his intention of preparing the boats for going away. They were immediately hoisted out and the fitting begun. Canvas bread-bags were made, in case it should be necessary suddenly to desert the vessels; and men were sent with the lead and line to the northward and eastward, to sound wherever they found cracks in the ice, that they might have notice before the ice took the ground; for, in that case, the ships must have instantly been crushed or overset.

On August 7th they began to haul the boats over the ice, Nelson having command of the four-oared cutter. The men behaved excellently well, like true British seamen: they seemed reconciled to the thought of leaving the ships, and had full confidence in their officers. About noon, the ice appeared rather more open near the vessels; and as the wind was easterly, though there was but little of it, the sails were set and they got about a mile to the westward. They moved very slowly, and were not now nearly so far to the westward as when they were first beset. However, all sail was kept upon them, to force them through whenever the ice slacked the least. Whatever exertions were made, it could not be possible to get the boats to the water's edge before the 14th; and if the situation of the ships should not alter by that time, it would not be justifiable to stay longer by them. The commander therefore resolved to carry on both attempts together, moving the boats constantly, and taking every opportunity of getting the ships through.

A party was sent out next day to the westward to examine the state of the ice: they returned with tidings that it was very heavy and close, consisting chiefly of large fields. The ships, however, moved something, and the ice itself was drifting westward. There was a thick fog, so that it was impossible to ascertain what advantage had been gained. It continued on the 9th; but the ships were moved a little through some very small openings: the mist cleared off in the afternoon, and it was then perceived that they had driven much more than could have been expected to the westward, and that the ice itself had driven still farther. In the course of the day they got past the boats, and took them on board again.

On the morrow the wind sprang up to the north-north-east. All sail was set, and the ships forced their way through a great deal of very heavy ice. They frequently struck, and with such force that one stroke broke the shank of the *Racehorse's* best bower anchor; but the vessels made way, and by noon they had cleared the ice and were out at sea.

The ships were paid off shortly after their return to England; and Nelson was then placed by his uncle with Captain Farmer, in the *Seahorse*, of twenty guns, then going out to the East Indies in the squadron under Sir Edward Hughes. His good conduct attracted the attention of the master (afterwards Captain Surridge), and, upon his recommendation, the captain rated him as midshipman.

At this time his countenance was florid, and his appearance rather stout and athletic; but when he had been about eighteen months in India he felt the effects of that climate, so perilous to European constitutions. The disease baffled all power of medicine; he was reduced almost to a skeleton; the use of his limbs was for some time entirely lost; and the only hope that remained was from a voyage home. Accordingly he was brought home by Captain Pigot, in the *Dolphin*; and had it not been for the attentive and careful kindness of that officer on the way, Nelson would never have lived to reach his native shores.

Soon after his return, on April 8th, 1777, he passed his examination for a lieutenancy. Captain Suckling sat at the head of the board; and when the examination had ended, in a manner highly honourable to Nelson, rose from his seat, and introduced him to the examining captains as his nephew. They expressed their wonder that he had not informed them of this relationship before; he replied that he did not wish the younker to be favoured; he knew his nephew would pass a good examination, and he had not been deceived.

First Steps Up the Ladder
A Chapter From Nelson's Career by Robert Southey

Though Nelson did not live to be an old man, he crowded his life with so much activity that it is quite impossible to follow it in detail within the limits of the present space. Active to restlessness, he wearied beyond endurance of perfunctory duty and official routine, and if active service did not come in his way he sought it. The death of his uncle, Captain Suckling, soon after he had obtained his lieutenancy, threw him upon his own resources, and compelled him to look out for himself. This naturally strengthened his self-reliance and helped to develop his character.

On the day following his examination for a lieutenancy Nelson was appointed to the *Lowestoffe* frigate,—Captain William Locher then fitting out for Jamaica,—from whence he passed to the Bristol flag-ship and soon became first lieutenant. On December 8th, 1778, he was appointed to the command of the *Badger* brig. While the *Badger* was lying in Montego Bay an incident occurred which showed the coolness and readiness of resource of the young officer. The *Glasgow*, a craft of twenty guns, having entered the bay and cast anchor, was found to be on fire, the steward having carelessly caused the conflagration while taking rum from the after hold. Many of the crew sought safety in flight, leaping into the water to escape the inevitable explosion of the magazine. Nelson, however, was soon upon the spot, when he compelled the remainder of the crew to throw the powder overboard and point the cannon upwards, thereby minimising the evil consequences of the catastrophe.

Shortly after this Nelson was employed in conveying five hundred men from Port Royal to Cape Gracias a Dios in Honduras, in furtherance of a project of General Dalling to take Fort San Juan and cut off the communication of the Spaniards between their northern and southern possessions in America.

The castle of San Juan is thirty-two miles below the Lake of Nicaragua, from which the river issues, and sixty-nine from its mouth. Boats reach the sea from thence in a day and a half; but their navigation back, even when unladen, is the labour of days. The English appeared before it on the 11th, two days after they had taken San Bartolomeo. Nelson's advice was, that it should instantly be carried by assault: but Nelson was not the commander, and it was thought proper to observe all the formalities of a siege. Ten days were wasted before this could be commenced: it was a work more of fatigue than of danger; but fatigue was more to be dreaded than the enemy. The rains set in, and, could the garrison have held out a little longer, disease would have rid them of their invaders.

Even the Indians sank under it, the victims of unusual exertion and of their own excesses. The place surrendered on the 24th. But victory procured to the conquerors none of the relief they expected; the castle was worse than a prison, and it contained nothing which could contribute to the recovery of the sick or the preservation of those who were yet unaffected. The huts, which served for hospitals, were surrounded with filth and with the putrefying hides of slaughtered cattle—almost sufficient of themselves to have engendered pestilence; and when, at last, orders were given to erect a convenient hospital, the contagion had become so general that there were none who could work at it; for, besides the few who were able to perform garrison duty, there were not orderly men enough to assist the sick.

Nelson was attacked with the prevailing dysentery when the news arrived that he had been appointed to succeed Captain Glover in the *Janus* of forty-four guns. He returned to the harbour the day before San Juan surrendered, and immediately sailed for Jamaica in the sloop that had brought the news of the appointment. His health, however, compelled him to forego his opportunity and return to England, where he spent four months in rest and recuperation. Nelson's next appointment was to the *Albemarle* of twenty-eight guns with which, as he said, as if to try his constitution he was now sent to the North Seas and kept there the whole winter. Nelson arrived at this station during the armed neutrality; and when he anchored off Elsineur, the Danish admiral sent on board, desiring to be informed what ships had arrived, and to have their force written down. Nelson said to the messenger:

"The *Albemarle* is one of his Britannic Majesty's ships: you are at liberty, sir, to count the guns as you go down the side; and you may assure the Danish admiral that, if necessary, they shall all be well served."

Other characteristic actions are recorded of Nelson at this time.

On his return to the Downs, while he was ashore visiting the senior officer, there came on so heavy a gale that almost all the vessels drove, and a store-ship came athwart-hawse of the *Albemarle*. Nelson feared she would drive on the Goodwin Sands: he ran to the beach; but even the Deal boatmen thought it impossible to get on board, such was the violence of the storm. At length some of the most intrepid offered to make the attempt for fifteen guineas; and, to the astonishment and fear of all the beholders, Nelson embarked during the height of the tempest. With great difficulty and imminent danger he succeeded in reaching her. She lost her bowsprit and foremast, but escaped further injury.

Nelson was now ordered to Quebec, and accordingly sailed for Canada. During her first cruise on that station the *Albemarle* captured a fishing-schooner, which contained, in her cargo, nearly all the property that her master possessed, and the poor fellow had a large family at home, anxiously expecting him. Nelson employed him as a pilot in Boston Bay, then restored him the schooner and cargo, and gave him a certificate to secure him against being captured by any other vessel. The man came off afterwards to the *Albemarle*, at the hazard of his life, with a present of sheep, poultry, and fresh provisions. A most valuable supply it proved; for the scurvy was raging on board: this was in the middle of August, and the ship's company had not had a fresh meal since the beginning of April. While here, Lord Hood introduced Nelson to Prince William Henry, Duke of Clarence, telling him that if he wished to ask any questions respecting naval tactics, Captain Nelson could give him as much information as any officer in the fleet.

Another characteristic act of Nelson occurred while he was cruising between Puerto Cabello and La Guayra, under French colours, for the purpose of obtaining information, when a king's launch, belonging to the Spaniards, passed near, and, being hailed in French, came alongside without suspicion, and answered all the questions asked concerning the number and force of the enemy's ships. The crew, however, were not a little surprised when they were taken on board, and found themselves prisoners. One of the party went by the name of the Count de Deux Ponts. He was, however, a prince of the German empire, and brother to the heir of the Electorate of Bavaria: his companions were French officers of distinction, and men of science, who had been collecting specimens in the various branches of natural history.

Nelson having entertained them with the best his table could afford, told them they were at liberty to depart with their boat and all that it contained; he only required them to promise that they would consider themselves as prisoners, if the commander-in-chief should refuse to acquiesce in their being thus liberated: a circumstance which was not by any means likely to happen. Tidings soon arrived that the preliminaries of peace had been signed; and the *Albemarle* returned to England, and was paid off.

Nelson's next appointment was to the *Boreas*, twenty-eight guns, bound for the Leeward Islands as a cruiser on the peace establishment. Here we have a happy picture of his treatment of the midshipmen who came under his influence.

If he perceived that a boy was afraid at first going aloft, he would say to him, in a friendly manner: "Well, sir, I am going a race to the mast-head, and beg that I may meet you there." The poor little fellow instantly began to climb, and got up how he could—Nelson never noticed in what manner, but, when they met in the top, spoke cheerfully to him, and would say how much any person was to be pitied who fancied that getting up was either dangerous or difficult. Every day he went into the school-room, to see that they were pursuing their nautical studies, and at noon he was always the first on deck with his quadrant. Whenever he paid a visit of ceremony, some of these youths always accompanied him.

The sense of duty, which was so strong an element in Nelson's character, led him into much trouble at this period of his career. The Navigation Act as then in existence had been allowed to become a dead letter in as far as America and Nova Scotia were concerned, and Nelson felt that it was the duty of the navy to enforce it. This led him into difficulties with his superiors, who resented his dictation, and with the traders whose interests he attacked. In the result he had to choose between disobeying his superiors and disobeying acts of parliament. "I determined," he says, "upon the former, trusting to the uprightness of my intentions, and believing that my country would not let me be ruined for protecting her commerce."

For this he would probably have been tried by court martial had not the spirit of the fleet been with him. As it was he was subject to civil proceedings, which made it impossible for him to leave his ship for a long time for fear of arrest and subjected him to annoyance for years after. The government, however, ultimately took up his defence and finally thanked the commander-in-chief for the services rendered by Nelson against his orders.

Nelson's attempts at this time to put down the abuses whereby the British Government were being defrauded by dishonest traders also made him many enemies; but in this as in most of his enterprises, he was ultimately successful; inducing the government to introduce proper systems of checking supplies.

About this time he found consolation for public worries in domestic felicity, betrothing the daughter of Mr. Herbert, the President of Nevis, then, though only in her eighteenth year, the widow of Dr. Nisbet, a physician. She had one child, a son, by name Josiah, who afterwards entered the navy. One day Mr. Herbert, who had hastened, half-dressed, to receive Nelson, exclaimed, on returning to his dressing-room, "Good God! if I did not find that great little man, of whom everybody is so afraid, playing in the next room, under the dining-table, with Mrs. Nisbet's child!" A few days afterwards Mrs. Nisbet herself was first introduced to him, and thanked him for the partiality which he had shown her little boy.

They were married on March 11th, 1787; Prince William Henry, who had come out to the West Indies the preceding winter, being present, by his own desire, to give away the bride. Nelson took his wife to his father's parsonage, meaning only to pay him a visit before they went to France; a project which he had formed for the sake of acquiring a competent knowledge of the French language. But his father could not bear to lose him thus unnecessarily. Mr. Nelson had long been an invalid, suffering under paralytic and asthmatic affections, which, for several hours after he rose in the morning, scarcely permitted him to speak. He had been given over by his physicians for this complaint nearly forty years before his death, and was, for many of his last years, obliged to spend all his winters at Bath.

The sight of his son, he declared, had given him new life. "But, Horatio," said he, "it would have been better that I had not been thus cheered, if I am so soon to be bereaved of you again. Let me, my good son, see you whilst I can. My age and infirmities increase, and I shall not last long." To such an appeal there could be no reply. Nelson took up his abode for a time at the parsonage, and amused himself with the sports and occupations of the country.

On Board the "Agamemnon"
By Robert Southey

THE SIEGE OF BASTIA.—THE SIEGE OF CALVI.—THE ANNEXATION OF CORSICA.—THE CAPTURE OF THE "ÇA IRA" AND THE "CENSEUR."

On January 30th, 1793, by the united interest of Prince William, now Duke of Clarence, and Lord Hood, Nelson was appointed to the *Agamemnon* of sixty-five guns and was ordered to the Mediterranean to serve under Lord Hood. While here, he was sent with despatches to Sir William Hamilton, our envoy at the court of Naples, and thus formed the acquaintance of Sir William and his wife. When returning from this mission, he fell in with five sail of the enemy and gave chase. He came near enough to one frigate to engage her, but after inflicting and receiving much damage was unable to follow up his advantage. Shortly after, he was detached with a small squadron to co-operate with General Paoli and the anti-Galician party in Corsica, an expedition—the immediate object of which was the conquest of the city of Bastia, then held by the French—in which Nelson showed what a determined sailor can do on shore.

Lord Hood submitted to General Dundas, who commanded the land forces, a plan for the reduction of this place; but the general declined co-operating, thinking the attempt impracticable without a reinforcement of two thousand men, which he expected from Gibraltar. Upon this Lord Hood determined to reduce it with the naval force under his command, and leaving part of his fleet off Toulon, sailed with the rest to Bastia. General d'Aubant, who succeeded General Dundas in the command of the land forces, held the same opinion as his predecessor and refused to furnish his lordship with a single soldier, cannon, or any stores. Lord Hood could only obtain a few artillerymen; so ordering on board the troops who, having been embarked as marines, were borne on the ships' books as part of their respective complements, he began the siege with eleven hundred and eighty-three soldiers, artillerymen, and marines, and two hundred and fifty sailors.

"We are but few," said Nelson, "but of the right sort; our general at St. Fiorenzo not giving us one of the five regiments he has there lying idle."

These men were landed on April 4th, under Lieutenant-Colonel Villettes and Nelson, who had now acquired from the army the title of brigadier. Guns were dragged by the sailors up heights where it appeared almost impossible to convey them; a work of the greatest difficulty, and one which Nelson said could never, in his opinion, have been accomplished by any but British seamen. The soldiers, though less dexterous in such service, because not accustomed, like sailors, to habitual dexterity, behaved with equal spirit. "Their zeal," said the brigadier, "is almost unexampled. There is not a man but considers himself as personally interested in the event, and as deserted by the general. It has, I am persuaded, made them equal to double their numbers."

La Combe St. Michel, the commissioner from the national convention, who was in the city, replied to the summons of the British admiral in these terms: "I have hot shot for your ships, and bayonets for your troops. When two-thirds of our men are killed, I will then trust to the generosity of the English." The siege, however, was not sustained with the firmness which such a reply seemed to augur. On May 19th a treaty of capitulation was begun, and that same evening the troops from St. Fiorenzo made their appearance on the hills; and, on the following morning, General d'Aubant arrived with the whole army to take possession of the town.

The events of the siege had justified the confidence of the sailors; but they themselves excused the opinion of the generals, when they saw what they had done. "I am all astonishment," said Nelson, "when I reflect upon what we have achieved: one thousand regulars, fifteen hundred national guards, and a large party of Corsican troops, four thousand in all, laying down their arms to twelve hundred soldiers, marines, and seamen! I always was of opinion, have ever acted up to it and never had any reason to repent it, that one Englishman was equal to three Frenchmen. Had this been an English town, I am sure it would not have been taken by them."

The *Agamemnon* was now despatched to co-operate at the siege of Calvi with General Sir Charles Stuart. Nelson had less responsibility here than at Bastia, and was acting with a man after his own heart, who was never sparing of himself, and slept every night in the advanced battery. But the service was not less hard than that of the former siege. "We will fag ourselves to death," said he to Lord Hood, "before any blame shall lie at our doors. I trust it will not be forgotten that twenty-five pieces of heavy ordnance have been dragged to the different batteries, mounted, and all but three fought by seamen, except one artilleryman to point the guns." The climate proved more destructive than the service; for this was during the period of the "lion sun," as they there call our season of the "dog days."

Of two thousand men above half were sick, and the rest like so many phantoms. Nelson described himself as the reed among the oaks, bowing before the storm when they were laid low by it. "All the prevailing disorders have attacked me," said he, "but I have not strength enough for them to fasten on." The loss from the enemy was not great; but Nelson received a serious injury: a shot struck the ground near him, and drove the sand and small gravel into one of his eyes. He spoke of it slightly at the time: writing the same day to Lord Hood, he only said that he got a little hurt that morning, not much; and the next day, he said, he should be able to attend his duty in the evening. In fact, he suffered it to confine him only one day; but the sight was lost.

After the fall of Calvi, his services were, by a strange omission, altogether overlooked and his name was not even mentioned in the list of wounded. Nelson felt himself neglected. "One hundred and ten days," said he, "I have been actually engaged, at sea and on shore, against the enemy; three actions against ships, two against Bastia in my ship, four boat actions, and two villages taken, and twelve sail of vessels burnt. I do not know that any one has done more. I have had the comfort to be always applauded by my commander-in-chief, but never to be rewarded; and, what is more mortifying, for services in which I have been wounded others have been praised, who, at the same time, were actually in bed, far from the scene of action. They have not done me justice. But, never mind. I'll have a *Gazette* of my own." How amply was this prediction realised!

As the result of this expedition, Corsica was annexed to the British Crown with the consent of the majority of the people, and received a constitution as free as our own. Some, however, favoured French occupation, and soon after France taking advantage of the discontent, sought the reconquest of the island. Corsica was now loudly threatened. The French had a superior fleet in the Mediterranean, and they sent it out with express orders to seek the English and engage them.

Accordingly, the Toulon fleet, consisting of seventeen ships of the line, and five smaller vessels, put to sea. Admiral Hotham, who had succeeded Lord Hood, received this information at Leghorn, and sailed immediately in search of them. He had with him fourteen sail of the line and one Neapolitan seventy-four; but his ships were only half manned, containing but seven thousand six hundred and fifty men, whereas the enemy had sixteen thousand nine hundred. He soon came in sight of them: a general action was expected; but after manoeuvring for a day in sight of the English fleet, they allowed themselves to be chased. Nelson followed the *Ça Ira* for several hours, inflicting and receiving considerable damage the result of which was that seven of the *Agamemnon* men were hurt, while the *Ça Ira* lost one hundred and ten, and was so cut up that she could not get a top mast aloft during the following night.

The next morning the French fleet was observed about five miles off the *Ça Ira*, and the *Censeur* which had her in tow being about three and a half miles distant. All sail was made to cut these ships off, and a partial engagement of the two fleets ensued. The *Agamemnon* was again engaged with her yesterday's antagonist; but she had to fight on both sides the ship at the same time. The *Ça Ira* and the *Censeur* fought most gallantly: the first lost nearly three hundred men, in addition to her former loss; the last, three hundred and fifty. Both at last struck, and Lieutenant Andrews, of the *Agamemnon*, hoisted English colours on board them both.

As soon as these vessels had struck, Nelson went to Admiral Hotham, and proposed that the two prizes should be left with the *Illustrious* and *Courageux*, which had been crippled in the action, and with four frigates, and that the rest of the fleet should pursue the enemy and follow up the advantage to the utmost. But his reply was—"We must be contented: we have done very well." "Now," said Nelson, "had we taken ten sail, and allowed the eleventh to escape, when it had been possible to have got at her, I could never have called it well done. Goodall backed me: I got him to write to the admiral; but it would not do. We should have had such a day as, I believe, the annals of England never produced."

Nelson's next expedition was to Genoa to co-operate with the Austrian and Sardinian forces; but his allies were unworthy of him and by their irresolution and delay continued to frustrate his best laid schemes. In an engagement between the Austrians and the French, General de Vins, the Austrian general, gave up the command in the middle of the battle, pleading ill-health. Nelson says:

> From that moment not a soldier stayed at his post: it was the devil take the hindmost. Many thousands ran away who had never seen the enemy; some of them thirty miles from the advanced posts. Had I not—though, I own, against my inclination—been kept at Genoa, from eight to ten thousand men would have been taken prisoners, and, amongst the number, General de Vins himself; but, by this means, the pass of the Bocchetta was kept open. The purser of the ship, who was at Vado, ran with the Austrians eighteen miles without stopping: the men without arms, officers without soldiers, women without assistance. The oldest officer, say they, never heard of so complete a defeat, and certainly without any reason. Thus has ended my campaign.

The defeat of General de Vins gave the enemy possession of the Genoese coast from Savona to Voltri; and it deprived the Austrians of their direct communication with the English fleet. The *Agamemnon*, therefore, could no longer be useful on this station, and so Nelson sailed for Leghorn to refit. When his ship went into dock, there was not a mast, yard, sail, or any part of the rigging but what stood in need of repair, having been cut to pieces with shot. The hull was so damaged that it had for some time been secured by cables, which were served or thrapped round it.

The Evacuation of Corsica and the Battle of Cape St. Vincent
By Robert Southey.

Sir John Jervis now became commander of the Mediterranean fleet, and Nelson joined him in Fiorenzo Bay. The manner in which Nelson was received is said to have excited some envy. One captain observed to him: "You did just as you pleased in Lord Hood's time, the same in Admiral Hotham's, and now again with Sir John Jervis; it makes no difference to you who is commander-in-chief."

Had Nelson consulted his own inclinations at this time, he would have returned for a short period of rest, but as Sir John Jervis put it, "We cannot spare you, either as captain or admiral," and so he resumed his station in the Gulf of Genoa.

The French had not followed up their successes in that quarter with their usual celerity. Scherer, who commanded there, owed his advancement to any other cause than his merit, was removed from a command for which his incapacity was afterwards clearly proved, and Bonaparte was appointed to succeed him. Bonaparte, with a celerity which had never before been witnessed in modern war, pursued his advantages to the uttermost; and, in a very short time, dictated to the court of Turin terms of peace, or rather of submission, by which all the strongest places of Piedmont were put into his hands.

On one occasion, and only on one, Nelson was able to impede the progress of this new conqueror. Six vessels, laden with cannon and ordnance-stores for the siege of Mantua, sailed from Toulon for St. Pier d'Arena. Assisted by Captain Cockburn, in the *Meleager*, he drove them under a battery, pursued them, silenced the batteries, and captured the whole. Military books, plans, and maps of Italy, with the different points marked upon them where former battles had been fought, sent by the Directory for Bonaparte's use, were found in the convoy. The loss of this artillery was one of the chief causes which compelled the French to raise the siege of Mantua.

The successes of Bonaparte on land led the British government to order the evacuation of Corsica, and Nelson undertook to protect the embarkation of British property. The viceroy, Sir Gilbert Elliott, deeply felt the impolicy and ignominy of this evacuation, and Nelson exclaimed, when he heard that the fleet was to leave the Mediterranean, "Do His Majesty's ministers know their own minds? They do not know what this fleet is capable of performing—anything and everything. Much as I shall rejoice to see England, I lament our present orders in sackcloth and ashes, so dishonourable to the dignity of England, whose fleets are equal to meet the world in arms."

Sir Gilbert Elliott believed that the great body of the Corsicans were perfectly satisfied with the British government, but when they found that the English intended to evacuate the island, they naturally and necessarily sent to make their peace with the French. The partisans of France found none to oppose them. A committee of thirty took upon them the government of Bastia, and sequestrated all the British property; armed Corsicans mounted guard at every place, and a plan was laid for seizing the viceroy. Nelson, who was appointed to superintend the evacuation, frustrated these projects.

At a time when everyone else despaired of saving stores, cannon, provisions, or property of any kind, and a privateer was moored across the mole-head to prevent all boats from passing, he sent word to the committee that if the slightest opposition were made to the embarkment and removal of British property, he would batter the town down. The privateer pointed her guns at the officer who carried this message, and muskets were levelled against his boats from the mole-head. Upon this Captain Sutton, of the *Egmont*, pulling out his watch, gave them a quarter of an hour to deliberate upon their answer.

In five minutes after the expiration of that time, the ships, he said, would open their fire. Upon this the very sentinels scampered off, and every vessel came out of the mole. A ship-owner complained to the commodore that the municipality refused to let him take his goods out of the custom-house. Nelson directed him to say that unless they were instantly delivered he would open his fire. The committee turned pale; and without answering a word gave him the keys. Their last attempt was to levy a duty upon the things that were re-embarked. He sent them word that he would pay them a disagreeable visit if there were any more complaints.

The committee then finding that they had to deal with a man who knew his own power and was determined to make the British name respected, desisted from the insolent conduct which they had assumed, and it was acknowledged that Bastia never had been so quiet and orderly since the English were in possession of it. In less than a week private property and public stores to the value of £200,000 had been safely removed.

The French, favoured by the Spanish fleet, which was at that time within twelve leagues of Bastia, pushed over troops from Leghorn, who landed near Cape Corse on the 18th, and, on the 20th, at one in the morning entered the citadel, an hour only after the British had spiked the guns and evacuated it. Nelson embarked at daybreak, being the last person who left the shore; having thus, as he said, seen the first and the last of Corsica.

Having thus ably effected this humiliating service, Nelson was ordered to hoist his broad pennant on board the *Minerve* frigate, Captain George Cockburn, and, with the *Blanche* under his command, proceed to Porto Ferrajo, and superintend the evacuation of that place also. On his way he fell in with two Spanish frigates, the *Sabina* and the *Ceres*. The *Minerve* engaged the former, which was commanded by Don Jacobo Stuart, a descendant of the Duke of Berwick. After an action of three hours, during which the Spaniards lost a hundred and sixty-four men, the *Sabina* struck. The Spanish captain, who was the only surviving officer, had hardly been conveyed on board the *Minerve*, when another enemy's frigate came up, compelled her to cast off the prize, and brought her a second time to action.

After half an hour's trial of strength, this new antagonist wore and hauled off; but a Spanish squadron of two ships of the line and two frigates came in sight. The *Blanche*, from which the *Ceres* had got off, was far to windward, and the *Minerve* escaped only by the anxiety of the enemy to recover their own ship. As soon as Nelson reached Porto Ferrajo, he sent his prisoner in a flag of truce to Carthagena, having returned him his sword; this he did in honour of the gallantry which Don Jacobo had displayed, and not without some feeling of respect for his ancestry. By the same flag of truce he sent back all the Spanish prisoners at Porto Ferrajo, in exchange for whom he received his own men who had been taken in the prize.

Nelson now sailed from Porto Ferrajo with a convoy for Gibraltar, and thence proceeded westward in search of the admiral. Off the mouth of the Straits he fell in with the Spanish fleet, and on February 13th, 1797, reaching the station off Cape St. Vincent, informed Sir John Jervis of its proximity.

He was now directed to shift his broad pennant on board the *Captain*, seventy-four, Captain R. W. Miller; and, before sunset, the signal was made to prepare for action, and to keep, during the night, in close order. At daybreak the enemy were in sight. The British force consisted of two ships of one hundred guns, two of ninety-eight, two of ninety, eight of seventy-four, and one sixty-four: fifteen of the line in all; with four frigates, a sloop, and a cutter. The Spaniards had one four-decker, of one hundred and thirty-six guns, six three-deckers of one hundred and twelve, two eighty-fours, eighteen seventy-fours: in all, twenty-seven ships of the line, with ten frigates and a brig.

Their admiral, Don Joseph de Cordova, had learnt from an American, on the 5th, that the English had only nine ships, which was indeed the case when his informer had seen them; for a reinforcement of five ships from England, under Admiral Parker, had not then joined, and the *Culloden* had parted company. Upon this information, the Spanish commander, instead of going into Cadiz, as was his intention when he sailed from Carthagena, determined to seek an enemy so inferior in force; and relying, with fatal confidence, upon the American account, he suffered his ships to remain too far dispersed, and in some disorder. When the morning of the 14th broke and discovered the English fleet, a fog for some time concealed their number.

The lookout ship of the Spaniards, fancying that her signal was disregarded, because so little notice seemed to be taken of it, made another signal that the English force consisted of forty sail of the line. The captain afterwards said he did this to rouse the admiral; it had the effect of perplexing him, and alarming the whole fleet. The absurdity of such an act shows what was the state of the Spanish navy under that miserable government, by which Spain was so long oppressed and degraded and finally betrayed. In reality, the general incapacity of the naval officers was so well known, that in a *pasquinade*, which about this time appeared at Madrid, wherein the different orders of the state were advertised for sale, the greater part of the sea-officers, with all their equipments, were offered as a gift; and it was added that any person who would please to take them should receive a handsome gratuity.

Before the enemy could form a regular order of battle, Sir John Jervis, by carrying a press of sail, came up with them, passed through their fleet, then tacked, and thus cut off nine of their ships from the main body. These ships attempted to form on the larboard tack, either with a design of passing through the British line, or to leeward of it, and thus rejoining their friends. Only one of them succeeded in this attempt, and that only because she was so covered with smoke that her intention was not discovered till she had reached the rear: the others were so warmly received that they put about, took to flight, and did not appear again in the action till its close.

The admiral was now able to direct his attention to the enemy's main body, which was still superior in number to his whole fleet, and more so in weight of metal. He made signal to tack in succession. Nelson, whose station was in the rear of the British line, perceived that the Spaniards were bearing up before the wind, with an intention of forming their line, going large, and joining their separated ships; or else, of getting off without an engagement. To prevent either of these schemes, he disobeyed the signal without a moment's hesitation, and ordered his ship to be wore. This at once brought him into action with the *Santissima Trinidad*, one hundred and thirty-six, the *San Joseph*, one hundred and twelve, the *Salvador del Mundo*, one hundred and twelve, the *San Nicolas*, eighty, the *San Isidro*, seventy-four, another seventy-four, and another first-rate.

Trowbridge, in the *Culloden*, immediately joined, and most nobly supported him; and for nearly an hour did the *Culloden* and *Captain* maintain what Nelson called "this apparently, but not really, unequal contest;"—such was the advantage of skill and discipline and the confidence which brave men derive from them. The *Blenheim* then passing between them and the enemy, gave them a respite, and poured in her fire upon the Spaniards. The *Salvador del Mundo* and *San Isidro* dropped astern, and were fired into, in a masterly style, by the *Excellent*, Captain Collingwood. The *San Isidro* struck; and Nelson thought that the *Salvador* struck also. "But Collingwood," says he, "disdaining the parade of taking possession of beaten enemies, most gallantly pushed up, with every sail set, to save his old friend and messmate, who was, to every appearance, in a critical situation;" for the *Captain* was at this time actually fired upon by three first-rates, by the *San Nicolas*, and by a seventy-four, within about pistol-shot of that vessel. The *Blenheim* was ahead, the *Culloden* crippled and astern.

Collingwood ranged up, and hauling up his main sail just astern passed within ten feet of the *San Nicolas*, giving her a most tremendous fire, then passing on for the *Santissima Trinidad*. The *San Nicolas* luffing up, the *San Joseph* fell on board her, and Nelson resumed his station abreast of them, and close alongside. The *Captain* was now incapable of farther service, either in the line or in chase: she had lost her foretop-mast; not a sail, shroud, or rope was left, and her wheel was shot away. Nelson, therefore, directed Captain Miller to put the helm a-starboard, and, calling for the boarders, ordered them to board.

Captain Berry, who had lately been Nelson's first lieutenant, was the first man who leaped into the enemy's mizen chains. Miller, when in the very act of going, was ordered by Nelson to remain. Berry was supported from the spritsail yard, which locked in the *San Nicolas's* main rigging. A soldier of the 69th broke the upper quarter-gallery window, and jumped in, followed by the commodore himself, and by others as fast as possible. The cabin doors were fastened, and the Spanish officers fired their pistols at them through the window; the doors were soon forced, and the Spanish brigadier fell while retreating to the quarter-deck. Nelson pushed on, and found Berry in possession of the poop, and the Spanish ensign hauling down. He passed on to the forecastle, where he met two or three Spanish officers, and received their swords.

The English were now in full possession of every part of the ship; and a fire of pistols and musketry opened upon them from the admiral's stern gallery of the *San Joseph*. Nelson having placed sentinels at the different ladders, and ordered Captain Miller to send more men into the prize, gave orders for boarding that ship from the *San Nicolas*. It was done in an instant, he himself leading the way, and exclaiming—"Westminster Abbey, or victory!" Berry assisted him into the main chains; and at that very moment a Spanish officer looked over the quarter-deck rail and said they surrendered. It was not long before he was on the quarter-deck, where the Spanish captain presented to him his sword, and told him the admiral was below, dying of his wounds. There, on the quarter-deck of an enemy's first-rate, he received the swords of the officers, giving them, as they were delivered, one by one, to William Fearney, one of his old "Agamemnons," who, with the utmost coolness, put them under his arm.

One of his sailors came up, and, with an Englishman's feeling, took him by the hand, saying he might not soon have such another place to do it in, and he was heartily glad to see him there. Twenty-four of the *Captain's* men were killed, and fifty-six wounded; a fourth part of the loss sustained by the whole squadron falling upon this ship. Nelson received only a few bruises.

The Spaniards had still eighteen or nineteen ships, which had suffered little or no injury; that part of the fleet which had been separated from the main body in the morning was now coming up, and Sir John Jervis made signal to bring-to. His ships could not have formed without abandoning those which they had captured, and running to leeward: the *Captain* was lying a perfect wreck on board her two prizes; and many of the other vessels were so shattered in their masts and rigging as to be wholly unmanageable. The Spanish admiral meantime, according to his official account, being altogether undecided in his own opinion respecting the state of the fleet, inquired of his captains whether it was proper to renew the action: nine of them answered explicitly that it was not; others replied that it was expedient to delay the business. The *Pelayo* and the *Principe Conquistador* were the only ships that were for fighting.

As soon as the action was discontinued Nelson went on board the admiral's ship. Sir John Jervis received him on the quarter-deck, took him in his arms, and said he could not sufficiently thank him. For this victory the commander-in-chief was rewarded with the title of Earl St. Vincent. In the official letter of Sir John Jervis Nelson was not mentioned. It is said that the admiral had seen an instance of the ill consequence of such selections, after Lord Howe's victory, and therefore would not name any individual, thinking it proper to speak to the public only in terms of general approbation. His private letter to the first lord of the Admiralty was, with his consent, published for the first time in a *Life of Nelson*, by Mr. Harrison. Here it is said that "Commodore Nelson, who was in the rear on the starboard tack, took the lead on the larboard, and contributed very much to the fortune of the day."

It is also said that he boarded the two Spanish ships successively; but the fact that Nelson wore without orders, and thus planned as well as accomplished the victory, is not explicitly stated. Perhaps it was thought proper to pass over this part of his conduct in silence, as a splendid fault: but such an example is not dangerous. The author of the work in which this letter was first made public, protests against those over-zealous friends "who would make the action rather appear as Nelson's battle than that of the illustrious commander-in-chief, who derives from it so deservedly his title. No man," he says, "ever less needed, or less desired, to strip a single leaf from the honoured wreath of any other hero, with the vain hope of augmenting his own, than the immortal Nelson; no man ever more merited the whole of that which a generous nation unanimously presented to Sir J. Jervis, than the Earl St. Vincent."

Certainly Earl St. Vincent well deserved the reward which he received: but it is not detracting from his merit to say that Nelson is as fully entitled to as much fame from this action as the commander-in-chief; not because the brunt of the action fell upon him; not because he was engaged with all the four ships which were taken, and took two of them, it may almost be said, with his own hand; but because the decisive movement which enabled him to perform all this, and by which the action became a victory, was executed in neglect of orders, and upon his own judgment, and at his peril. Earl St. Vincent deserved his earldom; but it is not to the honour of those by whom titles were distributed in those days that Nelson never obtained the rank of earl for either of those victories which he lived to enjoy, though the one was the most complete and glorious in the annals of naval history, and the other the most important in its consequences of any which was achieved during the whole war.

Before the news of the action reached England, Nelson was advanced to the rank of rear-Admiral, and now his gallantry was rewarded by the Order of the Bath. The sword of the Spanish rear-Admiral, presented to Nelson when he boarded his ship, and which Sir John Jervis insisted on his keeping, he presented to the mayor and corporation of Norwich, saying that he knew no place where it could give him or his family more pleasure to have it kept than in the capital city of the county where he was born. The freedom of that city was voted to him on that occasion.

But of all the numerous congratulations which he received, none could have affected him more deeply than that which came to him from his venerable father. "I thank my God," said that excellent man, "with all the power of a grateful soul, for the mercies He has most graciously bestowed on me in preserving you. Not only my few acquaintances here, but the people in general, met me at every corner with such handsome words that I was obliged to retire from the public eye. The height of glory to which your professional judgment, united with a proper degree of bravery, guarded by Providence, has raised you, few sons, my dear child, attain to, and fewer fathers live to see. Tears of joy have involuntarily trickled down my furrowed cheeks. Who could stand the force of such general congratulations? The name and services of Nelson have sounded throughout this city of Bath from the common ballad singer to the public theatre."

The good old man concluded by telling him that the field of glory in which he had so long been conspicuous was still open, and by giving him his blessing.

The Story of Santa Cruz
By Robert Southey

About the middle of the year 1797 Nelson hoisted his flag as rear-Admiral of the blue on board the *Theseus*. This ship had taken part in the mutiny in England, and being just arrived from home, some danger was apprehended from the temper of the men. This was one reason why Nelson was removed to her. He had not been on board many weeks before a paper, signed in the name of all the ship's company, was dropped on the quarter-deck, containing these words: "Success attend Admiral Nelson! God bless Captain Miller! We thank them for the officers they have placed over us. We are happy and comfortable, and will shed every drop of blood in our veins to support them; and the name of the *Theseus* shall be immortalised as high as her captain's."

While Nelson was in the *Theseus*, he was employed in the command of the inner squadron at the blockade of Cadiz. During this service the most perilous action occurred in which he was ever engaged. Making a night attack upon the Spanish gun-boats, his barge was attacked by an armed launch, under their commander, Don Miguel Tregoyen, carrying twenty-six men. Nelson had with him only his ten barge-men, Captain Freemantle, and his coxswain, John Sykes, an old and faithful follower, who twice saved the life of his admiral by parrying the blows that were aimed at him, and, at last, actually interposed his own head to receive the blow of a Spanish sabre, which he could not by any other means avert;—thus dearly was Nelson beloved. Notwithstanding the great disproportion of numbers, eighteen of the enemy were killed, all the rest wounded, and their launch taken.

Twelve days after this *rencontre*, Nelson sailed at the head of an expedition against Teneriffe. In this disastrous expedition, which took place in July 1797, Nelson was much embarrassed by difficulties of wind and tide, but though foiled in his plans still felt it a point of honour to make some attempt to capture the town. Perfectly aware how desperate a service this was likely to prove, before he left the *Theseus*, he called Lieutenant Nisbet into the cabin that he might assist in arranging and burning his mother's letters. Perceiving that the young man was armed he earnestly begged him to remain behind. "Should we both fall, Josiah," said he, "what would become of your poor mother? The care of the *Theseus* falls to you; stay, therefore, and take charge of her."

Nisbet replied, "Sir, the ship must take care of itself; I will go with you tonight, if I never go again."

He met his captains at supper on board the *Seahorse*; Captain Freemantle, whose wife, whom he had lately married in the Mediterranean, presided at table. At eleven o'clock the boats, containing between six and seven hundred men, with a hundred and eighty on board the *Fox* cutter, and from seventy to eighty in a boat which had been taken the day before, proceeded in six divisions toward the town, conducted by all the captains of the squadron, except Freemantle and Bowen, who attended with Nelson to regulate and lead the way to the attack. They were to land on the mole, and thence hasten, as fast as possible, into the great square; then form and proceed as should be found expedient. They were not discovered till about half-past one o'clock, when, being within half gun-shot of the landing place, Nelson directed the boats to cast off from each other, give a huzza, and push for the shore. But the Spaniards were excellently well prepared; the alarm bells answered the huzza, and a fire of thirty or forty pieces of cannon, with musketry from one end of the town to the other, opened upon the invaders. Nothing, however, could check the intrepidity with which they advanced.

The night was exceedingly dark; most of the boats missed the mole and went on shore through a raging surf, which stove all to the left of it. The admiral, Freemantle, Thompson, Bowen, and four or five other boats found the mole; they stormed it instantly and carried it, though it was defended, as they imagined, by four or five hundred men. Its guns, which were six-and-twenty pounders, were spiked; but such a heavy fire of musketry and grape was kept up from the citadel and the houses at the head of the mole, that nearly all the assailants were killed or wounded. In the act of stepping out of the boat Nelson received a shot through the right elbow, and fell; but, as he fell, he caught the sword, which he had just drawn, in his left hand, determined never to part with it while he lived, for it had belonged to his uncle, Captain

Suckling, and he valued it like a relic. Nisbet, who was close to him, placed him at the bottom of the boat, and laid his hat over the shattered arm, lest the sight of the blood, which gushed out in great abundance, should increase his faintness. He then examined the wound; and taking some silk handkerchiefs from his neck, bound them round tight above the lacerated vessels.

Had it not been for this presence of mind in his stepson, Nelson must have perished. One of his barge-men, by name Lovel, tore his shirt into shreds, and made a sling with them for the broken limb. They then collected five other seamen, by whose assistance they succeeded, at length, in getting the boat afloat; for it had grounded with the falling tide. Nisbet took one of the oars, and ordered the steersman to go close under the guns of the battery, that they might be safe from its tremendous fire. They pushed on for the *Theseus*. When they came alongside, Nelson peremptorily refused all assistance in getting on board. A single rope was thrown over the side, which he twisted round his left hand, saying, "Let me alone: I have yet my legs left, and one arm. Tell the surgeon to make haste and get his instruments. I know I must lose my right arm; so the sooner it is off the better."

The total loss of the English, in killed, wounded, and drowned, amounted to two hundred and fifty. Nelson made no mention of his own wound in his official despatches; but in a private letter to Lord St. Vincent—the first which he wrote with his left hand—he shows himself to have been deeply affected by the failure of this enterprise. "I am become," he said, "a burthen to my friends, and useless to my country; but by my last letter you will perceive my anxiety for the promotion of my son-in-law, Josiah Nisbet. When I leave your command, I become dead to the world:—'I go hence, and am no more seen.' If from poor Bowen's loss you think it proper to oblige me, I rest confident you will do it. The boy is under obligations to me; but he repaid me, by bringing me from the mole of Santa Cruz. I hope you will be able to give me a frigate to convey the remains of my carcass to England."

"A left-handed admiral," he said subsequently, "will never again be considered as useful; therefore, the sooner I get to a very humble cottage the better, and make room for a sounder man to serve the state."

Not having been in England till now, since he lost his eye, he went to receive a year's pay, as smart money; but could not obtain payment, because he had neglected to bring a certificate from a surgeon that the sight was actually destroyed. A little irritated that this form should be insisted upon; because, though the fact was not apparent, he thought it was sufficiently notorious, he procured a certificate, at the same time, for the loss of his arm; saying, they might just as well doubt one as the other. This put him in good humour with himself, and with the clerk who had offended him. On his return to the office, the clerk, finding it was only the annual pay of a captain, observed he thought it had been more.

"Oh!" replied Nelson, "this is only for an eye. In a few days I shall come for an arm; and in a little time longer, God knows, most probably for a leg." Accordingly, he soon afterwards went; and with perfect good humour exhibited the certificate of the loss of his arm.

The Story of the Battle of the Nile
By Robert Southey

Early in the year 1798 Sir Horatio Nelson hoisted his flag on board the *Vanguard*, and was ordered to rejoin Earl St.Vincent.

Immediately on his rejoining the fleet, he was despatched to the Mediterranean, with a small squadron, in order to ascertain, if possible, the object of the great expedition which at that time was fitting out, under Bonaparte, at Toulon. The defeat of this armament, whatever might be its destination, was deemed by the British government an object paramount to every other; and Earl St.Vincent was directed, if he thought it necessary to take his whole force into the Mediterranean, to relinquish, for that purpose, the blockade of the Spanish fleet, as a thing of inferior moment; but, if he should deem a detachment sufficient, "I think it almost unnecessary," said the first lord of the Admiralty, in his secret instructions, "to suggest to you the propriety of putting it under Sir Horatio Nelson." It is to the honour of Earl St. Vincent that he had already made the same choice.

The armament at Toulon consisted of thirteen ships of the line, seven forty-gun frigates, with twenty-four smaller vessels of war, and nearly two hundred transports. Nelson sailed from Gibraltar on May 9th, with the *Vanguard, Orion,* and *Alexander,* seventy-fours; the *Caroline, Flora, Emerald,* and *Terpsichore* frigates; and the *Bonne Citoyenne* sloop of war, to watch this formidable armament. On the 19th, when they were in the Gulf of Lyons, a gale came on from the north-west. It moderated so much on the 20th, as to enable them to get their topgallant masts and yards aloft. After dark, it again began to blow strong; but the ships had been prepared for a gale, and therefore Nelson's mind was easy.

Shortly after midnight, however, his main-top mast went over the side, and the mizen-top mast soon afterward. The night was so tempestuous, that it was impossible for any signal either to be seen or heard; and Nelson determined, as soon as it should be daybreak, to wear, and scud before the gale: but, at half-past three the foremast went in three pieces, and the bowsprit was found to be sprung in three places.

When day broke, they succeeded in wearing the ship with a remnant of the spritsail: this was hardly to have been expected. The *Vanguard* was at that time twenty-five leagues south of the islands of Hieres, with her head lying to the north-east, and if she had not wore, the ship must have drifted to Corsica. Captain Ball, in the *Alexander*, took her in tow, to carry her into the Sardinian harbour of St. Pietro. Here, by the exertions of Sir James Saumarez, Captain Ball, and Captain Berry, the *Vanguard* was refitted in four days; months would have been employed in refitting her in England.

The delay which was thus occasioned was useful to him in many respects: it enabled him to complete his supply of water, and to receive a reinforcement, which Earl St. Vincent, being himself reinforced from England, was enabled to send him. It consisted of the best ships of his fleet: the *Culloden*, seventy-four, Captain T. Trowbridge; *Goliath*, seventy-four, Captain T. Foley; *Minotaur*, seventy-four, Captain T. Louis; *Defence*, seventy-four, Captain John Peyton; *Bellerophon*, seventy-four, Captain H. D. E. Darby; *Majestic*, seventy-four, Captain G. B. Westcott; *Zealous*, seventy-four, Captain S. Hood; *Swiftsure*, seventy-four, Captain B. Hallowell; *Theseus*, seventy-four, Captain R. W. Miller; *Audacious*, seventy-four, Captain Davidge Gould. The *Leander*, fifty, Captain T. B. Thompson, was afterwards added. These ships were made ready for the service as soon as Earl St. Vincent received advice from England that he was to be reinforced. As soon as the reinforcement was seen from the masthead of the admiral's ship, off Cadiz Bay, signal was immediately made to Captain Trowbridge to put to sea; and he was out of sight before the ships from home cast anchor in the British station.

Trowbridge took with him no instructions to Nelson as to the course he was to steer, nor any certain account of the enemy's destination: everything was left to his own judgment. Unfortunately, the frigates had been separated from him in the tempest, and had not been able to rejoin: they sought him unsuccessfully in the Bay of Naples, where they obtained no tidings of his course, and he sailed without them.

The first news of the enemy's armament was, that it had surprised Malta. Nelson formed a plan for attacking it while at anchor at Gozo; but on June 22nd intelligence reached him that the French had left that island on the 16th, the day after their arrival. It was clear that their destination was eastward—he thought for Egypt—and for Egypt, therefore, he made all sail. Had the frigates been with him he could scarcely have failed to gain information of the enemy: for want of them, he only spoke three vessels on the way; two came from Alexandria, one from the Archipelago; and neither of them had seen anything of the French. He arrived off Alexandria on the 28th, and the enemy were not there, neither was there any account of them; but the governor was endeavouring to put the city in a state of defence, having received advice from Leghorn that the French expedition was intended against Egypt, after it had taken Malta. Nelson then shaped his course to the northward, for Caramania, and steered from thence along the southern side of Candia, carrying a press of sail, both night and day, with a contrary wind.

Baffled in his pursuit, he returned to Sicily. The Neapolitan ministry had determined to give his squadron no assistance, being resolved to do nothing which could possibly endanger their peace with the French Directory; by means, however, of Lady Hamilton's influence at court, he procured secret orders to the Sicilian governors; and, under those orders, obtained everything which he wanted at Syracuse—a timely supply, without which, he always said, he could not have recommenced his pursuit with any hope of success. "It is an old saying," said he in his letter, "*that the devil's children have the devil's luck.* I cannot to this moment learn, beyond vague conjecture, where the French fleet are gone to; and having gone a round of six hundred leagues at this season of the year, with an expedition incredible, here I am, as ignorant of the situation of the enemy as I was twenty-seven days ago."

On July 25th he sailed from Syracuse for the Morea. Anxious beyond measure, and irritated that the enemy should so long have eluded him, the tediousness of the nights made him impatient; and the officer of the watch was repeatedly called on to let him know the hour, and convince him, who measured time by his own eagerness, that it was not yet daybreak. The squadron made the gulf of Coron on the 28th. Trowbridge entered the port, and returned with the intelligence that the French had been seen about four weeks before steering to the south-east from Candia. Nelson then determined immediately to return to Alexandria; and the British fleet accordingly, with every sail set, stood once more for the coast of Egypt

On August 1st, about ten in the morning, they came in sight of Alexandria. The port had been vacant and solitary when they saw it last; it was now crowded with ships, and they perceived with exultation that the tri-colour flag was flying upon the walls. At four in the afternoon, Captain Hood in the *Zealous* made the signal for the enemy's fleet. For many preceding days Nelson had hardly taken either sleep or food: he now ordered his dinner to be served, while preparations were making for battle, and when his officers rose from the table and went to their separate stations, he said to them: "Before this time tomorrow I shall have gained a peerage or Westminster Abbey."

The French, steering direct for Candia, had made an angular passage for Alexandria; whereas Nelson, in pursuit of them, made straight for that place, and thus materially shortened the distance. The two fleets must actually have crossed on the night of June 22nd.

The French fleet arrived at Alexandria on July 1st; and Brueys, not being able to enter the port, which time and neglect had ruined, moored his ships in Aboukir Bay, in a strong and compact line of battle; the headmost vessel, according to his own account, being as close as possible to a shoal on the north-west, and the rest of the fleet forming a kind of curve along the line of deep water, so as not to be turned by any means in the south-west.

The advantage of numbers, both in ships, guns, and men, was in favour of the French. They had thirteen ships of the line and four frigates, carrying 1196 guns, and 11,230 men. The English had the same number of ships of the line, and one fifty-gun ship, carrying 1012 guns and 8068 men. The English ships were all seventy-fours: the French had three eighty-gun ships and one three-decker of one hundred and twenty.

During the whole pursuit it had been Nelson's practice, whenever circumstances would permit, to have his captains on board the *Vanguard*, and explain to them his own ideas of the different and best modes of attack, and such plans as he proposed to execute, on falling in with the enemy, whatever their situation might be. There is no possible position, it is said, which he did not take into calculation. His officers were thus fully acquainted with his principles of tactics; and such was his confidence in their abilities, that the only thing determined upon, in case they should find the French at anchor, was for the ships to form as most convenient for their mutual support, and to anchor by the stern. "First gain the victory," he said, "and then make the best use of it you can."

The moment he perceived the position of the French, that intuitive genius with which Nelson was endowed displayed itself; and it instantly struck him that where there was room for an enemy's ship to swing there was room for one of ours to anchor. The plan which he intended to pursue, therefore, was to keep entirely on the outer side of the French line, and station his ships, as far as he was able, one on the outer bow and another on the outer quarter, of each of the enemy's. This plan of doubling on the enemy's ships was projected by Lord Hood, when he designed to attack the French fleet at their anchorage in Gourjean road. Lord Hood found it impossible to make the attempt; but the thought was not lost upon Nelson, who acknowledged himself on this occasion indebted for it to his old and excellent commander. Captain Berry, when he comprehended the scope of the design, exclaimed with transport, "If we succeed, what will the world say!"

"There is no *if* in the case," replied the admiral; "that we shall succeed is certain: who may live to tell the story is a very different question."

As the squadron advanced they were assailed by a shower of shot and shells from the batteries on the island, and the enemy opened a steady fire from the starboard side of their whole line, within half gun-shot distance, full into the bows of our van ships. It was received in silence: the men on board every ship were employed aloft in furling sails, and below in tending the braces and making ready for anchoring. A miserable sight for the French, who, with all their skill, and all their courage, and all their advantages of numbers and situation, were upon that element, on which, when the hour of trial comes, a Frenchman has no hope.

A French brig was instructed to decoy the English, by manoeuvring so as to tempt them toward a shoal lying off the island of Bekier; but Nelson either knew the danger or suspected some deceit, and the lure was unsuccessful. Captain Foley led the way in the *Goliath*, outsailing the *Zealous*, which for some minutes disputed this post of honour with him. He had long conceived that if the enemy were moored in line of battle in with the land the best plan of attack would be to lead between them and the shore, because the French guns on that side were not likely to be manned, nor even ready for action. Intending, therefore, to fix himself on the inner bow of the *Guerrier*, he kept as near the edge of the bank as the depth of water would admit; but his anchor hung, and having opened his fire, he drifted to the second ship, the *Conquerant*, before it was clear, then anchored by the stern, inside of her, and in ten minutes shot away her mast.

Hood, in the *Zealous*, perceiving this, took the station which the *Goliath* intended to have occupied, and totally disabled the *Guerrier* in twelve minutes. The third ship which doubled the enemy's van was the *Orion*, Sir J. Saumarez; she passed to windward of the *Zealous*, and opened her larboard guns as long as they bore on the *Guerrier*, then passing inside the *Goliath*, sank a frigate which annoyed her, hauled round toward the French line, and anchoring inside, between the fifth and sixth ships from the *Guerrier*, took her station on the larboard bow of the *Franklin* and the quarter of the *Peuple Souverain*, receiving and returning the fire of both. The sun was now nearly down. The *Audacious*, Captain Gould, pouring a heavy fire into the *Guerrier* and the *Conquerant*, fixed herself on the larboard bow of the latter; and when that ship struck, passed on to the *Peuple Souverain*. The *Theseus*, Captain Miller, followed, brought down the *Guerrier's* remaining main and mizen masts, then anchored inside of the *Spartiate*, the third in the French line.

While these advanced ships doubled the French line the *Vanguard* was the first that anchored on the outer side of the enemy, within half pistol-shot of their third ship, the *Spartiate*. Nelson had six colours flying in different parts of his rigging, lest they should be shot away;— that they should be struck, no British admiral considers as a possibility. He veered half a cable, and instantly opened a tremendous fire; under cover of which the other four ships of his division, the *Minotaur*, *Bellerophon*, *Defence*, and *Majestic*, sailed on ahead of the admiral. In a few minutes every man stationed at the first six guns in the fore part of the *Vanguard's* deck was killed or wounded—these guns were three times cleared. Captain Louis, in the *Minotaur*, anchored next ahead, and took off the fire of the *Aquilon*, the fourth in the enemy's line. The *Bellerophon*, Captain Darby, passed ahead, and dropped her stern anchor on the starboard bow of the *Orient*, seventh in the line, Brueys' own ship, of one hundred and twenty guns, whose difference of force was in proportion of more than seven to three, and whose weight of ball, from the lower deck alone, exceeded that from the whole broadside of the *Bellerophon*.

Captain Peyton, in the *Defence*, took his station ahead of the *Minotaur*, and engaged the *Franklin*, the sixth in the line; by which judicious movement the British line remained unbroken. The *Majestic*, Captain Westcott, got entangled with the main rigging of one of the French ships astern of the *Orient*, and suffered dreadfully from that three-decker's fire; but she swung clear, and closely engaging the *Heureux*, the ninth ship on the starboard bow, received also the fire of the *Tonnant*, which was the eighth in the line. The other four ships of the British squadron, having been detached previous to the discovery of the French, were at a considerable distance when the action began. It commenced at half-past six; about seven, night closed, and there was no other light than that from the fire of the contending fleets.

Trowbridge, in the *Culloden*, then foremost of the remaining ships, was two leagues astern. He came on sounding, as the others had done: as he advanced, the increasing darkness increased the difficulty of the navigation, and suddenly, after having found eleven fathoms water, before the lead could be hove again, he was fast aground; nor could all his own exertions, joined to those of the *Leander* and the *Mutine* brig, which came to his assistance, get him off in time to bear a part in the action. His ship, however, served as a beacon to the *Alexander* and *Swiftsure*, which would else, from the course which they were holding, have gone considerably farther on the reef, and must inevitably have been lost.

These ships entered the bay, and took their stations, in the darkness, in a manner long spoken of with admiration by all who remembered it. Captain Hallowell, in the *Swiftsure*, as he was bearing down, fell in with what seemed to be a strange sail; Nelson had directed his ships to hoist four lights horizontally at the mizen peak, as soon as it became dark, and this vessel had no such distinction. Hallowell, however, with great judgment, ordered his men not to fire: if she was an enemy, he said, she was in too disabled a state to escape; but, from her sails being loose, and the way in which her head was, it was probable she might be an English ship. It was the *Bellerophon*, overpowered by the huge *Orient*: her lights had gone overboard, nearly two hundred of her crew were killed or wounded; all her masts and cables had been shot away; and she was drifting out of the line, towards the lee side of the bay. Her station, at this important time, was occupied by the *Swiftsure*, which opened a steady fire on the quarter of the *Franklin* and the bows of the French admiral.

At the same instant, Captain Ball, with the *Alexander*, passed under his stern, and anchored within side on his larboard quarter, raking him, and keeping up a severe fire of musketry upon his decks. The last ship which arrived to complete the destruction of the enemy was the *Leander*. Captain Thompson, finding that nothing could be done that night to get off the *Culloden*, advanced with the intention of anchoring athwart-hawse of the *Orient*. The *Franklin* was so near her ahead that there was not room for him to pass clear of the two; he, therefore, took his station athwart-hawse of the latter, in such a position as to rake both.

The two first ships of the French line had been dismasted within a quarter of an hour after the commencement of the action; and the others had in that time suffered so severely, that victory was already certain. The third, fourth, and fifth were taken possession of at half-past eight.

Meantime, Nelson received a severe wound on the head from a piece of langrage shot. Captain Berry caught him in his arms as he was falling. The great effusion of blood occasioned an apprehension that the wound was mortal. Nelson himself thought so: a large flap of the skin of the forehead, cut from the bone, had fallen over one eye, and the other being blind, he was in total darkness. When he was carried down, the surgeon—in the midst of a scene scarcely to be conceived by those who have never seen a cock-pit in time of action, and the heroism which is displayed amid its horrors,—with a natural and pardonable eagerness quitted the poor fellow then under his hands, that he might instantly attend the admiral. "No!" said Nelson, "I will take my turn with my brave fellows."

Nor would he suffer his own wound to be examined till every man who had been previously wounded was properly attended to. Fully believing that the wound was mortal, and that he was about to die, as he had ever desired, in battle and in victory, he called the chaplain, and desired him to deliver what he supposed to be his dying remembrance to Lady Nelson: he then sent for Captain Louis on board from the *Minotaur*, that he might thank him personally for the great assistance which he had rendered to the *Vanguard*; and, ever mindful of those who deserved to be his friends, appointed Captain Hardy from the brig to the command of his own ship, Captain Berry having to go home with the news of the victory.

When the surgeon came in due time to examine his wound (for it was in vain to entreat him to let it be examined sooner) the most anxious silence prevailed; and the joy of the wounded men, and of the whole crew, when they heard that the hurt was merely superficial, gave Nelson deeper pleasure than the unexpected assurance that his life was in no danger. The surgeon requested, and as far as he could, ordered him to remain quiet; but Nelson could not rest. He called for his secretary, Mr. Campbell, to write the despatches. Campbell had himself been wounded, and was so affected at the blind and suffering state of the admiral, that he was unable to write.

The chaplain was then sent for; but, before he came, Nelson, with his characteristic eagerness, took the pen, and contrived to trace a few words, marking his devout sense of the success which had already been obtained. He was now left alone; when suddenly a cry was heard on the deck that the *Orient* was on fire. In the confusion, he found his way up, unassisted and unnoticed; and, to the astonishment of every one, appeared on the quarter-deck, where he immediately gave orders that boats should be sent to the relief of the enemy.

It was soon after nine that the fire on board the *Orient* broke out. Brueys was dead: he had received three wounds, yet he would not leave his post; a fourth cut him almost in two. He desired not to be carried below, but to be left to die upon deck. The flames soon mastered his ship. Her sides had just been painted, and the oil-jars and paint-buckets were lying on the poop. By the prodigious light of this conflagration the situation of the two fleets could now be perceived, the colours of both being clearly distinguishable. About ten o'clock the ship blew up, with a shock which was felt to the very bottom of every vessel. Many of her officers and men jumped overboard, some clinging to the spars and pieces of wreck, with which the sea was strewn, others swimming to escape from the destruction which they momentarily dreaded. Some were picked up by our boats; and some even in the heat and fury of the action were dragged into the lower ports of the nearest British vessel by the British sailors.

The greater part of her crew, however, stood the danger till the last, and continued to fire from the lower deck. This tremendous explosion was followed by a silence not less awful: the firing immediately ceased on both sides, and the first sound which broke the silence was the dash of her shattered masts and yards falling into the water from the vast height to which they had been exploded. It is upon record that a battle between two armies was once broken off by an earthquake:—such an event would be felt like a miracle; but no incident in war, produced by human means, has ever equalled the sublimity of this co-instantaneous pause, and all its circumstances.

About seventy of the *Orient's* crew were saved by the English boats. Among the many hundreds who perished, were the commodore, Casa-Bianca, and his son, a brave boy, only ten years old. They were seen floating on a shattered mast when the ship blew up. She had money on board (the plunder of Malta) to the amount of £600,000 sterling.

The masses of burning wreck, which were scattered by the explosion, excited for some moments apprehensions in the English which they had never felt from any other danger. Two large pieces fell into the main and fore tops of the *Swiftsure*, without injuring any person. A port fire also fell into the main-royal of the *Alexander*: the fire which it occasioned was speedily extinguished. Captain Ball had provided, as far as human foresight could provide, against any such danger. All the shrouds and sails of his ship, not absolutely necessary for its immediate management, were thoroughly wetted, and so rolled up that they were as hard and as little inflammable as so many solid cylinders.

The firing recommenced with the ships to leeward of the centre, and continued till about three. At daybreak, the *Guillaume Tell* and the *Genereux*, the two rear ships of the enemy, were the only French ships of the line which had their colours flying; they cut their cables in the forenoon, not having been engaged, and stood out to sea, and two frigates with them. The *Zealous* pursued; but as there was no other ship in a condition to support Captain Hood, he was recalled. It was generally believed by the officers that if Nelson had not been wounded, not one of these ships could have escaped: the four certainly could not, if the *Culloden* had got into action, and if the frigates belonging to the squadron had been present, not one of the enemy's fleet would have left Aboukir Bay. These four vessels, however, were all that escaped; and the victory was the most complete and glorious in the annals of naval history.

"Victory," said Nelson, "is not a name strong enough for such a scene;" he called it a conquest. Of thirteen sail of the line, nine were taken and two burnt; of the four frigates, one was sunk, another, the *Artimese*, was burnt by her captain, who, having fired a broadside at the *Theseus*, struck his colours, then set fire to his ship and escaped with most of his crew to shore. The British loss in killed and wounded amounted to 895. Westcott was the only captain who fell; 3105 of the French, including the wounded, were sent on shore, and 5225 perished.

The shore, for an extent of four leagues, was covered with wreck; and the Arabs found employment for many days in burning on the beach the fragments which were cast up, for the sake of the iron. Part of the *Orient's* main mast was picked up by the *Swiftsure*. Captain Hallowell ordered his carpenter to make a coffin of it; the iron as well as wood was taken from the wreck of the same ship. It was finished as well and handsomely as the workman's skill and materials would permit, and Hallowell then sent it to the admiral with the following letter,—

> Sir, I have taken the liberty of presenting you a coffin made from the main mast of *L'Orient*, that when you have finished your military career in this world you may be buried in one of your trophies. But that that period may be far distant, is the earnest wish of your sincere friend, Benjamin Hallowell.

An offering so strange, and yet so suited to the occasion, was received by Nelson in the spirit with which it was sent. As if he felt it good for him, now that he was at the summit of his wishes, to have death before his eyes, he ordered the coffin to be placed upright in his cabin.

Nelson was now at the summit of glory: congratulations, rewards, and honours were showered upon him by all the states, and princes, and powers to whom his victory gave a respite. At home he was created Baron Nelson of the Nile and of Burnham Thorpe, with a pension of £2000 for his own life, and those of his two immediate successors. A grant of £10,000 was voted to Nelson by the East India Company; the Turkish Company presented him with a piece of plate; the city of London presented a sword to him and to each of his captains; gold medals were distributed to the captains; and the first lieutenants of all the ships were promoted, as had been done after Lord Howe's victory.

After the battle of the Nile, Nelson returned to Naples, where he renewed his friendship with Sir William and Lady Hamilton. Italy received him everywhere with open arms, and the most flattering welcome was given him by both court and people. The story of his stay in Italy, however, is the saddest chapter in his life, for it was here that his domestic happiness was destroyed, and his fine chivalrous nature received its only stain.

His birthday, which occurred a week after his arrival, was celebrated with one of the most splendid *fêtes* ever beheld at Naples. But, notwithstanding the splendour with which he was encircled, and the flattering honours with which all ranks welcomed him, Nelson was fully sensible of the depravity, as well as weakness, of those by whom he was surrounded. He said:

> What precious moments the courts of Naples and Vienna are losing! Three months would liberate Italy! but this court is so enervated, that the happy moment will be lost. I am very un-

well; and their miserable conduct is not likely to cool my irritable temper. It is a country of fiddlers and poets, libertines and scoundrels.

He saved the court from the inevitable consequences of misrule for a time, drove the French out of Rome, laid siege to Malta, and worked miracles of energy and skill in many ways, but he left Italy with the feeling that there was no pleasure in life.

Nelson was welcomed in England with every mark of popular honour. At Yarmouth, where he landed, every ship in the harbour hoisted her colours. The mayor and corporation waited upon him with the freedom of the town, and accompanied him in procession to church, with all the naval officers on shore and the principal inhabitants. Bonfires and illuminations concluded the day; and, on the morrow, the volunteer cavalry drew up and saluted him as he departed, and followed the carriage to the borders of the county. At Ipswich the people came out to meet him, drew him a mile into the town and three miles out. In London, he was feasted by the city, drawn by the populace from Ludgate Hill to Guildhall, and received the thanks of the common council for his great victory and a golden hilted sword studded with diamonds. Nelson had every earthly blessing except domestic happiness; he had forfeited that forever.

The Bombardment of Copenhagen
By Robert Southey

In the year 1801, Nelson, who had been made vice-Admiral of the blue, was sent to the Baltic, as second in command under Sir Hyde Parker, by Earl St. Vincent, now first lord of the Admiralty. The three northern courts had formed a confederacy for making England resign her naval rights. Of these courts Russia was guided by the passions of its emperor, Paul, a man not without fits of generosity and some natural goodness, but subject to the wildest humours of caprice and crazed by the possession of greater power than can ever be safely, or perhaps innocently, possessed by weak humanity. Denmark was French at heart; ready to co-operate in all the views of France, to recognise all her usurpations, and obey all her injunctions. Sweden, under a king whose principles were right and whose feelings were generous, but who had a taint of hereditary insanity, acted in acquiescence with the dictates of two powers whom it feared to offend.

The Danish Navy, at this time, consisted of twenty-three ships of the line with about thirty-one frigates and smaller vessels, exclusive of guardships. The Swedes had eighteen ships of the line, fourteen frigates and sloops, seventy-four galleys and smaller vessels, besides gunboats, and this force was in a far better state of equipment than the Danish. The Russians had eighty-two sail of the line and forty frigates. Of these there were forty-seven sail of the line at Cronstadt, Revel, Petersburg, and Archangel; but the Russian fleet was ill-manned, ill-officered, and ill-equipped. Such a combination under the influence of France would soon have become formidable; and never did the British cabinet display more decision than in instantly preparing to crush it.

The British fleet sailed on March 12th and Mr. Vansittart sailed in it; the government still hoping to obtain its ends by negotiation. Mr.

Vansittart left the fleet at the Scaw and preceded it in a frigate with a flag of truce. Precious time was lost by this delay which was to be purchased by the dearest blood of Britain and Denmark; according to the Danes themselves, the intelligence that a British fleet was seen off the Sound produced a much more general alarm in Copenhagen than its actual arrival in the roads; for their means of defence were, at that time, in such a state that they could hardly hope to resist, still less to repel, an enemy.

On the 21st, Nelson had a long conference with Sir Hyde; and the next day addressed a letter to him worthy of himself and of the occasion. Mr. Vansittart's report had then been received. It represented the Danish government as in the highest degree hostile, and their state of preparation as exceeding what our cabinet had supposed possible; for Denmark had profited with all activity, by the leisure which had so impoliticly been given her. "The more I have reflected," said Nelson to his commander, "the more I am confirmed in opinion that not a moment should be lost in attacking the enemy. They will every day and every hour be stronger; we shall never be so good a match for them as we are at this moment. The only consideration is how to get at them with the least risk to our ships."

Of the two courses open to them, that of proceeding past Cronenburg, and taking the deepest and straightest channel along the middle grounds and attacking the Danish line of floating batteries, or that of attempting the passage of the Belt, Sir Hyde Parker preferred the latter, Nelson and Captain Domett the former, though as Nelson put it, "Let it be by the Sound, by the Belt, or anyhow, only lose not an hour!" when it was finally decided to take the passage of the Sound.

The next day was wasted in despatching a flag of truce to the Governor of Cronenburg Castle, to ask whether he had received orders to fire at the British fleet, as the admiral must consider the first gun to be a declaration of war on the part of Denmark. A soldier-like and becoming answer was returned to this formality. The governor said that the British minister had not been sent away from Copenhagen but had obtained a passport at his own demand. He himself, as a soldier, could not meddle with politics: but he was not at liberty to suffer a fleet—of which the intention was not yet known—to approach the guns of the castle which he had the honour to command, and he requested, if the British admiral should think proper to make any proposals to the King of Denmark, that he might be apprised of it before the fleet approached nearer.

During this intercourse a Dane, who came on board the commander's ship, having occasion to express his business in writing found the pen blunt, and, holding it up, sarcastically said, "If your guns are not better pointed than your pens you will make little impression on Copenhagen!"

Nelson, who was now appointed to lead the van, shifted his flag to the *Elephant,* Captain Foley—a lighter ship than the *St. George,* and, therefore, fitter for the expected operations. The two following days were calm. Orders had been given to pass the Sound as soon as the wind would permit; and on the afternoon of the 29th the ships were cleared for action with an alacrity characteristic of British seamen. At daybreak on the 30th it blew a top-sail breeze from north-west. The signal was made and the fleet moved on in order of battle; Nelson's division in the van, Sir Hyde's in the centre, and Admiral Graves' in the rear.

The whole force consisted of fifty-one sail of various descriptions, of which sixteen were of the line. The greater part of the bomb and gun vessels took their stations off Cronenburg Castle, to cover the fleet; while others on the larboard were ready to engage the Swedish shore. The Danes, having improved every moment which ill-timed negotiation and baffling weather gave them, had lined their shore with batteries; and as soon as the *Monarch,* which was the leading ship, came abreast of them a fire was opened from about a hundred pieces of cannon and mortars. Our light vessels immediately in return opened their fire upon the castle.

The enemy's shot fell near enough to splash the water on board our ships; not relying upon any forbearance of the Swedes they meant to have kept the mid channel, but when they perceived that not a shot was fired from Helsinburg and that no batteries were to be seen on the Swedish shore, they inclined to that side, so as completely to get out of reach of the Danish guns. The uninterrupted blaze which was kept up from them till the fleet had passed served only to exhilarate our sailors and afford them matter for jest, as the shot fell in showers a full cable's length short of its destined aim.

About mid-day the whole fleet anchored between the island of Huen and Copenhagen. Sir Hyde, with Nelson, Admiral Graves, some of the senior captains, and the commanding officers of the artillery and the troops, then proceeded in a lugger to reconnoitre the enemy's means of defence; a formidable line of ships, *radeaux,* pontoons, galleys, fire-ships, and gun-boats, flanked and supported by extensive batteries, and occupying, from one extreme point to the other, an extent of nearly four miles.

A council of war was held in the afternoon. Nelson offered his services for the attack, requiring ten sail of the line and the whole of the smaller craft. Sir Hyde gave him two more line-of-battle ships than he asked for and left everything to his judgment.

The enemy's force was not the only, nor the greatest, obstacle with which the British fleet had to contend: there was another to be overcome before they could come in contact with it. The channel was little known and extremely intricate; all the buoys had been removed; and the Danes considered this difficulty as almost insuperable, thinking the channel impracticable for so large a fleet. Nelson himself saw the soundings made and the buoys laid down, boating it upon this exhausting service, day and night, till it was effected. When this was done, he thanked God for having enabled him to get through this difficult part of his duty. "It had worn him down," he said, "and was infinitely more grievous to him than any resistance which he could experience from the enemy."

On the morning of April 1st the whole fleet removed to an anchorage within two leagues of the town and off the north-west end of the Middle Ground: a shoal lying exactly before the town, at about three-quarters of a mile distance, and extending along its whole sea front. The King's Channel, where there is deep water, is between this shoal and the town; and here the Danes had arranged their line of defence, as near the shore as possible: nineteen ships and floating batteries, flanked, at the end nearest the town, by the Crown Batteries, which were two artificial islands at the mouth of the harbour—most formidable works; the larger one having, by the Danish account, sixty-six guns; but, as Nelson believed, eighty-eight.

The fleet having anchored, Nelson, with Riou in the *Amazon*, made his last examination of the ground; and about one o'clock, returning to his own ship, threw out the signal to weigh. It was received with a shout throughout the whole division; they weighed with a light and favourable wind. The narrow channel between the island of Saltholm and the Middle Ground had been accurately buoyed; the small craft pointed out the course distinctly; Riou led the way: the whole division coasted along the outer edge of the shoal, doubled its further extremity, and anchored there off Draco Point, just as the darkness closed—the headmost of the enemy's line not being more than two miles distant. The signal to prepare for action had been made early in the evening; and, as his own anchor dropped, Nelson called out, "I will fight them the moment I have a fair wind."

It had been agreed that Sir Hyde, with the remaining ships, should weigh on the following morning, at the same time as Nelson, to menace the Crown Batteries on his side and the four ships of the line which lay at the entrance of the arsenal, and to cover our own disabled ships as they came out of action.

The Danes, meantime, had not been idle: no sooner did the guns of Cronenburg make it known to the whole city that all negotiation was at an end, that the British fleet was passing the Sound, and that the dispute between the two crowns must now be decided by arms, than a spirit displayed itself most honourable to the Danish character. All ranks offered themselves to the service of their country; the university furnished a corps of twelve hundred youths, the flower of Denmark. It was one of those emergencies in which little drilling or discipline is necessary to render courage available: they had nothing to learn but how to manage the guns, and were employed day and night in practising them. When the movements of Nelson's squadron were perceived, it was known when and where the attack was to be expected, and the line of defence was manned indiscriminately by soldiers, sailors, and citizens.

This was an awful night for Copenhagen—far more so than for the British fleet, where the men were accustomed to battle and victory, and had none of those objects before their eyes which render death terrible. Nelson sat down to table with a large party of his officers; he was, as he was ever wont to be when on the eve of action, in high spirits, and drank to a leading wind and to the success of the morrow. After supper they returned to their respective ships, except Riou, who remained to arrange the order of battle with Nelson and Foley, and to draw up instructions: Hardy, meantime, went in a small boat to examine the channel between them and the enemy, approaching so near, that he sounded round their leading ship with a pole, lest the noise of throwing the lead should discover him.

The incessant fatigue of body as well as mind which Nelson had undergone during the last three days had so exhausted him that he was earnestly urged to go to his cot; and his old servant, Allen, using that kind of authority which long and affectionate services entitled and enabled him to assume on such occasions, insisted upon his complying. The cot was placed on the floor and he continued to dictate from it. About eleven Hardy returned and reported the practicability of the channel and the depth of water up to the enemy's line. About one the orders were completed; and half a dozen clerks in the foremost cabin proceeded to transcribe them, Nelson frequently calling out to them from his cot to hasten their work, for the wind was becoming fair. Instead of attempting to get a few hours of sleep he was constantly receiving reports on this important point. At daybreak it was announced as becoming perfectly fair. The clerks finished their work about six. Nelson, who was already up, breakfasted, and made signal for all captains.

Between eight and nine the pilots and masters were ordered on board the admiral's ship. The pilots were mostly men who had been mates in Baltic traders, and their hesitation about the bearing of the east end of the shoal and the exact line of deep water gave ominous warning of how little their knowledge was to be trusted. The signal for action had been made, the wind was fair—not a moment to be lost. Nelson urged them to be steady, to be resolute, and to decide; but they wanted the only ground for steadiness and decision in such cases, and Nelson had reason for regret that he had not trusted to Hardy's single report.

Captain Murray, in the *Edgar*, led the way; the *Agamemnon* was next in order; but, on the first attempt to leave her anchorage she could not weather the edge of the shoal, and Nelson had the grief to see his old ship, in which he had performed so many years' gallant services, immovably aground at a moment when her help was so greatly required. Signal was then made for the *Polyphemus*; and this change in the order of sailing was executed with the utmost promptitude; yet so much delay had thus been unavoidably occasioned, that the *Edgar* was for some time unsupported, and the *Polyphemus*, whose place should have been at the end of the enemy's line where their strength was the greatest, could get no further than the beginning, owing to the difficulty of the channel; there she occupied indeed an efficient station, but one where her presence was less required. The *Isis* followed, with better fortune, and took her own berth. The *Bellona*, Sir T. Thompson, kept too close on the starboard shoal, and grounded abreast of the outer ship of the enemy; this was the more vexatious, inasmuch as the wind was fair, the room ample, and three ships had led the way.

The *Russell*, following the *Bellona*, grounded in like manner; both were within reach of shot, but their absence from their intended stations was severely felt. Each ship had been ordered to pass her leader on the starboard side, because the water was supposed to shoal on the larboard shore. Nelson, who came next after these two ships, thought they had kept too far on the starboard direction, and made signal for them to close with the enemy, not knowing that they were aground; but when he perceived that they did not obey the signal, he ordered the *Elephant's* helm to starboard, and went within these ships, thus quitting the appointed order of sailing and guiding those which were to follow. The greater part of the fleet were probably, by this act of promptitude on his part, saved from going on shore. Each ship, as she arrived nearly opposite to her appointed station, let her anchor go by the stern and presented her broadside to the Danes. The distance between each was about half a cable. The action was fought at the distance of nearly a cable's length from the enemy.

At five minutes after ten the action began. The first half of our fleet was engaged in about half an hour; and by half-past eleven the battle became general. The plan of the attack had been complete, but seldom has any plan been more disconcerted by untoward accidents. Of twelve ships of the line, one was entirely useless, and two others in a situation where they could not render half the service which was required of them. Of the squadron of gun-brigs only one could get into action: the rest were prevented, by baffling currents, from weathering the eastern end of the shoal, and only two of the bomb-vessels could reach their station on the Middle Ground, and open their mortars on the arsenal, firing over both fleets.

Nelson's agitation had been extreme when he saw himself, before the action began, deprived of a fourth part of his ships of the line; but no sooner was he in battle, where his squadron was received with the fire of more than a thousand guns, than, as if that artillery, like music, had driven away all care and painful thoughts, his countenance brightened; and, as a bystander describes him, his conversation became joyous, animated, elevated, and delightful. The commander-in-chief, meantime, near enough to the scene of action to know the unfavourable accidents which had so materially weakened Nelson, and yet too distant to know the real state of the contending parties, suffered the most dreadful anxiety. To get to his assistance was impossible; both wind and current were against him.

Fear for the event, in such circumstances, would naturally preponderate in the bravest mind; and at one o'clock, perceiving that after three hours' endurance the enemy's fire was unslackened, he began to despair of success. "I will make the signal of recall," said he to his captain, "for Nelson's sake. If he is in a condition to continue the action successfully he will disregard it; if he is not, it will be an excuse for his retreat, and no blame can be imputed to him." Under a mistaken judgment, therefore, but with this disinterested and generous feeling he made the signal for retreat.

Nelson was at this time, in all the excitement of action, pacing the quarter-deck. A shot through the main mast knocked the splinters about; and he observed to one of his officers with a smile, "It is warm work, and this day may be the last to any of us at a moment;" and then stopping short at the gangway, added with emotion—"But mark you! I would not be elsewhere for thousands." About this time the signal lieutenant called out, that No. 39 (the signal for discontinuing the action) was thrown out by the commander-in-chief. He continued to walk the deck and appeared to take no notice of it. The signal officer met him at the next turn, and asked him if he should repeat it, "No," he replied, "acknowledge it."

Presently he called after him to know if the signal for close action was still hoisted; and being answered in the affirmative, said, "Mind you keep it so." He now paced the deck, moving the stump of his lost arm in a manner which always indicated great emotion. "Do you know," said he to Mr. Ferguson, "what is shown on board the commander-in-chief? No. 39!" Mr. Ferguson asked what that meant,—"Why, to leave off action!" Then, shrugging up his shoulders, he repeated the words—"Leave off action? Now, hang me if I do! You know, Foley," turning to the captain, "I have only one eye—I have a right to be blind sometimes;" and then, putting the glass to his blind eye, in that mood of mind which sports with bitterness, he exclaimed, "I really do not see the signal! Keep mine for closer battle flying! That's the way I answer such signals! Nail mine to the mast!"

Admiral Graves, who was so situated that he could not discern what was done on board the *Elephant*, disobeyed Sir Hyde's signal in like manner: whether by fortunate mistake, or by a like brave intention, has not been made known. The other ships of the line, looking only to Nelson, continued the action. The signal, however, saved Riou's little squadron but did not save its heroic leader. This squadron, which was nearest the commander-in-chief, obeyed, and hauled off. "What will Nelson think of us!" was Riou's mournful exclamation when he unwillingly drew off. He had been wounded in the head by a splinter, and was sitting on a gun encouraging his men, when, just as the *Amazon* showed her stern to the *Trekroner* battery, his clerk was killed by his side, and another shot swept away several marines who were hauling in the main-brace. "Come, then, my boys!" cried Riou, "let us die all together!" The words had scarcely been uttered before a raking shot cut him in two. Except it had been Nelson himself, the British navy could not have suffered a severer loss.

The action continued along the line with unabated vigour on our side and with the most determined resolution on the part of the Danes. They fought to great advantage because most of the vessels in their line of defence were without masts: the few which had any standing had their top-masts struck, and the hulls could only be seen at intervals.

The *Bellona* lost seventy-five men; the *Iris*, one hundred and ten; the *Monarch*, two hundred and ten. She was, more than any other line-of-battle ship, exposed to the great battery, and supporting, at the same time, the united fire of the *Holstein* and the *Zealand*, her loss this day exceeded that of any single ship during the whole war. Amid the tremendous carnage in this vessel some of the men displayed a singular instance of coolness: the pork and peas happened to be in the kettle; a shot knocked its contents about; they picked up the pieces, and ate and fought at the same time.

The prince-royal had taken his station upon one of the batteries, from whence he beheld the action and issued his orders. Denmark had never been engaged in so arduous a contest, and never did the Danes more nobly display their national courage. A youth of seventeen, by name Villemoes, particularly distinguished himself on this memorable day. He had volunteered to take the command of a floating battery, which was a raft consisting merely of a number of beams nailed together, with a flooring to support the guns: it was square, with a breastwork full of port-holes, and without masts—carrying twenty-four guns and one hundred and twenty men. With this he got under the stern of the *Elephant*, below the reach of the stern-chasers; and, under a heavy fire of small arms from the marines, fought his raft till the truce was announced, with such skill, as well as courage, as to excite Nelson's warmest admiration.

Between one and two the fire of the Danes slackened; about two it ceased from the greater part of their line, and some of their lighter ships were adrift. It was, however, difficult to take possession of those which struck, because the batteries on Amak Island protected them, and because an irregular fire was kept up from the ships themselves as the boats approached. This arose from the nature of the action; the crew were continually reinforced from the shore, and fresh men coming on board, did not inquire whether the flag had been struck, or, perhaps, did not heed it; many, or most of them, never having been engaged in war before.

By half-past two the action had ceased along that part of the line which was astern of the *Elephant*, but not with the ships ahead and the Crown Batteries. Nelson, seeing the manner in which his boats were fired upon when they went to take possession of the prizes, became angry, and said he must either send on shore to have this irregular proceeding stopped, or send a fire-ship and burn them. Half the shot from the *Trekroner* and from the batteries at Amak at this time struck the surrendered ships, four of which had got close together; and the fire of the English in return was equally, or even more, destructive to these poor devoted Danes. Nelson, who was as humane as he was brave, was shocked at this massacre—for such he called it—and, with a presence of mind peculiar to himself, and never more signally displayed than now, he retired into the stern galley, and wrote thus to the crown-prince:

> Vice-Admiral Lord Nelson has been commanded to spare Denmark when she no longer resists. The line of defence which covered her shores has struck to the British flag; but if the firing is continued on the part of Denmark he must set on fire all the prizes that he has taken, without having the power of saving the men who have so nobly defended them. The brave Danes are the brothers, and should never be the enemies, of the English.

A wafer was given him, but he ordered a candle to be brought from the cockpit and sealed the letter with wax, affixing a larger seal than he ordinarily used. "This," said he, "is no time to appear hurried and informal." Captain Sir Frederick Thesiger, who acted as his *aide-de-camp*, carried this letter with a flag of truce. Meantime the fire of the ships ahead and the approach of the *Ramilies* and *Defence* from Sir Hyde's division, which had now worked near enough to alarm the enemy, though not to injure them, silenced the remainder of the Danish line to the eastward of the *Trekroner*. That battery, however, continued its fire.

During Thesiger's absence, Nelson sent for Freemantle, from the *Ganges*, and consulted with him and Foley whether it was advisable to advance with those ships which had sustained least damage, against the yet uninjured part of the Danish line. They were decidedly of opinion that the best thing which could be done was, while the wind continued fair to remove the fleet out of the intricate channel, from which it had to retreat. In somewhat more than half an hour after Thesiger had been despatched, the Danish adjutant-general, Lindholm, came bearing a flag of truce; upon which the *Trekroner* ceased to fire and the action closed after four hours' continuance. He brought an inquiry from the prince, What was the object of Nelson's note? The British admiral wrote in reply:

> Lord Nelson's object in sending the flag of truce was humanity; he therefore consents that hostilities shall cease and that the wounded Danes may be taken on shore. And Lord Nelson will take his prisoners out of the vessels, and burn or carry off his prizes as he shall think fit. Lord Nelson, with humble duty to his royal highness the prince, will consider this the greatest victory he has ever gained if it may be the cause of a happy reconciliation and union between his own most gracious sovereign and His Majesty the King of Denmark.

Sir Frederick Thesiger was despatched a second time with the reply; and the Danish adjutant-general was referred to the commander-in-chief for a conference upon this overture. Lindholm, assenting to this, proceeded to the *London*, which was riding at anchor full four miles off; and Nelson, losing not one of the critical moments which he had thus gained, made signal for his leading ships to weigh in succession; they had the shoal to clear, they were much crippled, and their course was immediately under the guns of the *Trekroner*.

The *Monarch* led the way. This ship had received six-and-twenty shot between wind and water. She had not a shroud standing; there was a double-headed shot in the heart of her fore mast and the slightest wind would have sent every mast over her side. The imminent danger from which Nelson had extricated himself soon became apparent; the *Monarch* touched immediately upon a shoal, over which she was pushed by the *Ganges* taking her amid-ships; the *Glatton* went clear; but the other two, the *Defiance* and the *Elephant*, grounded about a mile from the *Trekroner*, and there remained fixed for many hours in spite of all the exertions of their wearied crews. The *Désirée* frigate also, at the other end of the line, having gone toward the close of the action to assist the *Bellona*, became fast on the same shoal.

Nelson left the *Elephant* soon after she took the ground to follow Lindholm. The heat of action was over; and that kind of feeling, which the surrounding scene of havoc was so well fitted to produce, pressed heavily upon his exhausted spirits. The sky had suddenly become overcast; white flags were waving from the mast-heads of so many shattered ships; the slaughter had ceased, but the grief was to come; for the account of the dead was not yet made up, and no man could tell for what friends he would have to mourn. There was another reflection also, which mingled with these melancholy thoughts and predisposed him to receive them. He was not here master of his own movements as at Egypt; he had won the day by disobeying his orders; and in so far as he had been successful, had convicted the commander-in-chief of an error in judgment. "Well," said he, as he left the *Elephant*, "I have fought contrary to orders and I shall perhaps be hanged! Never mind, let them!"

This was the language of a man, who, while he is giving utterance to an uneasy thought, clothes it half in jest because he half repents that it has been disclosed. His services had been too eminent on that day, his judgment too conspicuous, his success too signal, for any commander, however jealous of his own authority or envious of another's merits, to express anything but satisfaction and gratitude, which Sir Hyde heartily felt and sincerely expressed. It was speedily agreed that there should be a suspension of hostilities for four-and-twenty hours; that all the prizes should be surrendered and the wounded Danes carried on shore. Seventeen sail of the Danes were taken, burnt, or sunk in this battle.

The boats of Sir Hyde's division were actively employed all night in bringing out the prizes and in getting afloat the ships which were on shore. At daybreak, Nelson, who had slept in his own ship, the *St. George*, rowed to the *Elephant*, and his delight at finding her afloat seemed to give him new life. There he took a hasty breakfast, praising the men for their exertions, and then pushed off to the prizes which had not yet been removed. The English spent the day in refitting their own ships, securing the prizes, and distributing the prisoners; the Danes, in carrying on shore and disposing of the wounded and the dead. It had been a murderous action. Our loss, in killed and wounded, was nine hundred and fifty-three.

The loss of the Danes, including prisoners, amounted to about six thousand. The negotiations, meantime, went on; and it was agreed that Nelson should have an interview with the prince the following day. The preliminaries of the negotiation were adjusted at this interview. During the repast which followed, Nelson, with all the sincerity of his character, bore willing testimony to the valour of his foes. He told the prince that he had been in a hundred and five engagements but that this was the most tremendous of all.

"The French," he said, "fought bravely, but they could not have stood for one hour the fight which the Danes had supported for four." He requested that Villemoes might be introduced to him; and, shaking hands with the youth, told the prince that he ought to be made an admiral.

The prince replied: "If, my lord, I am to make all my brave officers admirals, I should have no captains or lieutenants in my service."

For the battle of Copenhagen, fought on April 2nd, 1801, Nelson was raised to the rank of viscount; an inadequate mark of reward for services so splendid and of such paramount importance to the dearest interests of England. There was, however, some prudence in dealing out honours to him step by step; had he lived long enough he would have fought his way up to a dukedom.

He had not been many weeks on shore before he was called upon to undertake a service for which no Nelson was required. Bonaparte, who was now first consul and in reality sole ruler of France, was making preparations upon a great scale for invading England; but his schemes in the Baltic had been baffled; fleets could not be created as they were wanted; and his armies, therefore, were to come over in gun-boats and such small craft as could be rapidly built or collected for the occasion. From the former governments of France such threats have only been matter of insult or policy: in Bonaparte they were sincere; for this adventurer, intoxicated with success, already began to imagine that all things were to be submitted to his fortune.

We had not at that time proved the superiority of our soldiers over the French, and the unreflecting multitude were not to be persuaded that an invasion could only be effected by numerous and powerful fleets. A general alarm was excited, and, in condescension to this unworthy feeling, Nelson was appointed to a command extending from Orfordness to Beachy Head, on both shores—a sort of service, he said, for which he felt no other ability than what might be found in his zeal. This zeal he continued to display without abatement until the Peace of Amiens gave him leisure to return home again.

The Story of the Battle of Trafalgar
By Robert Southey

In 1803 the short-lived Peace of Amiens came to an end, and Nelson was re-appointed to the command of the Mediterranean fleet. Hoisting his flag upon the *Victory* he busied himself for some time in preventing a combination of the French fleets. Notwithstanding his vigilance, the French ships escaped from Toulon and joined with those of Cadiz. Nelson followed them to the West Indies, but they were evidently more inclined to fence than to fight, and so contrived to elude him. Nelson, weary of cruising in search of the enemy, gave up the chase, and returned to England determined to rest awhile and recoup. All his stores were brought up from the *Victory*, and he found in his house at Merton the rest he required. Many days had not elapsed before Captain Blackwood, on his way to London with despatches, called on him at five in the morning.

Nelson, who was already dressed, exclaimed the moment he saw him: "I am sure you bring me news of the French and Spanish fleets! I think I shall yet have to beat them!" They had refitted at Vigo after an indecisive action with Sir Robert Calder, then proceeded to Ferrol, brought out the squadron from thence, and with it entered Cadiz in safety. "Depend on it, Blackwood," he repeatedly said, "I shall yet give M. Villeneuve a drubbing." But, when Blackwood had left him, he wanted resolution to declare his wishes to Lady Hamilton and his sisters, and endeavoured to drive away the thought. He had done enough; he said, "Let the man trudge it who has lost his budget!"

His countenance belied his lips and as he was pacing one of the walks in the garden, which he used to call the quarter-deck, Lady Hamilton came up to him and told him she saw he was uneasy. He smiled, and said, "No, he was as happy as possible; he was surrounded by those he loved, his health was better since he had been on shore, and he would not give sixpence to call the king his uncle."

She replied that she did not believe him, that she knew he was longing to get at the combined fleets, that he considered them as his own property, that he would be miserable if any man but himself did the business, and that he ought to have them as the price and reward of his two years' long watching and his hard chase. "Nelson," said she, "however we may lament your absence, offer your services; they will be accepted and you will gain a quiet heart by it; you will have a glorious victory, and then you may return here and be happy."

His services were as willingly accepted as they were offered; and Lord Barham, giving him the list of the navy, desired him to choose his own officers. "Choose yourself, my lord," was his reply; "the same spirit actuates the whole profession; you cannot choose wrong."

Early on September 14th Nelson reached Portsmouth, and having despatched his business on shore, endeavoured to elude the populace by taking a by-way to the beach; but a crowd collected in his train, pressing forward to obtain sight of his face; many were in tears, and many knelt down before him and blessed him as he passed. England has had many heroes, but never one who so entirely possessed the love of his fellow-countrymen as Nelson.

All men knew that his heart was as humane as it was fearless; that there was not in his nature the slightest alloy of selfishness or cupidity; but that, with perfect and entire devotion, he served his country with all his heart, and with all his soul, and with all his strength; and, therefore, they loved him as truly and as fervently as he loved England. They pressed upon the parapet to gaze after him when his barge pushed off, and he was returning their cheers by waving his hat. The sentinels who endeavoured to prevent them from trespassing upon this ground, were wedged among the crowd; and an officer, who, not very prudently upon such an occasion, ordered them to drive the people down with their bayonets, was compelled speedily to retreat, for the people would not be debarred from gazing till the last moment upon the hero—the darling hero—of England!

Nelson arrived off Cadiz on September 29th—his birthday. Fearing that if the enemy knew his force they might be deterred from venturing to sea, he kept out of sight of land, desired Collingwood to fire no salute and hoist no colours; and wrote to Gibraltar to request that the force of the fleet might not be inserted there in the *Gazette*. His reception in the Mediterranean fleet was as gratifying as the farewell of his countrymen at Portsmouth: the officers, who came on board to welcome him, forgot his rank as commander in their joy at seeing him again. On the day of his arrival, Villeneuve received orders to put to sea the first opportunity. Villeneuve, however, hesitated when he heard that Nelson had resumed the command. He called a council of war; and their determination was, that it would not be expedient to leave Cadiz unless they had reason to believe themselves stronger by one-third than the British force.

In the public measures of this country secrecy is seldom practicable, and seldom attempted: here, however, by the precautions of Nelson and the wise measures of the Admiralty, the enemy were for once kept in ignorance; for, as the ships appointed to reinforce the Mediterranean fleet were despatched singly, each as soon as it was ready, their collected number was not stated in the newspapers and their arrival was not known to the enemy. But the enemy knew that Admiral Louis, with six sail, had been detached for stores and water to Gibraltar. Accident also contributed to make the French admiral doubt whether Nelson himself had actually taken the command. An American, lately arrived from England, maintained that it was impossible—for he had seen him only a few days before in London, and at that time there was no rumour of his going again to sea.

The station which Nelson had chosen was some fifty or sixty miles to the west of Cadiz, near Cape St. Mary's. At this distance he hoped to decoy the enemy out, while he guarded against the danger of being caught with a westerly wind near Cadiz and driven within the Straits. The blockade of the port was rigorously enforced, in hopes that the combined fleet might be forced to sea by want. The Danish vessels, therefore, which were carrying provisions from the French ports in the bay, under the name of Danish property, to all the little ports from Ayamonte to Algeziras, from whence they were conveyed in coasting boats to Cadiz, were seized. Without this proper exertion of power, the blockade would have been rendered nugatory by the advantage thus taken of the neutral flag. The supplies from France were thus effectually cut off. There was now every indication that the enemy would speedily venture out: officers and men were in the highest spirits at the prospect of giving them a decisive blow; such, indeed, as would put an end to all further contest upon the seas.

Nelson, writing on October 6th said:

> I verily believe that the country will soon be put to some expense on my account; either a monument, or a new pension

and honours; for I have not the smallest doubt but that a very few days, almost hours, will put us in battle. The success no man can insure; but for the fighting them, if they can be got at, I pledge myself. The sooner the better: I don't like to have these things upon my mind.

At this time he was not without some cause of anxiety; he was in want of frigates—the eyes of the fleet, as he always called them—to the want of which the enemy before were indebted for their escape and Bonaparte for his arrival in Egypt. He had only twenty-three ships—others were on the way; but they might come too late; and though Nelson never doubted of victory, mere victory was not what he looked to, he wanted to annihilate the enemy's fleet.

On the 9th, Nelson sent Collingwood what he called, in his diary, the Nelson-touch.

> I send you my plan of attack, as far as a man dare venture to guess at the very uncertain position the enemy may be found in; but it is to place you perfectly at ease respecting my intentions, and to give full scope to your judgment for carrying them into effect. We can, my dear Coll, have no little jealousies. We have only one great object in view—that of annihilating our enemies and getting a glorious peace for our country. No man has more confidence in another than I have in you; and no man will render your services more justice than your very old friend, Nelson and Bronte.

The order of sailing was to be the order of battle; the fleet in two lines with an advanced squadron of eight of the fastest sailing two-deckers. The second in command, having the entire direction of his line, was to break through the enemy, about the twelfth ship from their rear; he would lead through the centre, and the advanced squadron was to cut off three or four ahead of the centre. This plan was to be adapted to the strength of the enemy, so that they should always be one-fourth superior to those whom they cut off. Nelson said that "his admirals and captains, knowing his precise object to be that of a close and decisive action, would supply any deficiency of signals and act accordingly. In case signals cannot be seen or clearly understood, no captain can do wrong if he places his ship alongside that of an enemy."

One of the last orders of this admirable man was that the name and family of every officer, seaman, and marine who might be killed or wounded in action, should be, as soon as possible, returned to him, in order to be transmitted to the chairman of the patriotic fund, for the benefit of the sufferer or his family.

About half-past nine in the morning of the 19th, the *Mars*, being the nearest to the fleet of the ships which formed the line of communication with the frigates in-shore, repeated the signal that the enemy were coming out of port. The wind was at this time very light, with partial breezes, mostly from the south-south-west. Nelson ordered the signal to be made for a chase in the south-east quarter. About two the repeating ships announced that the enemy were at sea. All night the British fleet continued under all sail, steering to the south-east. At daybreak they were in the entrance of the Straits, but the enemy were not in sight. About seven one of the frigates made signal that the enemy were bearing north. Upon this the *Victory* hove to; and shortly afterwards Nelson made sail again to the northward. In the afternoon the wind blew fresh from the south-west, and the English began to fear that the foe might be forced to return to port. A little before sunset, however, Blackwood, in the *Euryalus*, telegraphed that they appeared determined to go to the westward

The admiral said in his diary:

And that they shall not do if it is in the power of Nelson and Bronte to prevent them.

Nelson had signified to Blackwood that he depended upon him to keep sight of the enemy. They were observed so well that all their motions were made known to him; and, as they wore twice, he inferred that they were aiming to keep the port of Cadiz open and would retreat there as soon as they saw the British fleet; for this reason he was very careful not to approach near enough to be seen by them during the night. At daybreak the combined fleets were distinctly seen from the *Victory's* deck, formed in a close line of battle ahead, on the starboard tack, about twelve miles to leeward and standing to the south. Our fleet consisted of twenty-seven sail of the line and four frigates; theirs of thirty-three and seven large frigates. Their superiority was greater in size and weight of metal than in numbers. They had four thousand troops on board; and the best riflemen who could be procured, many of them Tyrolese, were dispersed through the ships.

Soon after daylight Nelson came upon deck. October 21st was a festival in his family, because on that day his uncle, Captain Suckling, in the *Dreadnought*, with two other line-of-battle ships, had beaten off a French squadron of four sail of the line and three frigates. Nelson, with that sort of superstition from which few persons are entirely exempt, had more than once expressed his persuasion that this was to be the day of his battle also; and he was well pleased at seeing his prediction about to be verified. The wind was now from the west, light breezes, with a long, heavy swell. Signal was made to bear down upon the enemy in two lines, and the fleet set all sail. Collingwood, in the *Royal Sovereign*, led the lee line of thirteen ships; the *Victory* led the weather line of fourteen. Having seen that all was as it should be, Nelson retired to his cabin, and wrote the following prayer:—

> May the great God whom I worship grant to my country and for the benefit of Europe in general a great and glorious victory, and may no misconduct in any one tarnish it; and may humanity after victory be the predominant feature in the British fleet! For myself individually, I commit my life to Him that made me; and may His blessing alight on my endeavours for serving my country faithfully! To Him I resign myself and the just cause which is entrusted to me to defend. Amen. Amen. Amen.

Having thus discharged his devotional duties, he proceeded to recite at length in his diary the services rendered to him and through him to the English nation by Lady Hamilton, commending her to the care of the government. This entry was witnessed by Henry Blackwood and T. M. Hardy.

Blackwood arrived on board the *Victory* about six o'clock. He found Nelson in good spirits, but very calm; not in that exhilaration which he had felt upon entering into battle at Aboukir and Copenhagen. He knew that his own life would be particularly aimed at, and seems to have looked for death with almost as sure an expectation as for victory. His whole attention was fixed upon the enemy. They tacked to the northward and formed their line on the larboard tack; thus bringing the shoals of Trafalgar and St. Pedro under the lee of the British, and keeping the port of Cadiz open for themselves. This was judiciously done; and Nelson, aware of the advantages it gave them, made signal to prepare to anchor.

Villeneuve was a skilful seaman; worthy of serving a better master and a better cause. His plan of defence was as well conceived and as original as the plan of attack. He formed the fleet in a double line; every alternate ship being about a cable's length to windward of her second ahead and astern. Nelson, certain of a triumphant issue to the day, asked Blackwood what he should consider as a victory. That officer answered, that, considering the handsome way in which battle was offered by the enemy, their apparent determination for a fair trial of strength and the situation of the land, he thought it would be a glorious result if fourteen were captured. He replied: "I shall not be satisfied with less than twenty." Soon afterwards he asked him if he did not think there was a signal wanting. Captain Blackwood made answer that he thought the whole fleet seemed very clearly to understand what they were about.

These words were scarcely spoken before that signal was made which will be remembered as long as the language, or even the memory, of England shall endure—Nelson's last signal:—

England expects every man will do his duty!

It was received throughout the fleet with a shout of answering acclamation, made sublime by the spirit which it breathed and the feeling which it expressed. "Now," said Lord Nelson, "I can do no more. We must trust to the great Disposer of all events and the justice of our cause. I thank God for this opportunity of doing my duty."

The French admiral, from the *Bucentaure*, beheld the new manner in which his enemy was advancing—Nelson and Collingwood each leading his line—and pointing them out to his officers he is said to have exclaimed that such conduct could not fail to be successful. Yet Villeneuve had made his own dispositions with the utmost skill, and the fleets under his command waited for the attack with perfect coolness. Ten minutes before twelve they opened their fire. Eight or nine of the ships immediately ahead of the *Victory*, and across her bows fired single guns at her, to ascertain whether she was yet within their range.

As soon as Nelson perceived that their shot passed over him, he desired Blackwood and Captain Prowse, of the *Sirius*, to repair to their respective frigates, and, on their way, to tell all the captains of the line-of-battle ships that he depended on their exertions, and that, if by the prescribed mode of attack they found it impracticable to get into action immediately, they might adopt whatever they thought best, provided it led them quickly and closely longside an enemy. Standing on the front poop, Blackwood took him by the hand, saying he hoped soon to return and find him in possession of twenty prizes. He replied, "God bless you, Blackwood; I shall never see you again."

Nelson's column was steered about two points more to the north than Collingwood's, in order to cut off the enemy's escape into Cadiz:

the lee line, therefore, was first engaged. "See," cried Nelson, pointing to the *Royal Sovereign* as she steered right for the centre of the enemy's line, cut through it astern of the *Santa Anna*, three-decker, and engaged her at the muzzle of her guns on the starboard side—"See how that noble fellow, Collingwood, carries his ship into action!" Collingwood, delighted at being first in the heat of the fire, and knowing the feelings of his commander and old friend, turned to his captain, and exclaimed: "Rotherham, what would Nelson give to be here!" Both these brave officers, perhaps, at this moment, thought of Nelson with gratitude for a circumstance which had occurred on the preceding day.

Admiral Collingwood, with some of the captains, having gone on board the *Victory* to receive instructions, Nelson inquired of him where his captain was, and was told in reply that they were not upon good terms with each other. "Terms!" said Nelson; "good terms with each other!" Immediately he sent a boat for Captain Rotherham, led him, as soon as he arrived, to Collingwood, and saying: "Look; yonder are the enemy!" bade them shake hands like Englishmen.

The enemy continued to fire a gun at a time at the *Victory*, till they saw that a shot had passed through her main-top-gallant sail; then they opened their broadsides, aiming chiefly at her rigging, in the hope of disabling her before she could close with them. Nelson, as usual, had hoisted several flags, lest one should be shot away. The enemy showed no colours till late in the action, when they began to feel the necessity of having them to strike. For this reason, the *Santissima Trinidad*, Nelson's old acquaintance, as he used to call her, was distinguishable only by her four decks; and to the bow of this opponent he ordered the *Victory* to be steered.

Meantime, an incessant raking fire was kept up upon the *Victory*. The admiral's secretary was one of the first who fell: he was killed by a cannon shot while conversing with Hardy. Captain Adair of the marines, with the help of a sailor, endeavoured to remove the body from Nelson's sight, who had a great regard for Mr. Scott; but he anxiously asked, "Is that poor Scott that's gone?" and being informed that it was indeed so, exclaimed, "Poor fellow!" Presently, a double-headed shot struck a party of marines, who were drawn up on the poop, and killed eight of them: upon which Nelson immediately desired Captain Adair to disperse his men round the ship, that they might not suffer so much from being together.

A few minutes afterwards a shot struck the fore-brace bits on the quarter-deck, and passed between Nelson and Hardy, a splinter from the bit tearing off Hardy's buckle and bruising his foot. Both stopped and looked anxiously at each other: each supposed the other to be wounded. Nelson then smiled, and said: "This is too warm work, Hardy, to last long."

The *Victory* had not yet returned a single gun; fifty of her men had been by this time killed or wounded, and her main-top mast with all her studding sails and their booms shot away. Nelson declared that, in all his battles, he had seen nothing which surpassed the cool courage of his crew on this occasion. At four minutes after twelve she opened her fire from both sides of her deck. It was not possible to break the enemy's line without running on board one of their ships; Hardy informed him of this and asked him which he would prefer. Nelson replied: "Take your choice, Hardy, it does not signify much."

The master was ordered to put the helm to port, and the *Victory* ran on board the *Redoubtable* just as her tiller-ropes were shot away. The French ship received her with a broadside, then instantly let down her lower-deck ports, for fear of being boarded through them, and never afterwards fired a great gun during the action. Her tops, like those of all the enemy's ships, were filled with riflemen. Nelson never placed musketry in his tops; he had a strong dislike to the practice; not merely because it endangers setting fire to the sails, but also because it is a murderous sort of warfare, by which individuals may suffer and a commander now and then be picked off, but which never can decide the fate of a general engagement.

Captain Harvey, in the *Temeraire*, fell on board the *Redoubtable* on the other side. Another enemy was in like manner on board the *Temeraire*, so that these four ships formed as compact a tier as if they had been moored together, their heads all lying the same way. The lieutenants of the *Victory* seeing this, depressed their guns of the middle and lower decks, and fired with a diminished charge, lest the shot should pass through and injure the *Temeraire*. And because there was danger that the *Redoubtable* might take fire from the lower-deck guns, the muzzles of which touched her side when they were run out, the fireman of each gun stood ready with a bucket of water, which, as soon as the gun was discharged, he dashed into the hole made by the shot. An incessant fire was kept up from the *Victory* from both sides; her larboard guns playing upon the *Bucentaure* and the huge *Santissima Trinidad*.

It had been part of Nelson's prayer that the British fleet might be distinguished by humanity in the victory he expected. Setting an example himself, he twice gave orders to cease firing upon the *Redoubtable*, supposing that she had struck, because her great guns were silent; for, as she carried no flag, there was no means of instantly ascertaining the fact.

From this ship, which he had thus twice spared, he received his death. A ball fired from her mizen-top, which, in the then situation of the two vessels, was not more than fifteen yards from that part of the deck where he was standing, struck the epaulette on his left shoulder, about a quarter after one, just in the heat of action. He fell upon his face on the spot which was covered with his poor secretary's blood. Hardy, who was a few steps from him, turning round, saw three men raising him up.

"They have done for me at last, Hardy!" said he.

"I hope not!" cried Hardy.

"Yes," he replied, "my back-bone is shot through!"

Yet even now, not for a moment losing his presence of mind, he observed, as they were carrying him down the ladder, that the tiller-ropes, which had been shot away, were not yet replaced, and ordered that new ones should be rove immediately. Then, that he might not be seen by the crew, he took out his handkerchief, and covered his face and his stars. Had he but concealed these badges of honour from the enemy, England, perhaps, would not have had cause to receive with sorrow the news of the Battle of Trafalgar. The cockpit was crowded with wounded and dying men, over whose bodies he was with some difficulty conveyed and laid upon a pallet in the midshipman's berth.

It was soon perceived, upon examination, that the wound was mortal. This, however, was concealed from all except Captain Hardy, the chaplain, and the medical attendants. He himself being certain, from the sensation in his back, and the gush of blood he felt momently within his breast, that no human care could avail him, insisted that the surgeon should leave him, and attend to those to whom he might be useful. "For," said he, "you can do nothing for me." All that could be done was to fan him with paper and frequently to give him lemonade to alleviate his intense thirst. He was in great pain, and expressed much anxiety for the event of the action, which now began to declare itself.

As often as a ship struck, the crew of the *Victory* hurrahed; and at every hurrah a visible expression of joy gleamed in the eyes, and marked the countenance of the dying hero. But he became impatient to see Captain Hardy; and as that officer though often sent for could not leave the deck, Nelson feared that some fatal cause prevented him, and repeatedly cried: "Will no one bring Hardy to me? He must be killed! He is surely dead!" An hour and ten minutes elapsed from the time when Nelson received his wound before Hardy could come to him. They shook hands in silence; Hardy in vain struggling to suppress the feelings of that most painful and yet sublimest moment.

"Well, Hardy," said Nelson, "how goes the day with us?"

"Very well," replied Hardy; "ten ships have struck, but five of the van have tacked and show an intention to bear down upon the *Victory*. I have called two or three of our fresh ships round, and have no doubt of giving them a drubbing."

"I hope," said Nelson, "none of our ships have struck?"

Hardy answered, "There was no fear of that."

Then, and not till then, Nelson spoke of himself. "I am a dead man, Hardy," said he; "I am going fast; it will be all over with me soon. Come nearer to me. Let my dear Lady Hamilton have my hair, and all other things belonging to me." Hardy observed that he hoped Mr. Beatty could yet hold out some prospect of life. "Oh, no!" he replied; "it is impossible; my back is shot through. Beatty will tell you so." Captain Hardy then once more shook hands with him, and with a heart almost bursting, hastened upon deck.

By this time all feeling below the breast was gone; and Nelson having made the surgeon ascertain this, said to him, "You know I am gone. I know it. I feel something rising in my breast" (putting his hand on his left side) "which tells me so." And upon Beatty's inquiring whether his pain was very great, he replied, "So great, that he wished he was dead. Yet," said he, in a lower voice, "one would like to live a little longer, too!" And after a few minutes, in the same undertone, he added: "What would become of poor Lady Hamilton if she knew my situation!" Next to his country, she occupied his thoughts.

Captain Hardy, some fifty minutes after he had left the cockpit, returned, and, again taking the hand of his dying friend and commander, congratulated him on having gained a complete victory. How many of the enemy were taken he did not know, as it was impossible to perceive them distinctly, but fourteen or fifteen at least. "That's well!" cried Nelson; "but I bargained for twenty." And then in a stronger voice, he said: "Anchor, Hardy; anchor." Hardy, upon this, hinted that Admiral Collingwood would take upon himself the direction of affairs. "Not while I live, Hardy," said the dying Nelson, ineffectually endeavouring to raise himself from the bed. "Do you anchor." His previous order for preparing to anchor had shown how clearly he foresaw the necessity of this.

Presently, calling Hardy back, he said to him, in a low voice: "Don't throw me overboard;" and he desired that he might be buried by his parents, unless it should please the king to order otherwise. Then reverting to private feelings—"Take care of my dear Lady Hamilton, Hardy; take care of poor Lady Hamilton. Kiss me, Hardy," said he. Hardy knelt down and kissed his cheek; and Nelson said: "Now I am satisfied. Thank God, I have done my duty!" Hardy stood over him in silence for a moment or two, then knelt again, and kissed his forehead. "Who is that?" said Nelson; and being informed, he replied: "God bless you, Hardy." And Hardy then left him forever.

Nelson now desired to be turned upon his right side, and said: "I wish I had not left the deck; for I shall soon be gone." Death was, indeed, rapidly approaching. He said to the chaplain: "Doctor, I have *not* been a *great* sinner;" and after a short pause, "Remember that I leave Lady Hamilton and my daughter Horatia as a legacy to my country." His articulation now became difficult; but he was distinctly heard to say: "Thank God, I have done my duty!" Nelson expired at thirty minutes after four, three hours and a quarter after he had received his wound.

Within a quarter of an hour after Nelson was wounded, about fifty of the *Victory's* men fell by the enemy's musketry. They, however, on their part, were not idle; and it was not long before there were only two Frenchmen left alive in the mizen-top of the *Redoubtable*. One of them was the man who had given the fatal wound; he did not live to boast of what he had done. An old quarter-master had seen him fire, and easily recognised him, because he wore a glazed cocked hat and a white frock. This quarter-master and two midshipmen, Mr. Collingwood and Mr. Pollard, were the only persons left in the *Victory's* poop; the two midshipmen kept firing at the top, and he supplied them with cartridges.

One of the Frenchmen attempting to make his escape down the rigging, was shot by Mr. Pollard, and fell on the poop. But the old quarter-master, as he cried out, "That's he, that's he," and pointed at the other, who was coming forward to fire again, received a shot in his mouth, and fell dead. Both the midshipmen then fired at the same time, and the fellow dropped in the top. When they took possession of the prize they went into the mizen-top, and found him dead, with one ball through his head and another through his breast.

The *Redoubtable* struck within twenty minutes after the fatal shot had been fired from her. During that time she had been twice on fire; in her forechains, and in her forecastle. The French, as they had done in other battles, made use in this of fire-balls and other combustibles—implements of destruction which other nations from a sense of honour and humanity have laid aside—which add to the sufferings of the wounded without determining the issue of the combat; which none but the cruel would employ, and which never can be successful against the brave. Once they succeeded in setting fire, from the *Redoubtable*, to some ropes and canvas on the *Victory's* booms. The cry ran through the ship and reached the cockpit.

But even this dreadful cry produced no confusion; the men displayed that perfect self-possession in danger by which English seamen are characterised; they extinguished the flames on board their own ship, and then hastened to extinguish them in the enemy, by throwing buckets of water from the gangway. When the *Redoubtable* had struck, it was not practicable to board her from the *Victory*; for though the two ships touched, the upper works of both fell in so much that there was a great space between their gangways, and she could not be boarded from the lower or middle decks because her ports were down. Some of our men went to Lieutenant Quilliam and offered to swim under her bows, and get up there; but it was thought unfit to hazard lives in this manner.

What our men would have done from gallantry, some of the crew of the *Santissima Trinidad* did to save themselves. Unable to stand the tremendous fire of the *Victory*, whose larboard guns played against this great four-decker, and not knowing how else to escape them nor where else to betake themselves for protection, many of them leapt overboard and swam to the *Victory*, and were actually helped up her sides by the English during the action. The Spaniards began the battle with less vivacity than their unworthy allies, but continued it with greater firmness. The *Argonauta* and *Bahama* were defended till they had each lost about four hundred men; the *San Juan Nepomuceno* lost three hundred and fifty.

Often as the superiority of British courage has been proved against France upon the seas, it was never more conspicuous than in this decisive conflict. Five of our ships were engaged muzzle to muzzle with five of the French. In all five the Frenchmen lowered their lower-deck ports and deserted their guns; while our men continued deliberately to load and fire till they had made the victory secure.

The total British loss in the battle of Trafalgar amounted to one thousand five hundred and eighty-seven. Twenty of the enemy struck. Unhappily the fleet did not anchor, as Nelson, almost with his dying breath, had enjoined; a gale came on from the south-west; some of the prizes went down, some went on shore; one effected its escape into Cadiz; others were destroyed—four only were saved, and those by the greatest exertions. The wounded Spaniards were sent ashore, an assurance being given that they should not serve till regularly exchanged; and the Spaniards, with a generous feeling which would not, perhaps, have been found in any other people, offered the use of their hospitals for our wounded, pledging the honour of Spain that they should be carefully attended there.

When the storm, after the action, drove some of the prizes upon the coast, they declared that the English, who were thus thrown into their hands, should not be considered as prisoners of war; and the Spanish soldiers gave up their own beds to their shipwrecked enemies. The Spanish vice-Admiral, Alva, died of his wounds. Villeneuve was sent to England and permitted to return to France. The French Government say that he destroyed himself on the way to Paris, dreading the consequences of a court martial; but there is every reason to believe that the tyrant, who never acknowledged the loss of the battle of Trafalgar, added Villeneuve to the numerous victims of his murderous policy.

ALSO FROM LEONAUR
AVAILABLE IN SOFTCOVER OR HARDCOVER WITH DUST JACKET

ESCAPE FROM THE FRENCH by Edward Boys—A Young Royal Navy Midshipman's Adventures During the Napoleonic War.

THE VOYAGE OF H.M.S. PANDORA by Edward Edwards R. N. & George Hamilton, edited by Basil Thomson—In Pursuit of the Mutineers of the Bounty in the South Seas—1790-1791.

MEDUSA by J. B. Henry Savigny and Alexander Correard and Charlotte-Adélaïde Dard —Narrative of a Voyage to Senegal in 1816 & The Sufferings of the Picard Family After the Shipwreck of the Medusa.

THE SEA WAR OF 1812 VOLUME 1 by A. T. Mahan—A History of the Maritime Conflict.

THE SEA WAR OF 1812 VOLUME 2 by A. T. Mahan—A History of the Maritime Conflict.

WETHERELL OF H. M. S. HUSSAR by John Wetherell—The Recollections of an Ordinary Seaman of the Royal Navy During the Napoleonic Wars.

THE NAVAL BRIGADE IN NATAL by C. R. N. Burne—With the Guns of H. M. S. Terrible & H. M. S. Tartar during the Boer War 1899-1900.

THE VOYAGE OF H. M. S. BOUNTY by William Bligh—The True Story of an 18th Century Voyage of Exploration and Mutiny.

SHIPWRECK! by William Gilly—The Royal Navy's Disasters at Sea 1793-1849.

KING'S CUTTERS AND SMUGGLERS: 1700-1855 by E. Keble Chatterton—A unique period of maritime history-from the beginning of the eighteenth to the middle of the nineteenth century when British seamen risked all to smuggle valuable goods from wool to tea and spirits from and to the Continent.

CONFEDERATE BLOCKADE RUNNER by John Wilkinson—The Personal Recollections of an Officer of the Confederate Navy.

NAVAL BATTLES OF THE NAPOLEONIC WARS by W. H. Fitchett—Cape St. Vincent, the Nile, Cadiz, Copenhagen, Trafalgar & Others.

PRISONERS OF THE RED DESERT by R. S. Gwatkin-Williams—The Adventures of the Crew of the Tara During the First World War.

U-BOAT WAR 1914-1918 by James B. Connolly/Karl von Schenk—Two Contrasting Accounts from Both Sides of the Conflict at Sea During the Great War.

AVAILABLE ONLINE AT **www.leonaur.com**
AND FROM ALL GOOD BOOK STORES

www.ingramcontent.com/pod-product-compliance
Lightning Source LLC
Chambersburg PA
CBHW021958160426
43197CB00007B/171